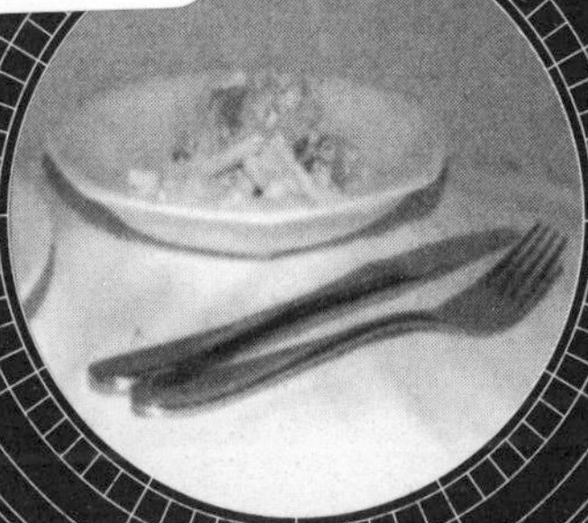

鷹野常雄

Tsuneo Takano

I don't mind being asked which I prefer, potato salad or macaroni salad, but you should at least tell me that it's coming with pasta.

You shouldn't be asking such questions anyway, but if you're going to, I'd rather be asked what kind of *pasta* I prefer!

Ω

Tsuneo Takano

Born in Tokyo.
No hobbies.
No expression.
No interests.
No harm.
Nothing to say.

Takeshi Obata was born in 1969 in Niigata, Japan, and is the artist of the wildly popular SHONEN JUMP title *Hikaru no Go,* which won the 2003 Tezuka Shinsei "New Hope" award and the Shogakukan Manga award. Obata is also the artist of *Arabian Majin Bokentan Lamp Lamp, Ayatsuri Sakon, Cyborg Jichan G,* and the smash hit manga *Death Note.*

RALΩGRAD

Vol. 1

The SHONEN JUMP ADVANCED
Manga Edition

Story By **TSUNEO TAKANO**
Art By **TAKESHI OBATA**

English Adaptation/Kelly Sue DeConnick
Translation/Tony Cusdin, HC Language Solutions, Inc.
Touch-up Art & Lettering/Elizabeth Watasin
Cover & Logo Design/Ronnie Casson
Interior Design/Sam Elzway
Editors/Urian Brown & Yuki Murashige

Editor in Chief, Books/Alvin Lu
Editor in Chief, Magazines/Marc Weidenbaum
VP of Publishing Licensing/Rika Inouye
VP of Sales/Gonzalo Ferreyra
Sr. VP of Marketing/Liza Coppola
Publisher/Hyoe Narita

Printed in the U.S.A.

Published by VIZ Media, LLC
P.O. Box 77010
San Francisco, CA 94107

SHONEN JUMP ADVANCED Manga Edition
10 9 8 7 6 5 4 3 2 1
First printing, February 2008

THE WORLD'S MOST
CUTTING-EDGE MANGA

SHONEN
JUMP
ADVANCED
www.shonenjump.com

VIZ
MEDIA
www.viz.com

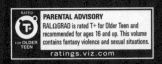

RalΩGrad

SHONEN JUMP ADVANCED
Manga Edition

Story by
Tsuneo Takano

Art by
Takeshi Obata

Vol. 1
Promise

Ral Ω Grad

Vol. 1
Promise

Contents

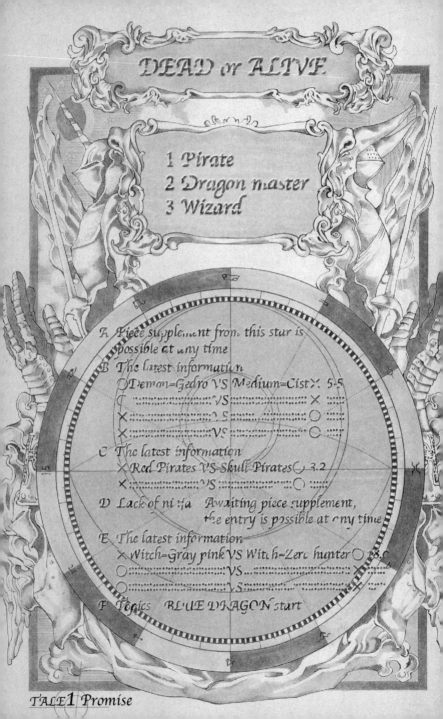

DEAD or ALIVE

1 Pirate
2 Dragon master
3 Wizard

A Piece supplement from this star is possible at any time

B The latest information
Demon=Gedro VS Medium=Cist ✕ 5·5
............................VS............................✕
✕............................VS............................○
✕............................VS............................○

C The latest information
✕ Red Pirates VS Skull Pirates ○ 3·2
✕............................VS............................○

D Lack of ninja Awaiting piece supplement, the entry is possible at any time

E The latest information
✕ Witch=Gray pink VS Witch=Zero hunter ○ 18·0
○............................VS............................✕
○............................VS............................

F Topics BLUE DRAGON start

TALE 1 Promise

TALE 1 Promise

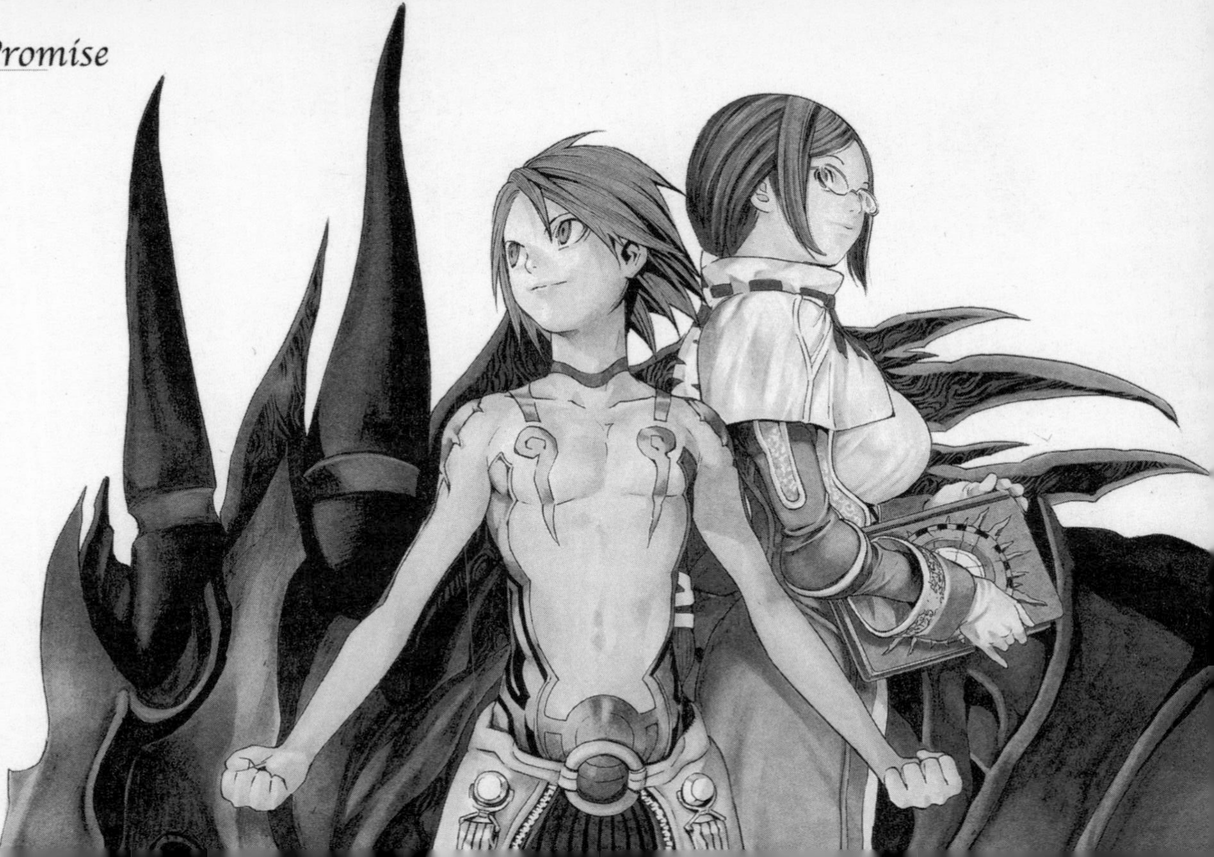

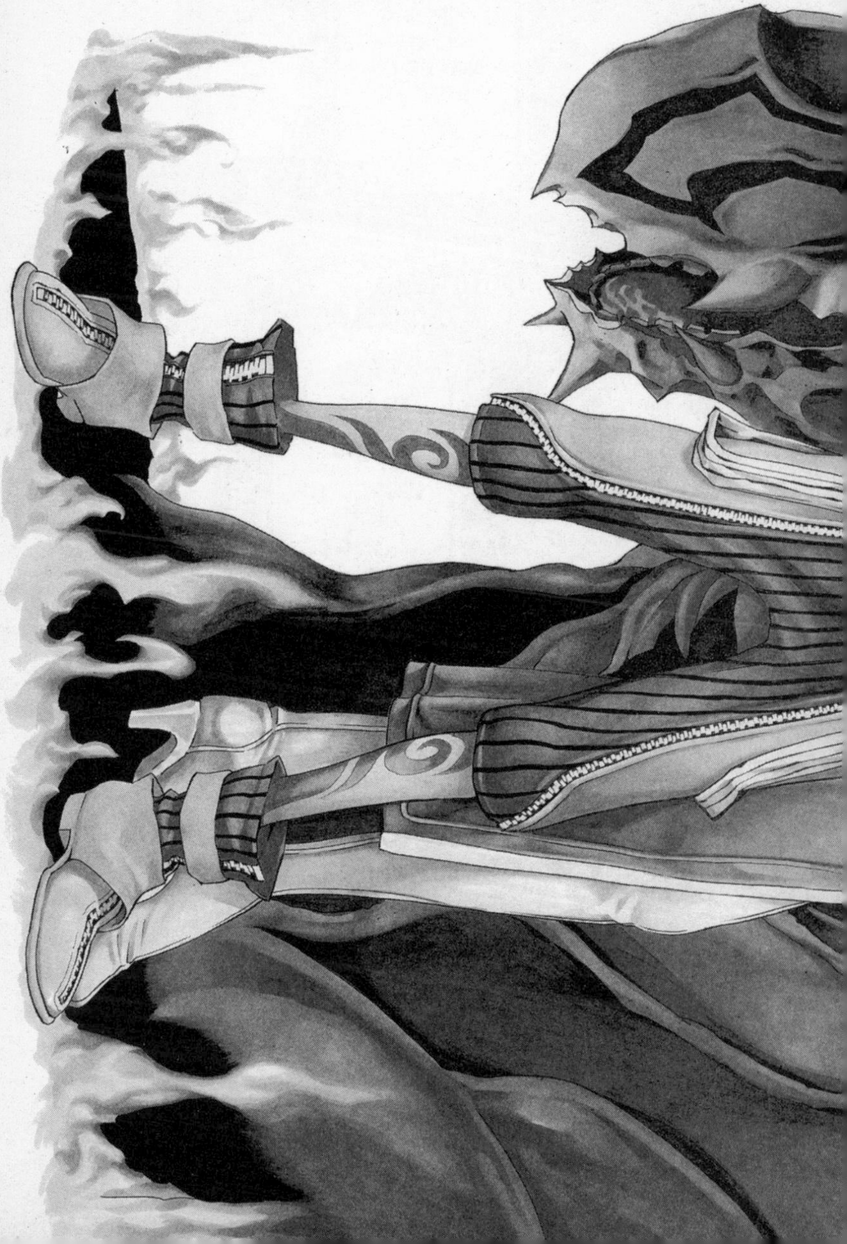

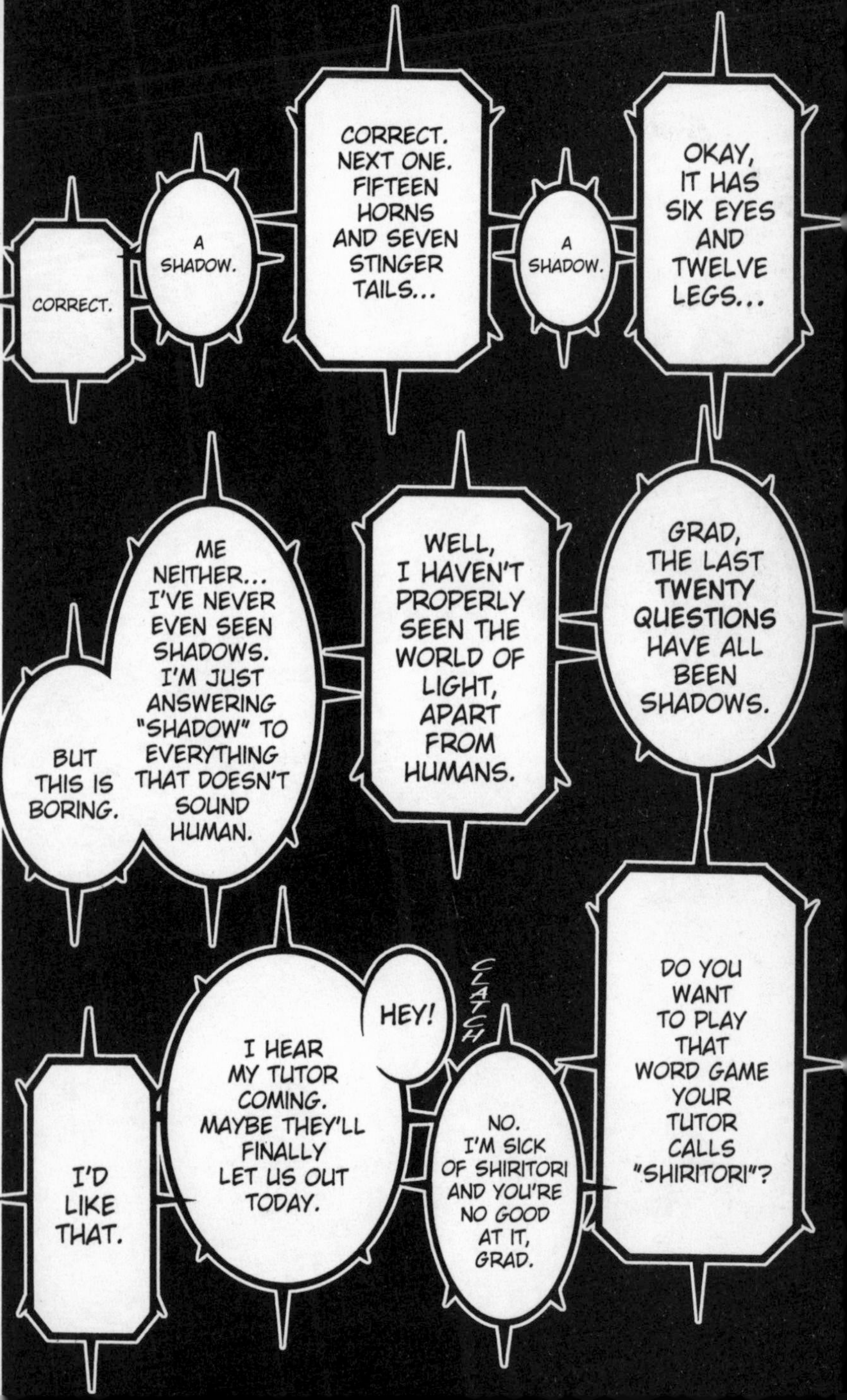
OKAY, IT HAS SIX EYES AND TWELVE LEGS...
A SHADOW.
CORRECT. NEXT ONE. FIFTEEN HORNS AND SEVEN STINGER TAILS...
A SHADOW.
CORRECT.
GRAD, THE LAST TWENTY QUESTIONS HAVE ALL BEEN SHADOWS.
WELL, I HAVEN'T PROPERLY SEEN THE WORLD OF LIGHT, APART FROM HUMANS.
ME NEITHER... I'VE NEVER EVEN SEEN SHADOWS. I'M JUST ANSWERING "SHADOW" TO EVERYTHING THAT DOESN'T SOUND HUMAN.
BUT THIS IS BORING.
DO YOU WANT TO PLAY THAT WORD GAME YOUR TUTOR CALLS "SHIRITORI"?
NO. I'M SICK OF SHIRITORI AND YOU'RE NO GOOD AT IT, GRAD.
CLATCH
HEY!
I HEAR MY TUTOR COMING. MAYBE THEY'LL FINALLY LET US OUT TODAY.
I'D LIKE THAT.

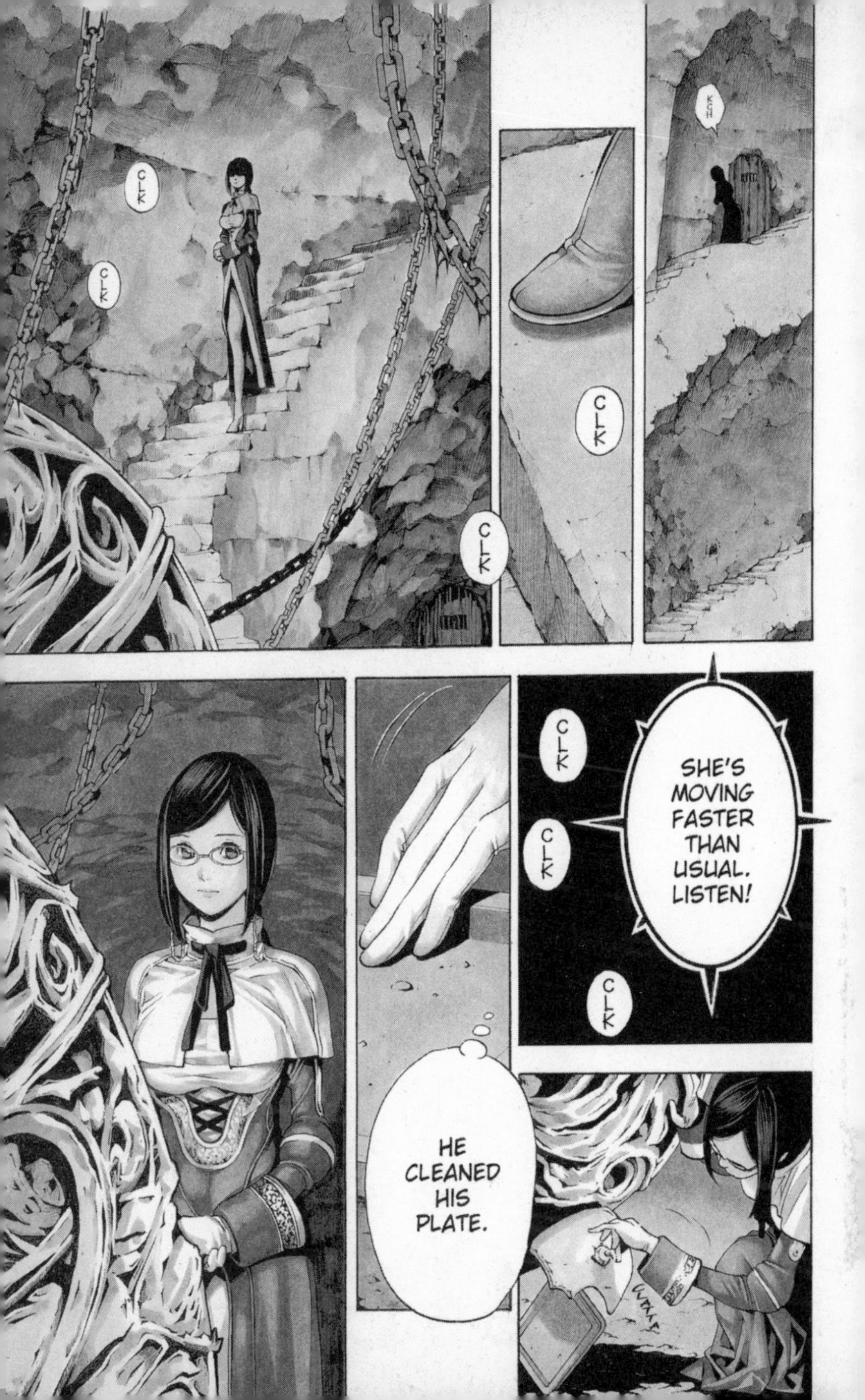
KCH
CLK
CLK
CLK
CLK
CLK
CLK
SHE'S MOVING FASTER THAN USUAL. LISTEN!
CLK
HE CLEANED HIS PLATE.

Ral Ω Grad

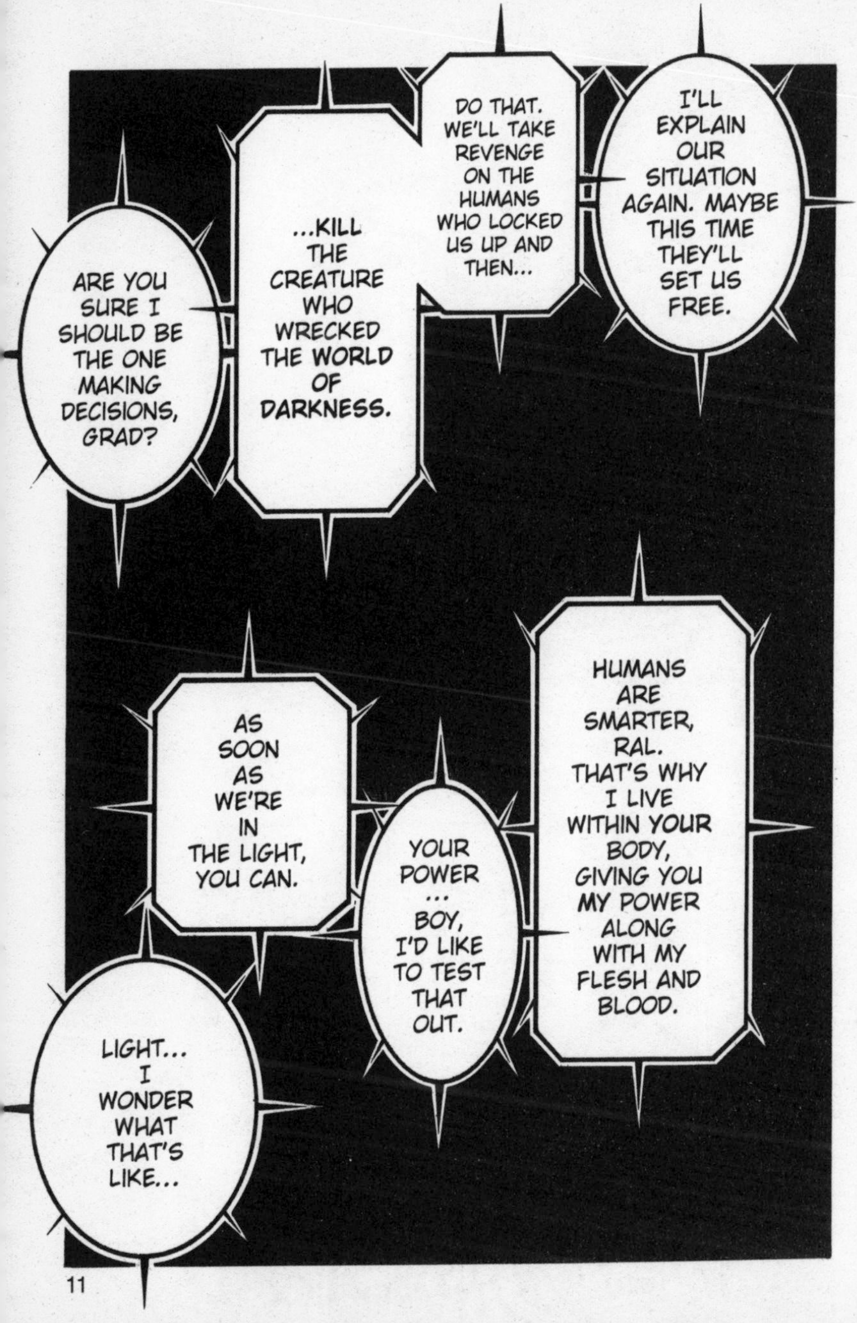
I'LL EXPLAIN OUR SITUATION AGAIN. MAYBE THIS TIME THEY'LL SET US FREE.
DO THAT. WE'LL TAKE REVENGE ON THE HUMANS WHO LOCKED US UP AND THEN...
...KILL THE CREATURE WHO WRECKED THE WORLD OF DARKNESS.
ARE YOU SURE I SHOULD BE THE ONE MAKING DECISIONS, GRAD?
HUMANS ARE SMARTER, RAL. THAT'S WHY I LIVE WITHIN YOUR BODY, GIVING YOU MY POWER ALONG WITH MY FLESH AND BLOOD.
YOUR POWER... BOY, I'D LIKE TO TEST THAT OUT.
AS SOON AS WE'RE IN THE LIGHT, YOU CAN.
LIGHT... I WONDER WHAT THAT'S LIKE...

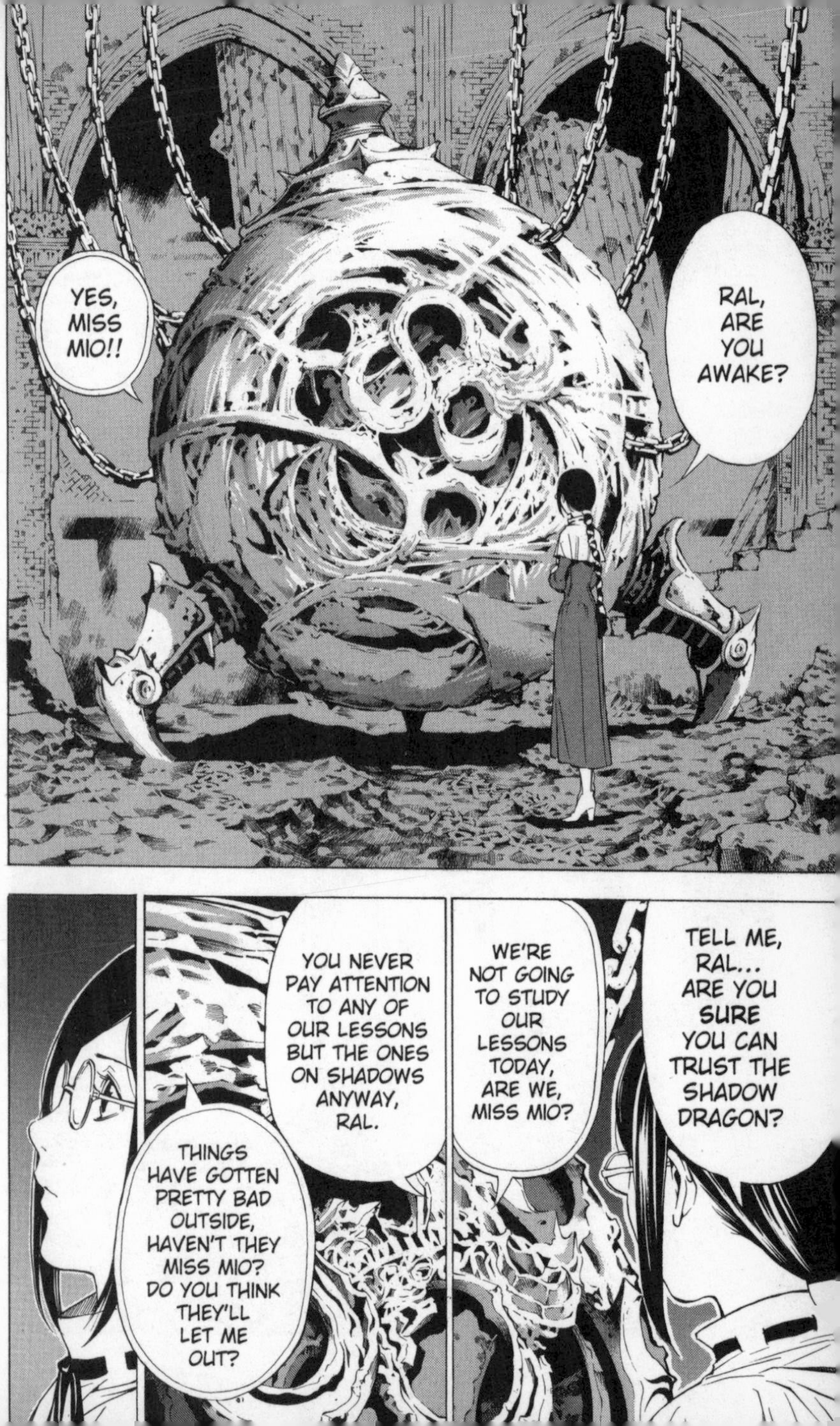
RAL, ARE YOU AWAKE?
YES, MISS MIO!!
TELL ME, RAL... ARE YOU SURE YOU CAN TRUST THE SHADOW DRAGON?
WE'RE NOT GOING TO STUDY OUR LESSONS TODAY, ARE WE, MISS MIO?
YOU NEVER PAY ATTENTION TO ANY OF OUR LESSONS BUT THE ONES ON SHADOWS ANYWAY, RAL.
THINGS HAVE GOTTEN PRETTY BAD OUTSIDE, HAVEN'T THEY MISS MIO? DO YOU THINK THEY'LL LET ME OUT?

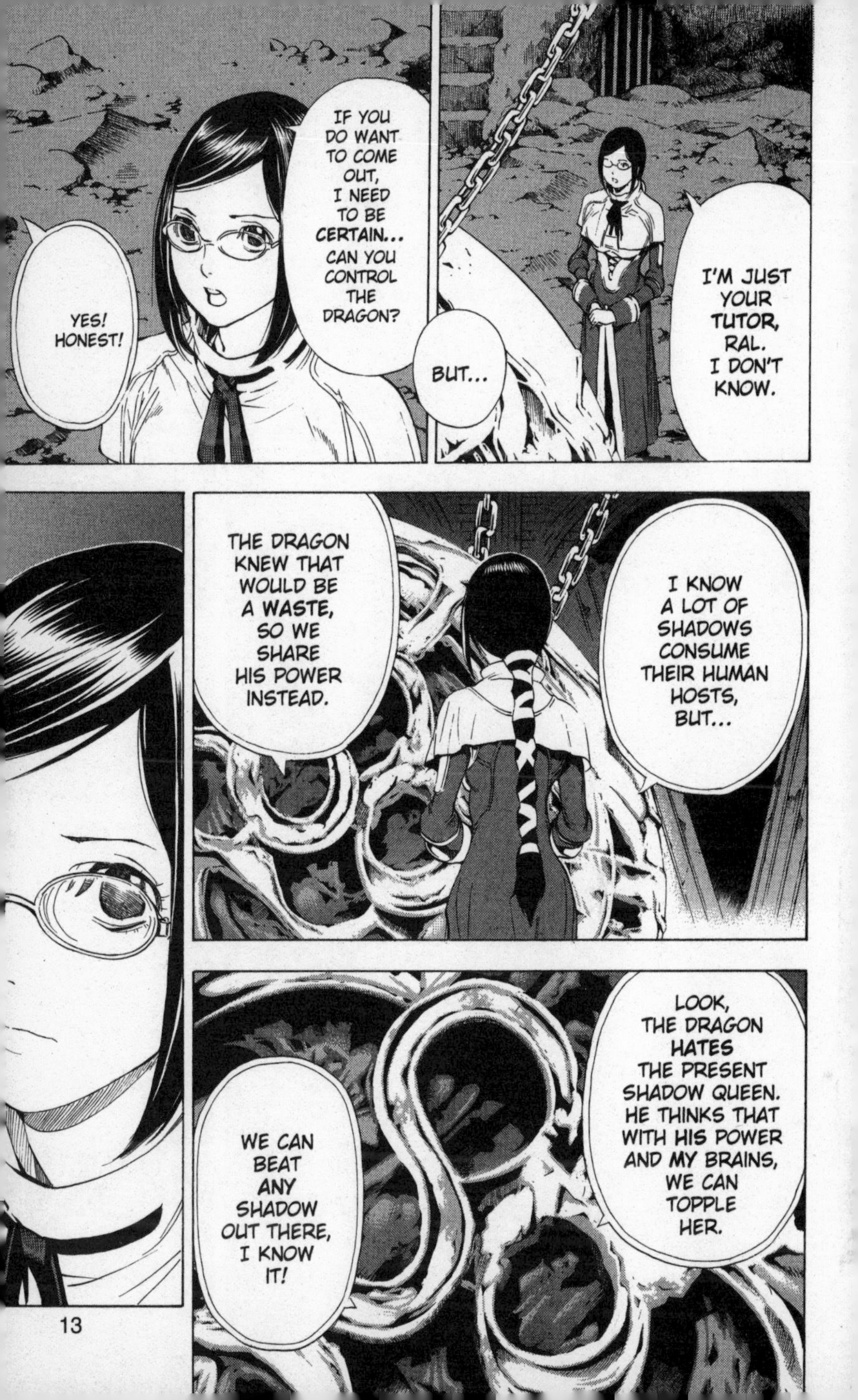
I'M JUST YOUR TUTOR, RAL. I DON'T KNOW.
BUT...
IF YOU DO WANT TO COME OUT, I NEED TO BE CERTAIN... CAN YOU CONTROL THE DRAGON?
YES! HONEST!
I KNOW A LOT OF SHADOWS CONSUME THEIR HUMAN HOSTS, BUT...
THE DRAGON KNEW THAT WOULD BE A WASTE, SO WE SHARE HIS POWER INSTEAD.
LOOK, THE DRAGON HATES THE PRESENT SHADOW QUEEN. HE THINKS THAT WITH HIS POWER AND MY BRAINS, WE CAN TOPPLE HER.
WE CAN BEAT ANY SHADOW OUT THERE, I KNOW IT!

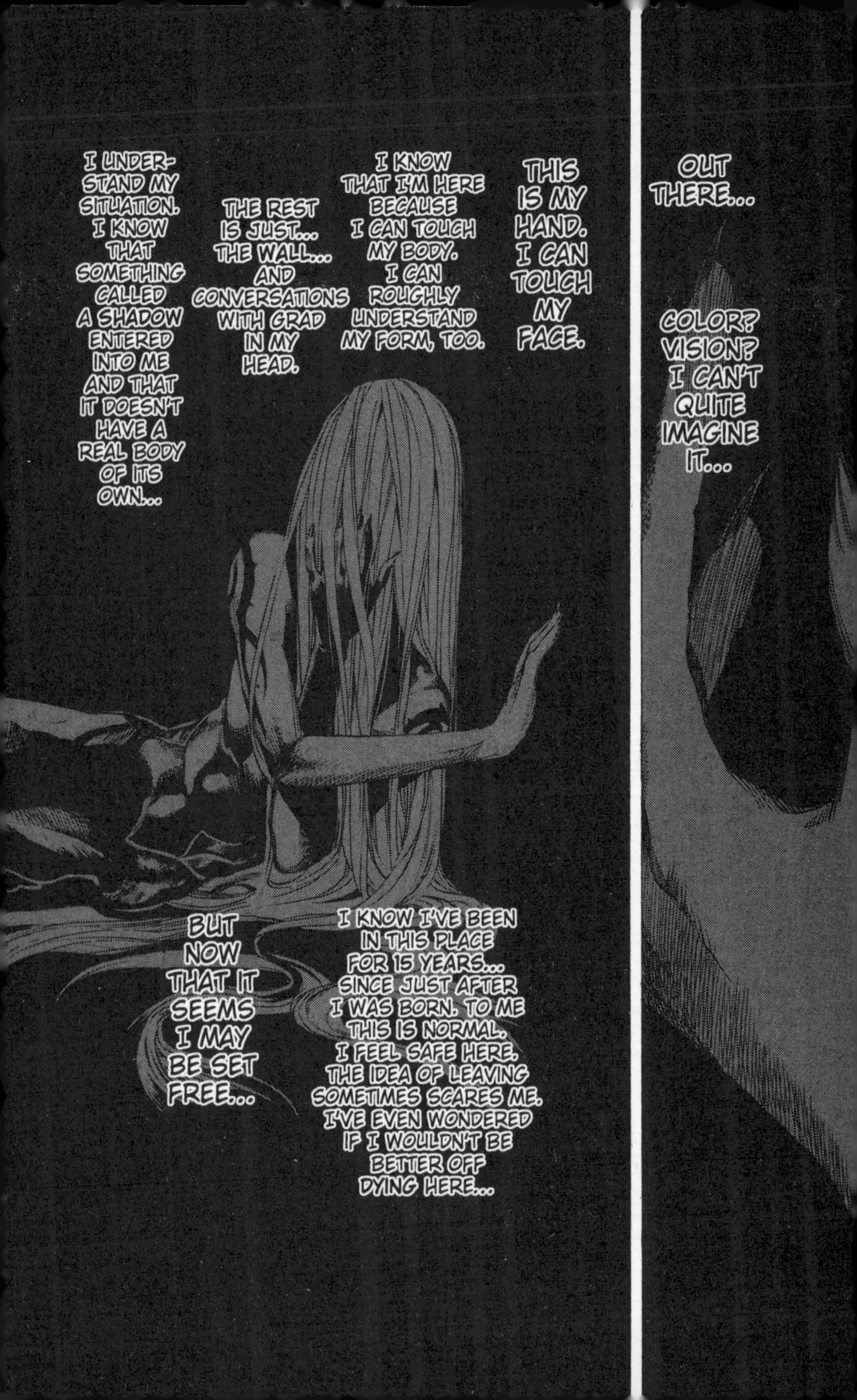
OUT THERE...
COLOR? VISION? I CAN'T QUITE IMAGINE IT...
THIS IS MY HAND. I CAN TOUCH MY FACE.
I KNOW THAT I'M HERE BECAUSE I CAN TOUCH MY BODY. I CAN ROUGHLY UNDERSTAND MY FORM, TOO.
THE REST IS JUST... THE WALL... AND CONVERSATIONS WITH GRAD IN MY HEAD.
I UNDER-STAND MY SITUATION. I KNOW THAT SOMETHING CALLED A SHADOW ENTERED INTO ME AND THAT IT DOESN'T HAVE A REAL BODY OF ITS OWN...
I KNOW I'VE BEEN IN THIS PLACE FOR 15 YEARS... SINCE JUST AFTER I WAS BORN. TO ME THIS IS NORMAL. I FEEL SAFE HERE. THE IDEA OF LEAVING SOMETIMES SCARES ME. I'VE EVEN WONDERED IF I WOULDN'T BE BETTER OFF DYING HERE...
BUT NOW THAT IT SEEMS I MAY BE SET FREE...

MIO!

YES?

GLANK

LORD ROY WISHES TO SPEAK WITH YOU IMMEDIATELY.

VERY WELL.

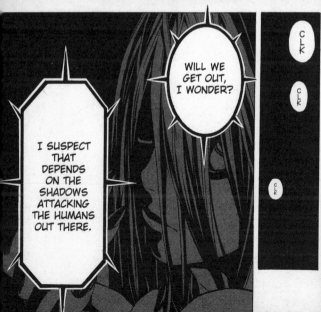

WILL WE GET OUT, I WONDER?

I SUSPECT THAT DEPENDS ON THE SHADOWS ATTACKING THE HUMANS OUT THERE.

CLK

CLK

CLK

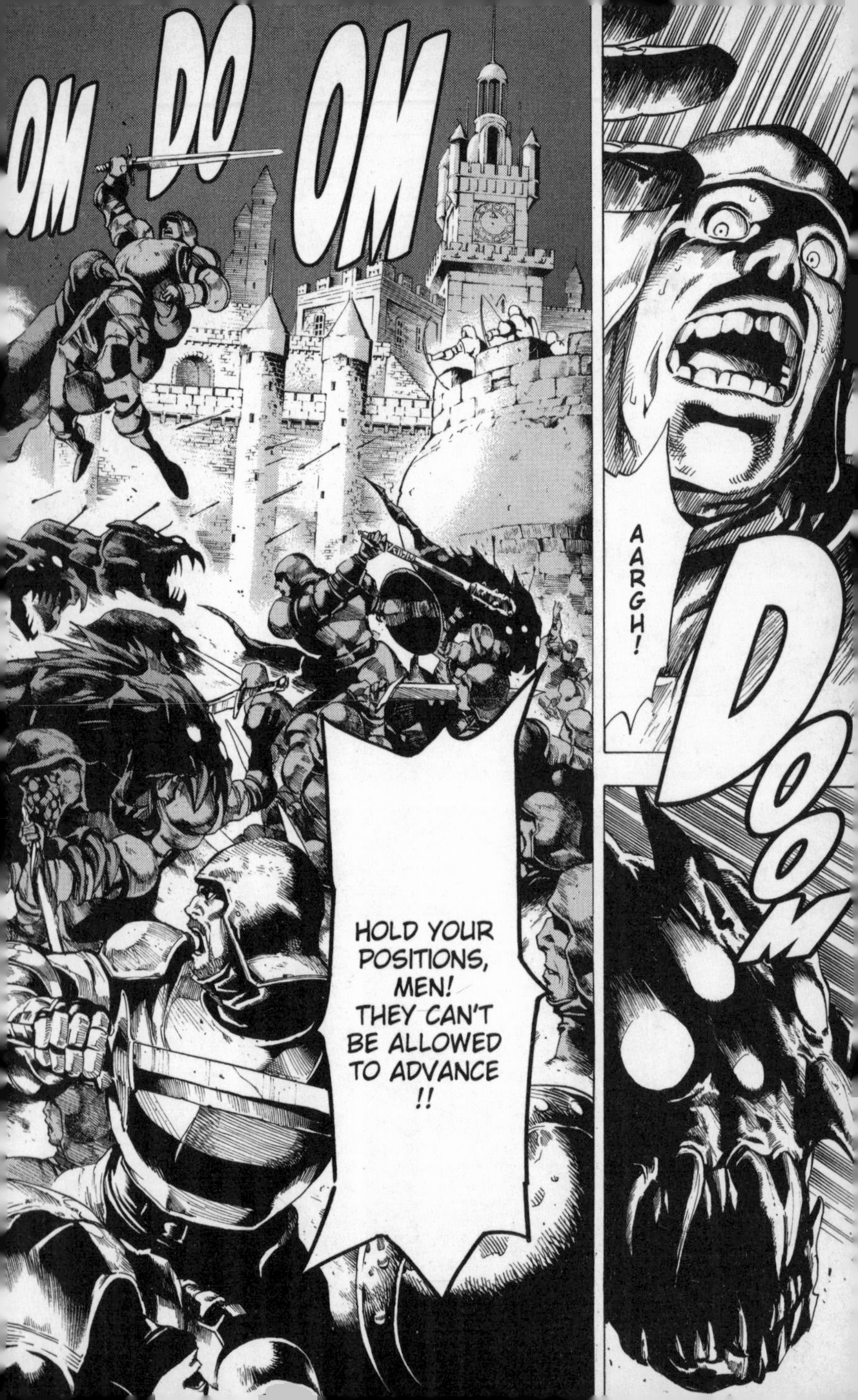
AARGH!
DOOOM
OM DO OM
HOLD YOUR POSITIONS, MEN! THEY CAN'T BE ALLOWED TO ADVANCE !!

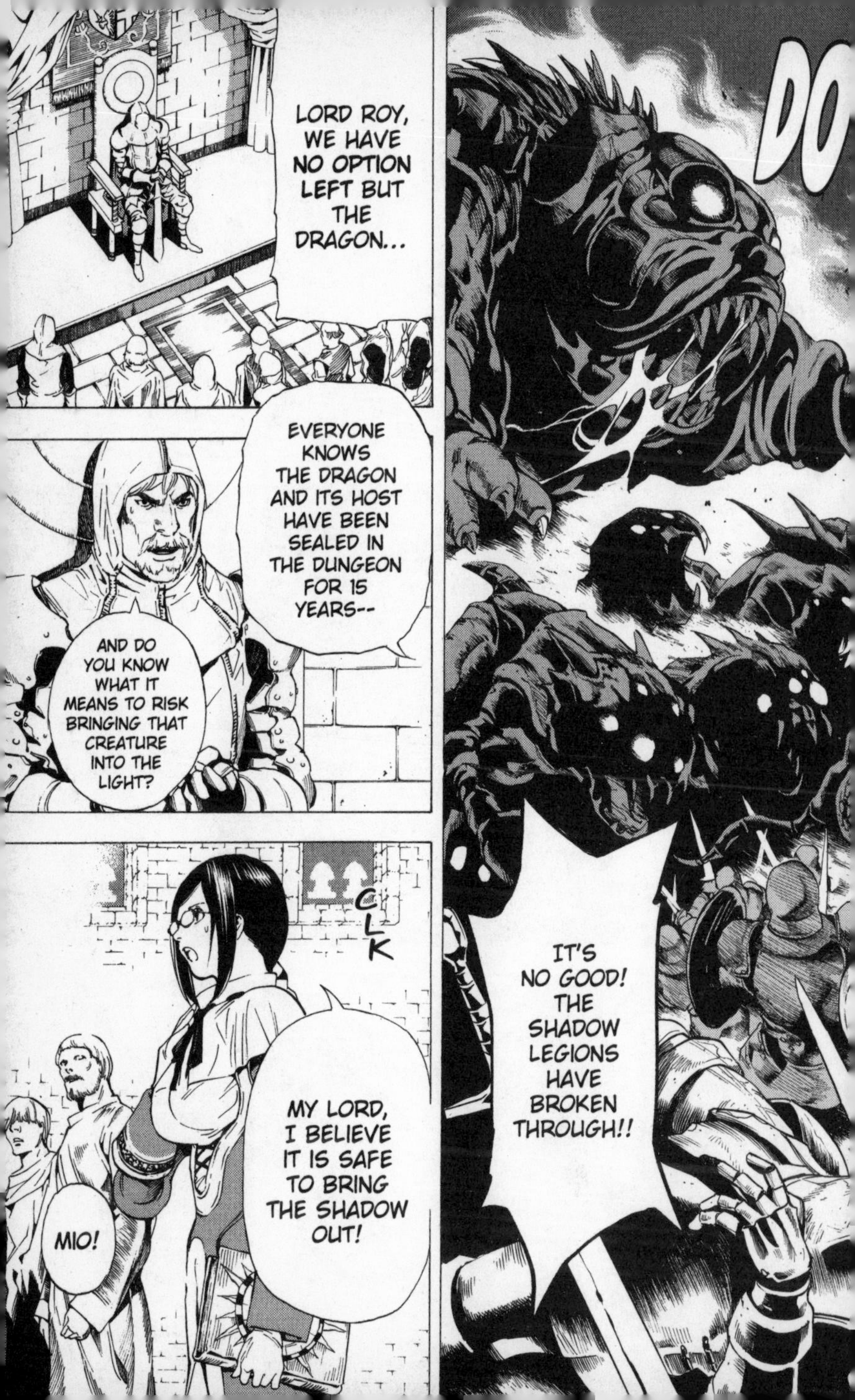
DO
IT'S NO GOOD! THE SHADOW LEGIONS HAVE BROKEN THROUGH!!
LORD ROY, WE HAVE NO OPTION LEFT BUT THE DRAGON...
EVERYONE KNOWS THE DRAGON AND ITS HOST HAVE BEEN SEALED IN THE DUNGEON FOR 15 YEARS--
AND DO YOU KNOW WHAT IT MEANS TO RISK BRINGING THAT CREATURE INTO THE LIGHT?
CLK
MY LORD, I BELIEVE IT IS SAFE TO BRING THE SHADOW OUT!
MIO!

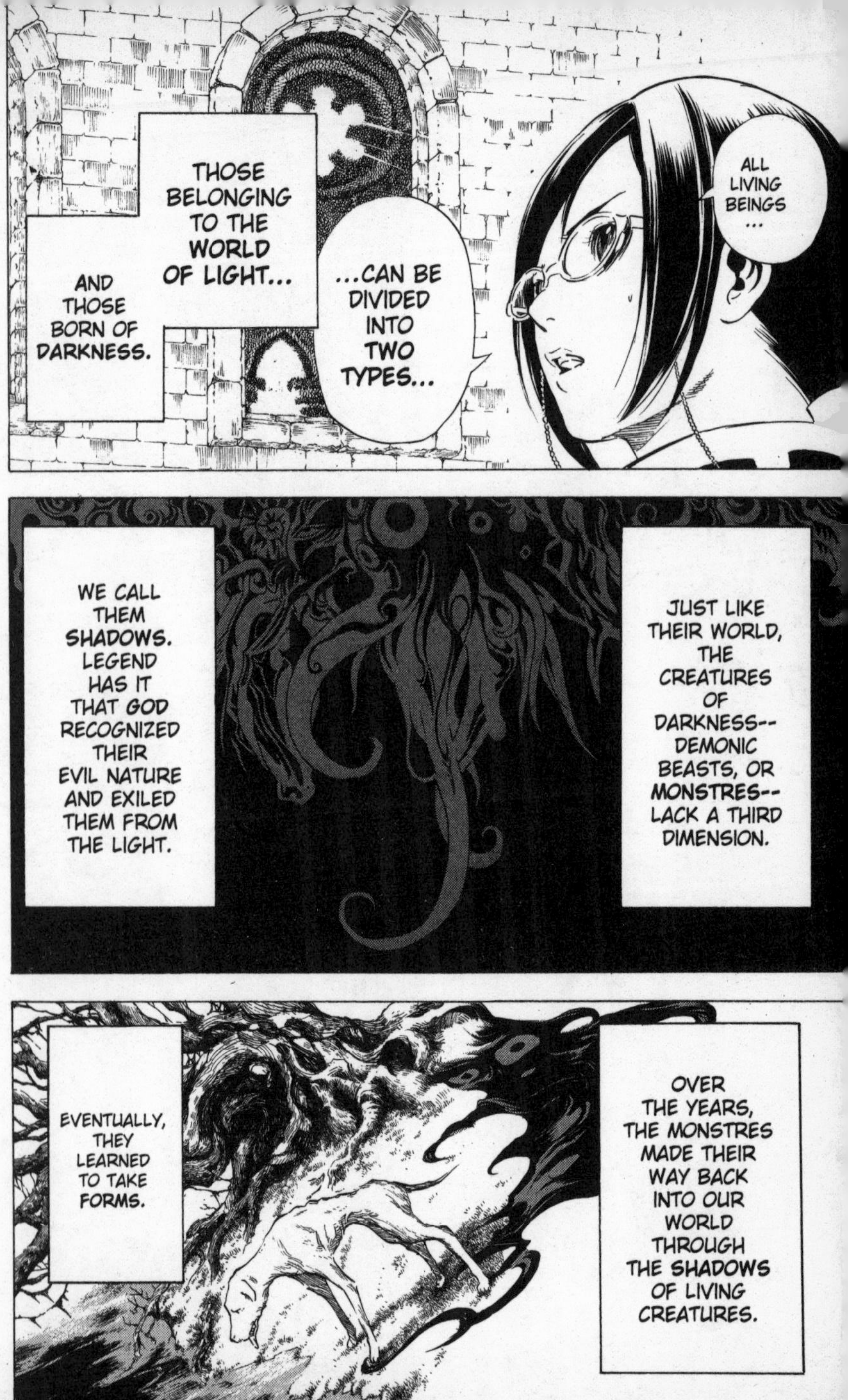
ALL LIVING BEINGS...
...CAN BE DIVIDED INTO TWO TYPES...
THOSE BELONGING TO THE WORLD OF LIGHT...
AND THOSE BORN OF DARKNESS.
JUST LIKE THEIR WORLD, THE CREATURES OF DARKNESS--DEMONIC BEASTS, OR MONSTRES--LACK A THIRD DIMENSION.
WE CALL THEM SHADOWS. LEGEND HAS IT THAT GOD RECOGNIZED THEIR EVIL NATURE AND EXILED THEM FROM THE LIGHT.
OVER THE YEARS, THE MONSTRES MADE THEIR WAY BACK INTO OUR WORLD THROUGH THE SHADOWS OF LIVING CREATURES.
EVENTUALLY, THEY LEARNED TO TAKE FORMS.

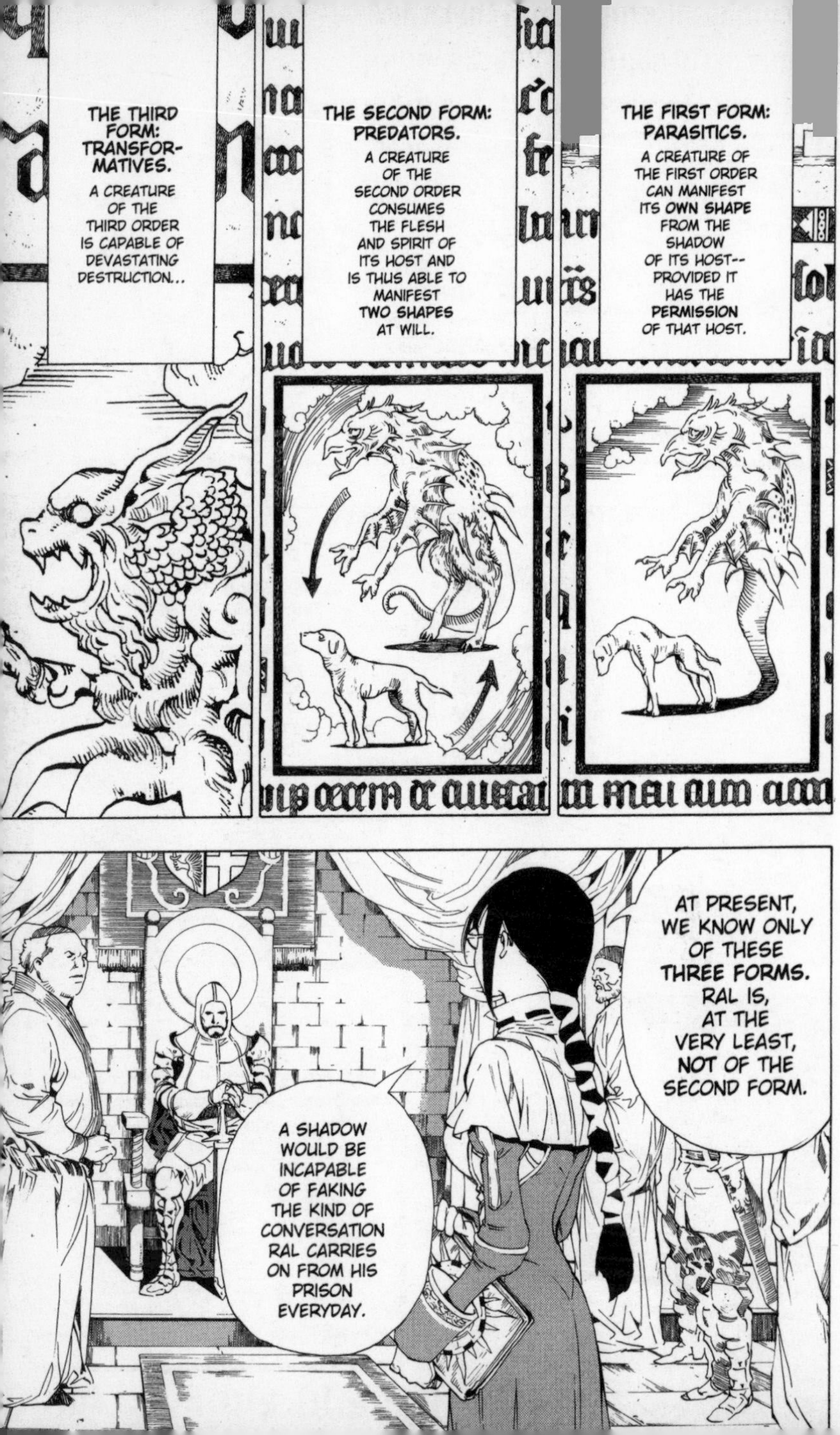
THE FIRST FORM: PARASITICS.
A CREATURE OF THE FIRST ORDER CAN MANIFEST ITS OWN SHAPE FROM THE SHADOW OF ITS HOST-- PROVIDED IT HAS THE PERMISSION OF THAT HOST.
THE SECOND FORM: PREDATORS.
A CREATURE OF THE SECOND ORDER CONSUMES THE FLESH AND SPIRIT OF ITS HOST AND IS THUS ABLE TO MANIFEST TWO SHAPES AT WILL.
THE THIRD FORM: TRANSFOR-MATIVES.
A CREATURE OF THE THIRD ORDER IS CAPABLE OF DEVASTATING DESTRUCTION...
AT PRESENT, WE KNOW ONLY OF THESE THREE FORMS. RAL IS, AT THE VERY LEAST, NOT OF THE SECOND FORM.
A SHADOW WOULD BE INCAPABLE OF FAKING THE KIND OF CONVERSATION RAL CARRIES ON FROM HIS PRISON EVERYDAY.

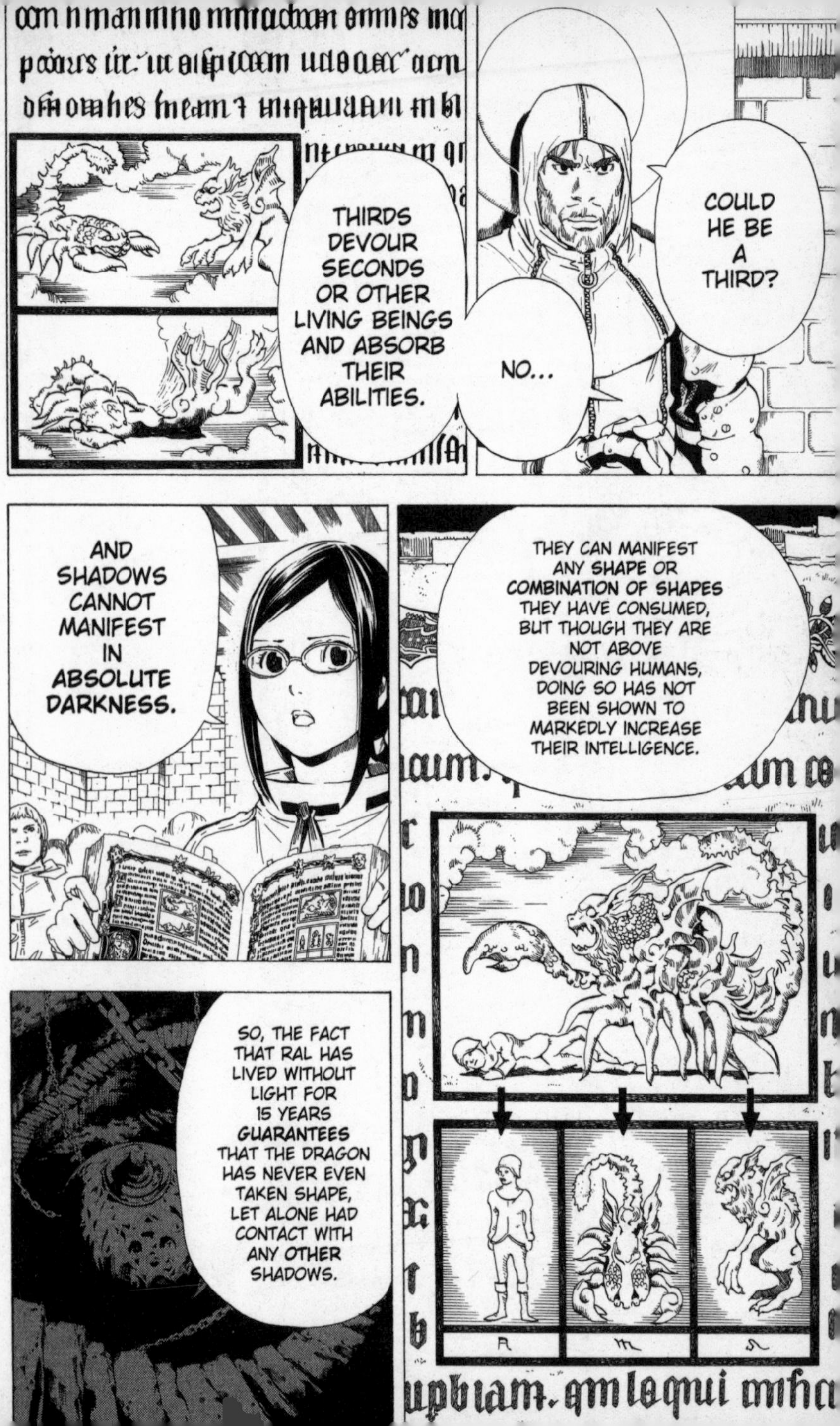
COULD HE BE A THIRD?
NO...
THIRDS DEVOUR SECONDS OR OTHER LIVING BEINGS AND ABSORB THEIR ABILITIES.
THEY CAN MANIFEST ANY SHAPE OR COMBINATION OF SHAPES THEY HAVE CONSUMED, BUT THOUGH THEY ARE NOT ABOVE DEVOURING HUMANS, DOING SO HAS NOT BEEN SHOWN TO MARKEDLY INCREASE THEIR INTELLIGENCE.
AND SHADOWS CANNOT MANIFEST IN ABSOLUTE DARKNESS.
SO, THE FACT THAT RAL HAS LIVED WITHOUT LIGHT FOR 15 YEARS GUARANTEES THAT THE DRAGON HAS NEVER EVEN TAKEN SHAPE, LET ALONE HAD CONTACT WITH ANY OTHER SHADOWS.

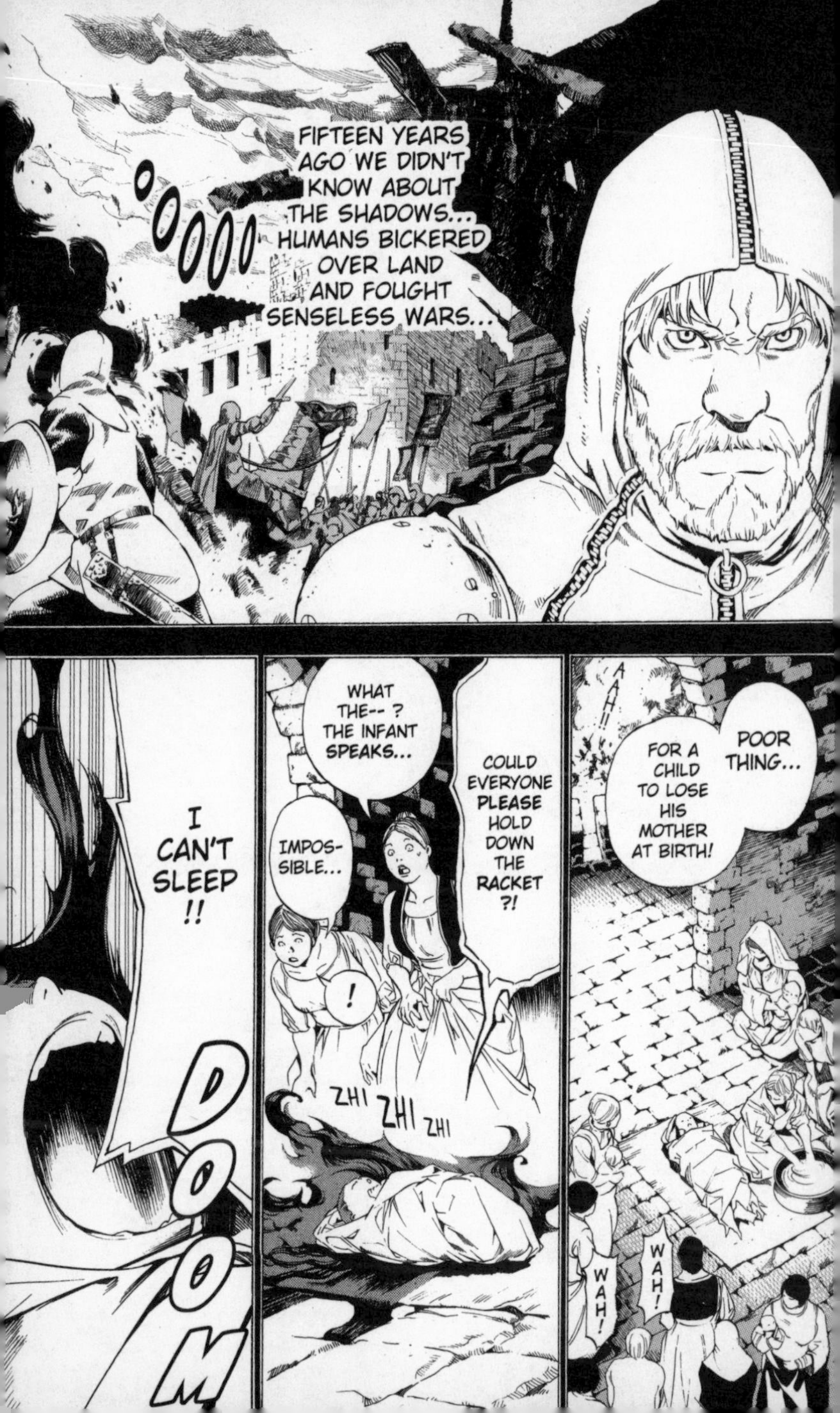
FIFTEEN YEARS AGO WE DIDN'T KNOW ABOUT THE SHADOWS... HUMANS BICKERED OVER LAND AND FOUGHT SENSELESS WARS...
OOOOO
POOR THING...
FOR A CHILD TO LOSE HIS MOTHER AT BIRTH!
AAH!!
WAH!
WAH!
COULD EVERYONE PLEASE HOLD DOWN THE RACKET ?!
WHAT THE-- ? THE INFANT SPEAKS...
IMPOSSIBLE...
!
ZHI ZHI ZHI
I CAN'T SLEEP !!
DOOOM

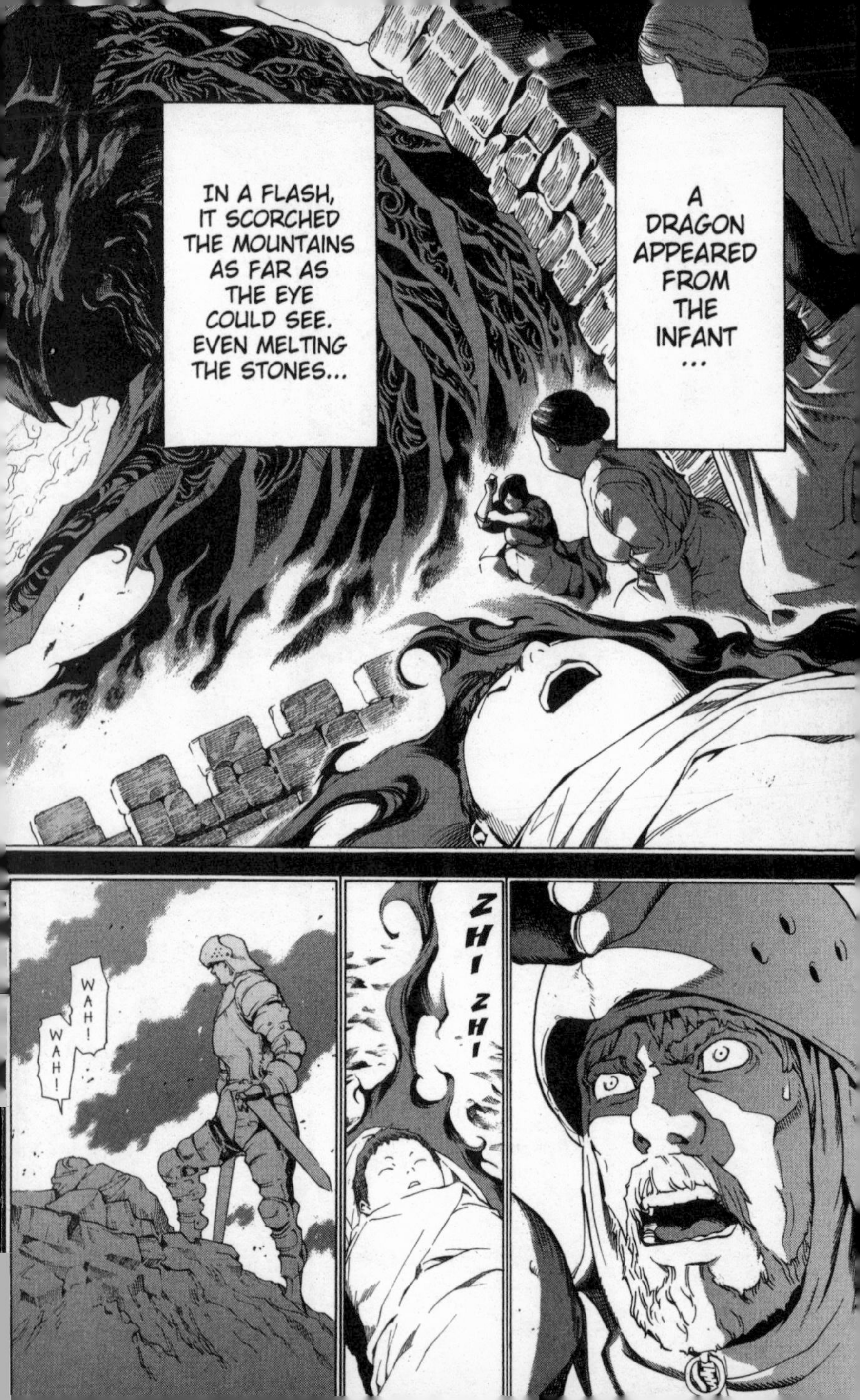
A DRAGON APPEARED FROM THE INFANT...
IN A FLASH, IT SCORCHED THE MOUNTAINS AS FAR AS THE EYE COULD SEE. EVEN MELTING THE STONES...
ZHI ZHI
WAH!
WAH!

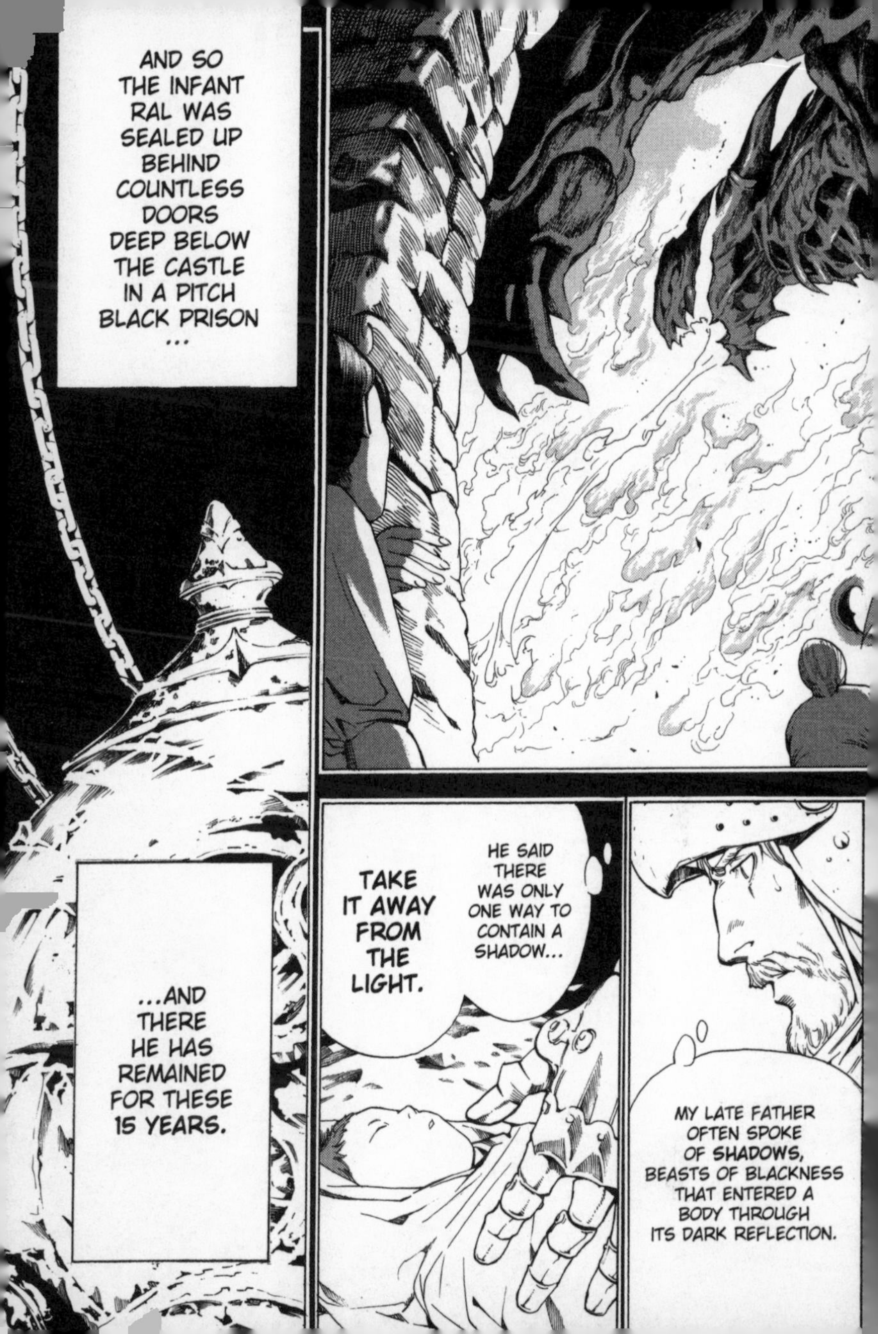
MY LATE FATHER OFTEN SPOKE OF SHADOWS, BEASTS OF BLACKNESS THAT ENTERED A BODY THROUGH ITS DARK REFLECTION.
HE SAID THERE WAS ONLY ONE WAY TO CONTAIN A SHADOW...
TAKE IT AWAY FROM THE LIGHT.
AND SO THE INFANT RAL WAS SEALED UP BEHIND COUNTLESS DOORS DEEP BELOW THE CASTLE IN A PITCH BLACK PRISON ...
...AND THERE HE HAS REMAINED FOR THESE 15 YEARS.

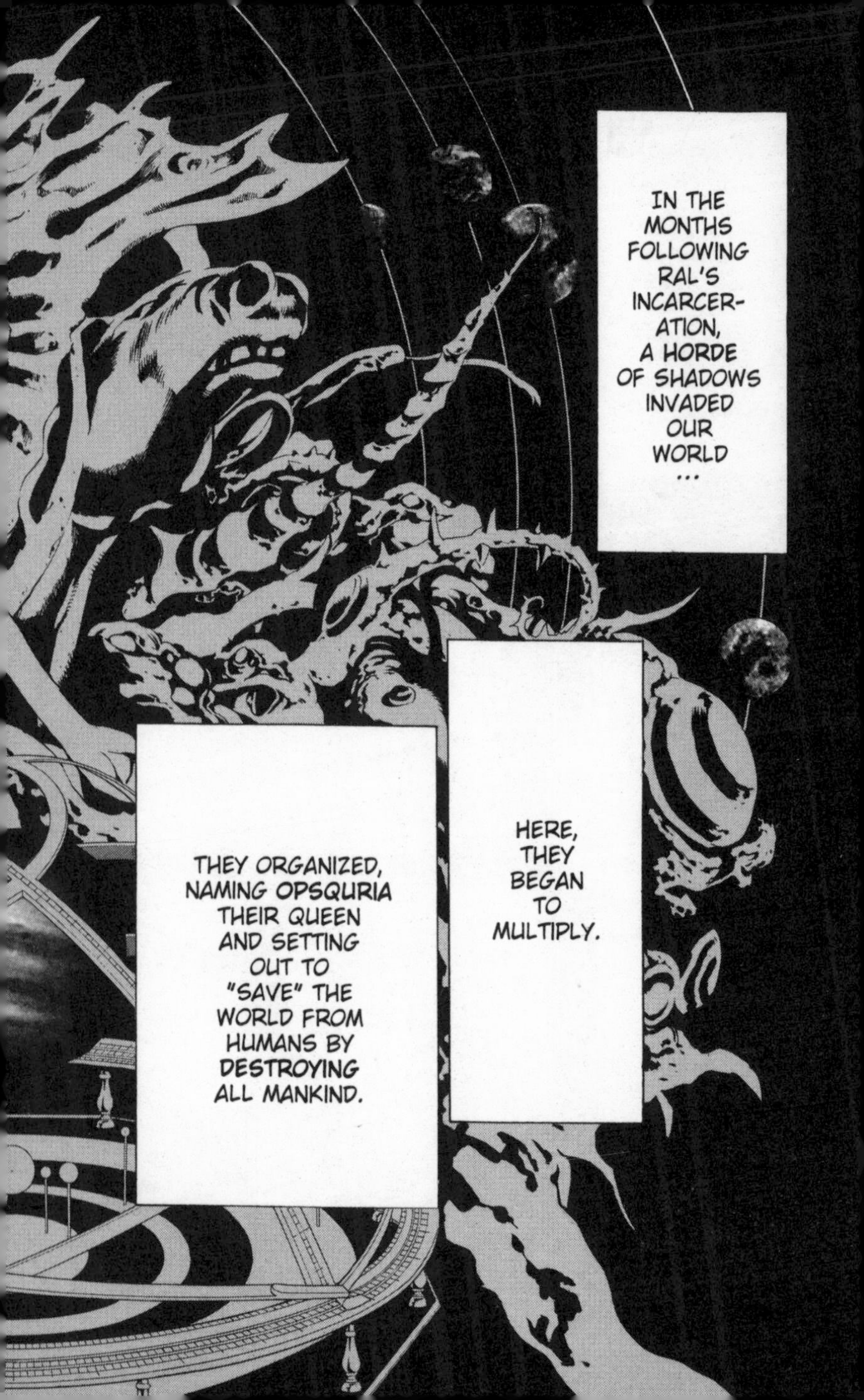
IN THE MONTHS FOLLOWING RAL'S INCARCER-ATION, A HORDE OF SHADOWS INVADED OUR WORLD ...
HERE, THEY BEGAN TO MULTIPLY.
THEY ORGANIZED, NAMING OPSQURIA THEIR QUEEN AND SETTING OUT TO "SAVE" THE WORLD FROM HUMANS BY DESTROYING ALL MANKIND.

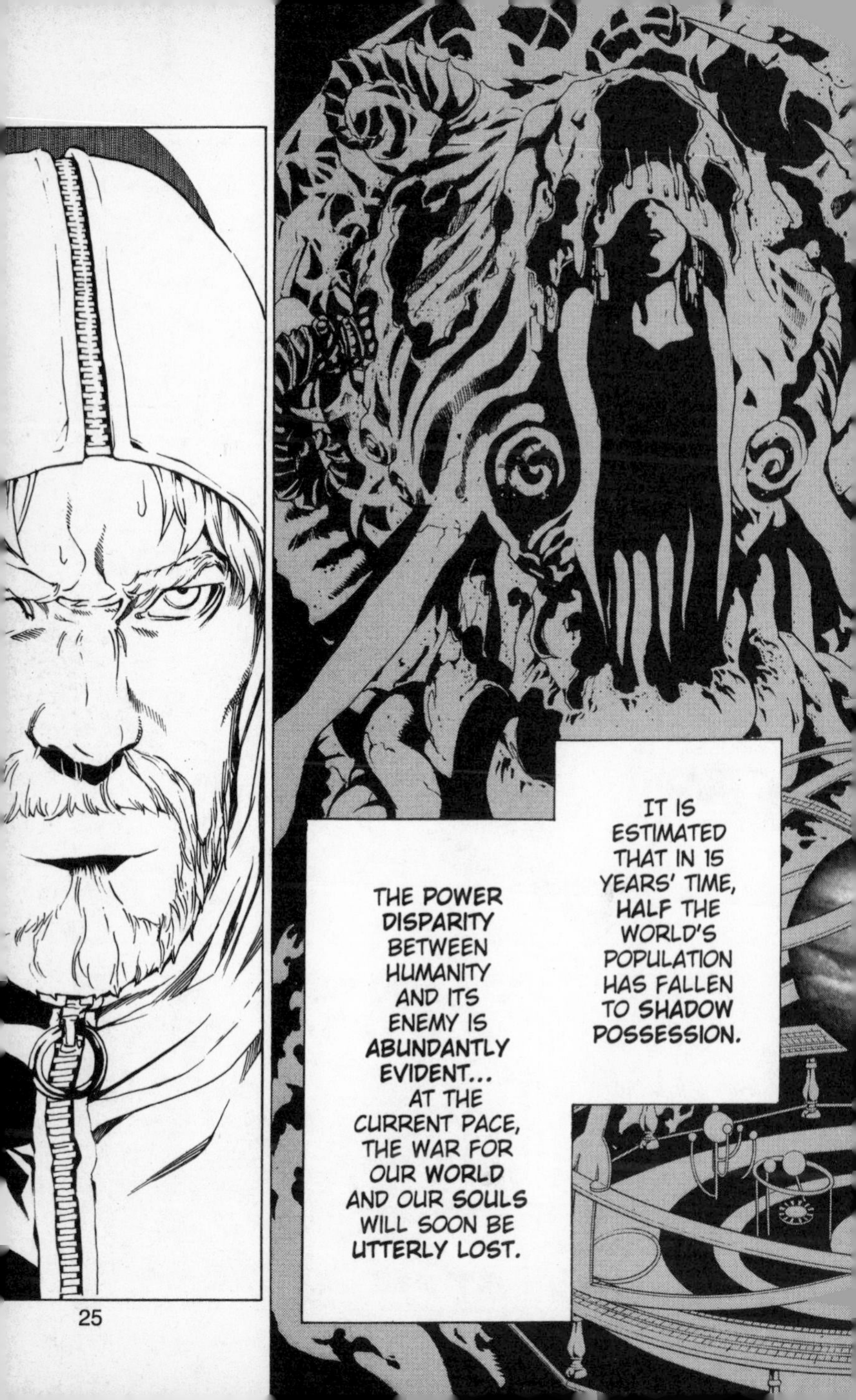
IT IS ESTIMATED THAT IN 15 YEARS' TIME, HALF THE WORLD'S POPULATION HAS FALLEN TO SHADOW POSSESSION.
THE POWER DISPARITY BETWEEN HUMANITY AND ITS ENEMY IS ABUNDANTLY EVIDENT... AT THE CURRENT PACE, THE WAR FOR OUR WORLD AND OUR SOULS WILL SOON BE UTTERLY LOST.

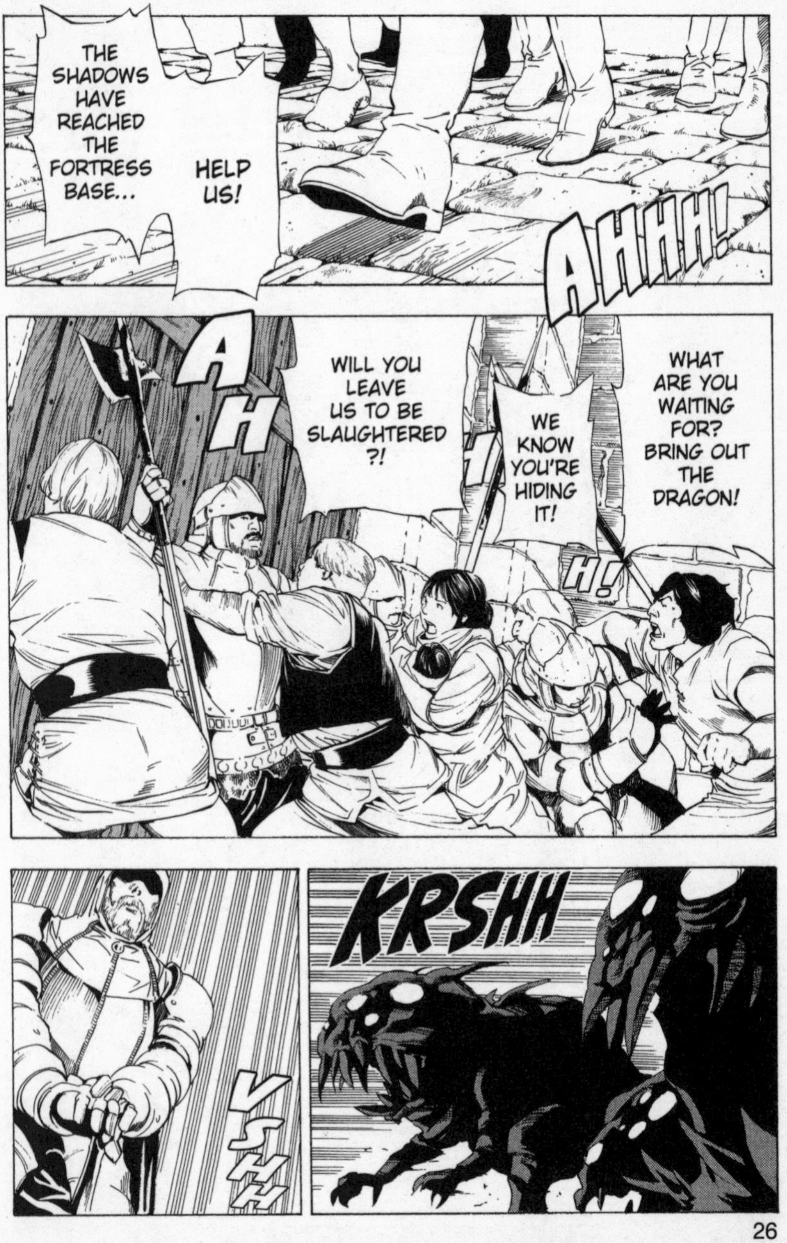
THE SHADOWS HAVE REACHED THE FORTRESS BASE...
HELP US!
AHHH!
WHAT ARE YOU WAITING FOR? BRING OUT THE DRAGON!
WE KNOW YOU'RE HIDING IT!
WILL YOU LEAVE US TO BE SLAUGHTERED?!
AH
H!
KRSHH
VSHH

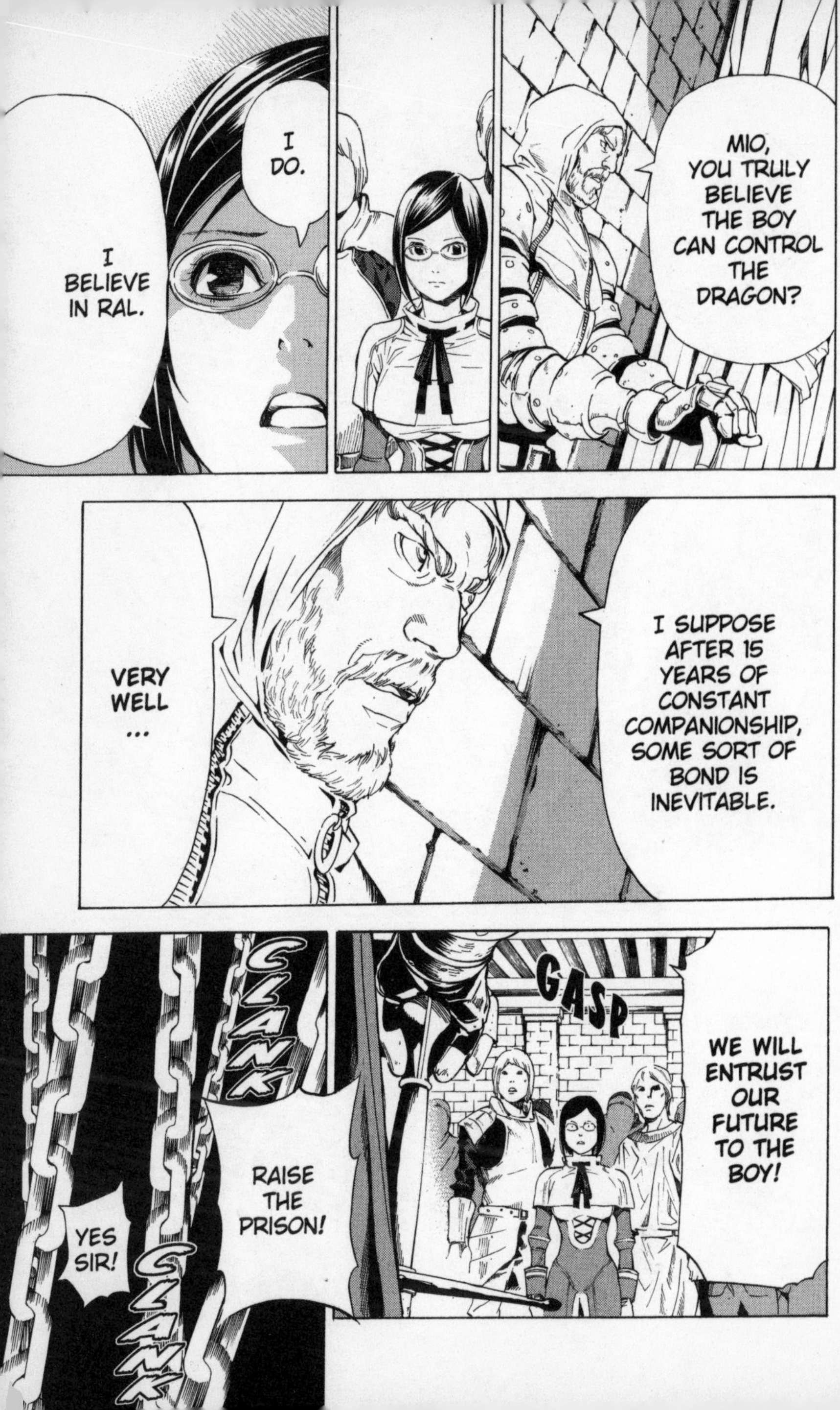
MIO, YOU TRULY BELIEVE THE BOY CAN CONTROL THE DRAGON?
I DO.
I BELIEVE IN RAL.
I SUPPOSE AFTER 15 YEARS OF CONSTANT COMPANIONSHIP, SOME SORT OF BOND IS INEVITABLE.
VERY WELL ...
GASP
WE WILL ENTRUST OUR FUTURE TO THE BOY!
CLANK
RAISE THE PRISON!
YES SIR!
CLANK

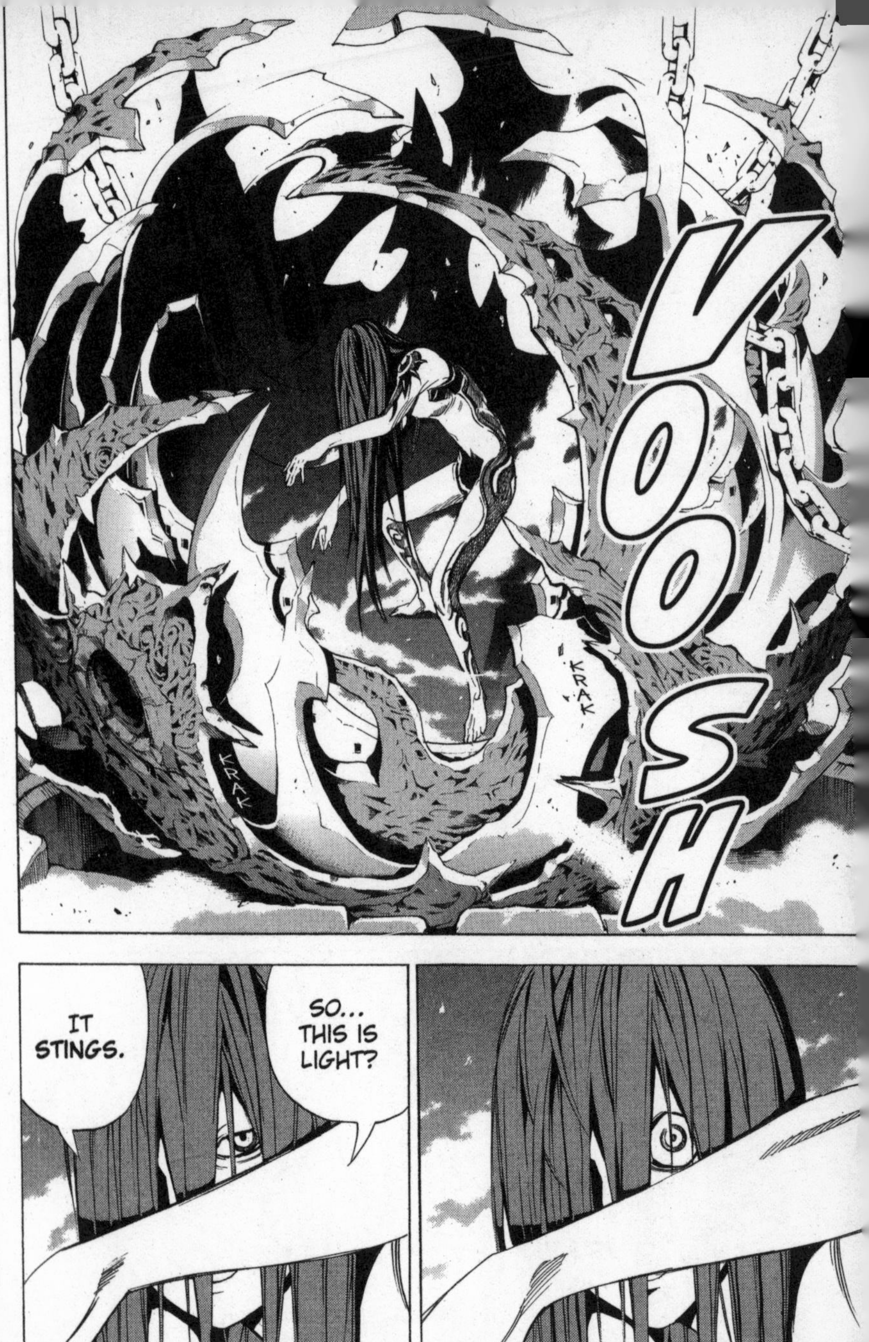
VOOSH
KRAK
KRAK
SO... THIS IS LIGHT?
IT STINGS.

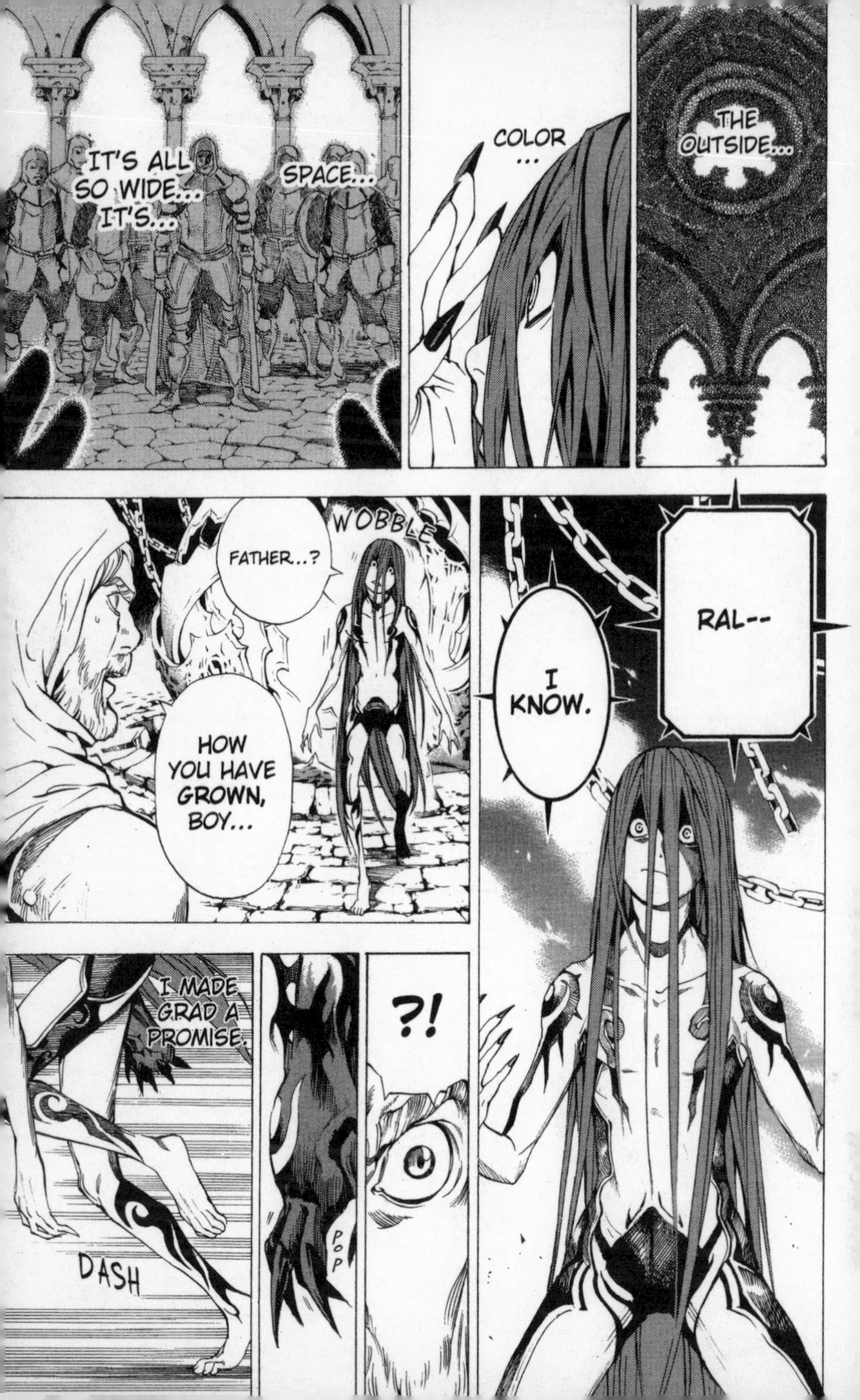
THE OUTSIDE...
COLOR ...
IT'S ALL SO WIDE... IT'S...
SPACE...
RAL--
I KNOW.
WOBBLE
FATHER..?
HOW YOU HAVE GROWN, BOY...
?!
POP
I MADE GRAD A PROMISE.
DASH

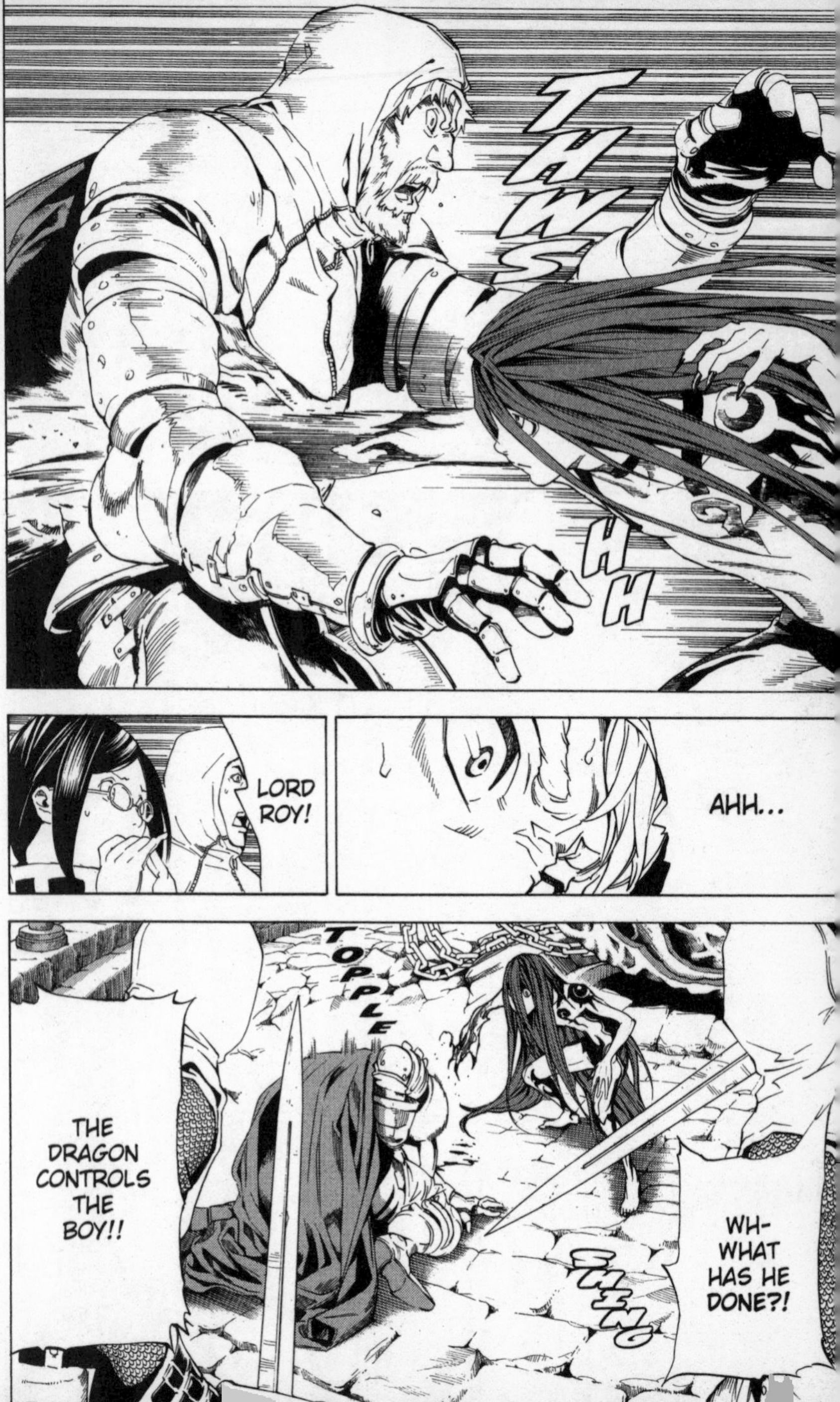
THWASHH
AHH...
LORD ROY!
WH-WHAT HAS HE DONE?!
TOPPLE
CHING
THE DRAGON CONTROLS THE BOY!!

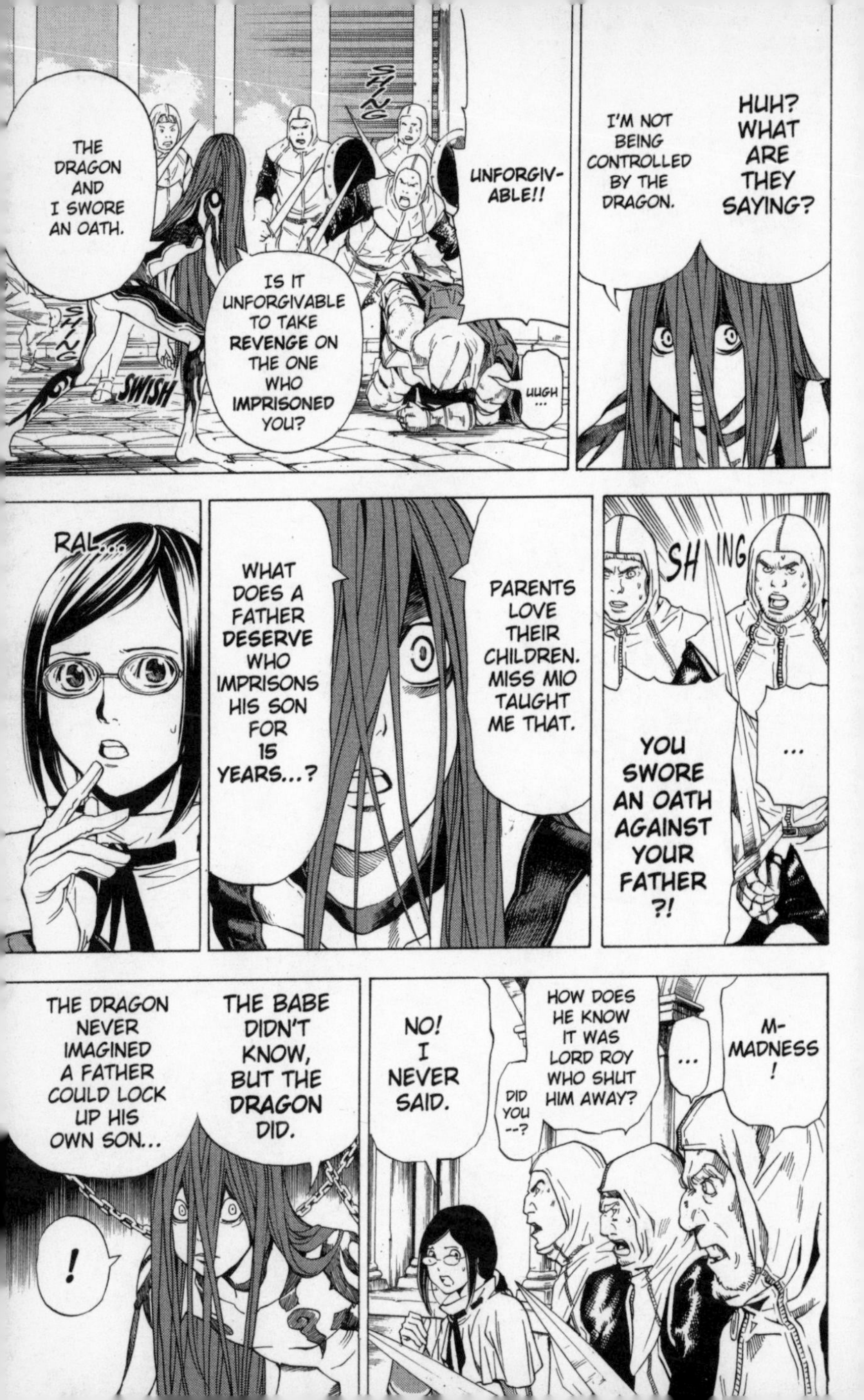
HUH? WHAT ARE THEY SAYING?
I'M NOT BEING CONTROLLED BY THE DRAGON.
SHING
UNFORGIV-ABLE!!
THE DRAGON AND I SWORE AN OATH.
IS IT UNFORGIVABLE TO TAKE REVENGE ON THE ONE WHO IMPRISONED YOU?
UUGH...
SHING
SWISH
SHING
...
YOU SWORE AN OATH AGAINST YOUR FATHER?!
PARENTS LOVE THEIR CHILDREN. MISS MIO TAUGHT ME THAT.
WHAT DOES A FATHER DESERVE WHO IMPRISONS HIS SON FOR 15 YEARS...?
RAL...
M-MADNESS!
...
HOW DOES HE KNOW IT WAS LORD ROY WHO SHUT HIM AWAY?
DID YOU --?
NO! I NEVER SAID.
THE BABE DIDN'T KNOW, BUT THE DRAGON DID.
THE DRAGON NEVER IMAGINED A FATHER COULD LOCK UP HIS OWN SON...
!

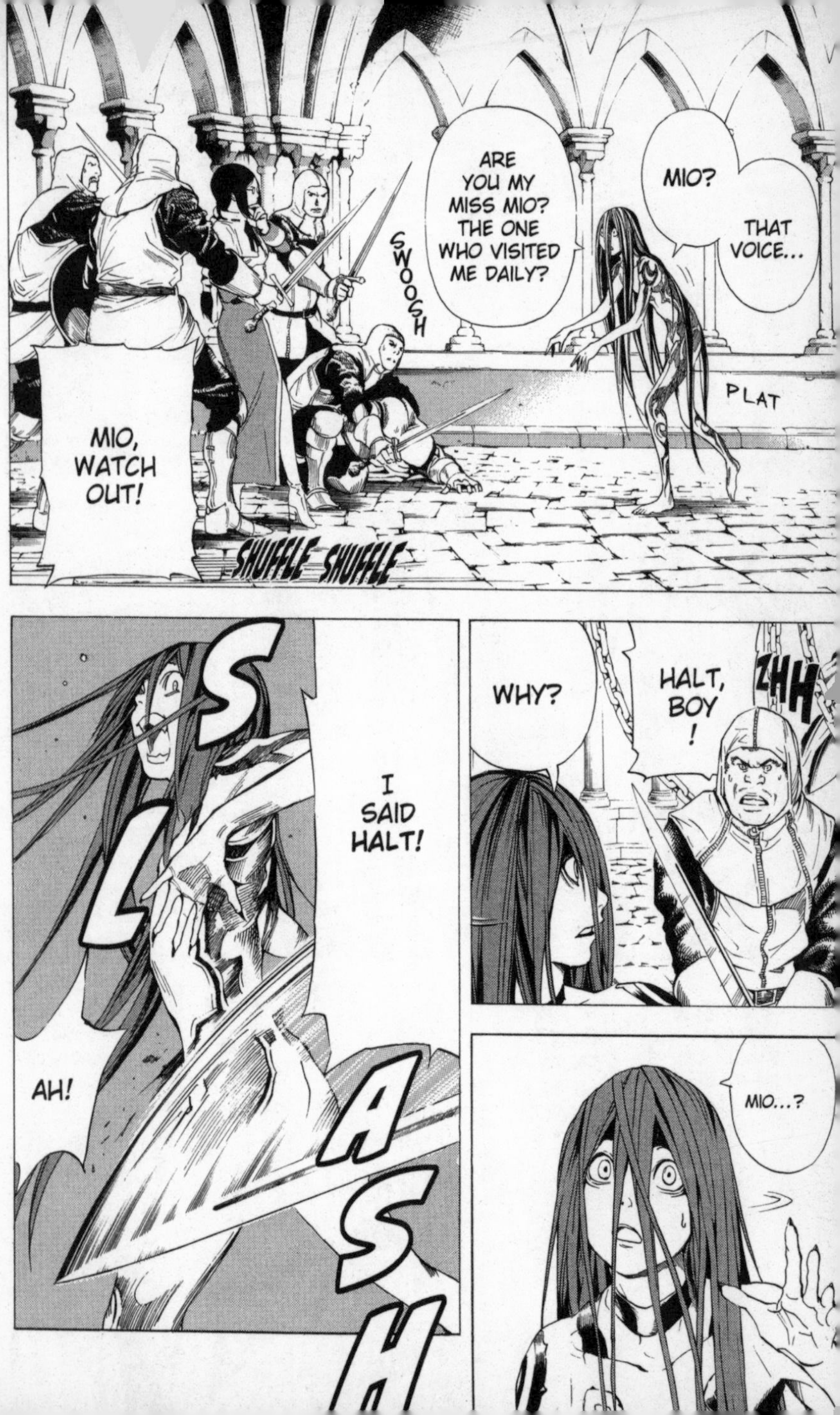
MIO?
THAT VOICE...
ARE YOU MY MISS MIO? THE ONE WHO VISITED ME DAILY?
SWOOSH
PLAT
MIO, WATCH OUT!
SHUFFLE SHUFFLE
ZHH
HALT, BOY!
WHY?
MIO...?
I SAID HALT!
SLASH
AH!

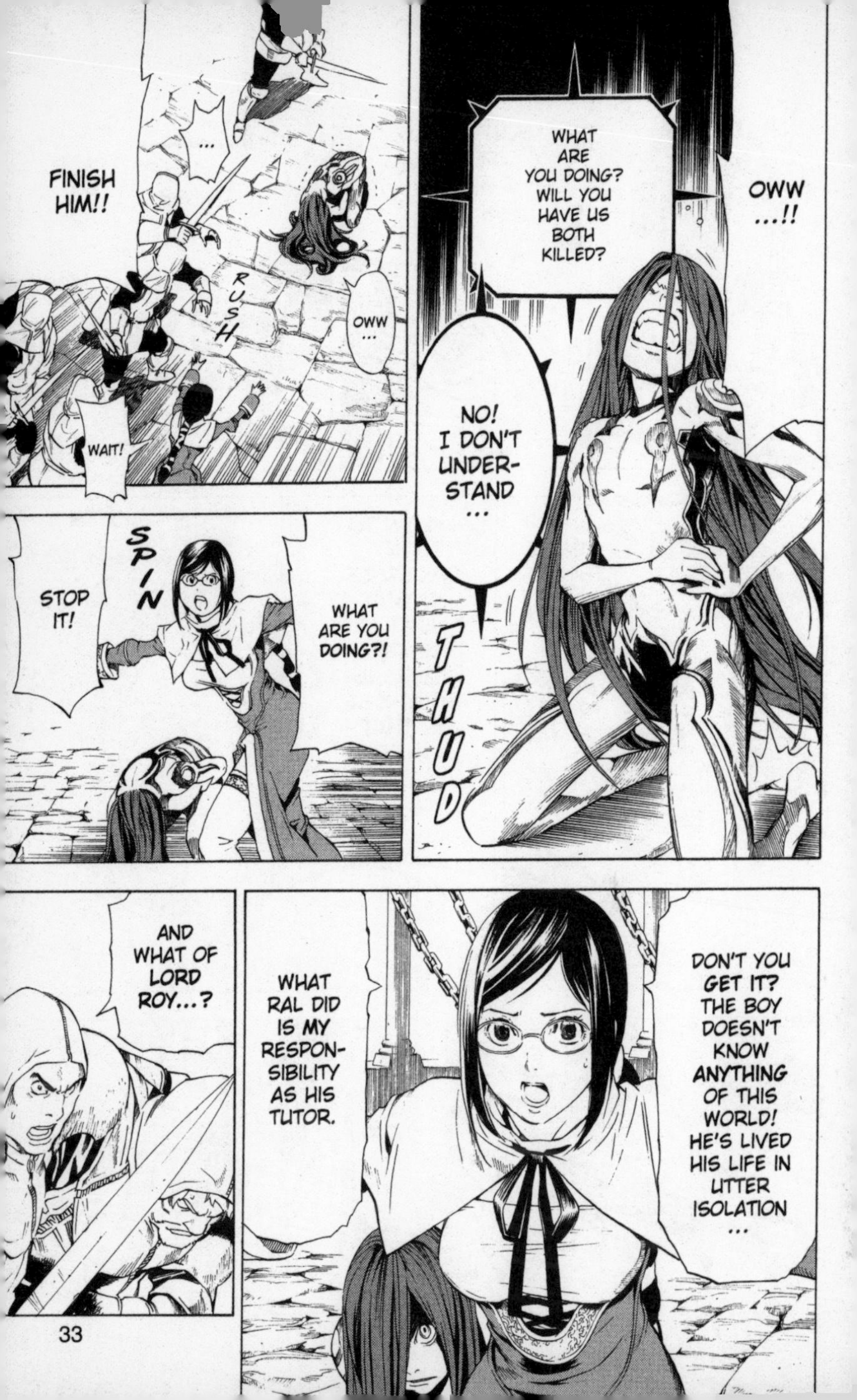
OWW ...!!
WHAT ARE YOU DOING? WILL YOU HAVE US BOTH KILLED?
NO! I DON'T UNDER-STAND ...
THUD
OWW ...
...
RUSH
FINISH HIM!!
WAIT!
WHAT ARE YOU DOING?!
SPIN
STOP IT!
DON'T YOU GET IT? THE BOY DOESN'T KNOW ANYTHING OF THIS WORLD! HE'S LIVED HIS LIFE IN UTTER ISOLATION ...
WHAT RAL DID IS MY RESPONSIBILITY AS HIS TUTOR.
AND WHAT OF LORD ROY...?

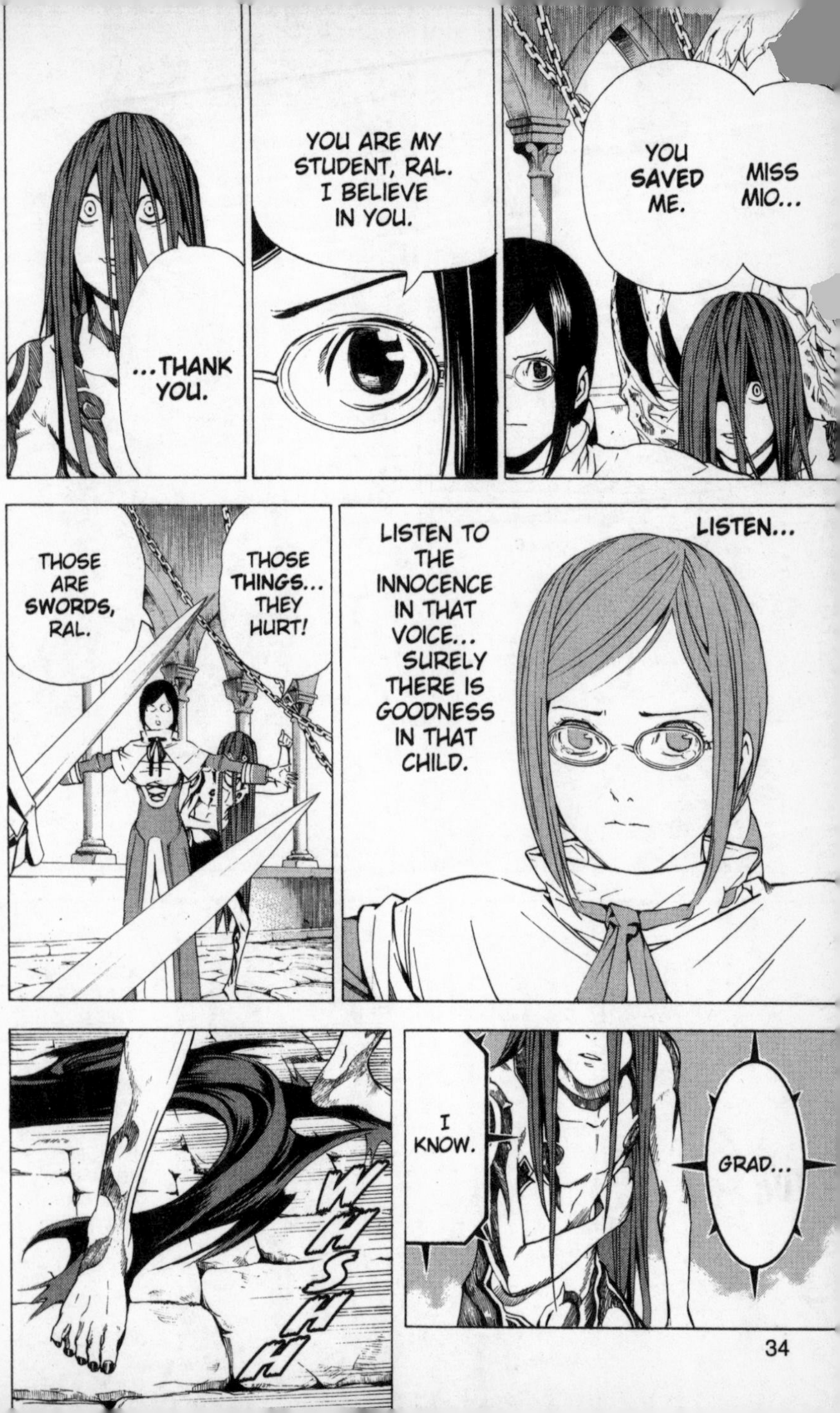
MISS MIO... YOU SAVED ME.
YOU ARE MY STUDENT, RAL. I BELIEVE IN YOU.
...THANK YOU.
LISTEN...
LISTEN TO THE INNOCENCE IN THAT VOICE... SURELY THERE IS GOODNESS IN THAT CHILD.
THOSE THINGS... THEY HURT!
THOSE ARE SWORDS, RAL.
GRAD...
I KNOW.
WHSHHH

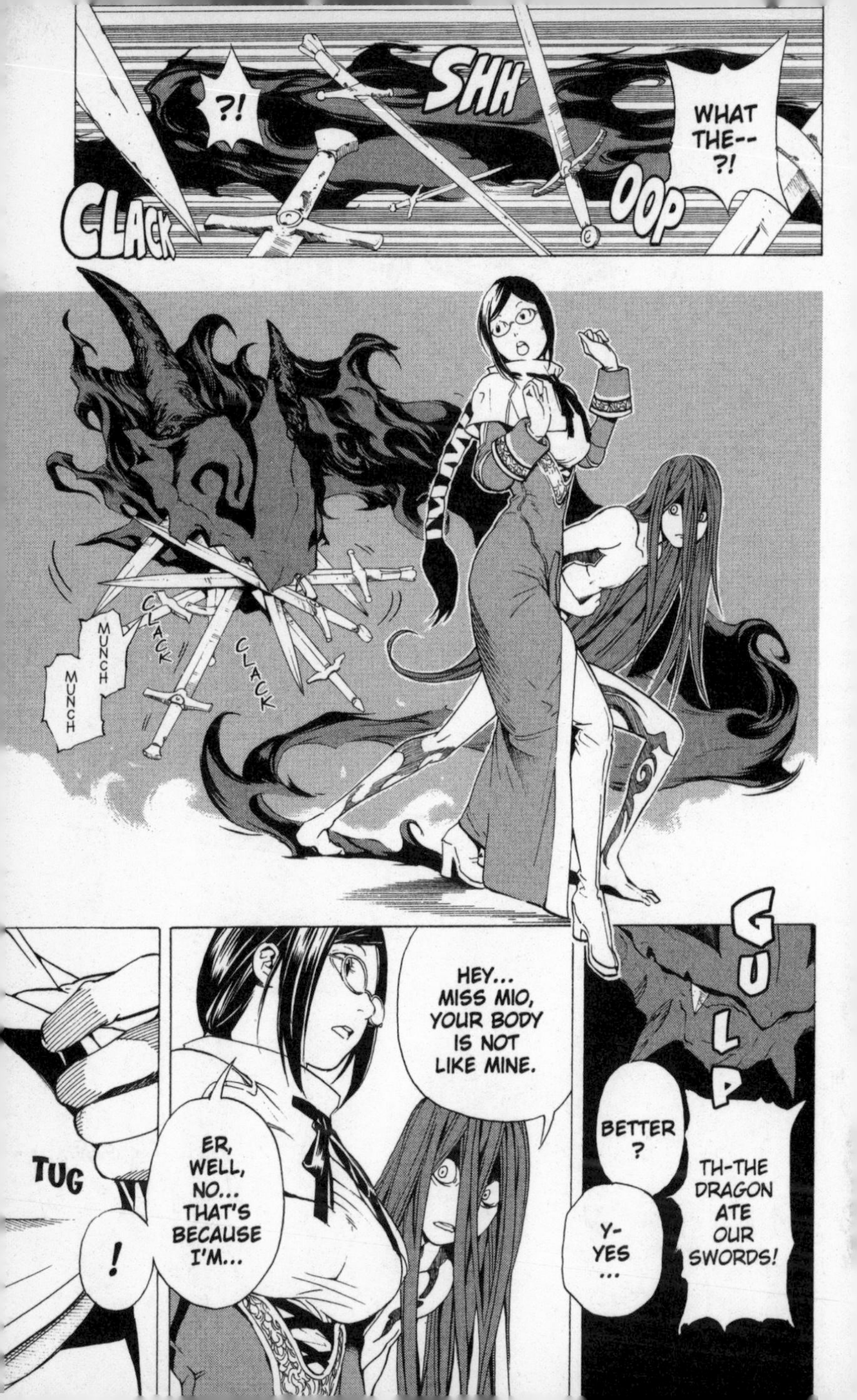
WHAT THE-- ?!
SHH
OOP
?!
CLACK
CLACK
CLACK
MUNCH
MUNCH
GULP
BETTER?
TH-THE DRAGON ATE OUR SWORDS!
Y-YES...
HEY... MISS MIO, YOUR BODY IS NOT LIKE MINE.
ER, WELL, NO... THAT'S BECAUSE I'M...
TUG
!

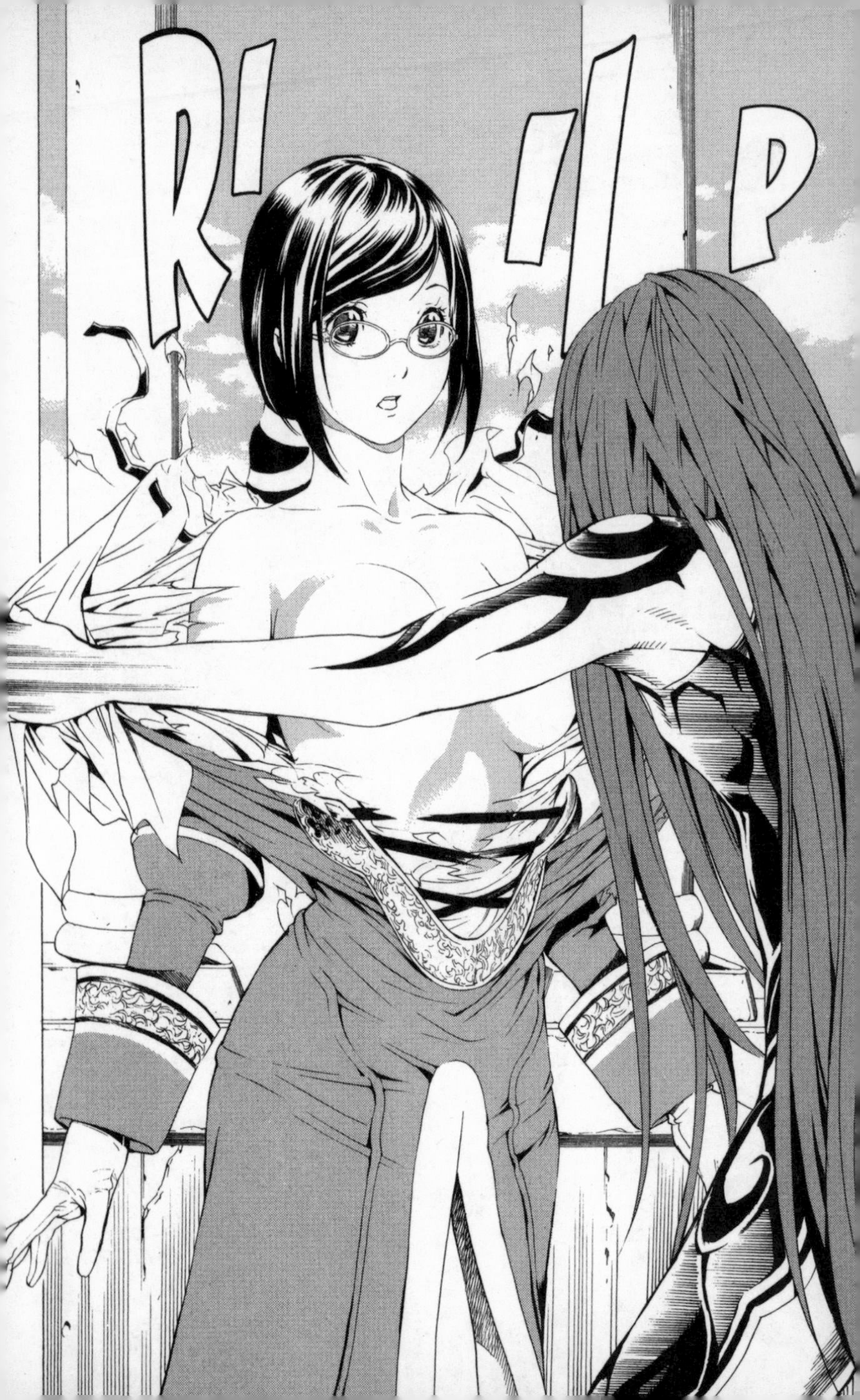
RIIP

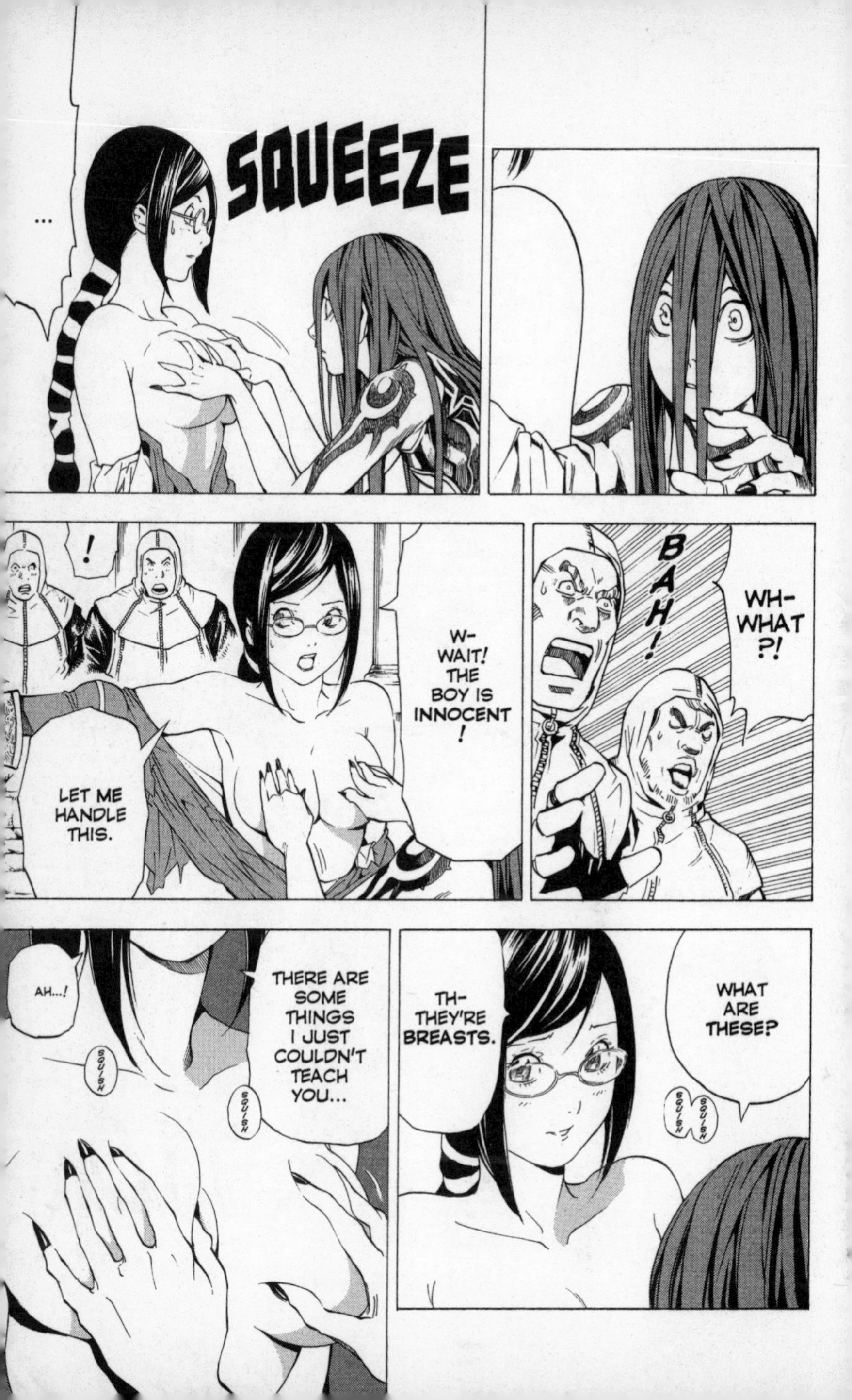
SQUEEZE
...
BAH!
WH-WHAT?!
!
W-WAIT! THE BOY IS INNOCENT!
LET ME HANDLE THIS.
WHAT ARE THESE?
SQUISH
SQUISH
TH-THEY'RE BREASTS.
THERE ARE SOME THINGS I JUST COULDN'T TEACH YOU...
SQUISH
AH...!
SQUISH

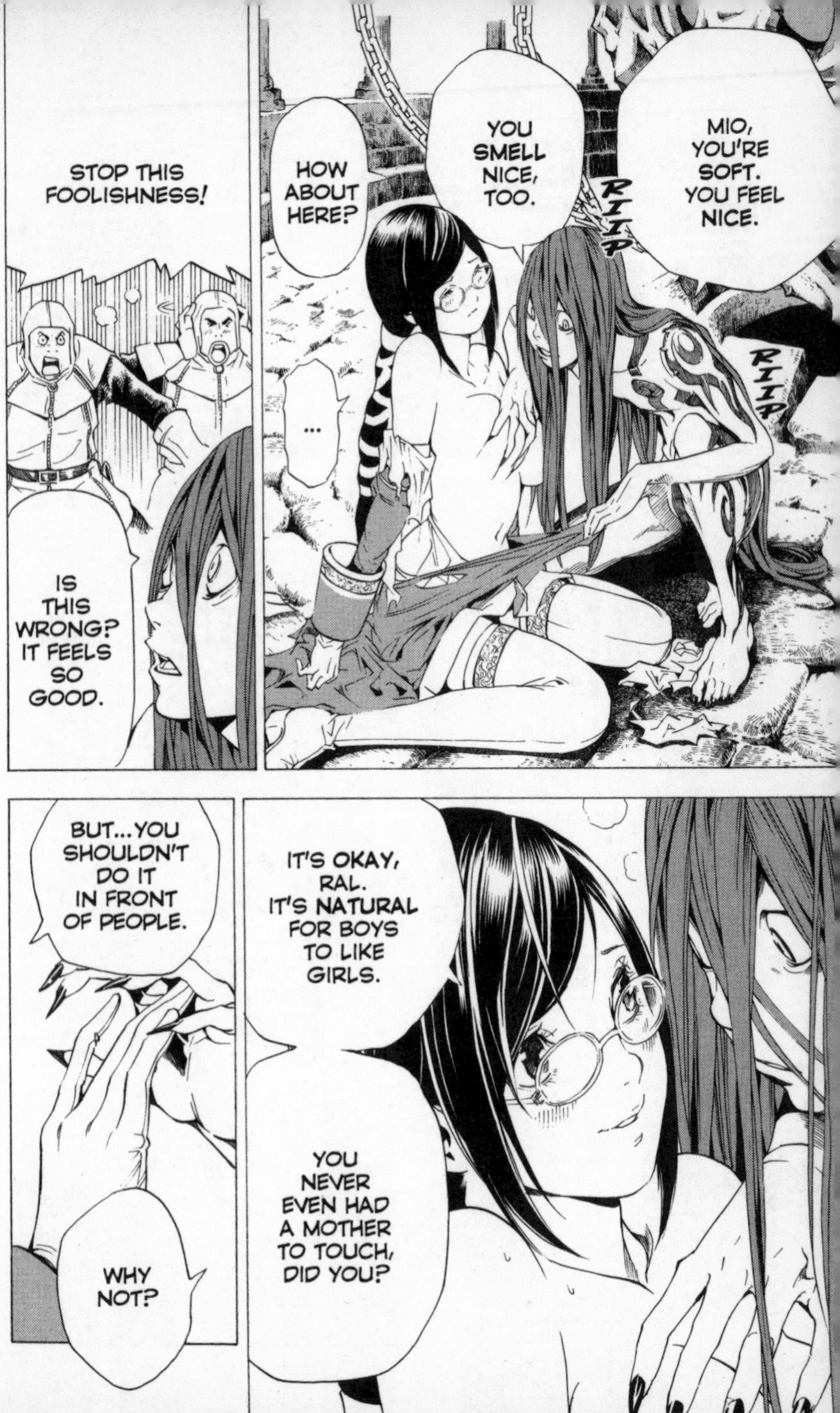
MIO, YOU'RE SOFT. YOU FEEL NICE.
RIIIP
YOU SMELL NICE, TOO.
HOW ABOUT HERE?
...
RIIIP
STOP THIS FOOLISHNESS!
IS THIS WRONG? IT FEELS SO GOOD.
IT'S OKAY, RAL. IT'S NATURAL FOR BOYS TO LIKE GIRLS.
YOU NEVER EVEN HAD A MOTHER TO TOUCH, DID YOU?
BUT...YOU SHOULDN'T DO IT IN FRONT OF PEOPLE.
WHY NOT?

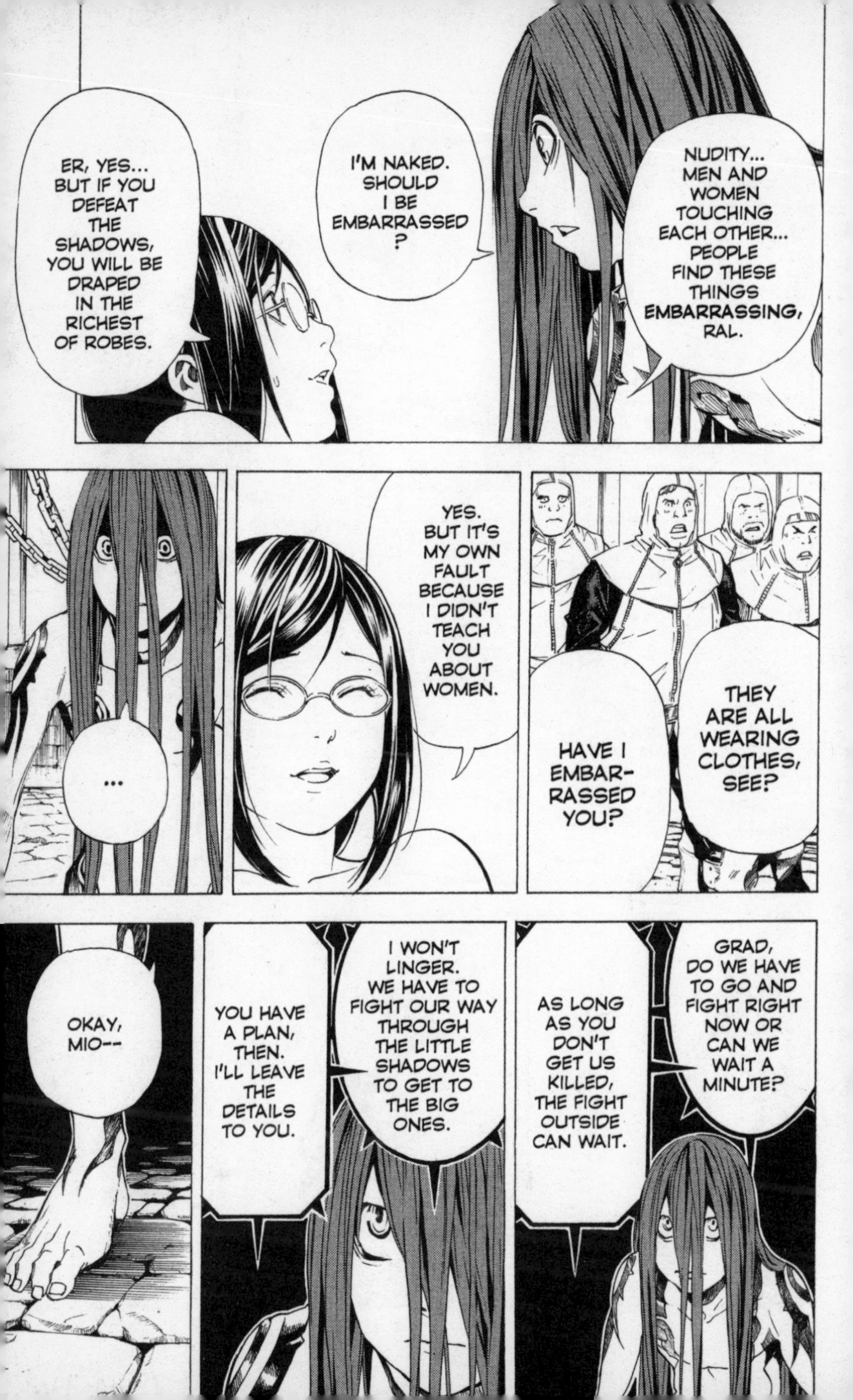
NUDITY... MEN AND WOMEN TOUCHING EACH OTHER... PEOPLE FIND THESE THINGS EMBARRASSING, RAL.
I'M NAKED. SHOULD I BE EMBARRASSED?
ER, YES... BUT IF YOU DEFEAT THE SHADOWS, YOU WILL BE DRAPED IN THE RICHEST OF ROBES.
THEY ARE ALL WEARING CLOTHES, SEE?
HAVE I EMBARRASSED YOU?
YES. BUT IT'S MY OWN FAULT BECAUSE I DIDN'T TEACH YOU ABOUT WOMEN.
...
GRAD, DO WE HAVE TO GO AND FIGHT RIGHT NOW OR CAN WE WAIT A MINUTE?
AS LONG AS YOU DON'T GET US KILLED, THE FIGHT OUTSIDE CAN WAIT.
I WON'T LINGER. WE HAVE TO FIGHT OUR WAY THROUGH THE LITTLE SHADOWS TO GET TO THE BIG ONES.
YOU HAVE A PLAN, THEN. I'LL LEAVE THE DETAILS TO YOU.
OKAY, MIO--

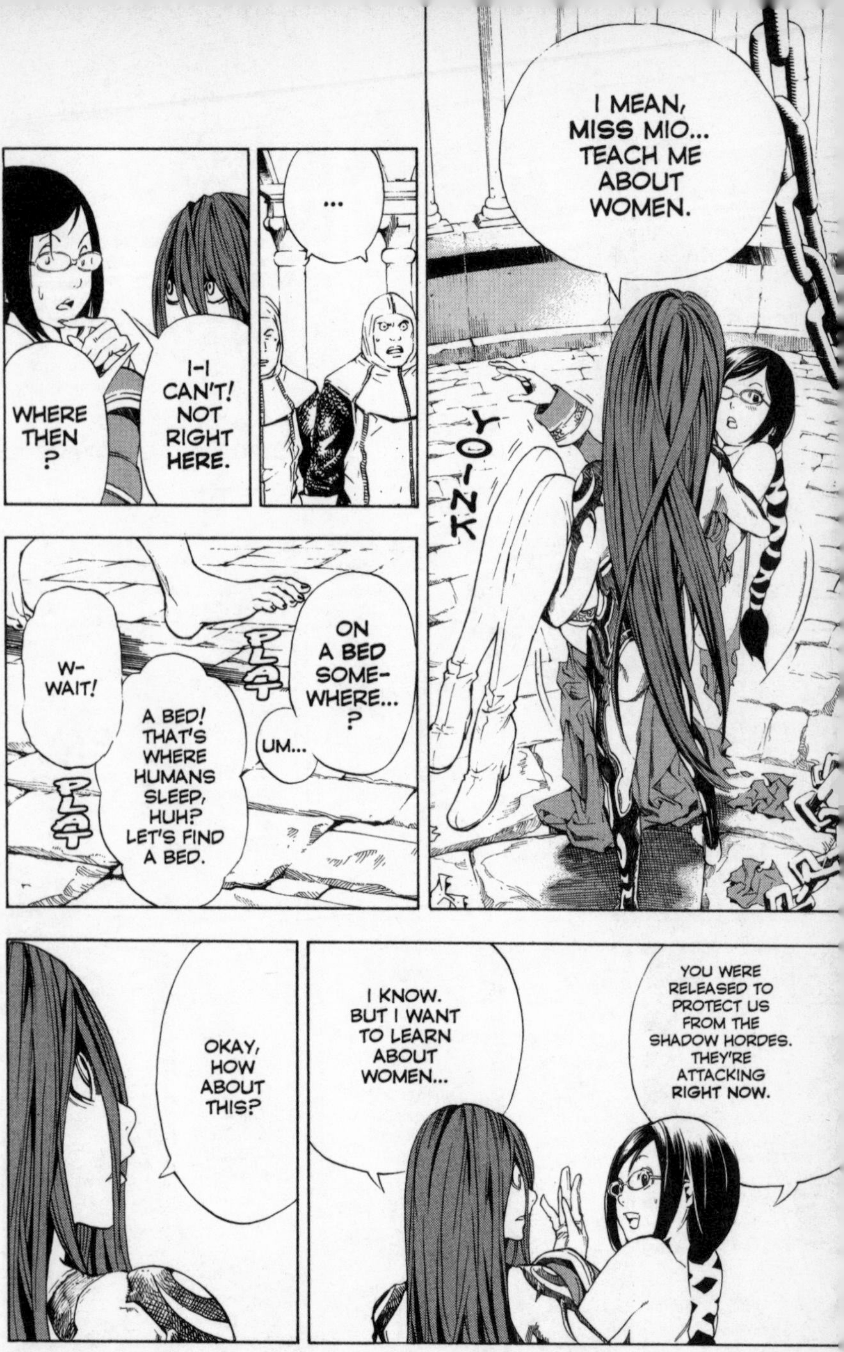
I MEAN, MISS MIO... TEACH ME ABOUT WOMEN.
YOINK
...
I-I CAN'T! NOT RIGHT HERE.
WHERE THEN?
ON A BED SOMEWHERE...?
UM...
PLAT
A BED! THAT'S WHERE HUMANS SLEEP, HUH? LET'S FIND A BED.
W-WAIT!
PLAT
YOU WERE RELEASED TO PROTECT US FROM THE SHADOW HORDES. THEY'RE ATTACKING RIGHT NOW.
I KNOW. BUT I WANT TO LEARN ABOUT WOMEN...
OKAY, HOW ABOUT THIS?

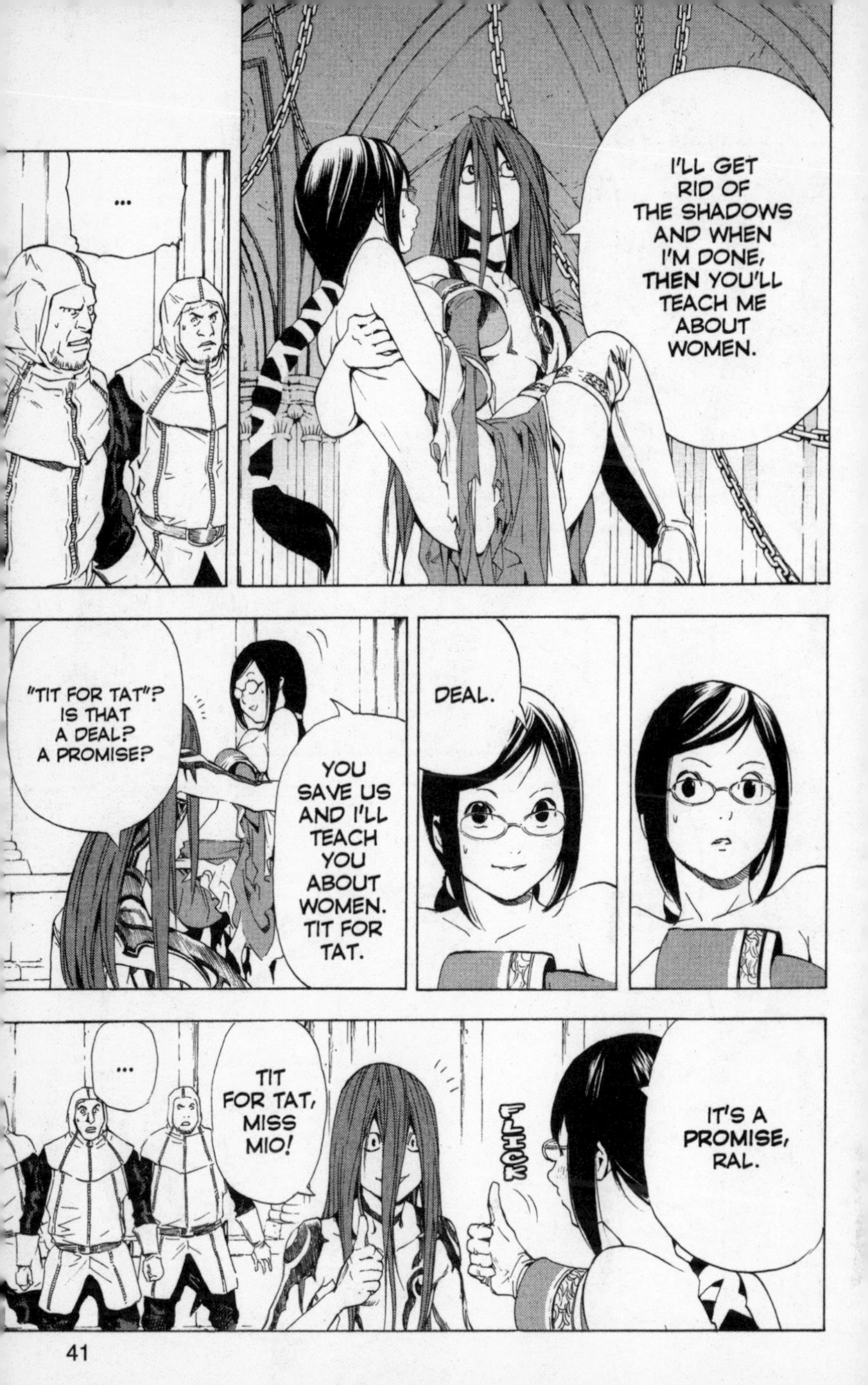

I'LL GET RID OF THE SHADOWS AND WHEN I'M DONE, THEN YOU'LL TEACH ME ABOUT WOMEN.
...
DEAL.
YOU SAVE US AND I'LL TEACH YOU ABOUT WOMEN. TIT FOR TAT.
"TIT FOR TAT"? IS THAT A DEAL? A PROMISE?
IT'S A PROMISE, RAL.
FLICK
TIT FOR TAT, MISS MIO!
...

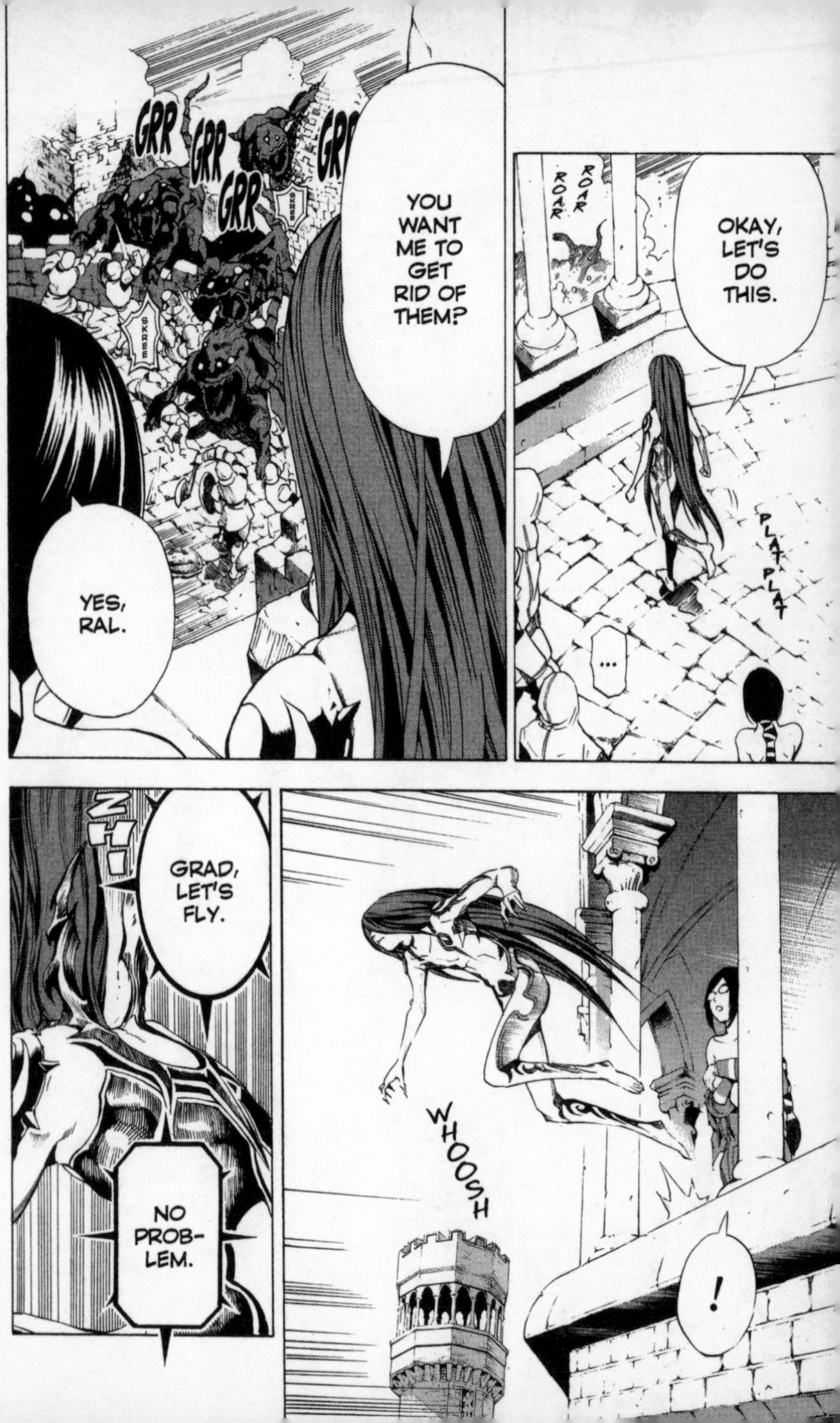
GRR
GRR
GRR
GRR
SKREE
SKREE
YOU WANT ME TO GET RID OF THEM?
YES, RAL.
ROAR
ROAR
OKAY, LET'S DO THIS.
PLAT PLAT
...
WHOOSH
!
GRAD, LET'S FLY.
NO PROB-LEM.

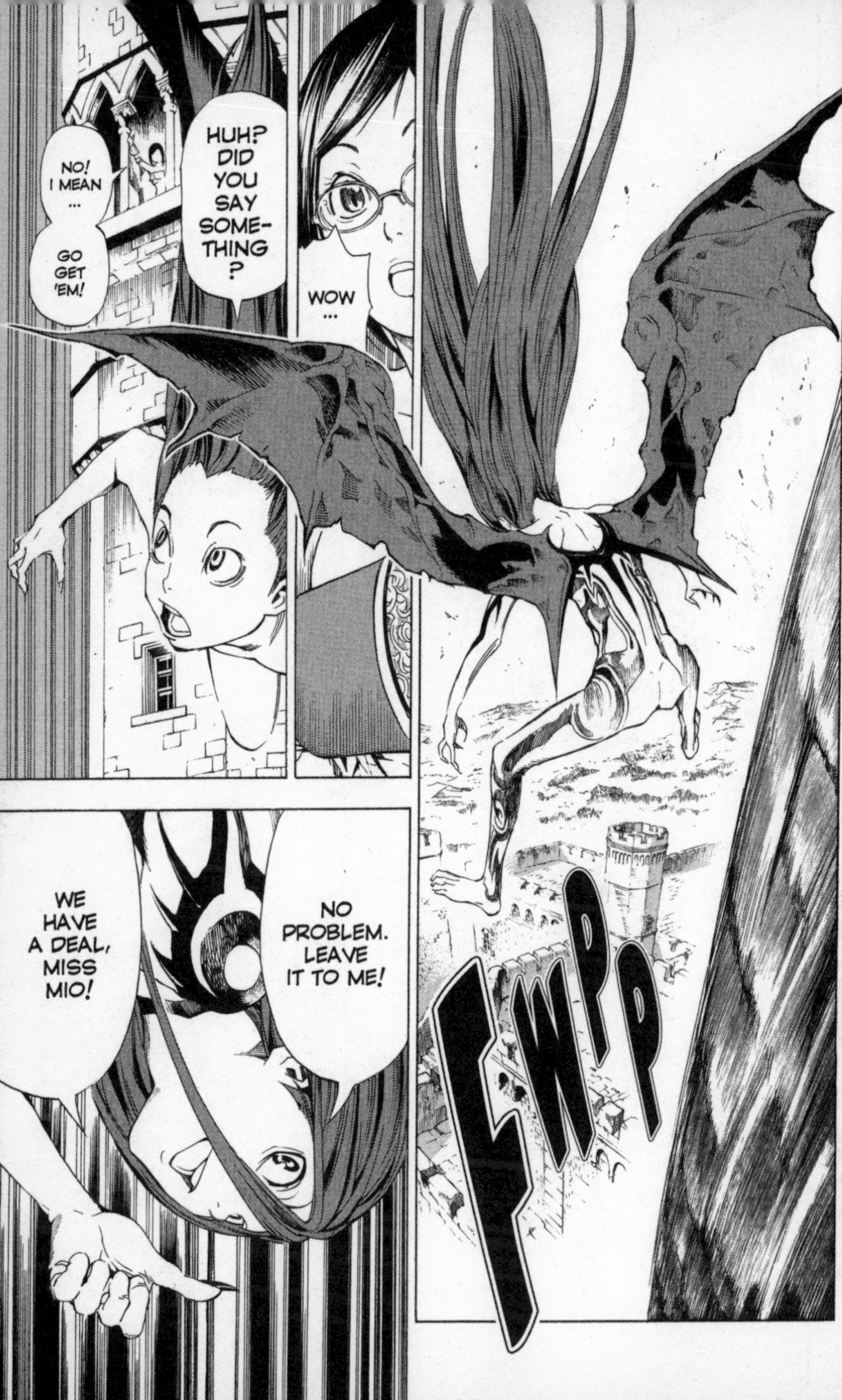
FWPP
WOW ...
HUH? DID YOU SAY SOMETHING?
NO! I MEAN ...
GO GET 'EM!
NO PROBLEM. LEAVE IT TO ME!
WE HAVE A DEAL, MISS MIO!

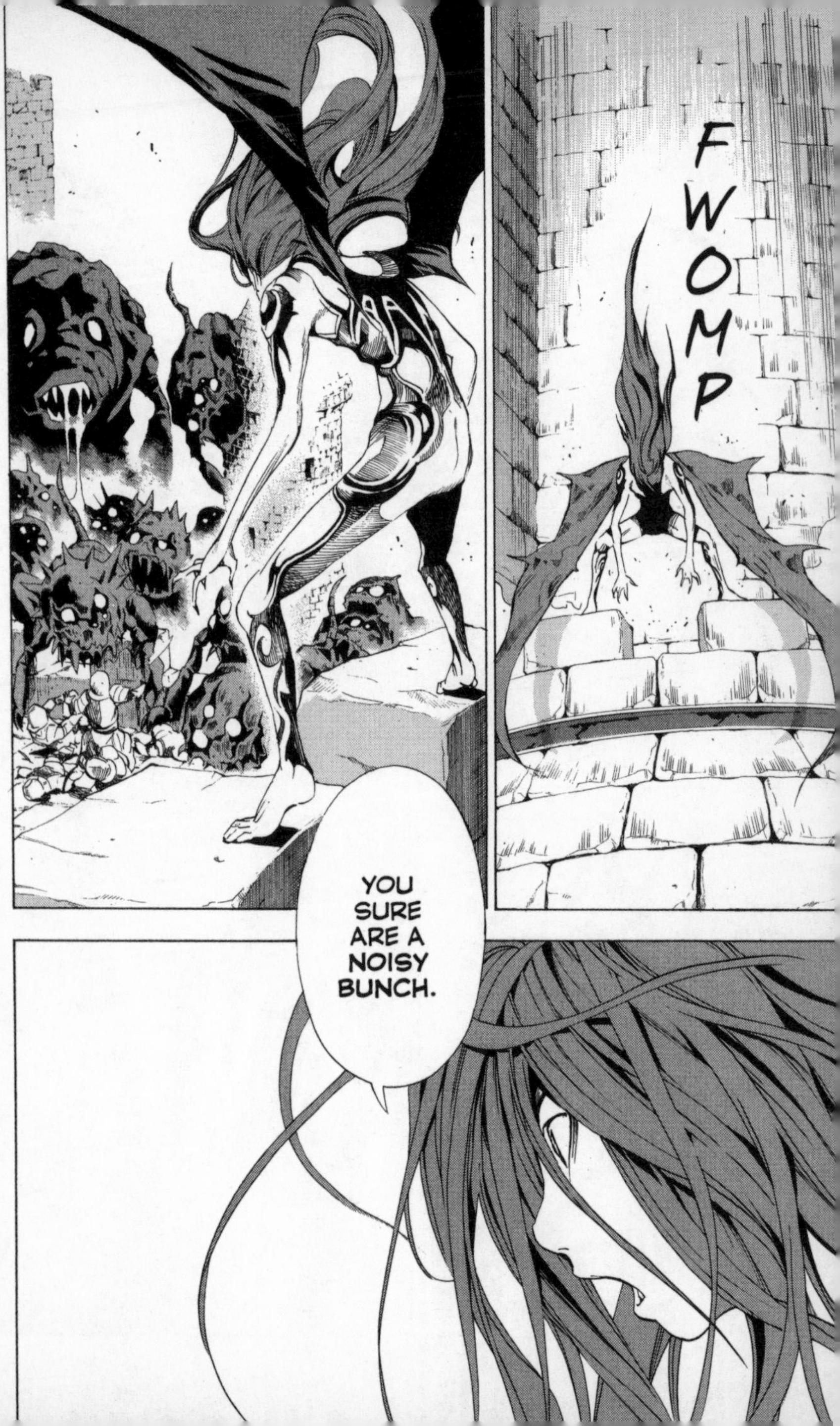
FWOMP
YOU SURE ARE A NOISY BUNCH.

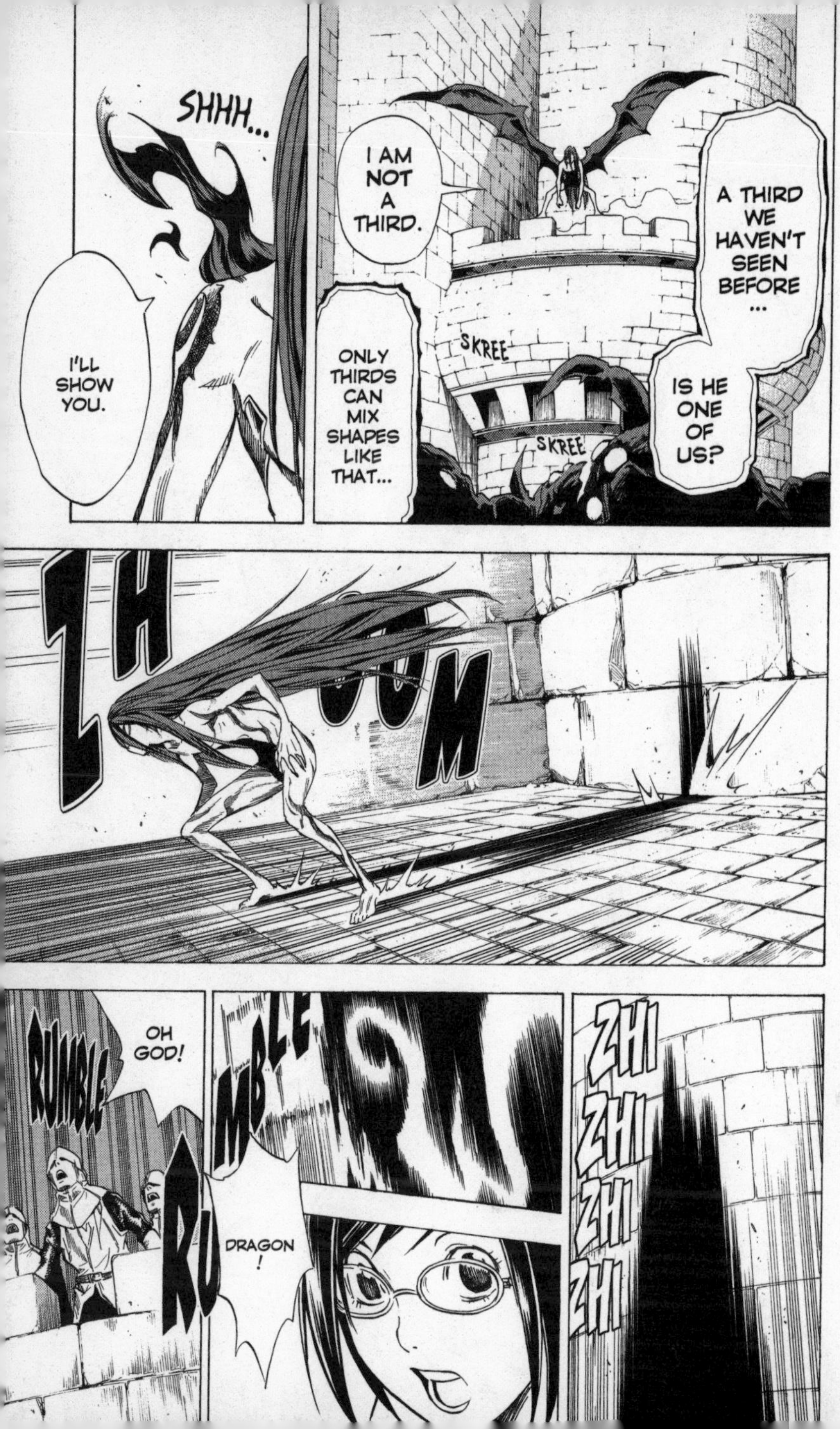

A THIRD WE HAVEN'T SEEN BEFORE ...
IS HE ONE OF US?
SKREE
SKREE
I AM NOT A THIRD.
ONLY THIRDS CAN MIX SHAPES LIKE THAT...
SHHH...
I'LL SHOW YOU.
ZHOOM
ZHI ZHI ZHI ZHI ZHI ZHI
RUMBLE
DRAGON!
RUMBLE
OH GOD!

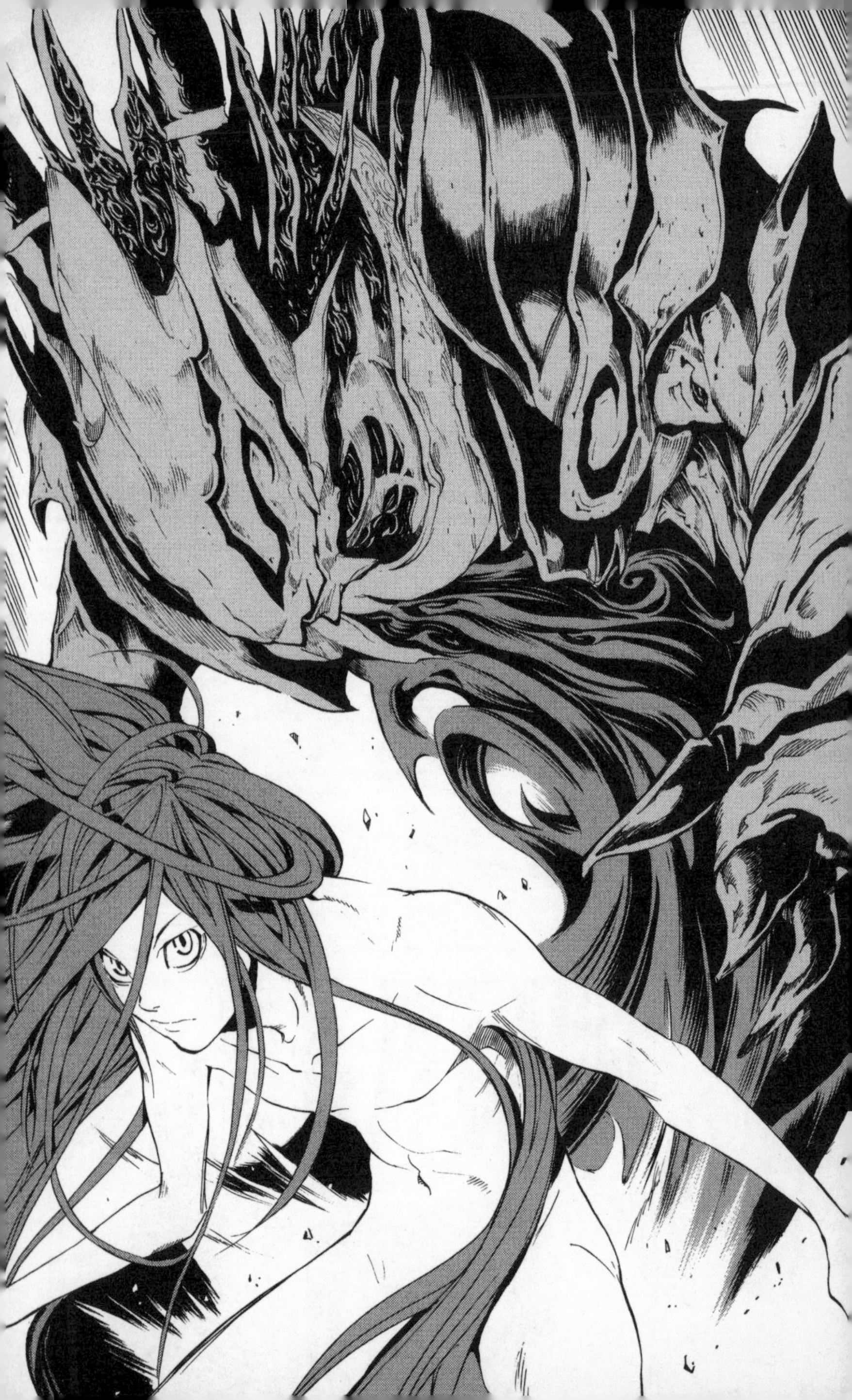

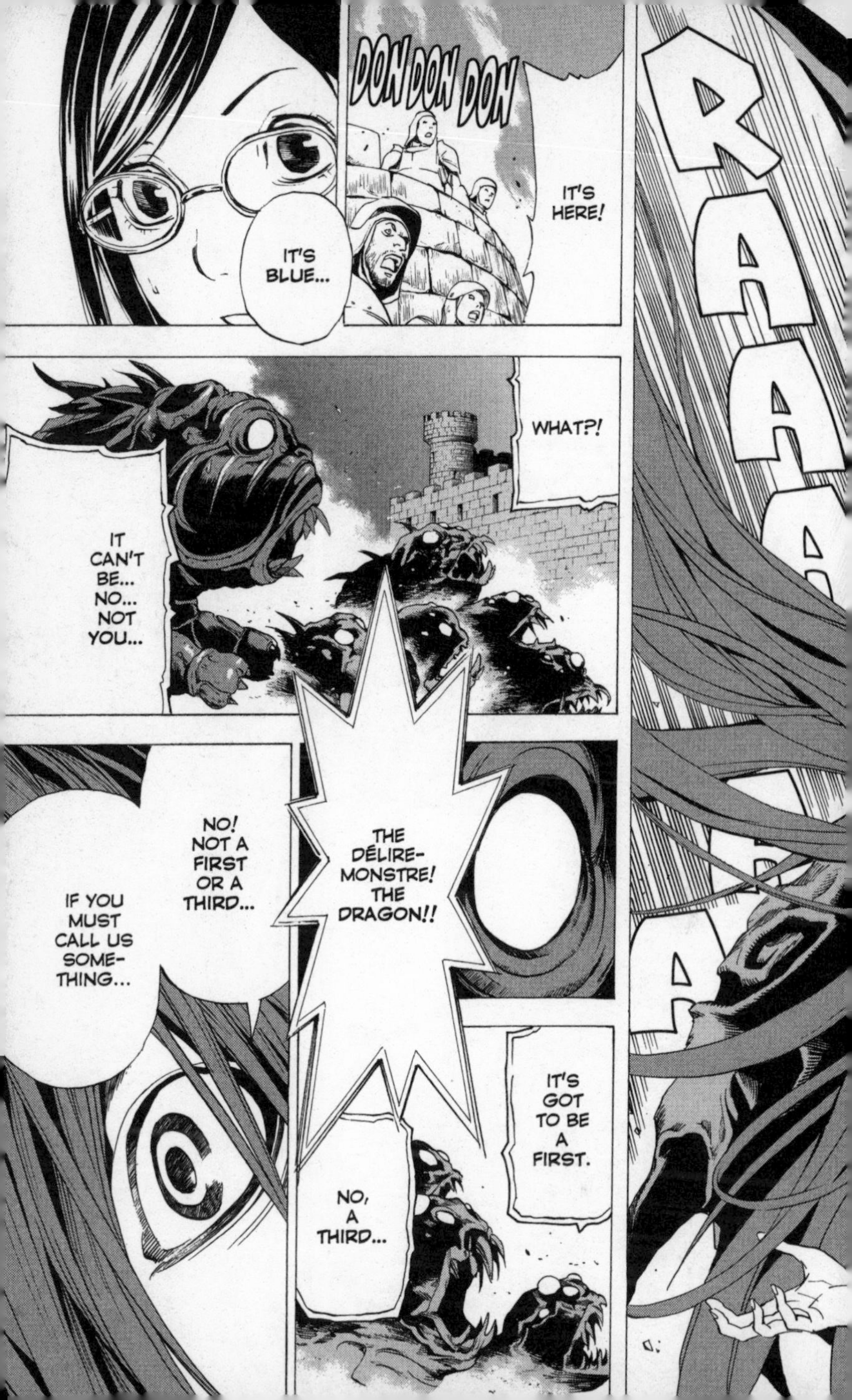
RAAAA
DON DON DON
IT'S HERE!
IT'S BLUE...
WHAT?!
IT CAN'T BE... NO... NOT YOU...
THE DÉLIRE-MONSTRE! THE DRAGON!!
IT'S GOT TO BE A FIRST.
NO, A THIRD...
NO! NOT A FIRST OR A THIRD...
IF YOU MUST CALL US SOMETHING...

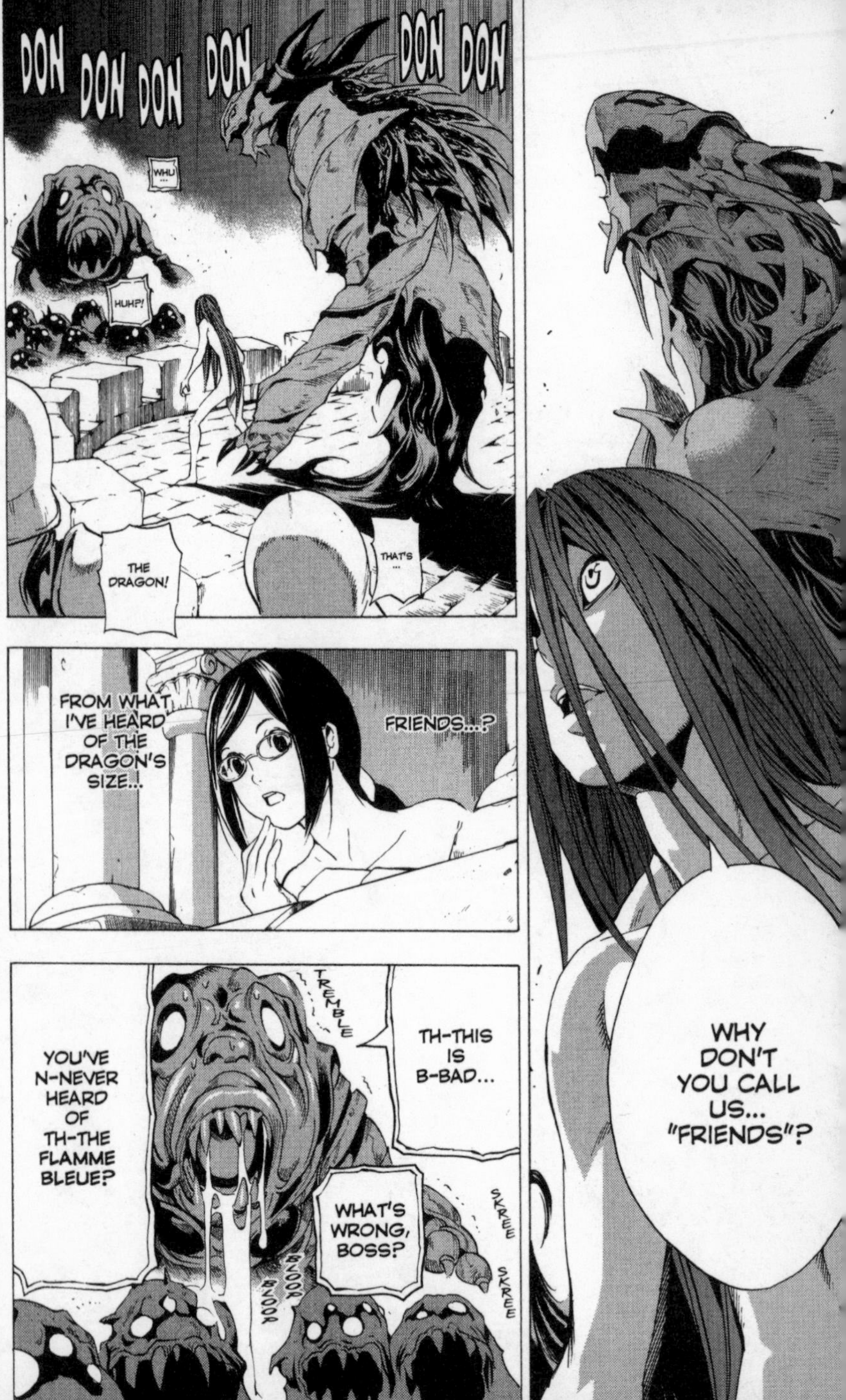
WHY DON'T YOU CALL US... "FRIENDS"?
DON DON DON DON DON DON
WHU...
HUH?!
THAT'S...
THE DRAGON!
FRIENDS...?
FROM WHAT I'VE HEARD OF THE DRAGON'S SIZE...
TREMBLE
TH-THIS IS B-BAD...
YOU'VE N-NEVER HEARD OF TH-THE FLAMME BLEUE?
SKREE SKREE
WHAT'S WRONG, BOSS?
BLOOR BLOOR

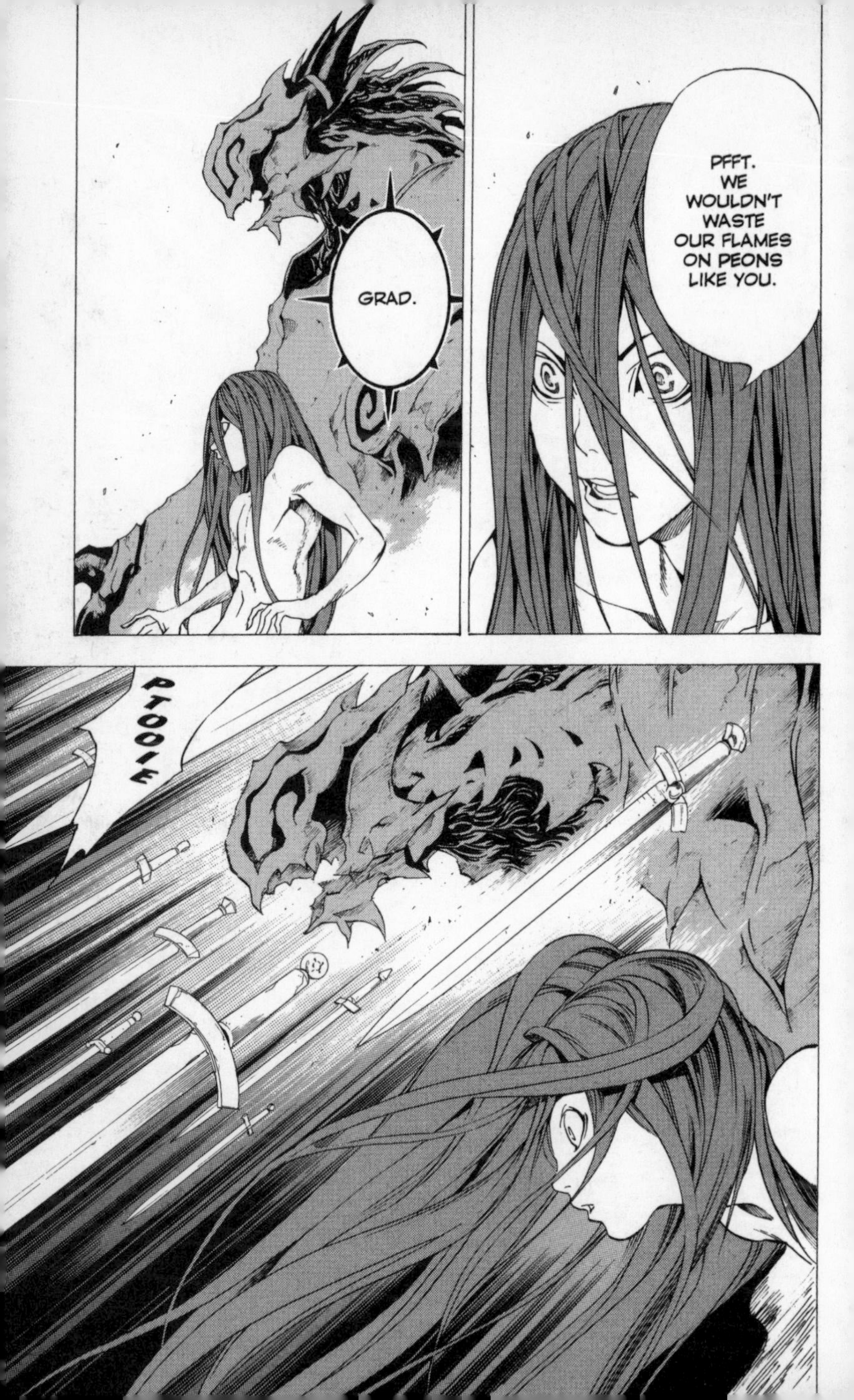
PFFT. WE WOULDN'T WASTE OUR FLAMES ON PEONS LIKE YOU.
GRAD.
PTOOIE

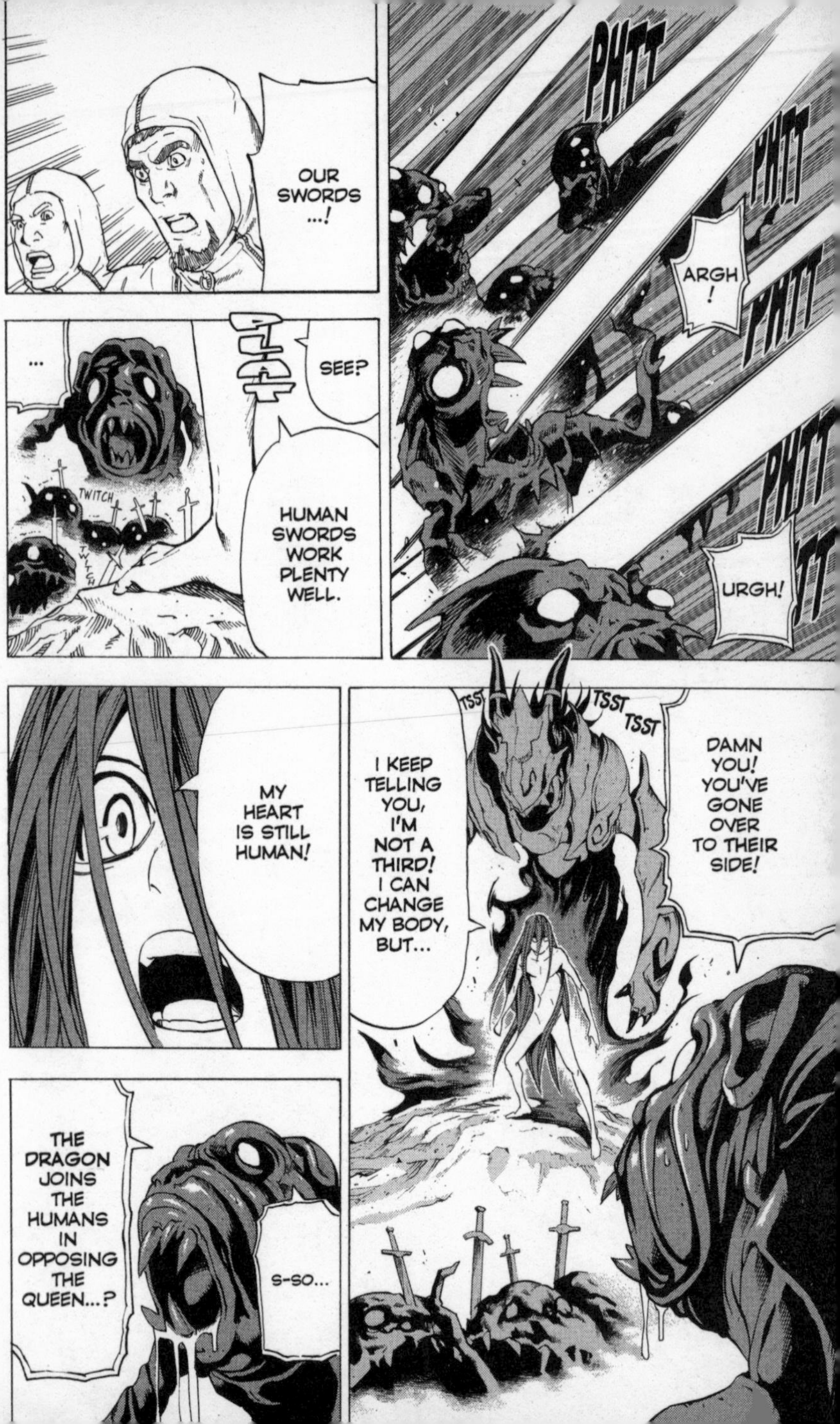
PHTT
PHTT
ARGH!
PHTT
PHTT
URGH!
OUR SWORDS...!
SEE?
HUMAN SWORDS WORK PLENTY WELL.
TWITCH
TWITCH
...
TSST TSST
DAMN YOU! YOU'VE GONE OVER TO THEIR SIDE!
TSST
I KEEP TELLING YOU, I'M NOT A THIRD! I CAN CHANGE MY BODY, BUT...
MY HEART IS STILL HUMAN!
S-SO...
THE DRAGON JOINS THE HUMANS IN OPPOSING THE QUEEN...?

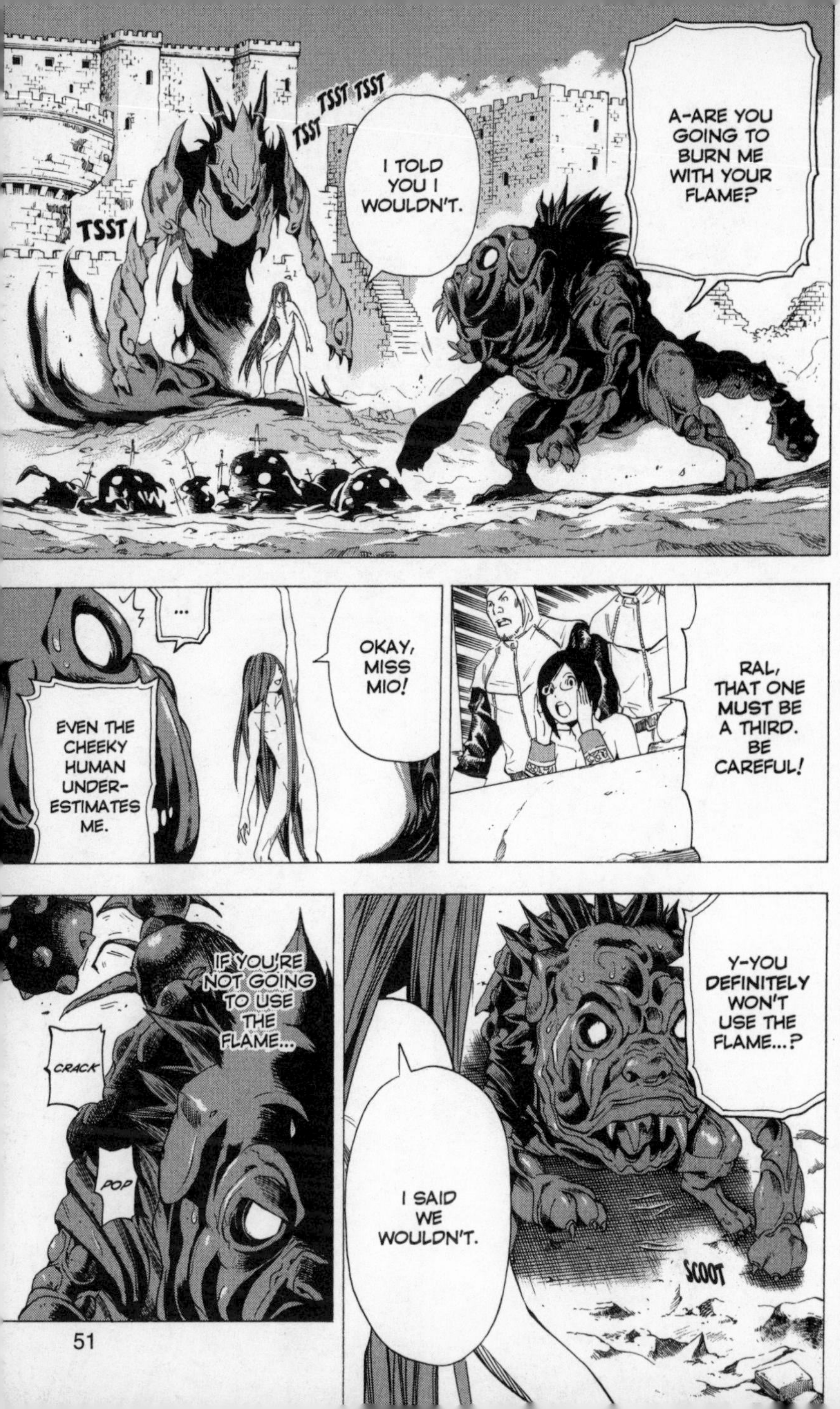
A-ARE YOU GOING TO BURN ME WITH YOUR FLAME?
TSST TSST
TSST
I TOLD YOU I WOULDN'T.
TSST
RAL, THAT ONE MUST BE A THIRD. BE CAREFUL!
OKAY, MISS MIO!
...
EVEN THE CHEEKY HUMAN UNDER-ESTIMATES ME.
Y-YOU DEFINITELY WON'T USE THE FLAME...?
I SAID WE WOULDN'T.
SCOOT
IF YOU'RE NOT GOING TO USE THE FLAME...
CRACK
POP

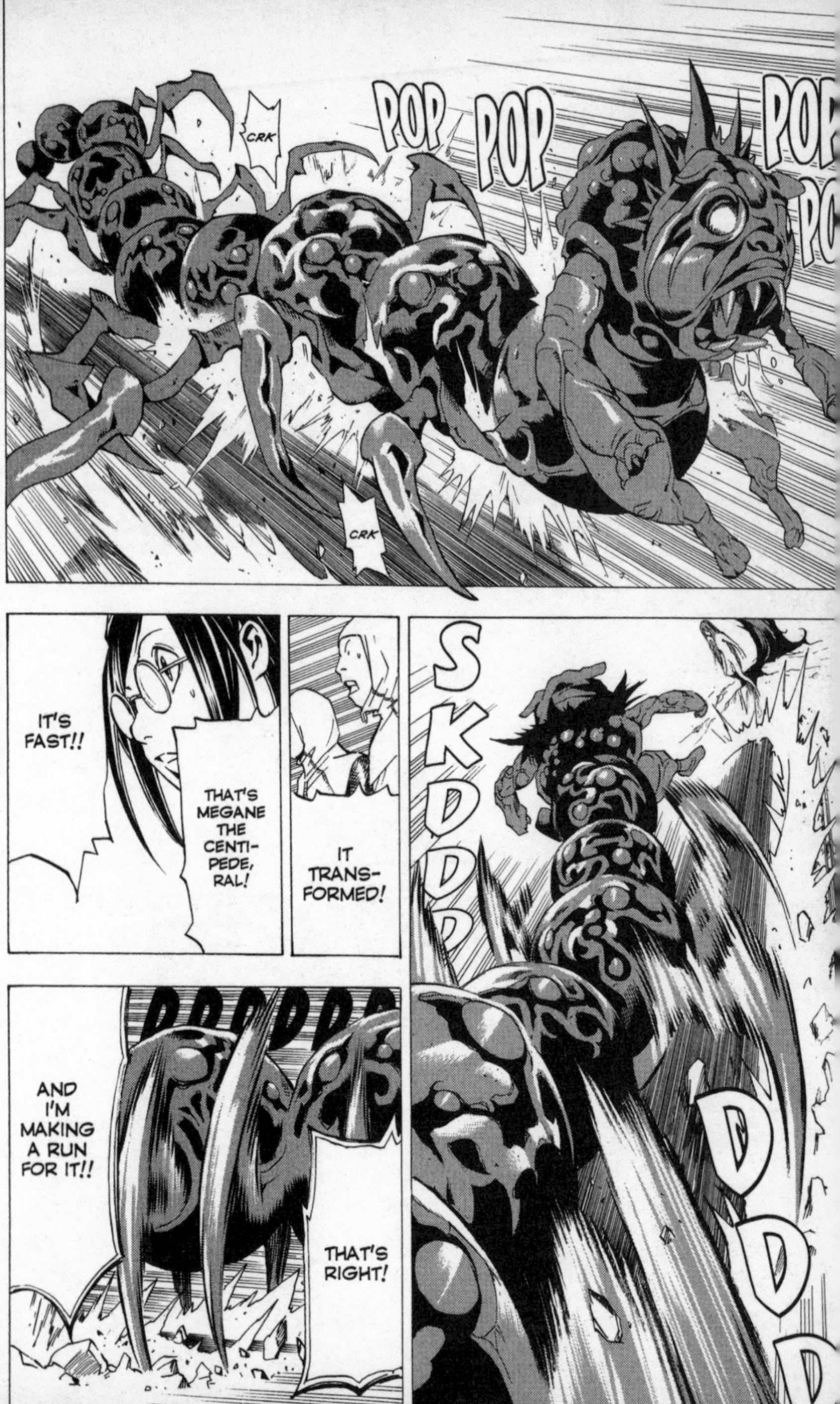
POP
PO
POP
POP
CRK
CRK
SKDDD
DDDD
IT TRANSFORMED!
THAT'S MEGANE THE CENTIPEDE, RAL!
IT'S FAST!!
THAT'S RIGHT!
AND I'M MAKING A RUN FOR IT!!

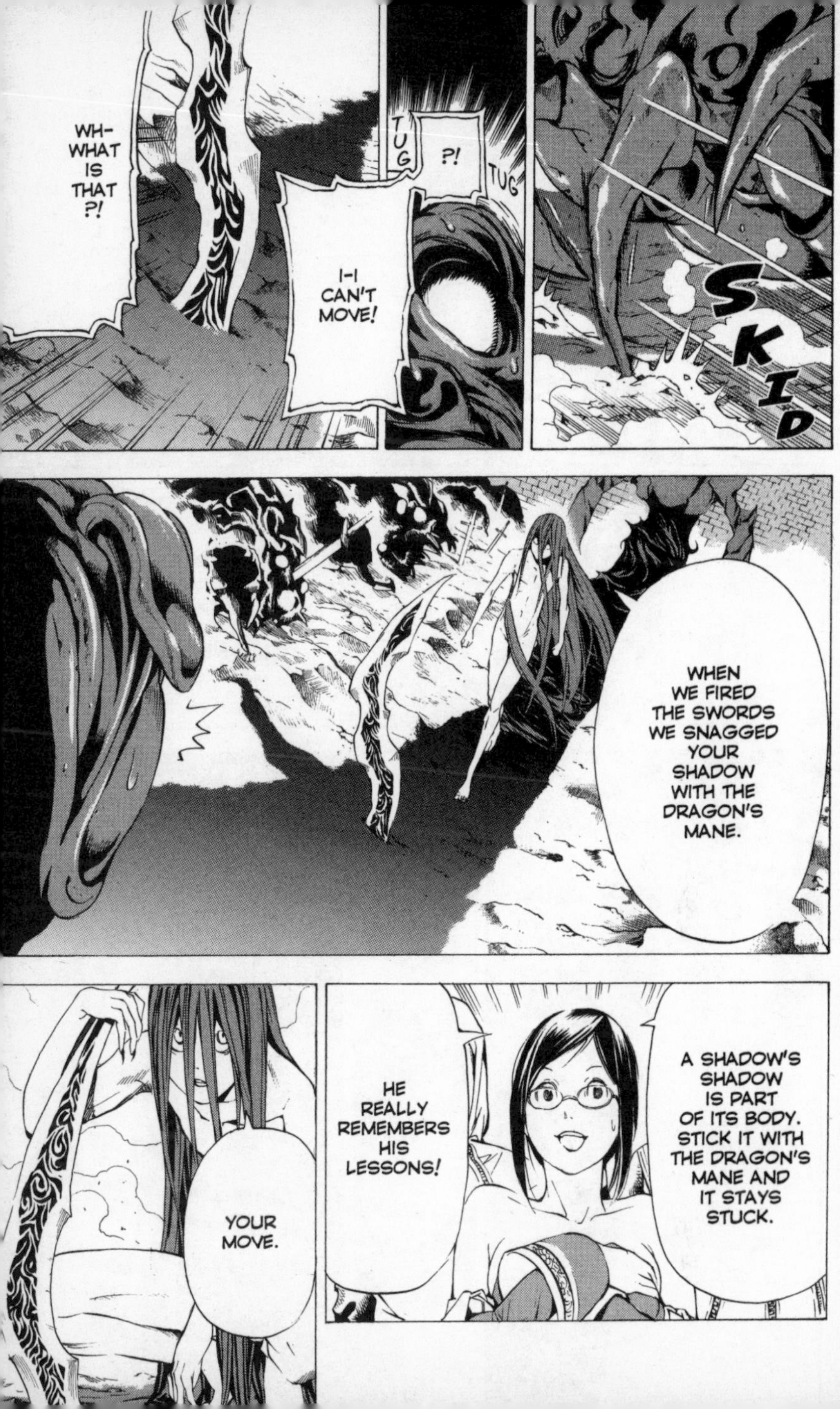
SKID
TUG
?!
TUG
I-I CAN'T MOVE!
WH-WHAT IS THAT?!
WHEN WE FIRED THE SWORDS WE SNAGGED YOUR SHADOW WITH THE DRAGON'S MANE.
A SHADOW'S SHADOW IS PART OF ITS BODY. STICK IT WITH THE DRAGON'S MANE AND IT STAYS STUCK.
HE REALLY REMEMBERS HIS LESSONS!
YOUR MOVE.

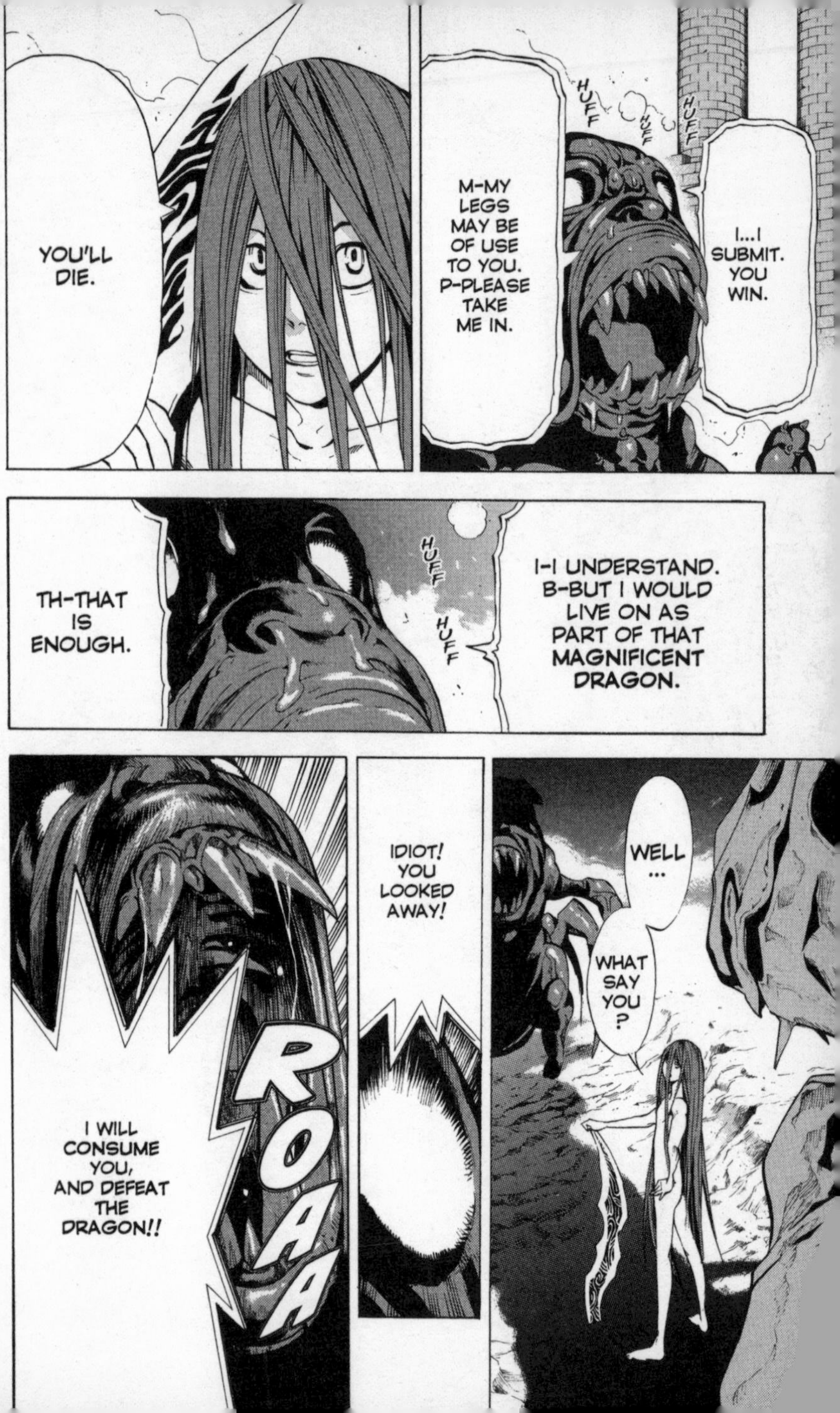
HUFF
HUFF
HUFF
I...I SUBMIT. YOU WIN.
M-MY LEGS MAY BE OF USE TO YOU. P-PLEASE TAKE ME IN.
YOU'LL DIE.
I-I UNDERSTAND. B-BUT I WOULD LIVE ON AS PART OF THAT MAGNIFICENT DRAGON.
HUFF
HUFF
TH-THAT IS ENOUGH.
WELL ...
WHAT SAY YOU ?
IDIOT! YOU LOOKED AWAY!
ROAA
I WILL CONSUME YOU, AND DEFEAT THE DRAGON!!

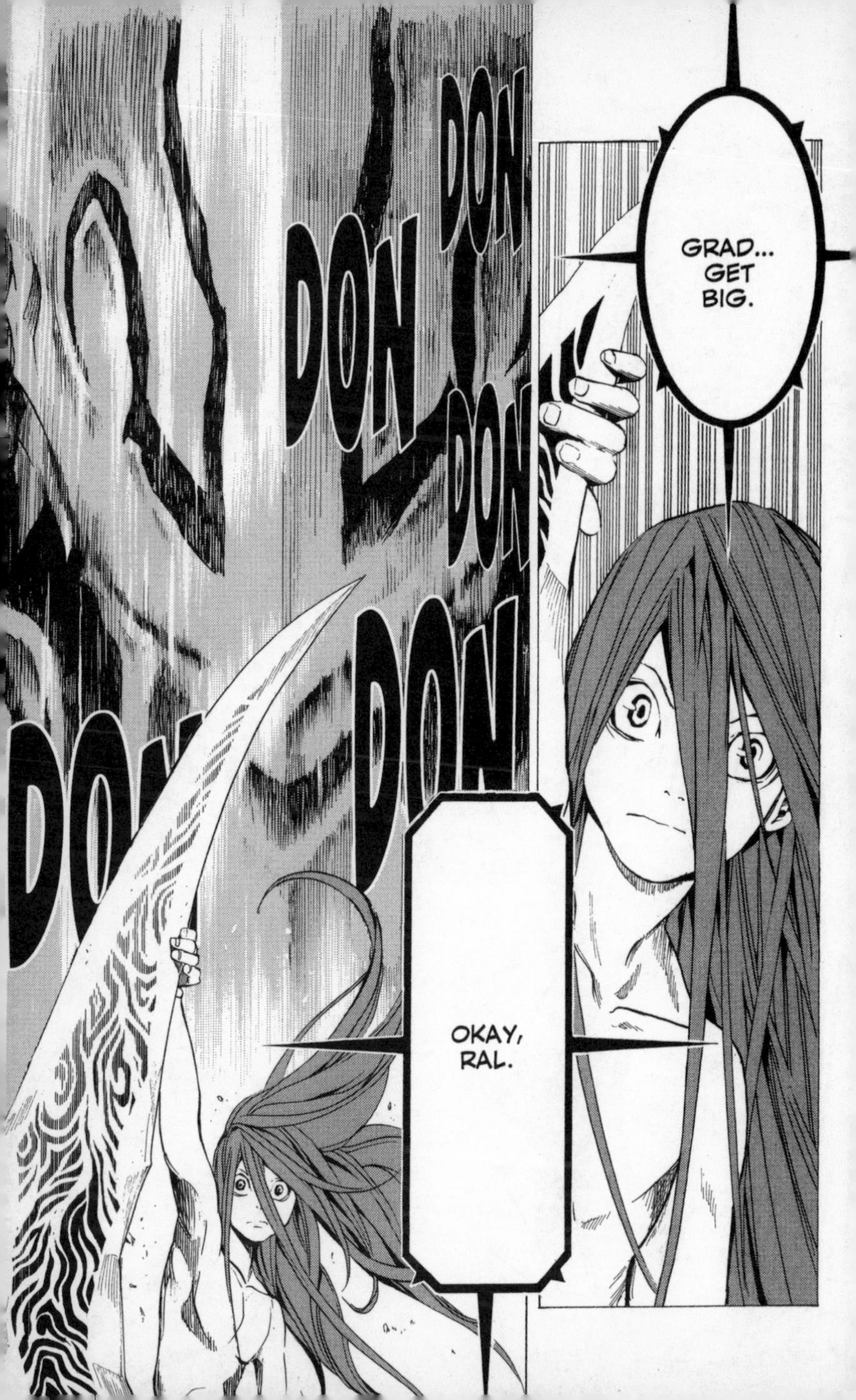
GRAD... GET BIG.
DON DON
DON DON
DON
DON
OKAY, RAL.

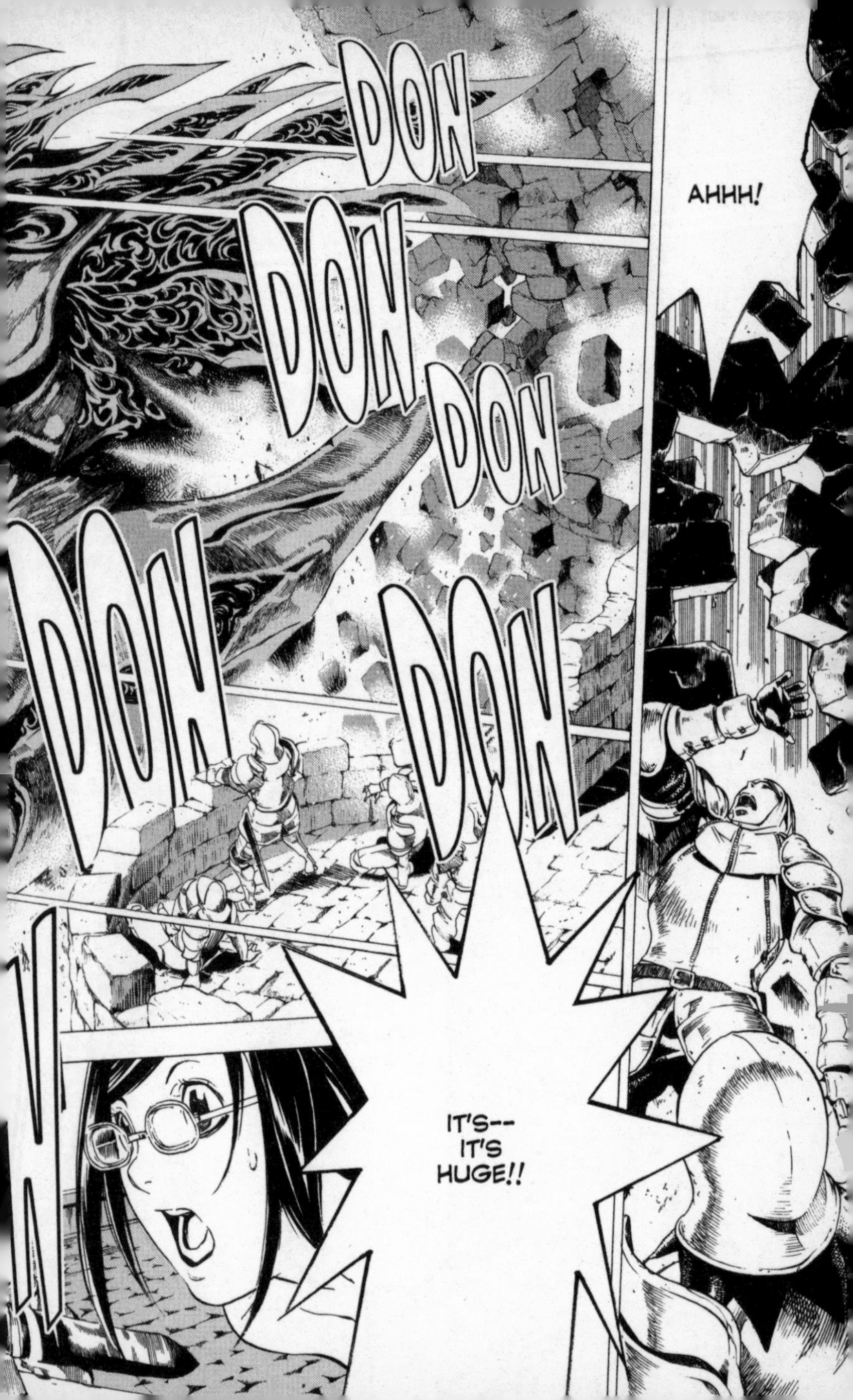
AHHH!
DON
DON
DON
DON
DON
IT'S-- IT'S HUGE!!

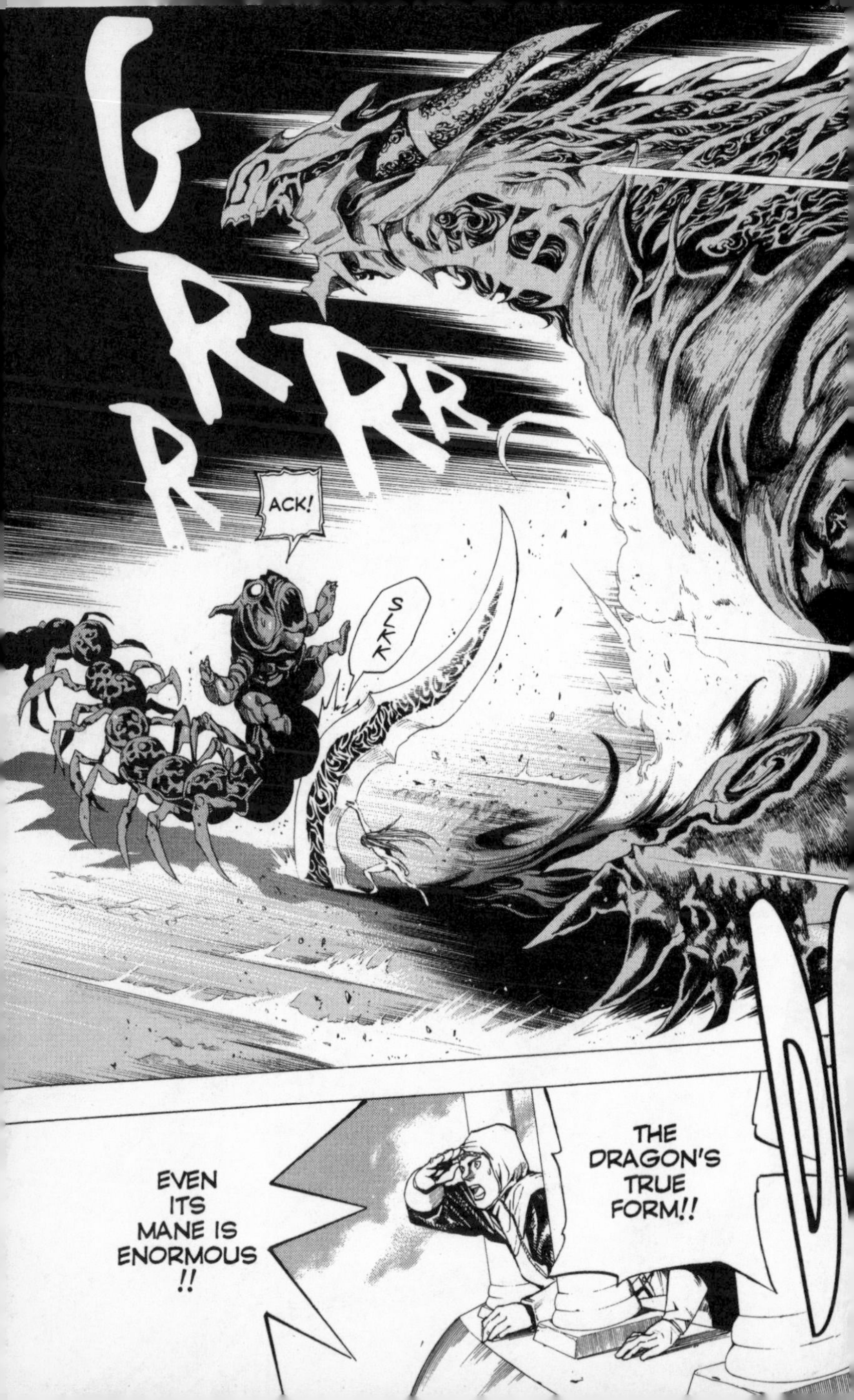
GRRRRR
ACK!
SLKK
THE DRAGON'S TRUE FORM!!
EVEN ITS MANE IS ENORMOUS!!

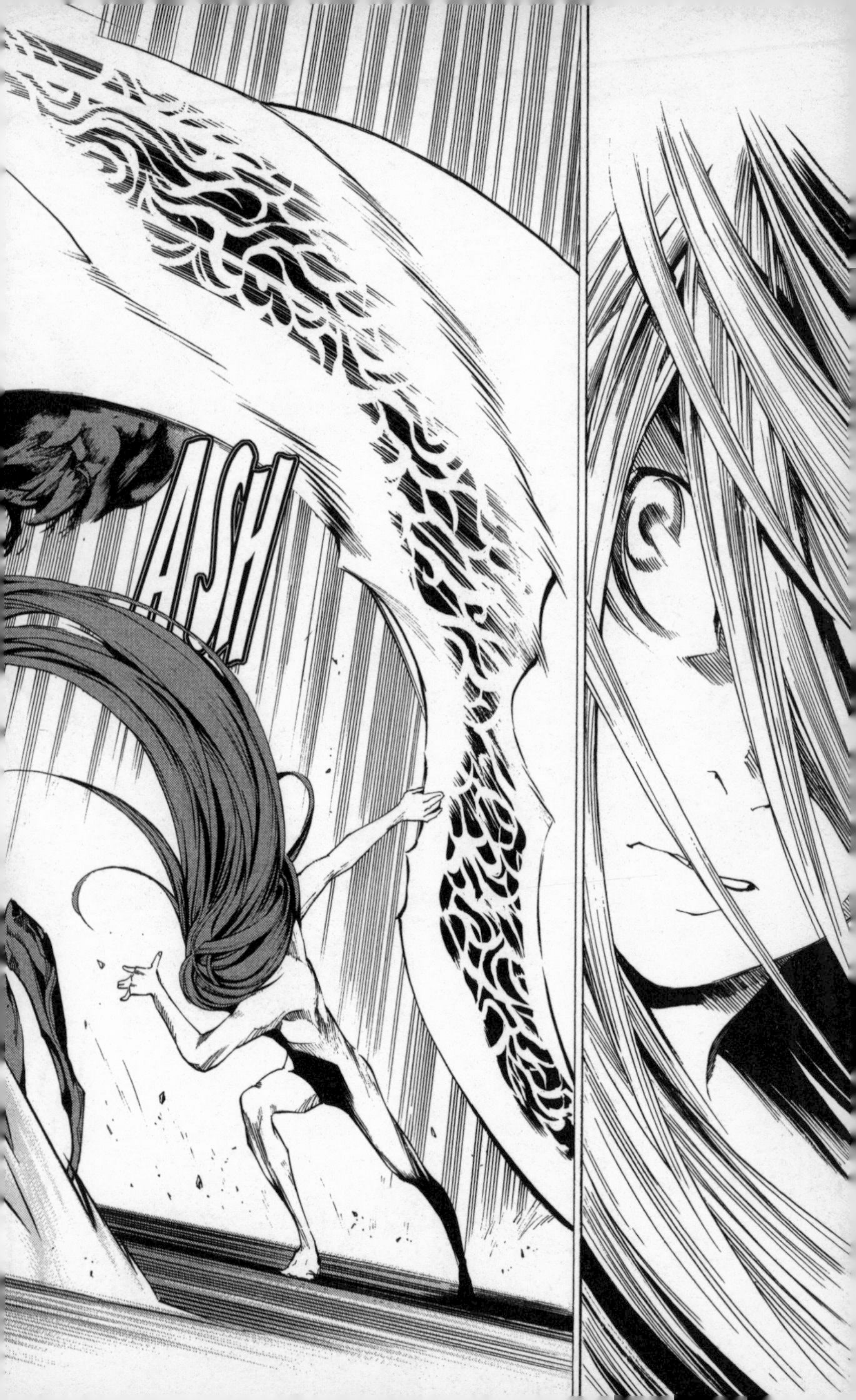
ASH

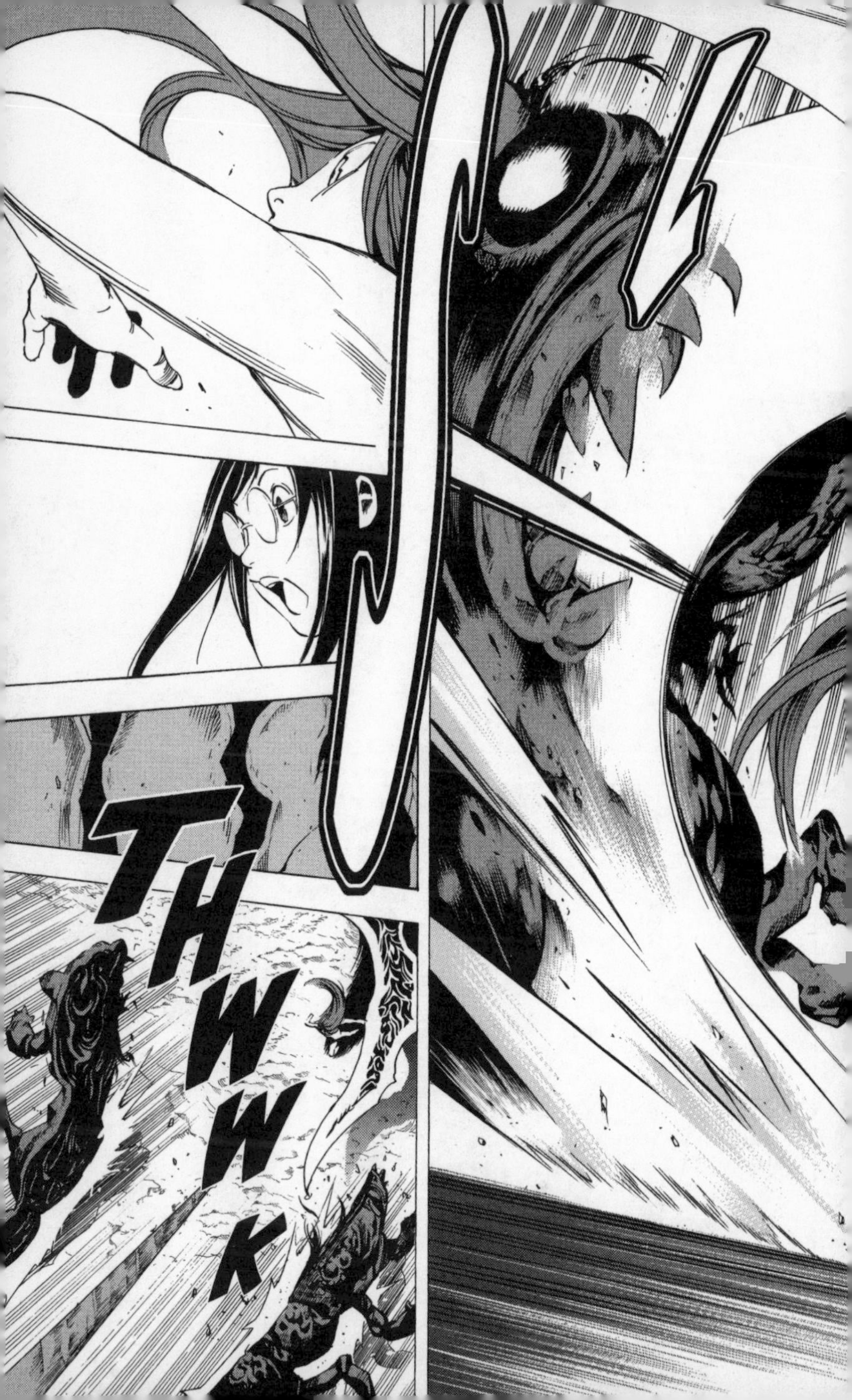
THWWK

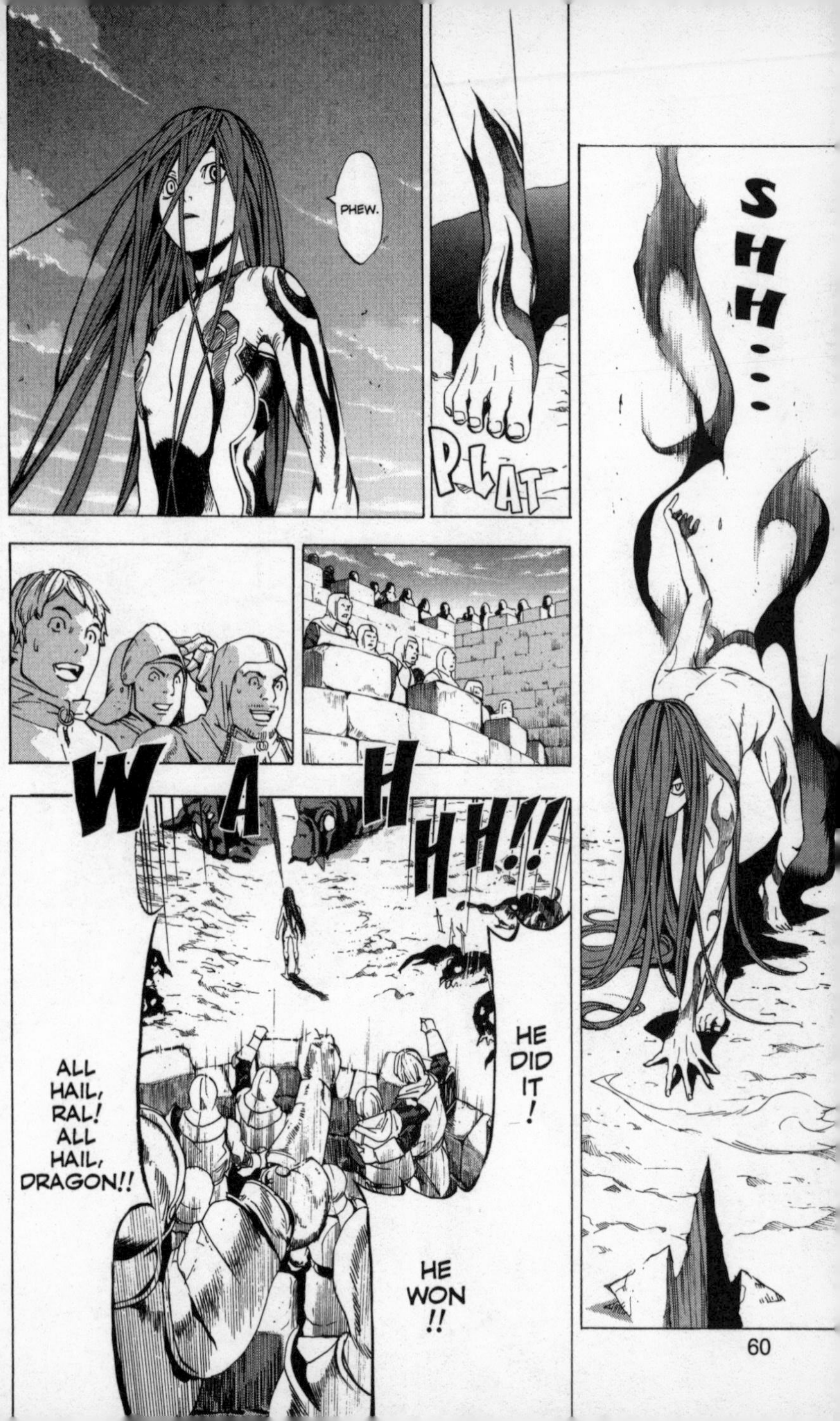
SHH...
PLAT
PHEW.
WAHHH!!
HE DID IT!
ALL HAIL, RAL! ALL HAIL, DRAGON!!
HE WON!!

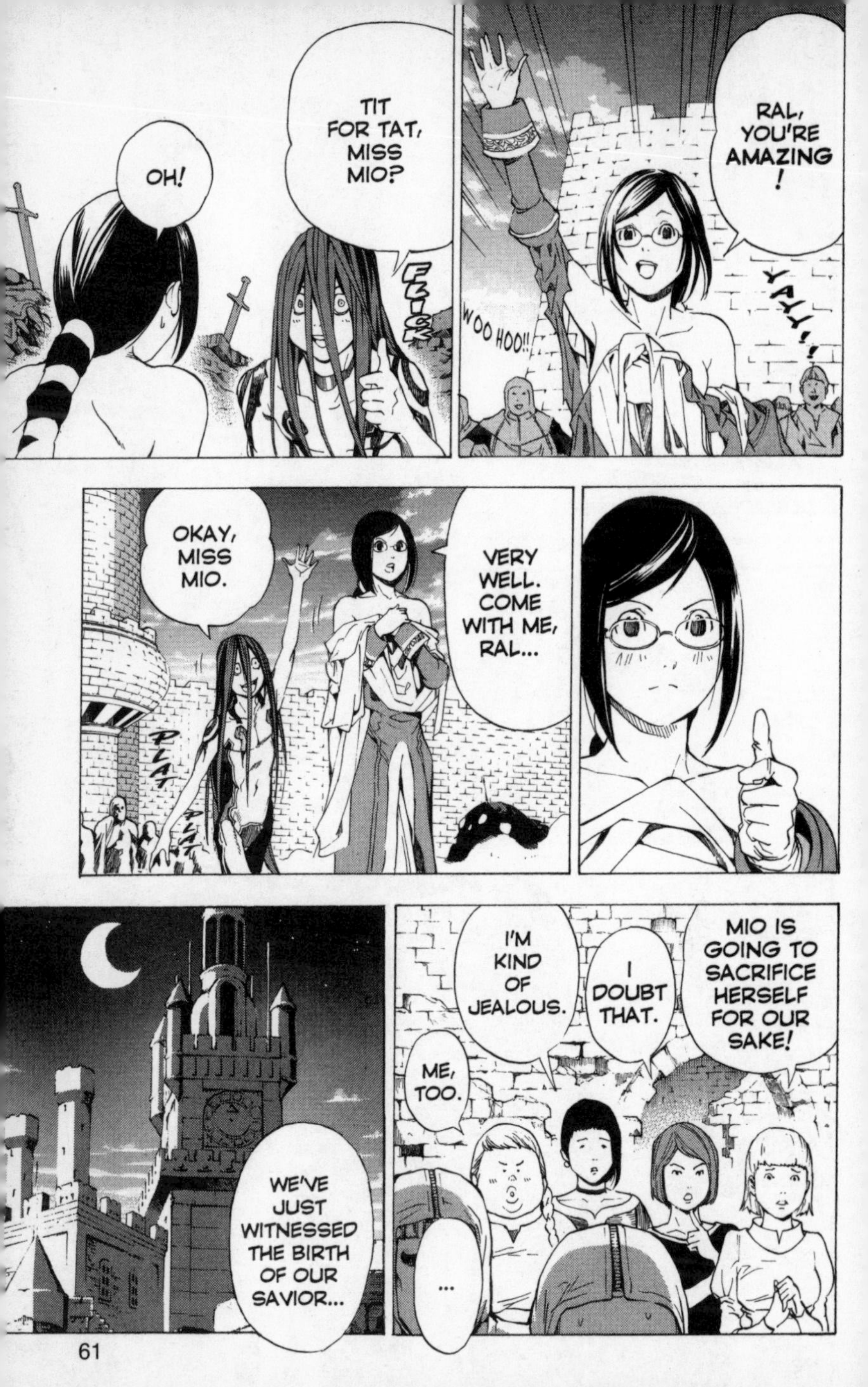
RAL, YOU'RE AMAZING!
YAYY!!
WOO HOO!!
TIT FOR TAT, MISS MIO?
OH!
VERY WELL. COME WITH ME, RAL...
OKAY, MISS MIO.
PLAT
PLAT
MIO IS GOING TO SACRIFICE HERSELF FOR OUR SAKE!
I DOUBT THAT.
I'M KIND OF JEALOUS.
ME, TOO.
...
WE'VE JUST WITNESSED THE BIRTH OF OUR SAVIOR...

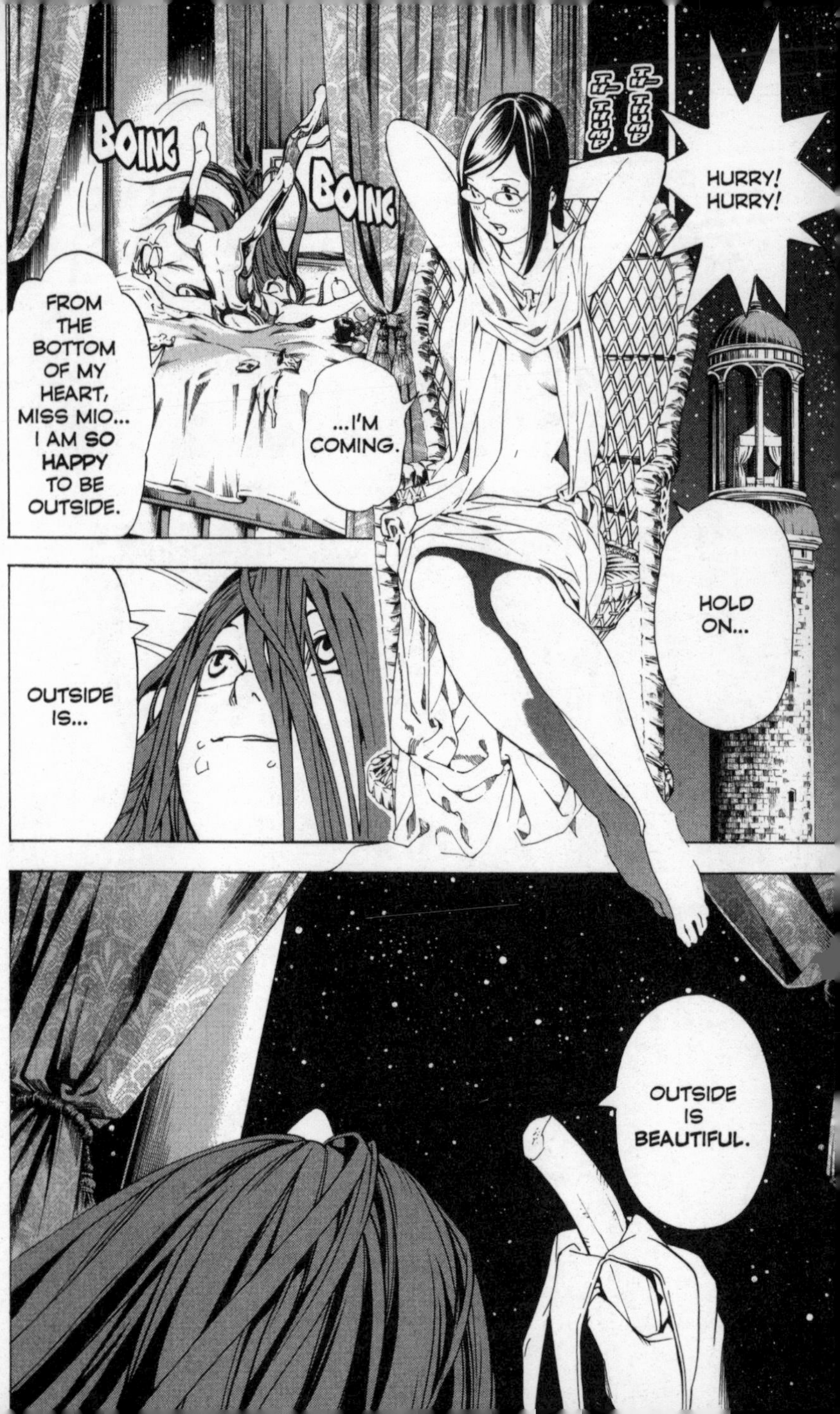
HURRY! HURRY!
TU-THUMP TU-THUMP
BOING BOING
...I'M COMING.
FROM THE BOTTOM OF MY HEART, MISS MIO... I AM SO HAPPY TO BE OUTSIDE.
HOLD ON...
OUTSIDE IS...
OUTSIDE IS BEAUTIFUL.

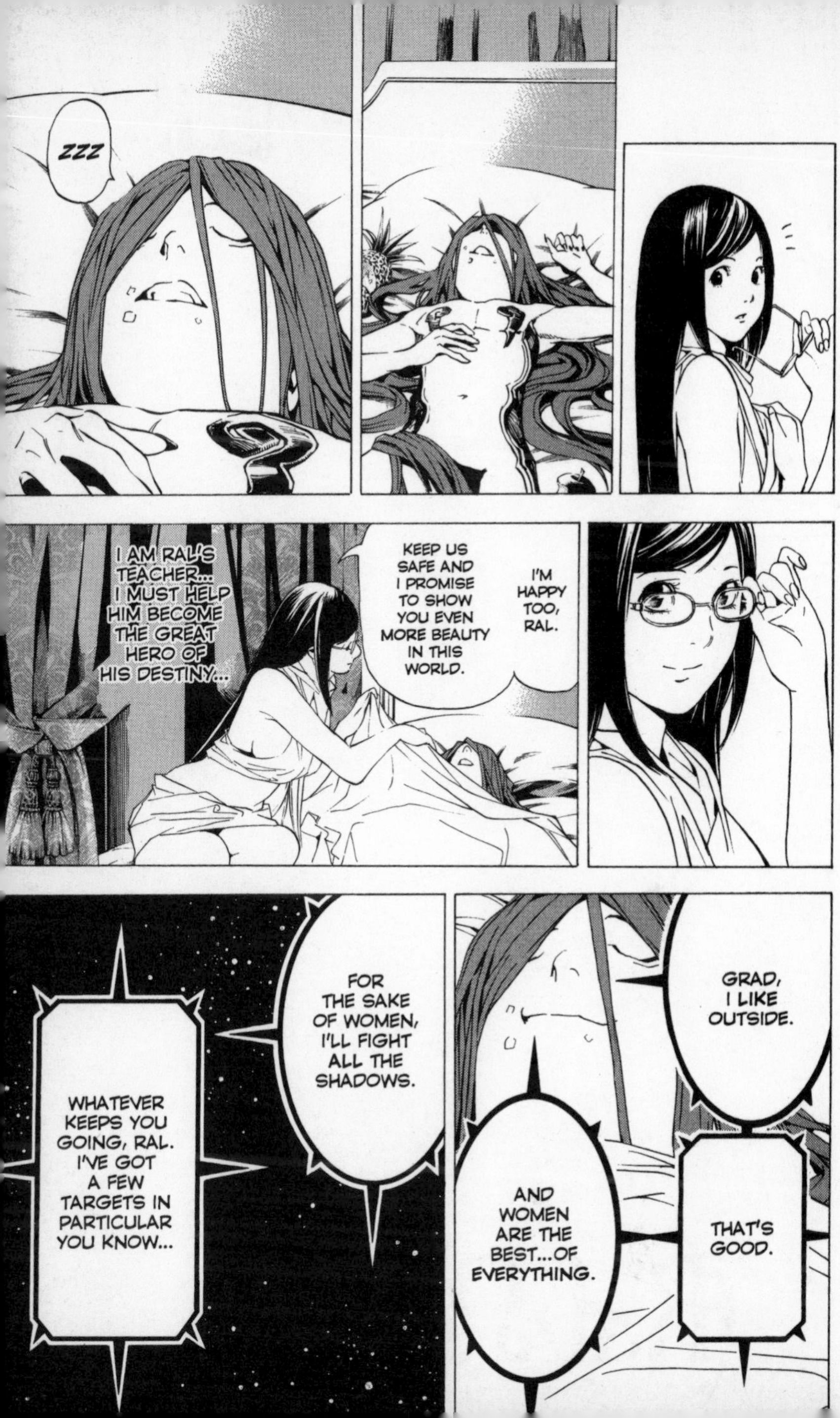
ZZZ
I'M HAPPY TOO, RAL.
KEEP US SAFE AND I PROMISE TO SHOW YOU EVEN MORE BEAUTY IN THIS WORLD.
I AM RAL'S TEACHER... I MUST HELP HIM BECOME THE GREAT HERO OF HIS DESTINY...
GRAD, I LIKE OUTSIDE.
THAT'S GOOD.
AND WOMEN ARE THE BEST...OF EVERYTHING.
FOR THE SAKE OF WOMEN, I'LL FIGHT ALL THE SHADOWS.
WHATEVER KEEPS YOU GOING, RAL. I'VE GOT A FEW TARGETS IN PARTICULAR YOU KNOW...

RalΩGrad

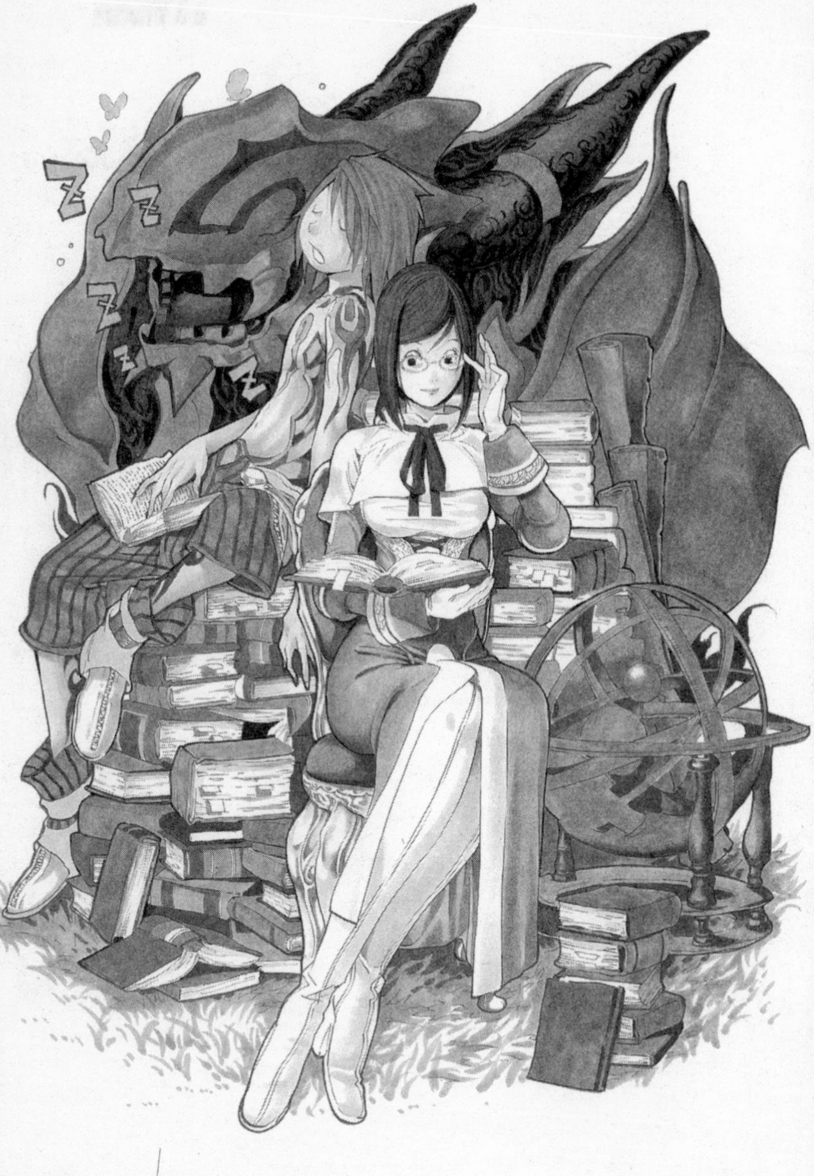

TALE 2 Back

THE FIRST FORM: PARASITICS

- A SHADOW OF THE FIRST ORDER ENTERS ITS HOST THROUGH THE LIVING BEING'S SHADOW. THE TWO SOULS CO-EXIST IN ONE BODY.

- WITH SOME LIMITATIONS, A FIRST CAN MANIFEST ITS SHAPE FROM THE SHADOW OF ITS HOST, BUT IT MUST HAVE BUILT UP ADEQUATE POWER WITHIN THE HOST AND IT MUST HAVE THE HOST'S PERMISSION.

- IN THE ABSENCE OF LIGHT, THE HOST PRODUCES NO SHADOW AND THE FIRST CANNOT TAKE SHAPE NOR DISPLAY ITS TALENTS.

- FIRSTS CAN MOVE FROM ONE LIVING BEING INTO ANOTHER. THEY ACQUIRE THE ABILITIES OF ANYONE OR ANYTHING THEY CONSUME.

- WHEN THE WORLD OF DARKNESS IS RESTORED, FIRSTS CAN RETURN TO THEIR HOME.

THE SECOND FORM: PREDATORS

- A SHADOW OF THE SECOND ORDER CONSUMES ITS HOST FROM THE INSIDE, TAKING THE HOST'S FLESH AND SPIRIT AS ITS OWN. A SECOND CAN MANIFEST EITHER ITS OWN SHAPE OR THAT OF ITS HOST, WITH NO CONSTRAINTS OF TIME OR LIGHT.

- IT SHOULD BE NOTED, HOWEVER, THAT IF A SECOND HAS BECOME A SECOND IN A PLACE OF DARKNESS WITHIN THE WORLD OF LIGHT, IT CANNOT MANIFEST SHAPE UNTIL IT RETURNS TO A PLACE OF LIGHT.

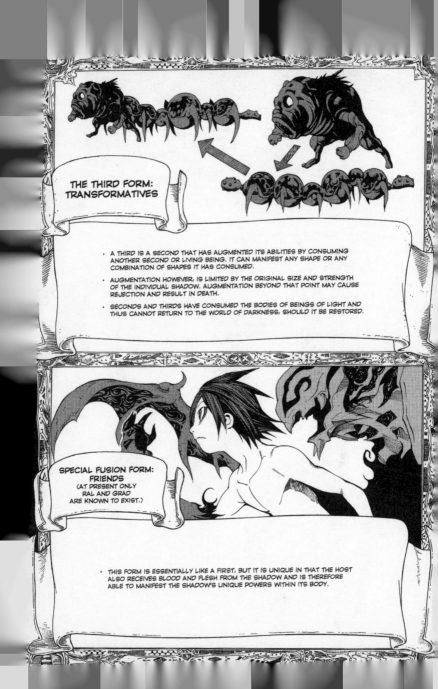

THE THIRD FORM: TRANSFORMATIVES

- A THIRD IS A SECOND THAT HAS AUGMENTED ITS ABILITIES BY CONSUMING ANOTHER SECOND OR LIVING BEING. IT CAN MANIFEST ANY SHAPE OR ANY COMBINATION OF SHAPES IT HAS CONSUMED.

- AUGMENTATION HOWEVER, IS LIMITED BY THE ORIGINAL SIZE AND STRENGTH OF THE INDIVIDUAL SHADOW. AUGMENTATION BEYOND THAT POINT MAY CAUSE REJECTION AND RESULT IN DEATH.

- SECONDS AND THIRDS HAVE CONSUMED THE BODIES OF BEINGS OF LIGHT AND THUS CANNOT RETURN TO THE WORLD OF DARKNESS, SHOULD IT BE RESTORED.

SPECIAL FUSION FORM: FRIENDS
(AT PRESENT ONLY RAL AND GRAD ARE KNOWN TO EXIST.)

- THIS FORM IS ESSENTIALLY LIKE A FIRST, BUT IT IS UNIQUE IN THAT THE HOST ALSO RECEIVES BLOOD AND FLESH FROM THE SHADOW AND IS THEREFORE ABLE TO MANIFEST THE SHADOW'S UNIQUE POWERS WITHIN ITS BODY.

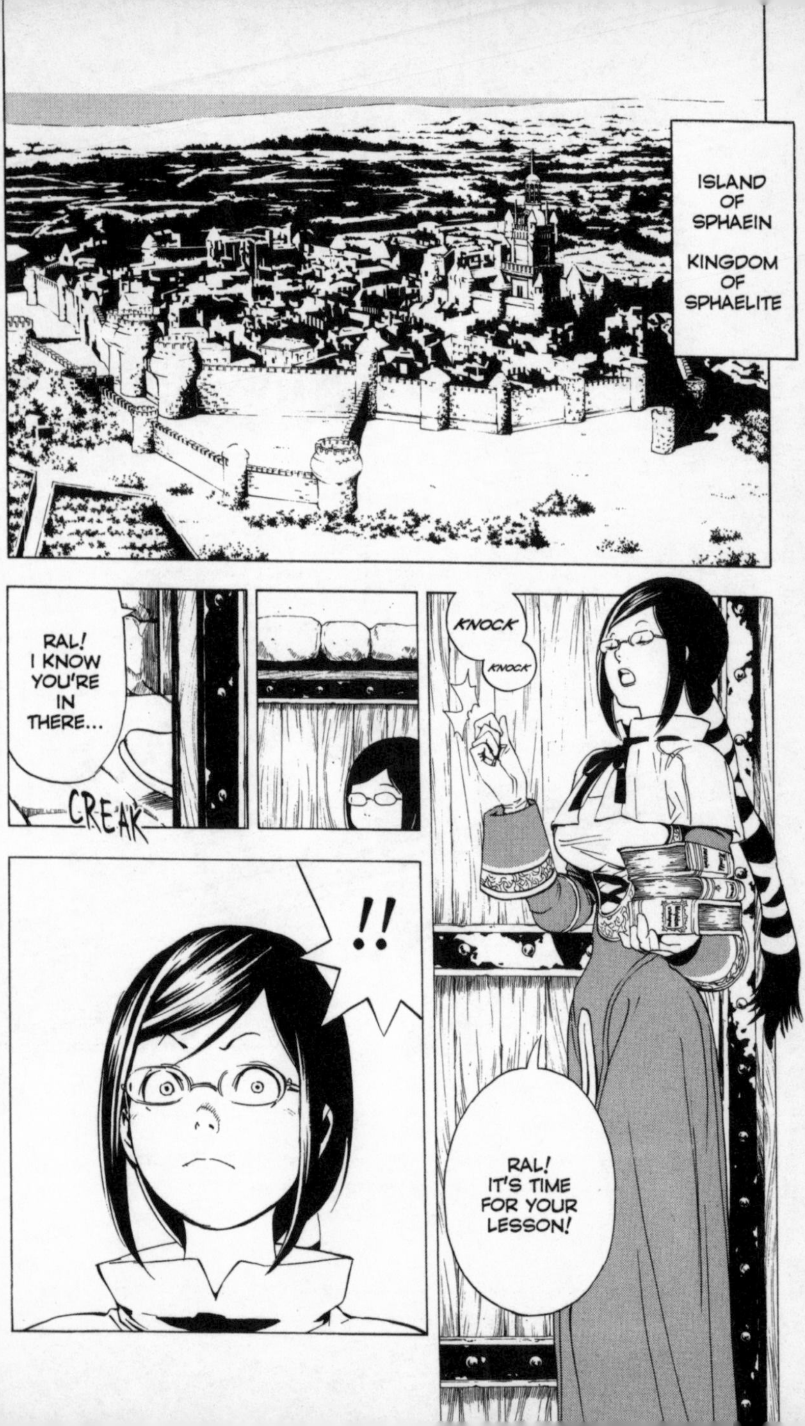
ISLAND OF SPHAEIN
KINGDOM OF SPHAELITE
KNOCK
KNOCK
RAL! IT'S TIME FOR YOUR LESSON!
RAL! I KNOW YOU'RE IN THERE...
CREAK
!!

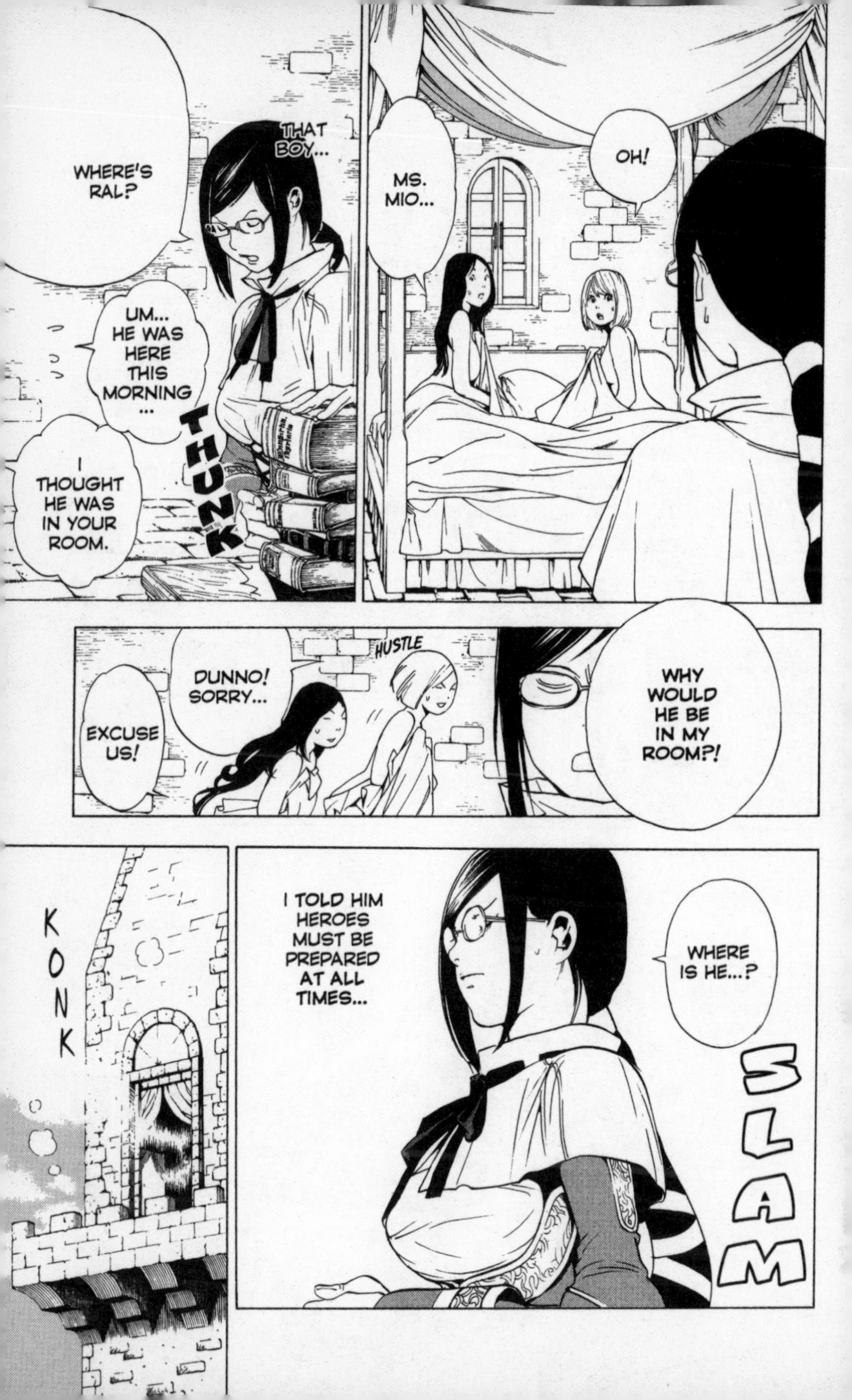
OH!
MS. MIO...
THAT BOY...
WHERE'S RAL?
UM... HE WAS HERE THIS MORNING ...
THUNK
I THOUGHT HE WAS IN YOUR ROOM.
WHY WOULD HE BE IN MY ROOM?!
HUSTLE
DUNNO! SORRY...
EXCUSE US!
WHERE IS HE...?
SLAM
I TOLD HIM HEROES MUST BE PREPARED AT ALL TIMES...
KONK

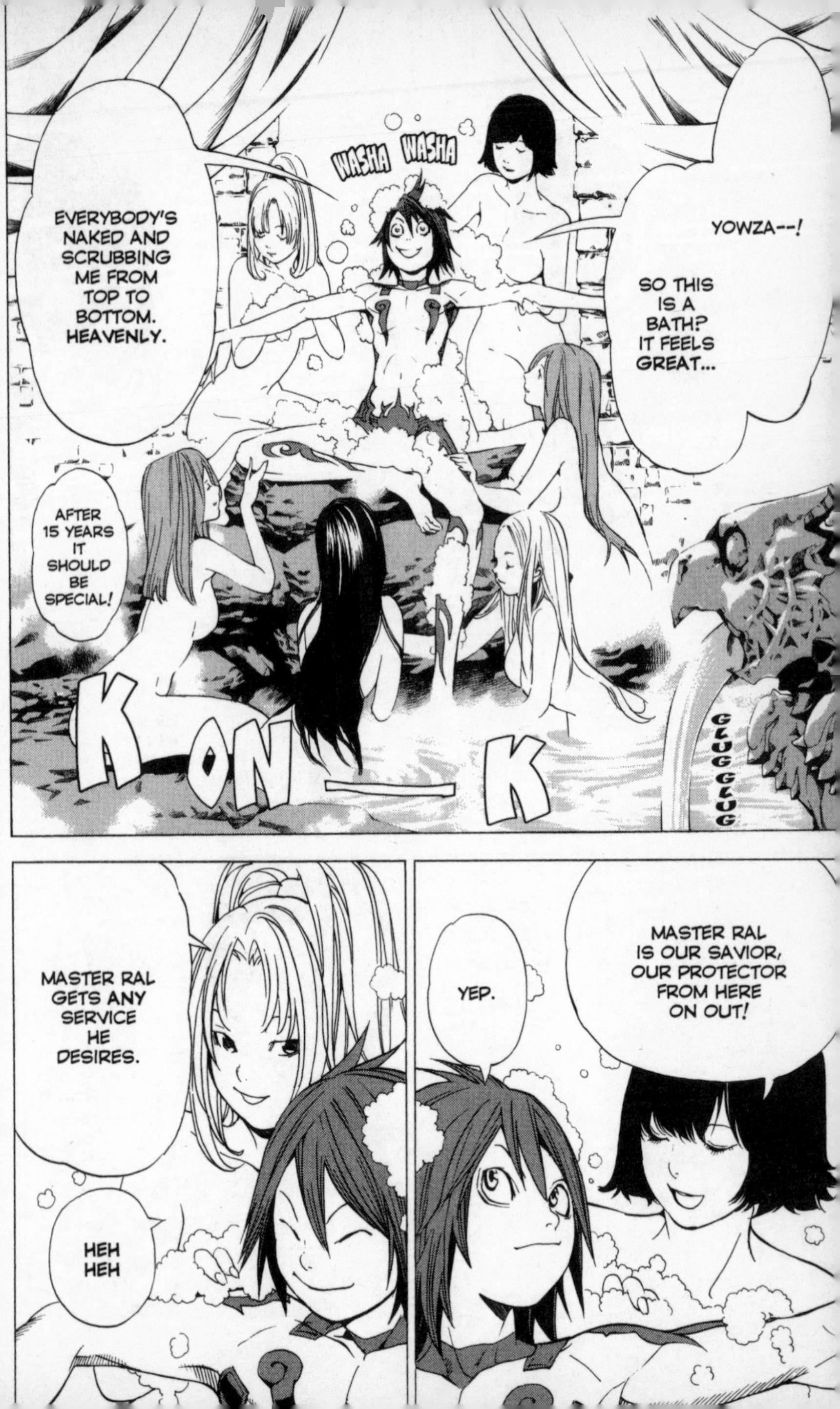
YOWZA--!
SO THIS IS A BATH? IT FEELS GREAT...
WASHA WASHA
EVERYBODY'S NAKED AND SCRUBBING ME FROM TOP TO BOTTOM. HEAVENLY.
AFTER 15 YEARS IT SHOULD BE SPECIAL!
GLUG GLUG
KONK
MASTER RAL IS OUR SAVIOR, OUR PROTECTOR FROM HERE ON OUT!
YEP.
MASTER RAL GETS ANY SERVICE HE DESIRES.
HEH HEH

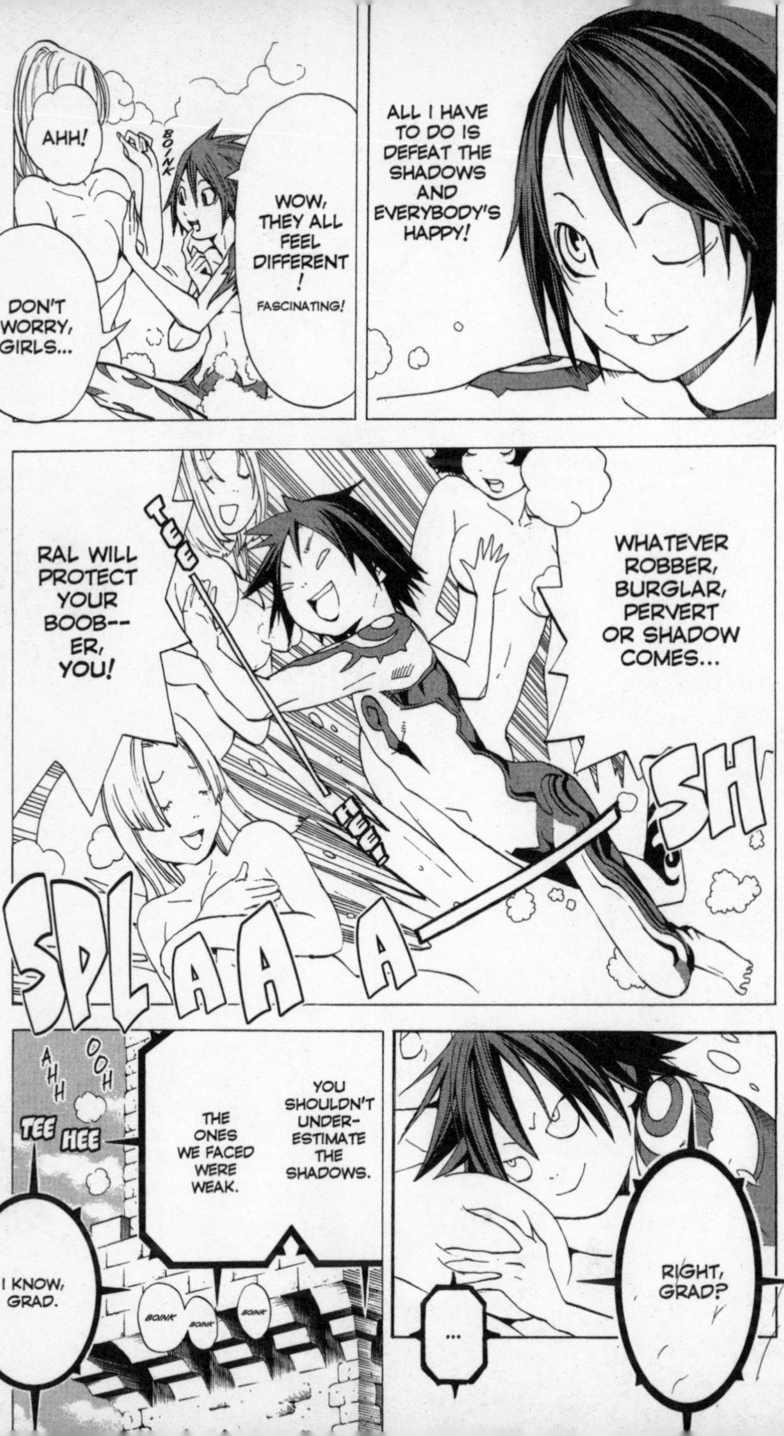
ALL I HAVE TO DO IS DEFEAT THE SHADOWS AND EVERYBODY'S HAPPY!
WOW, THEY ALL FEEL DIFFERENT!
FASCINATING!
BOINK
AHH!
DON'T WORRY, GIRLS...
WHATEVER ROBBER, BURGLAR, PERVERT OR SHADOW COMES...
RAL WILL PROTECT YOUR BOOB-- ER, YOU!
TEE
SH
SPLAAA
RIGHT, GRAD?
...
YOU SHOULDN'T UNDER-ESTIMATE THE SHADOWS.
THE ONES WE FACED WERE WEAK.
OOH
AHH
TEE HEE
BOINK
BOINK
BOINK
I KNOW, GRAD.

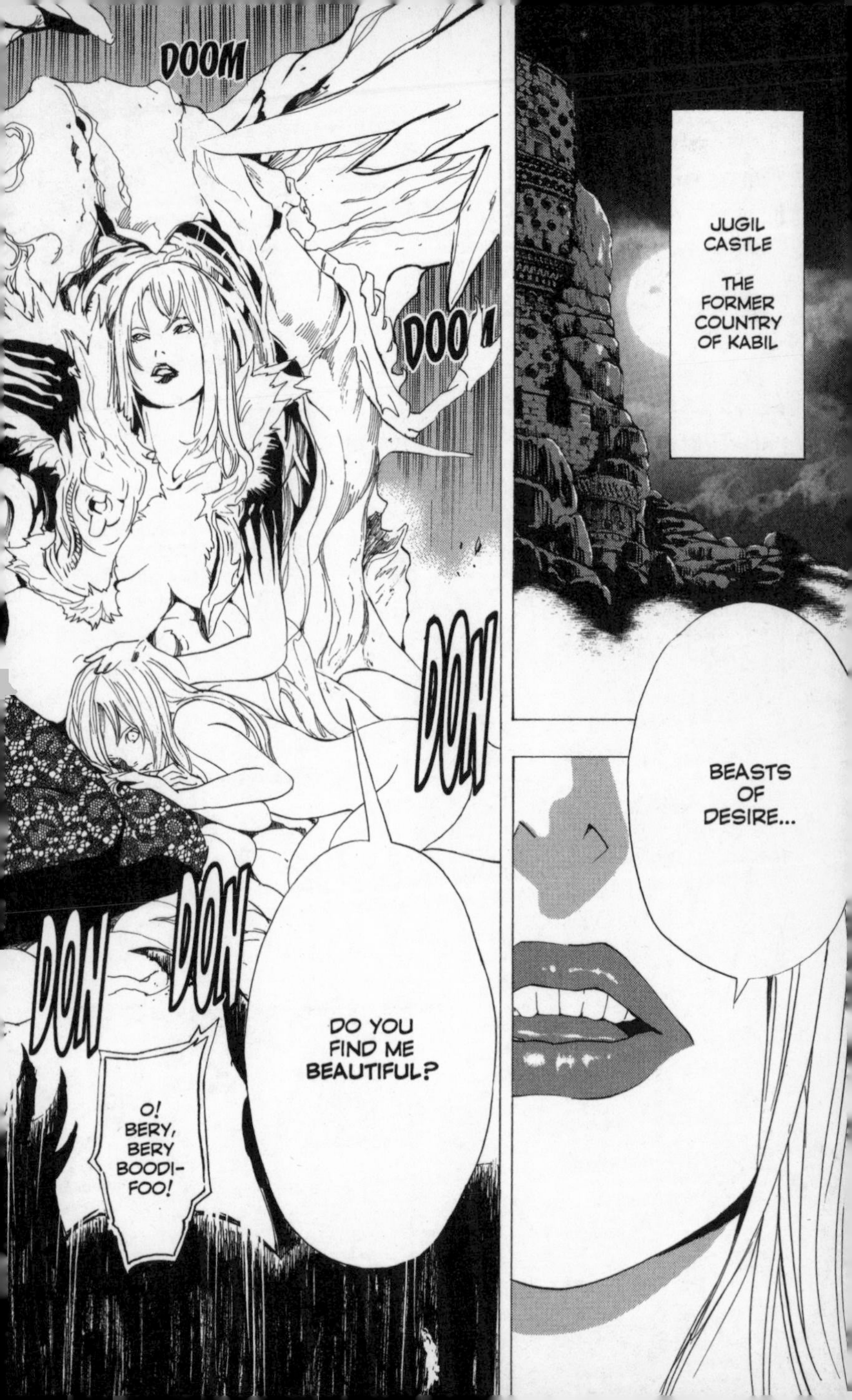
JUGIL CASTLE
THE FORMER COUNTRY OF KABIL
BEASTS OF DESIRE...
DOOM
DOO
DOH
DO YOU FIND ME BEAUTIFUL?
DOH
DOH
O! BERY, BERY BOODI-FOO!

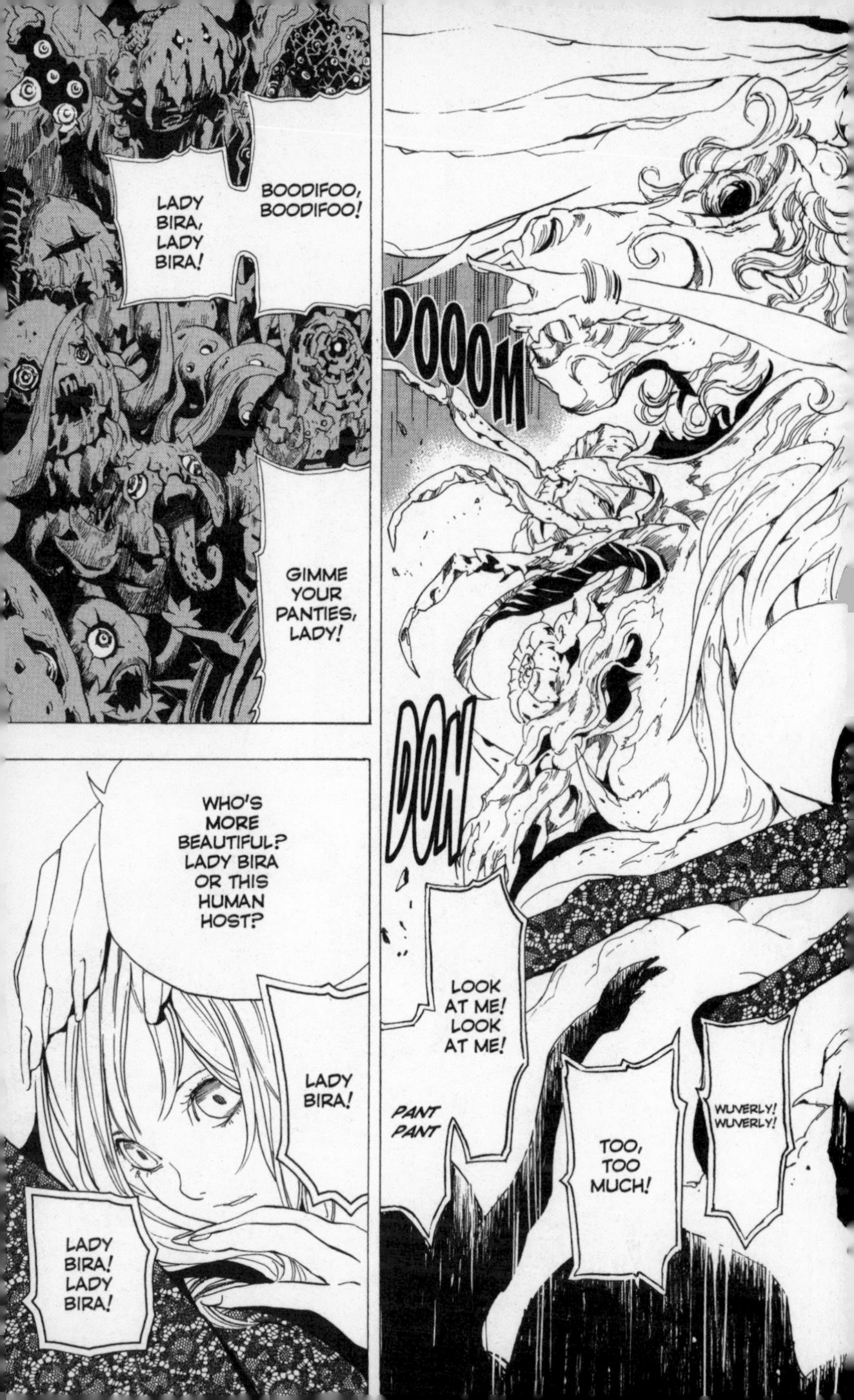
DOOOM
DOCH
LOOK AT ME! LOOK AT ME!
WUVERLY! WUVERLY!
TOO, TOO MUCH!
PANT PANT
BOODIFOO, BOODIFOO!
LADY BIRA, LADY BIRA!
GIMME YOUR PANTIES, LADY!
WHO'S MORE BEAUTIFUL? LADY BIRA OR THIS HUMAN HOST?
LADY BIRA!
LADY BIRA! LADY BIRA!

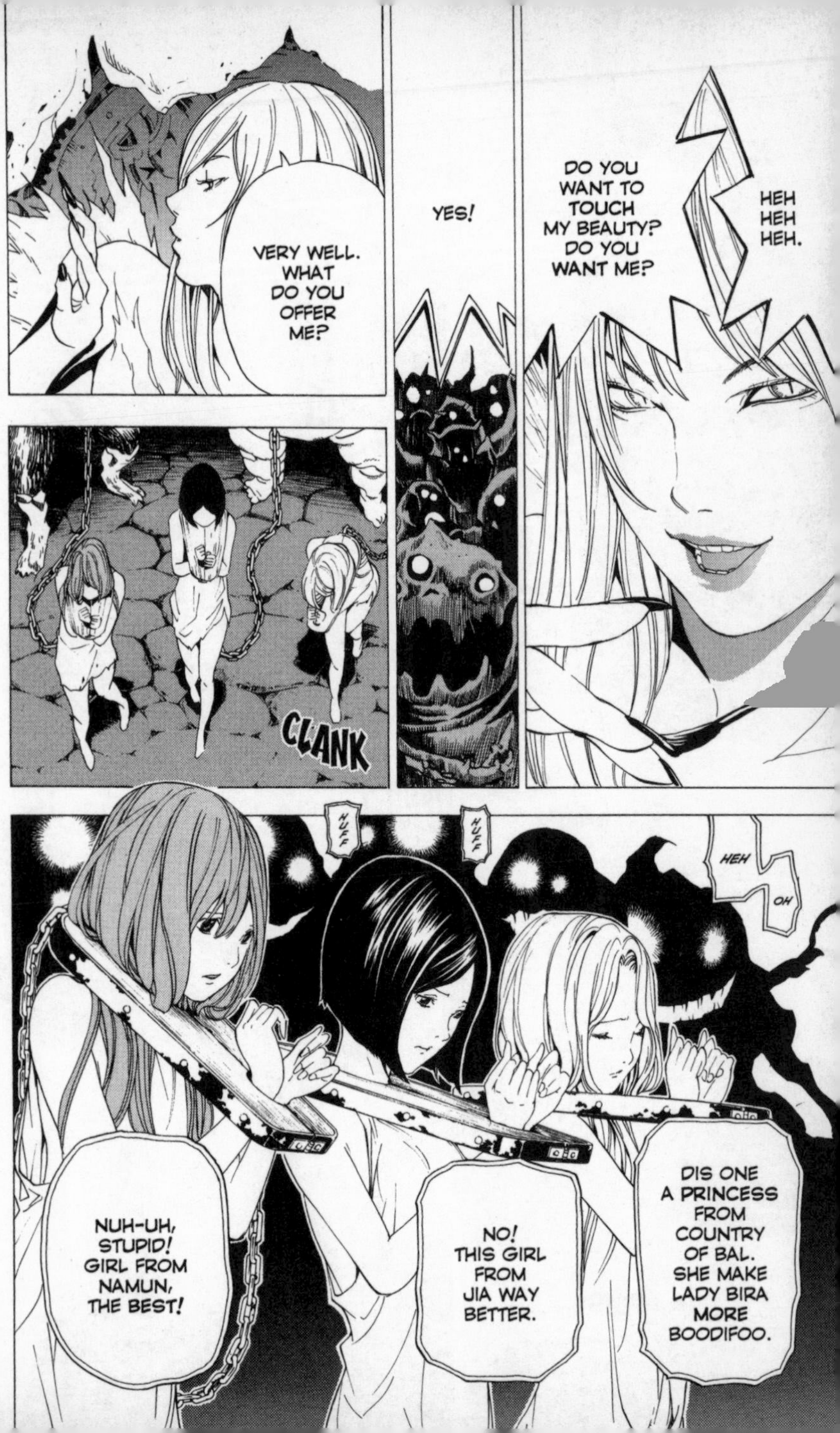
HEH HEH HEH.
DO YOU WANT TO TOUCH MY BEAUTY? DO YOU WANT ME?
YES!
VERY WELL. WHAT DO YOU OFFER ME?
CLANK
HUFF
HUFF
HEH
OH
DIS ONE A PRINCESS FROM COUNTRY OF BAL. SHE MAKE LADY BIRA MORE BOODIFOO.
NO! THIS GIRL FROM JIA WAY BETTER.
NUH-UH, STUPID! GIRL FROM NAMUN, THE BEST!

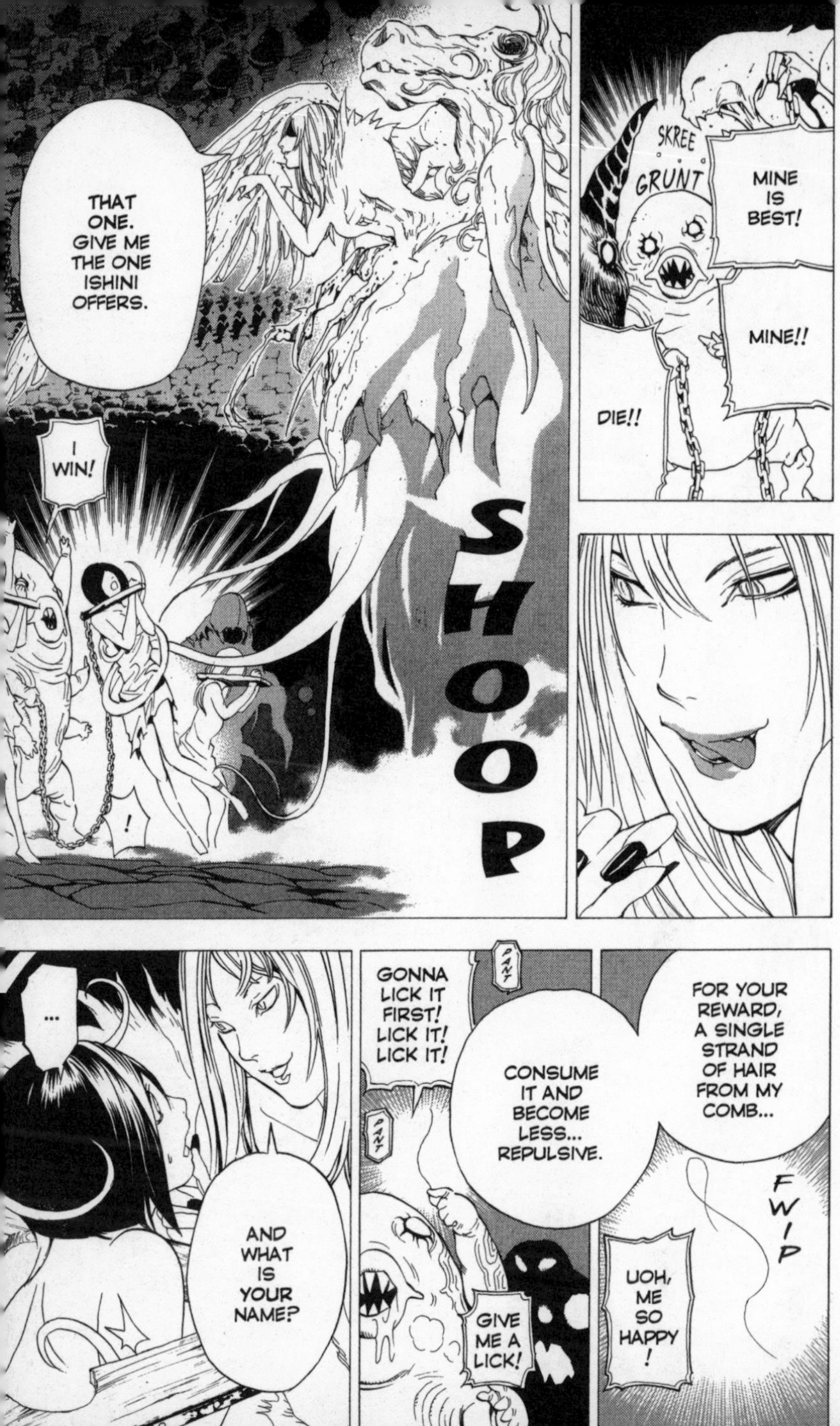
SKREE
GRUNT
MINE IS BEST!
MINE!!
DIE!!
THAT ONE. GIVE ME THE ONE ISHINI OFFERS.
SHOOP
I WIN!
!
FOR YOUR REWARD, A SINGLE STRAND OF HAIR FROM MY COMB...
CONSUME IT AND BECOME LESS... REPULSIVE.
FWIP
UOH, ME SO HAPPY!
PANT
GONNA LICK IT FIRST! LICK IT! LICK IT!
PANT
GIVE ME A LICK!
...
AND WHAT IS YOUR NAME?

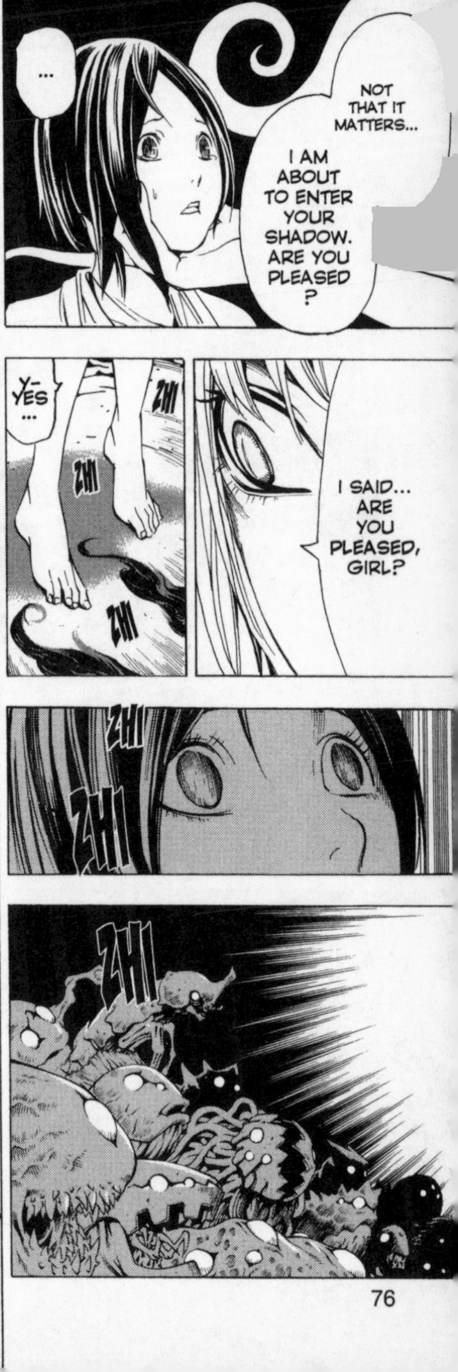
NOT THAT IT MATTERS...
I AM ABOUT TO ENTER YOUR SHADOW. ARE YOU PLEASED?
...
I SAID... ARE YOU PLEASED, GIRL?
Y-YES ...
ZHI
ZHI
ZHI
ZHI
ZHI
ZHI
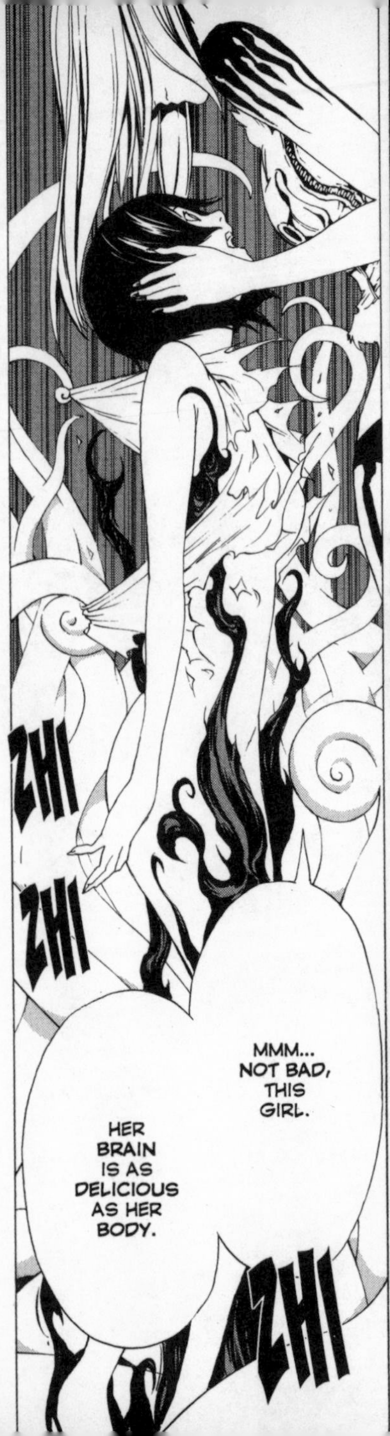
ZHI
ZHI
MMM... NOT BAD, THIS GIRL.
HER BRAIN IS AS DELICIOUS AS HER BODY.
ZHI

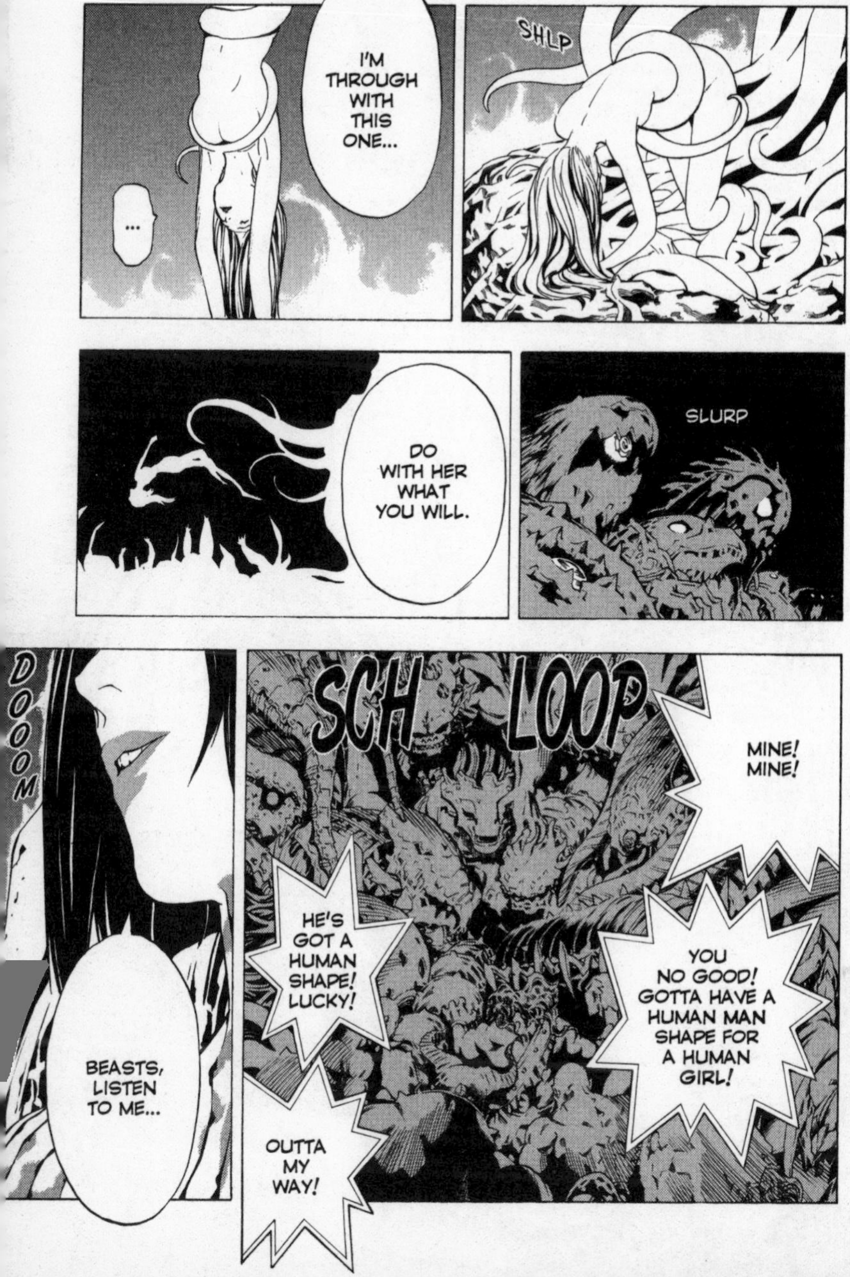
SHLP
I'M THROUGH WITH THIS ONE...
...
SLURP
DO WITH HER WHAT YOU WILL.
SCH LOOP
MINE! MINE!
YOU NO GOOD! GOTTA HAVE A HUMAN MAN SHAPE FOR A HUMAN GIRL!
HE'S GOT A HUMAN SHAPE! LUCKY!
OUTTA MY WAY!
DOOOOM
BEASTS, LISTEN TO ME...

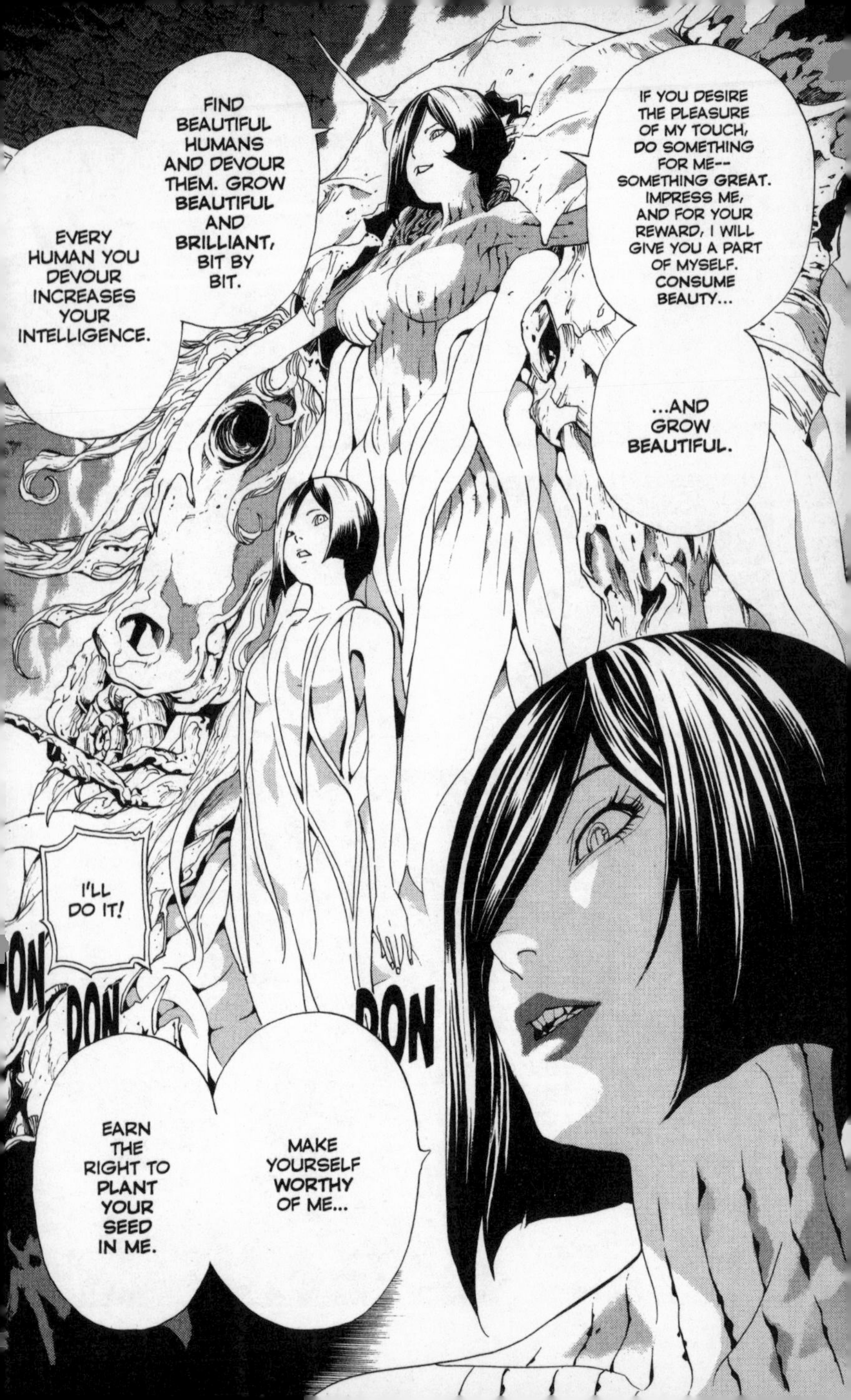
IF YOU DESIRE THE PLEASURE OF MY TOUCH, DO SOMETHING FOR ME-- SOMETHING GREAT. IMPRESS ME, AND FOR YOUR REWARD, I WILL GIVE YOU A PART OF MYSELF. CONSUME BEAUTY...
...AND GROW BEAUTIFUL.
FIND BEAUTIFUL HUMANS AND DEVOUR THEM. GROW BEAUTIFUL AND BRILLIANT, BIT BY BIT.
EVERY HUMAN YOU DEVOUR INCREASES YOUR INTELLIGENCE.
I'LL DO IT!
DON
DON
ON
MAKE YOURSELF WORTHY OF ME...
EARN THE RIGHT TO PLANT YOUR SEED IN ME.

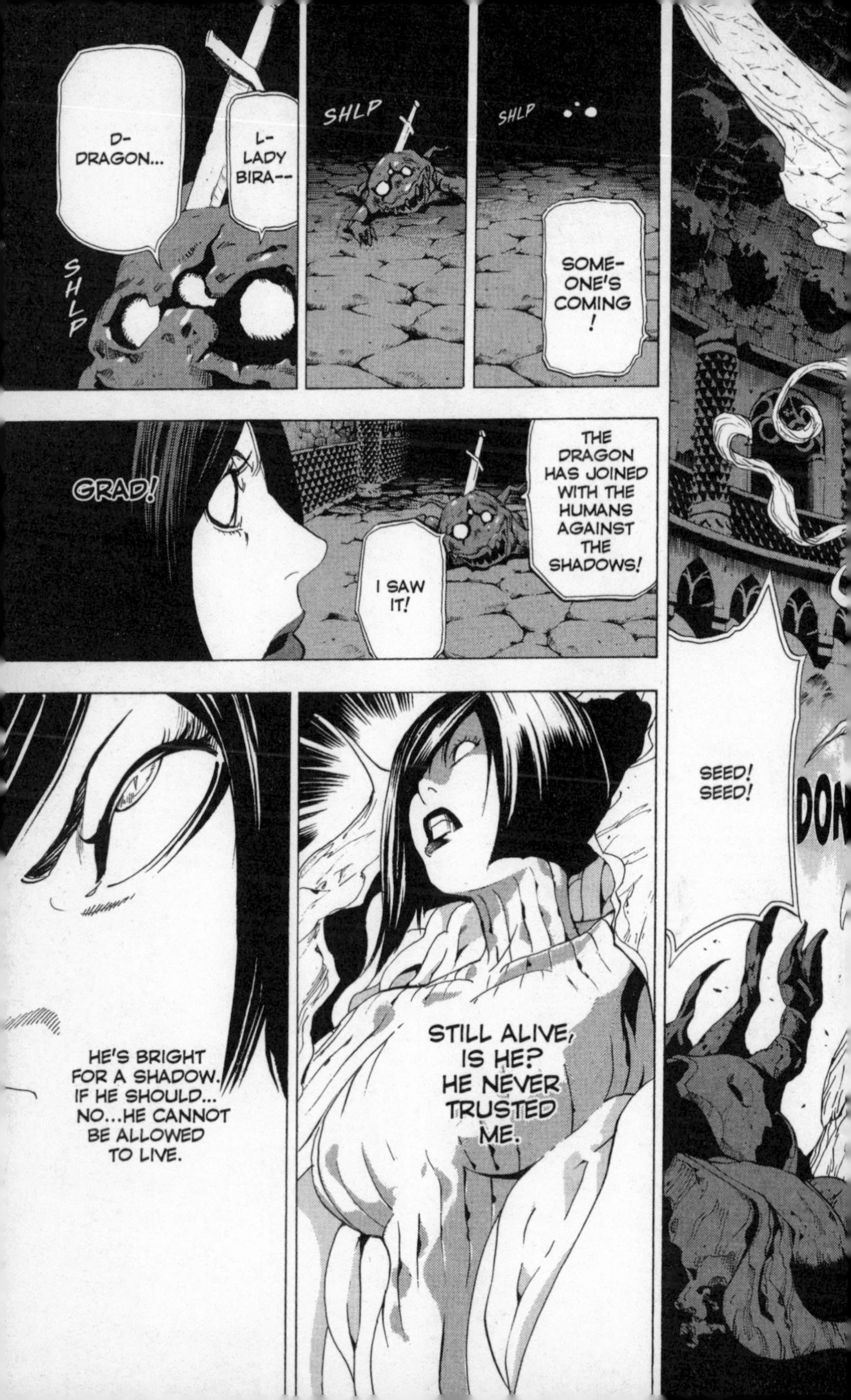
SEED! SEED!
DON
SHLP
SOME-ONE'S COMING!
SHLP
L-LADY BIRA--
D-DRAGON...
SHLP
THE DRAGON HAS JOINED WITH THE HUMANS AGAINST THE SHADOWS!
I SAW IT!
GRAD!
STILL ALIVE, IS HE? HE NEVER TRUSTED ME.
HE'S BRIGHT FOR A SHADOW. IF HE SHOULD... NO...HE CANNOT BE ALLOWED TO LIVE.

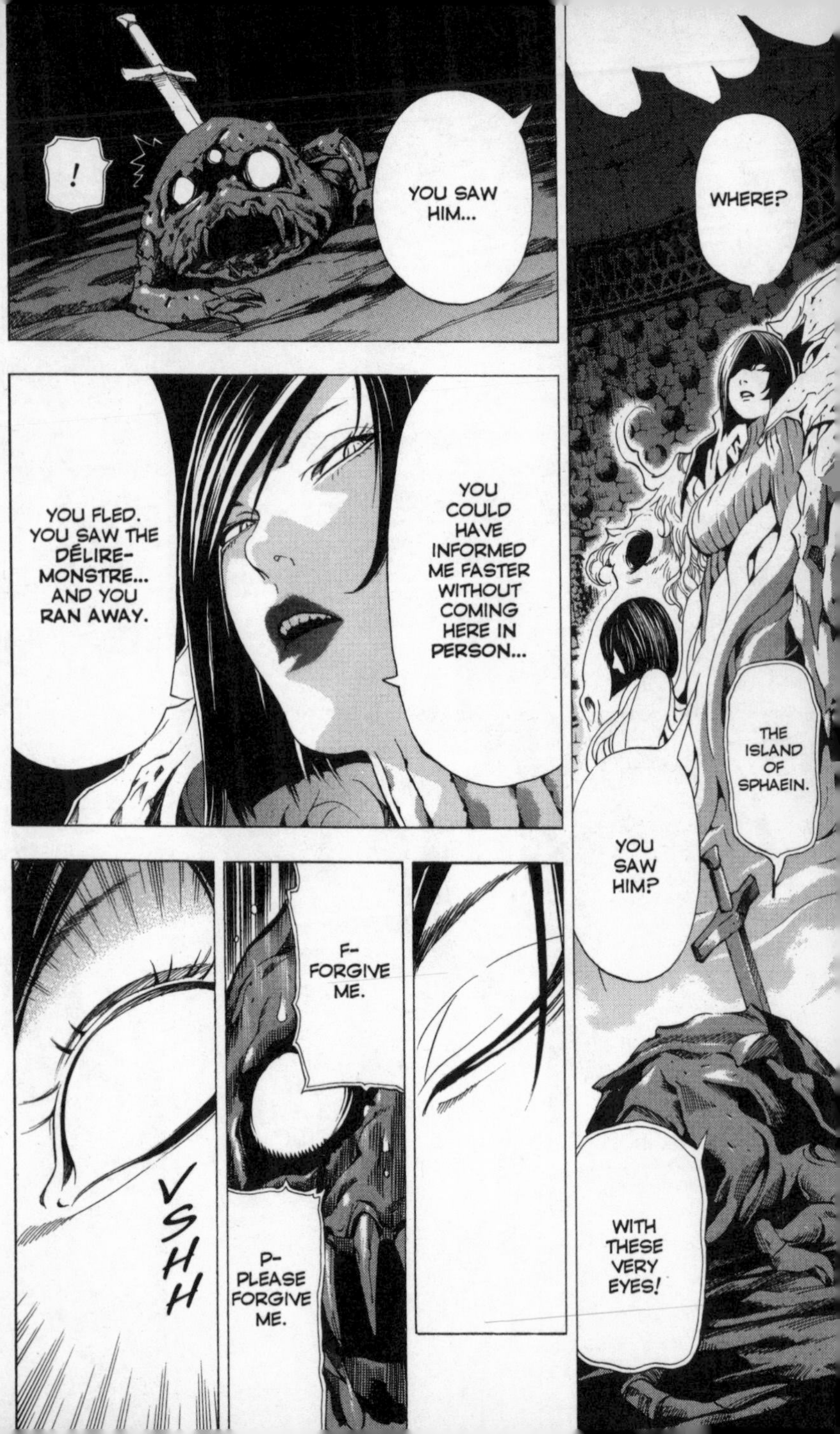
WHERE?
THE ISLAND OF SPHAEIN.
YOU SAW HIM?
WITH THESE VERY EYES!
YOU SAW HIM...
!
YOU COULD HAVE INFORMED ME FASTER WITHOUT COMING HERE IN PERSON...
YOU FLED. YOU SAW THE DÉLIRE-MONSTRE... AND YOU RAN AWAY.
F-FORGIVE ME.
P-PLEASE FORGIVE ME.
VSHH

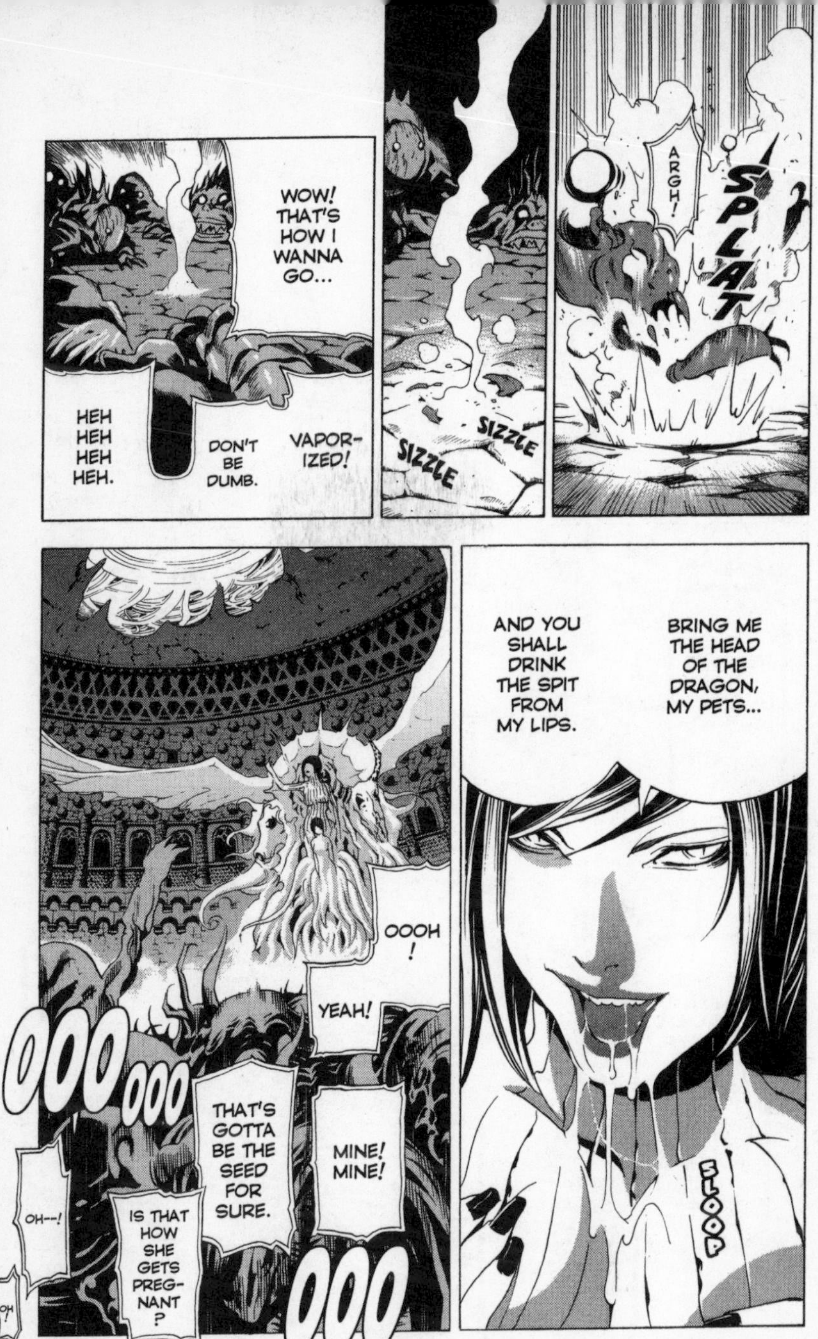
SPLAT
ARGH!
SIZZLE
SIZZLE
WOW! THAT'S HOW I WANNA GO...
VAPORIZED!
DON'T BE DUMB.
HEH HEH HEH HEH.
BRING ME THE HEAD OF THE DRAGON, MY PETS...
AND YOU SHALL DRINK THE SPIT FROM MY LIPS.
SLOOP
OOOH!
YEAH!
OOOOOO
MINE! MINE!
THAT'S GOTTA BE THE SEED FOR SURE.
IS THAT HOW SHE GETS PREGNANT?
OH--!
OH!
OOO

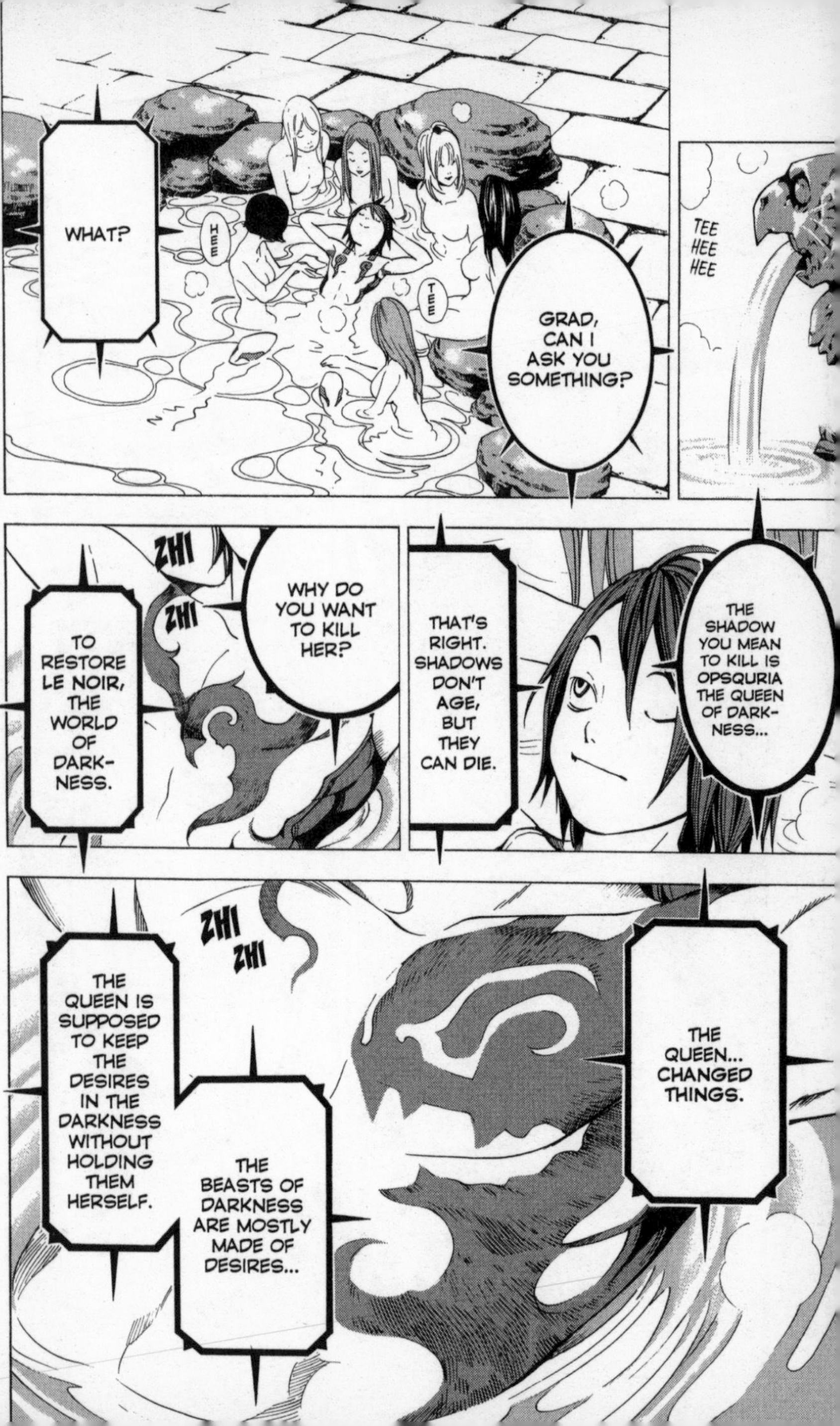
TEE HEE HEE
GRAD, CAN I ASK YOU SOMETHING?
HEE
TEE
WHAT?
THE SHADOW YOU MEAN TO KILL IS OPSQURIA THE QUEEN OF DARKNESS...
THAT'S RIGHT. SHADOWS DON'T AGE, BUT THEY CAN DIE.
WHY DO YOU WANT TO KILL HER?
ZHI
ZHI
TO RESTORE LE NOIR, THE WORLD OF DARKNESS.
THE QUEEN... CHANGED THINGS.
ZHI
ZHI
THE QUEEN IS SUPPOSED TO KEEP THE DESIRES IN THE DARKNESS WITHOUT HOLDING THEM HERSELF.
THE BEASTS OF DARKNESS ARE MOSTLY MADE OF DESIRES...

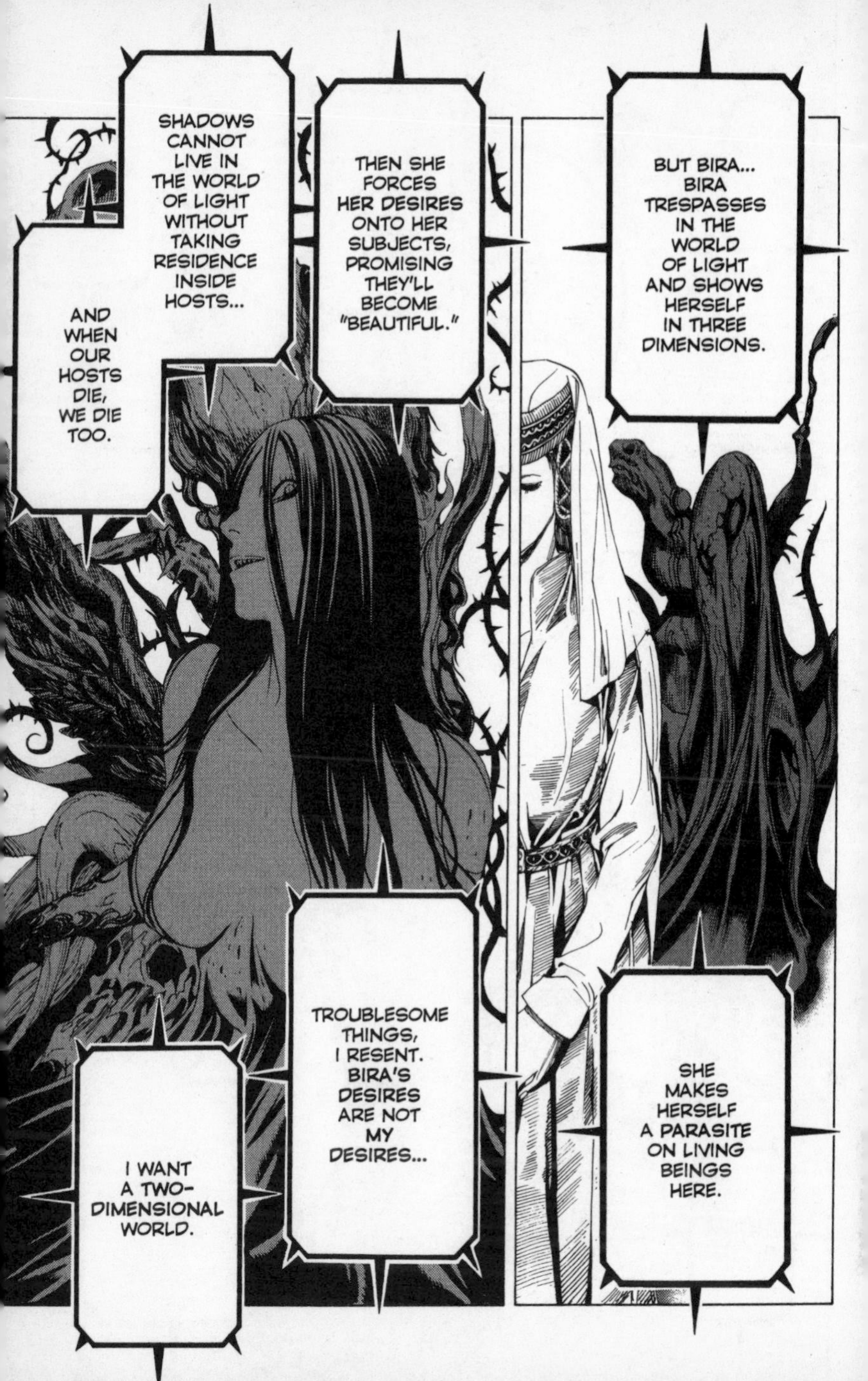
SHADOWS CANNOT LIVE IN THE WORLD OF LIGHT WITHOUT TAKING RESIDENCE INSIDE HOSTS...
AND WHEN OUR HOSTS DIE, WE DIE TOO.
BUT BIRA... BIRA TRESPASSES IN THE WORLD OF LIGHT AND SHOWS HERSELF IN THREE DIMENSIONS.
SHE MAKES HERSELF A PARASITE ON LIVING BEINGS HERE.
THEN SHE FORCES HER DESIRES ONTO HER SUBJECTS, PROMISING THEY'LL BECOME "BEAUTIFUL."
TROUBLESOME THINGS, I RESENT. BIRA'S DESIRES ARE NOT MY DESIRES...
I WANT A TWO-DIMENSIONAL WORLD.

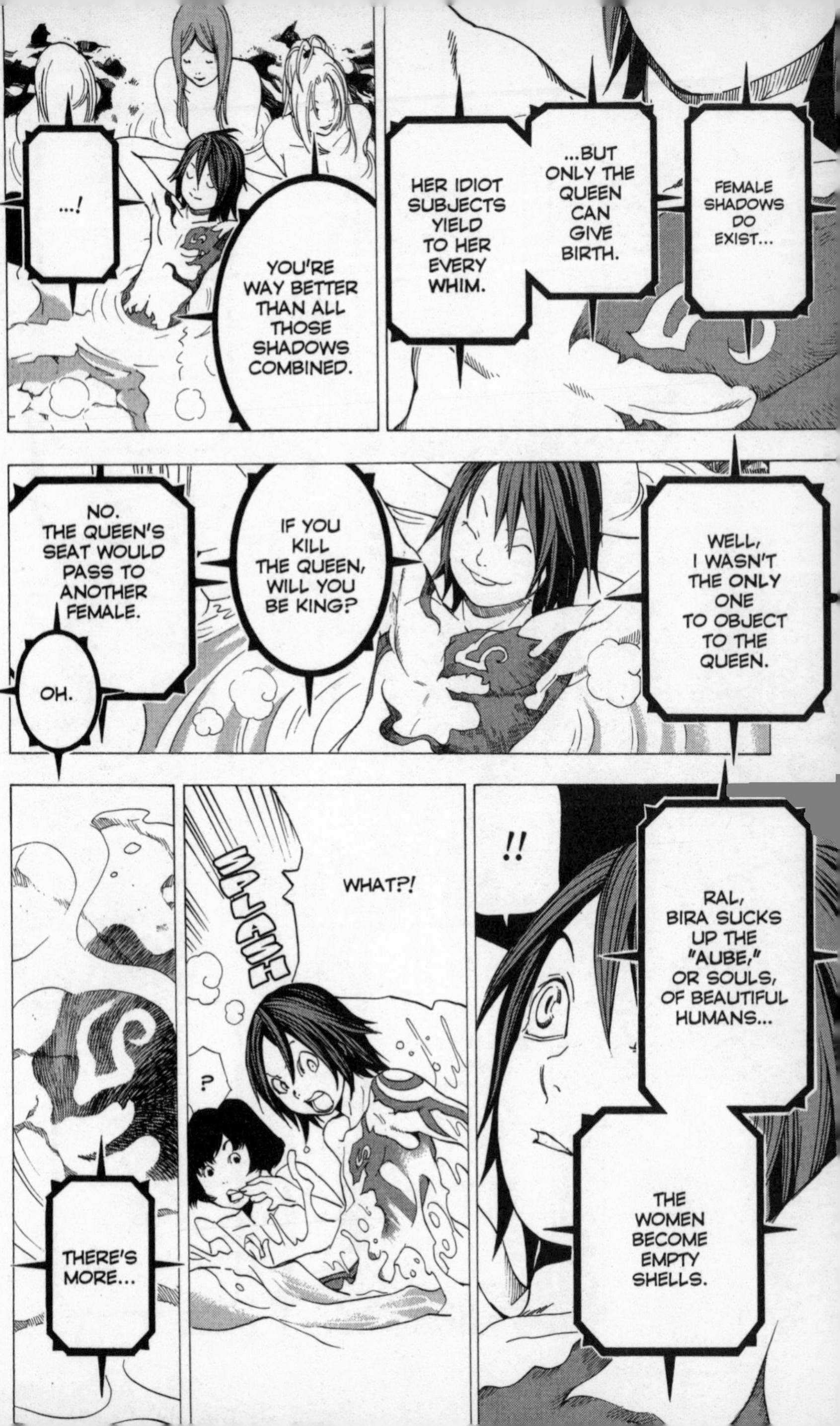
FEMALE SHADOWS DO EXIST...
...BUT ONLY THE QUEEN CAN GIVE BIRTH.
HER IDIOT SUBJECTS YIELD TO HER EVERY WHIM.
YOU'RE WAY BETTER THAN ALL THOSE SHADOWS COMBINED.
...!
WELL, I WASN'T THE ONLY ONE TO OBJECT TO THE QUEEN.
IF YOU KILL THE QUEEN, WILL YOU BE KING?
NO. THE QUEEN'S SEAT WOULD PASS TO ANOTHER FEMALE.
OH.
!!
RAL, BIRA SUCKS UP THE "AUBE," OR SOULS, OF BEAUTIFUL HUMANS...
THE WOMEN BECOME EMPTY SHELLS.
WHAT?!
SPLASH
?
THERE'S MORE...

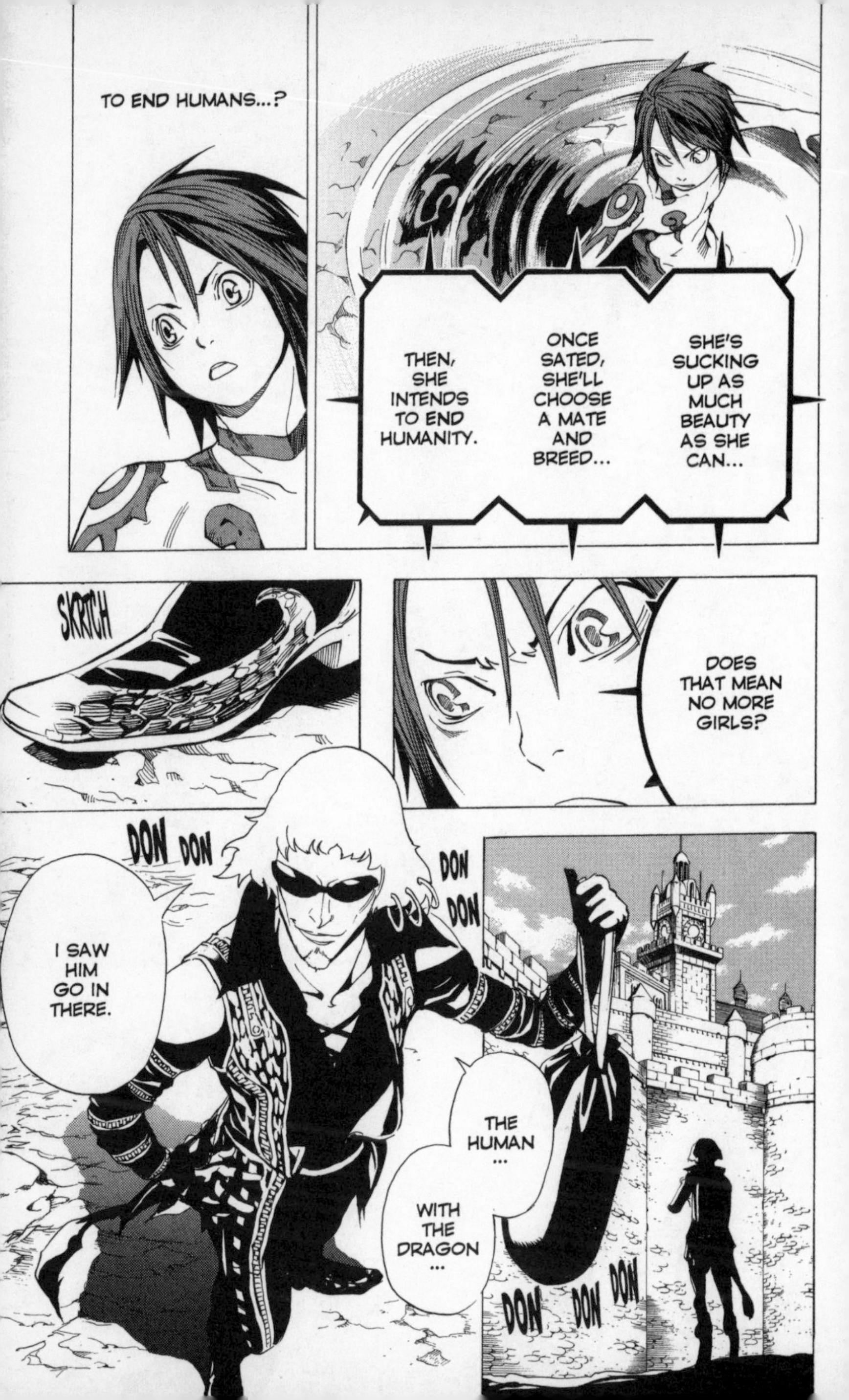
SHE'S SUCKING UP AS MUCH BEAUTY AS SHE CAN...
ONCE SATED, SHE'LL CHOOSE A MATE AND BREED...
THEN, SHE INTENDS TO END HUMANITY.
TO END HUMANS...?
DOES THAT MEAN NO MORE GIRLS?
SKRTCH
DON DON
THE HUMAN ...
WITH THE DRAGON ...
DON DON DON
DON DON
I SAW HIM GO IN THERE.

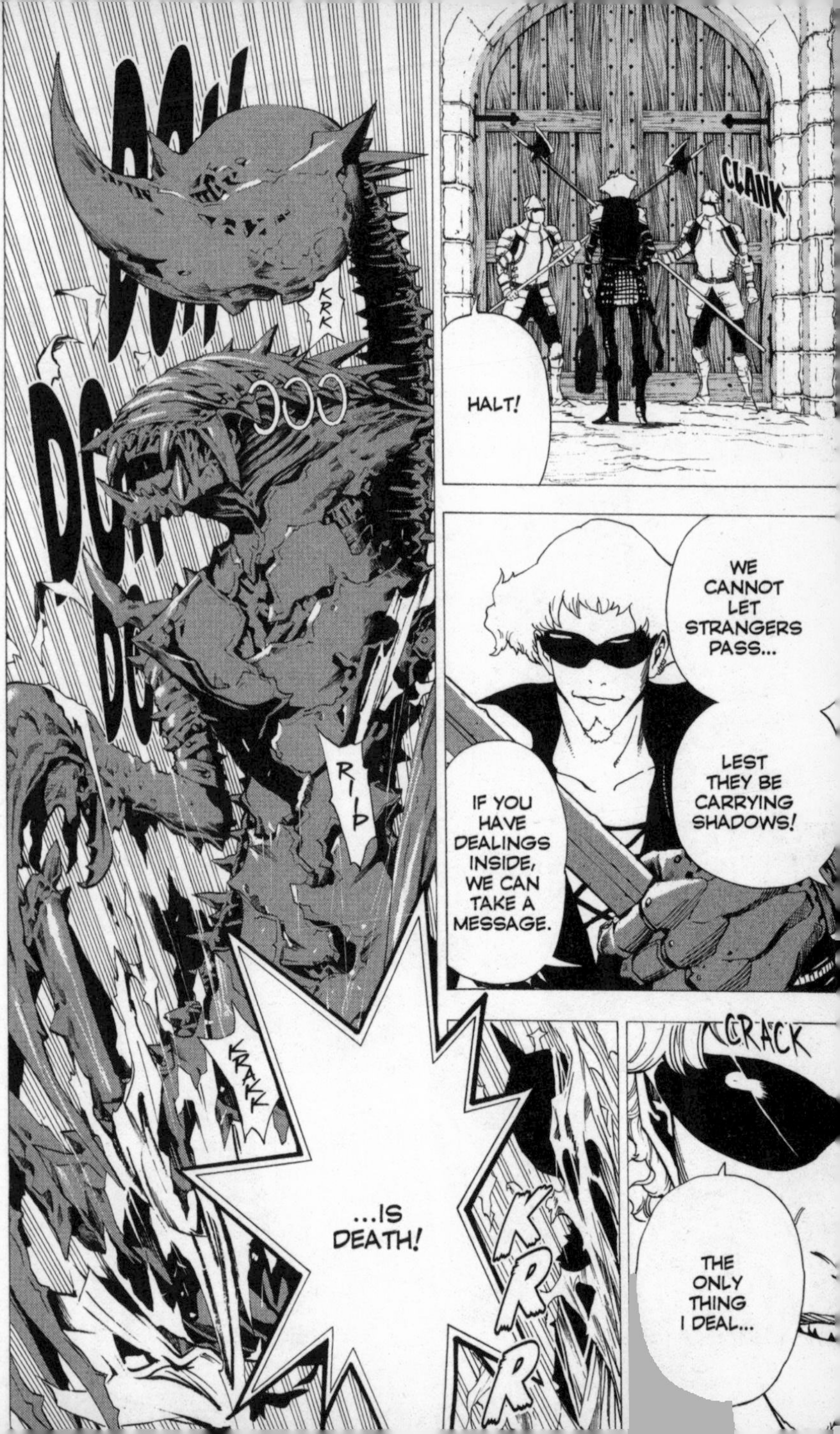
CLANK
HALT!
WE CANNOT LET STRANGERS PASS...
LEST THEY BE CARRYING SHADOWS!
IF YOU HAVE DEALINGS INSIDE, WE CAN TAKE A MESSAGE.
CRACK
THE ONLY THING I DEAL...
KRR
KRK
RIP
KRAKK
...IS DEATH!

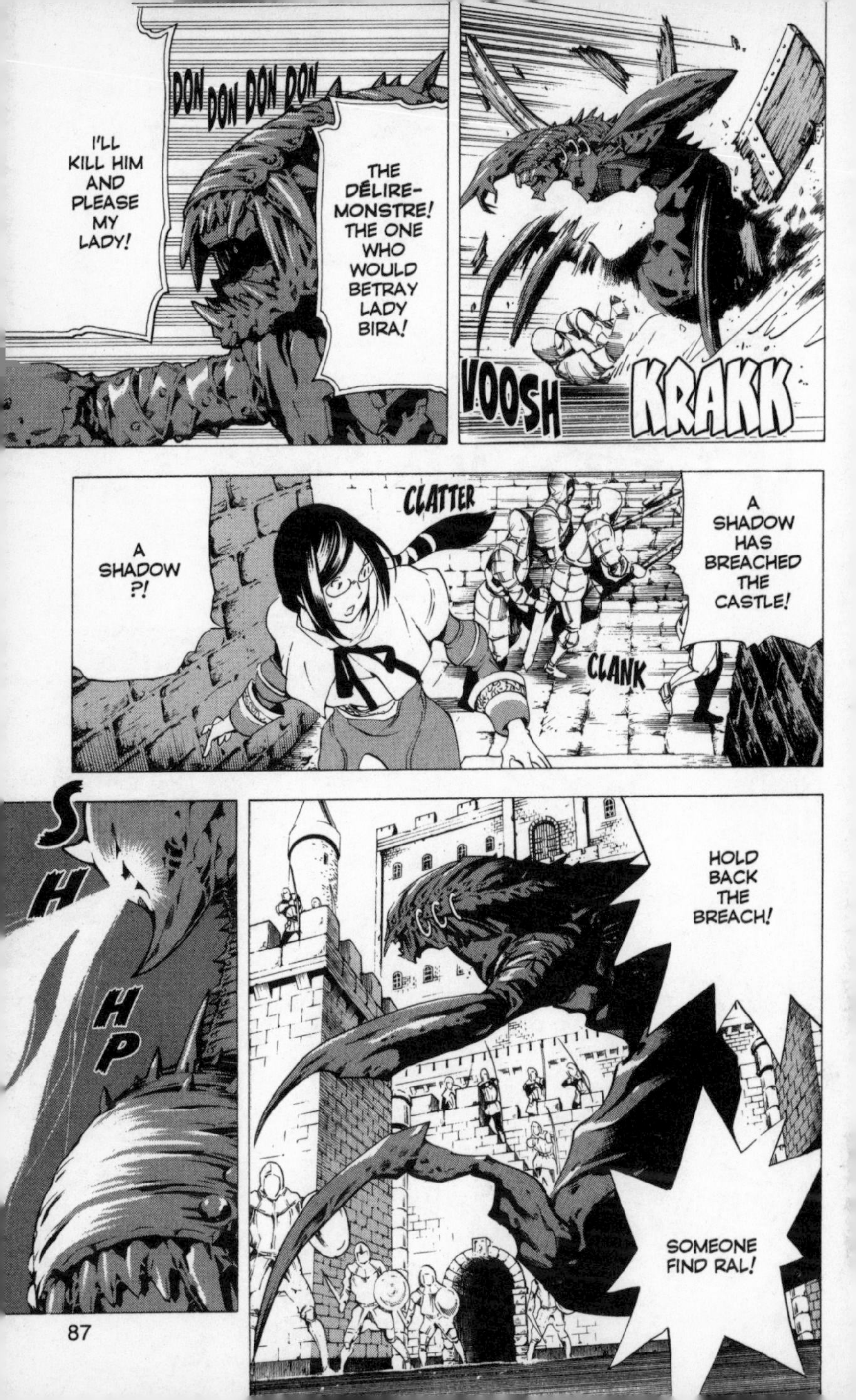
VOOSH
KRAKK
DON DON DON DON
THE DÉLIRE-MONSTRE! THE ONE WHO WOULD BETRAY LADY BIRA!
I'LL KILL HIM AND PLEASE MY LADY!
A SHADOW HAS BREACHED THE CASTLE!
CLATTER
CLANK
A SHADOW ?!
HOLD BACK THE BREACH!
SOMEONE FIND RAL!
SHHP

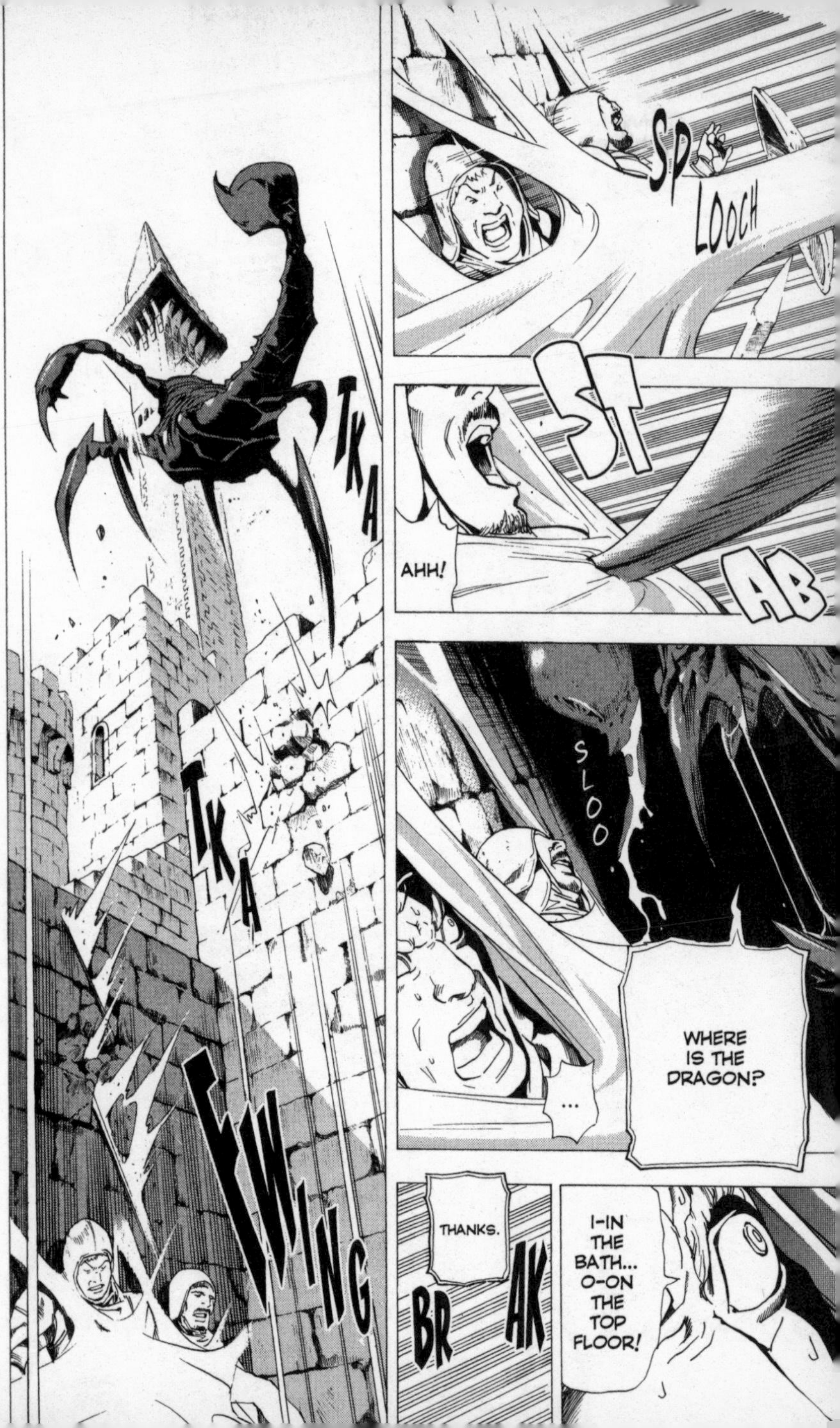
SPLOOCH
STAB
AHH!
SLOO
...
WHERE IS THE DRAGON?
I-IN THE BATH... O-ON THE TOP FLOOR!
BRAK
THANKS.
TKA
TKA
TWING

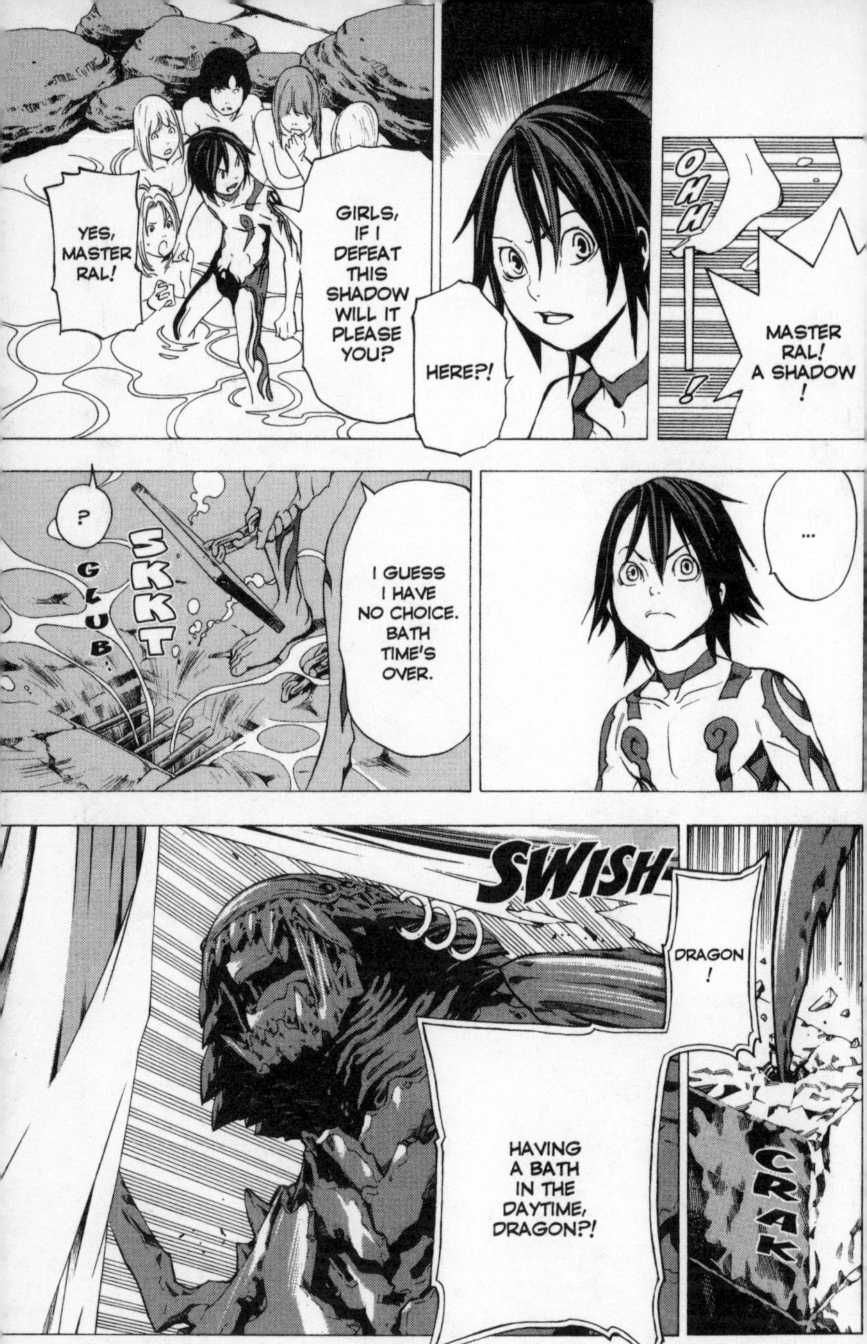
OHH—!
MASTER RAL! A SHADOW!
HERE?!
GIRLS, IF I DEFEAT THIS SHADOW WILL IT PLEASE YOU?
YES, MASTER RAL!
...
I GUESS I HAVE NO CHOICE. BATH TIME'S OVER.
SKKT
?
GLUB..
DRAGON!
CRAK
SWISH
HAVING A BATH IN THE DAYTIME, DRAGON?!

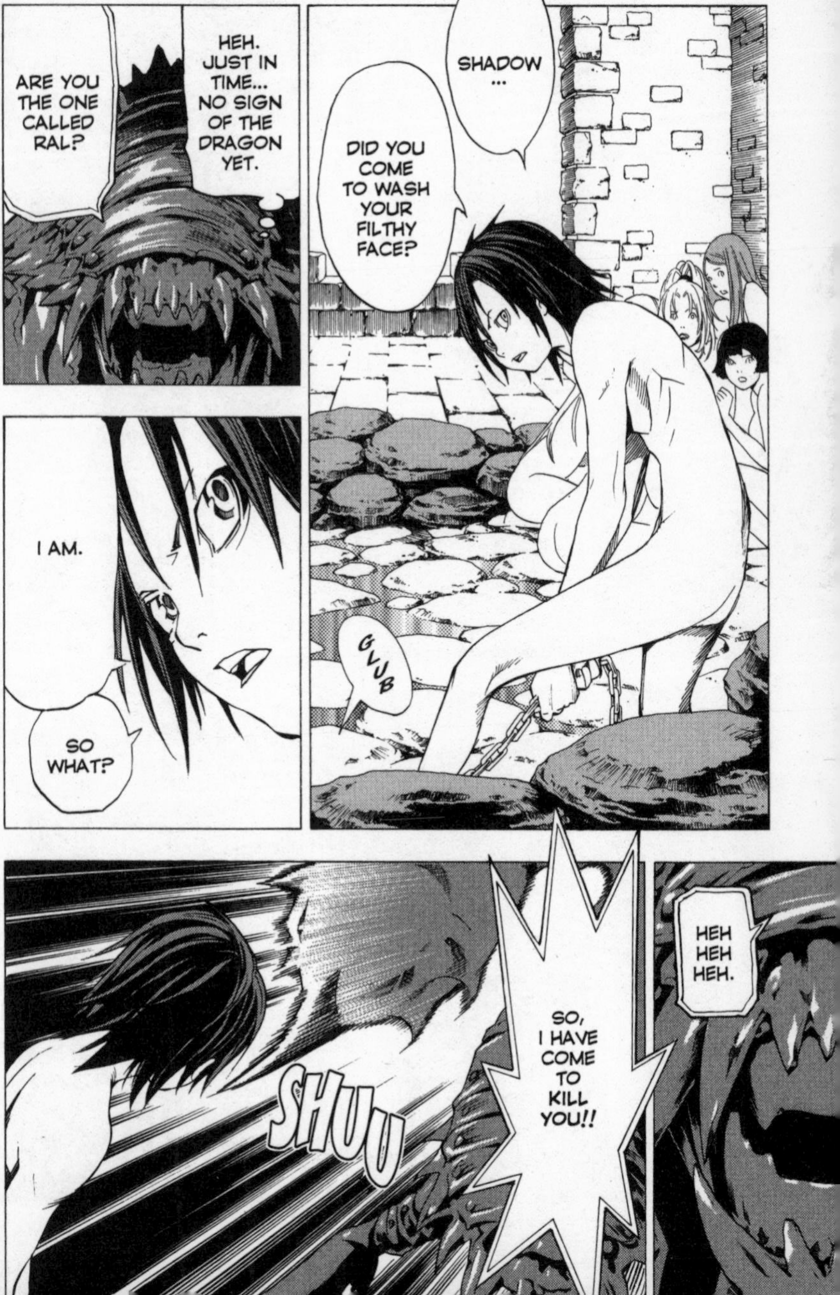
SHADOW ...
DID YOU COME TO WASH YOUR FILTHY FACE?
GLUB
HEH. JUST IN TIME... NO SIGN OF THE DRAGON YET.
ARE YOU THE ONE CALLED RAL?
I AM.
SO WHAT?
HEH HEH HEH.
SO, I HAVE COME TO KILL YOU!!
SHUU

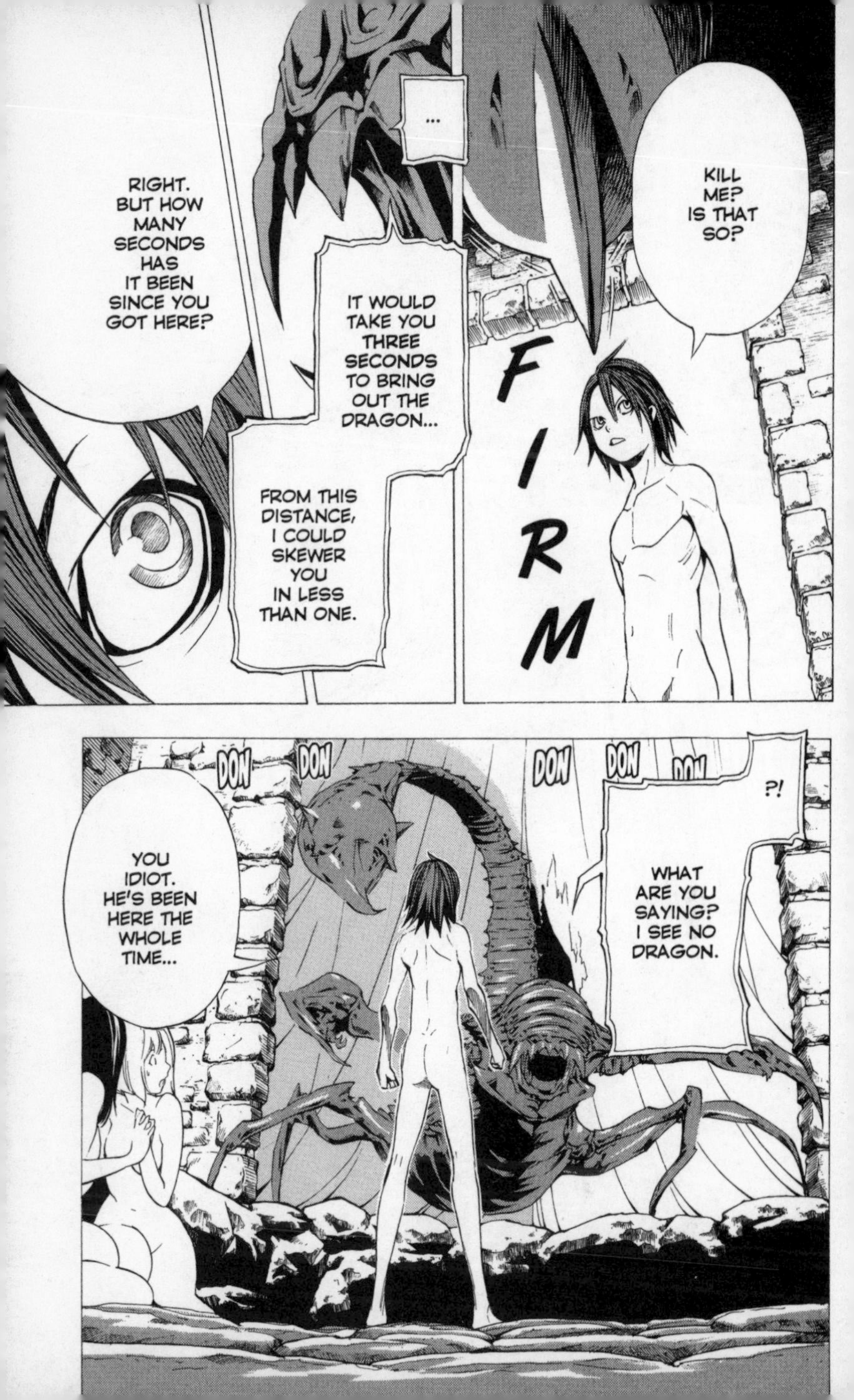
KILL ME? IS THAT SO?
FIRM
...
IT WOULD TAKE YOU THREE SECONDS TO BRING OUT THE DRAGON...
FROM THIS DISTANCE, I COULD SKEWER YOU IN LESS THAN ONE.
RIGHT. BUT HOW MANY SECONDS HAS IT BEEN SINCE YOU GOT HERE?
DON
DON
DON
DON
DON
?!
WHAT ARE YOU SAYING? I SEE NO DRAGON.
YOU IDIOT. HE'S BEEN HERE THE WHOLE TIME...

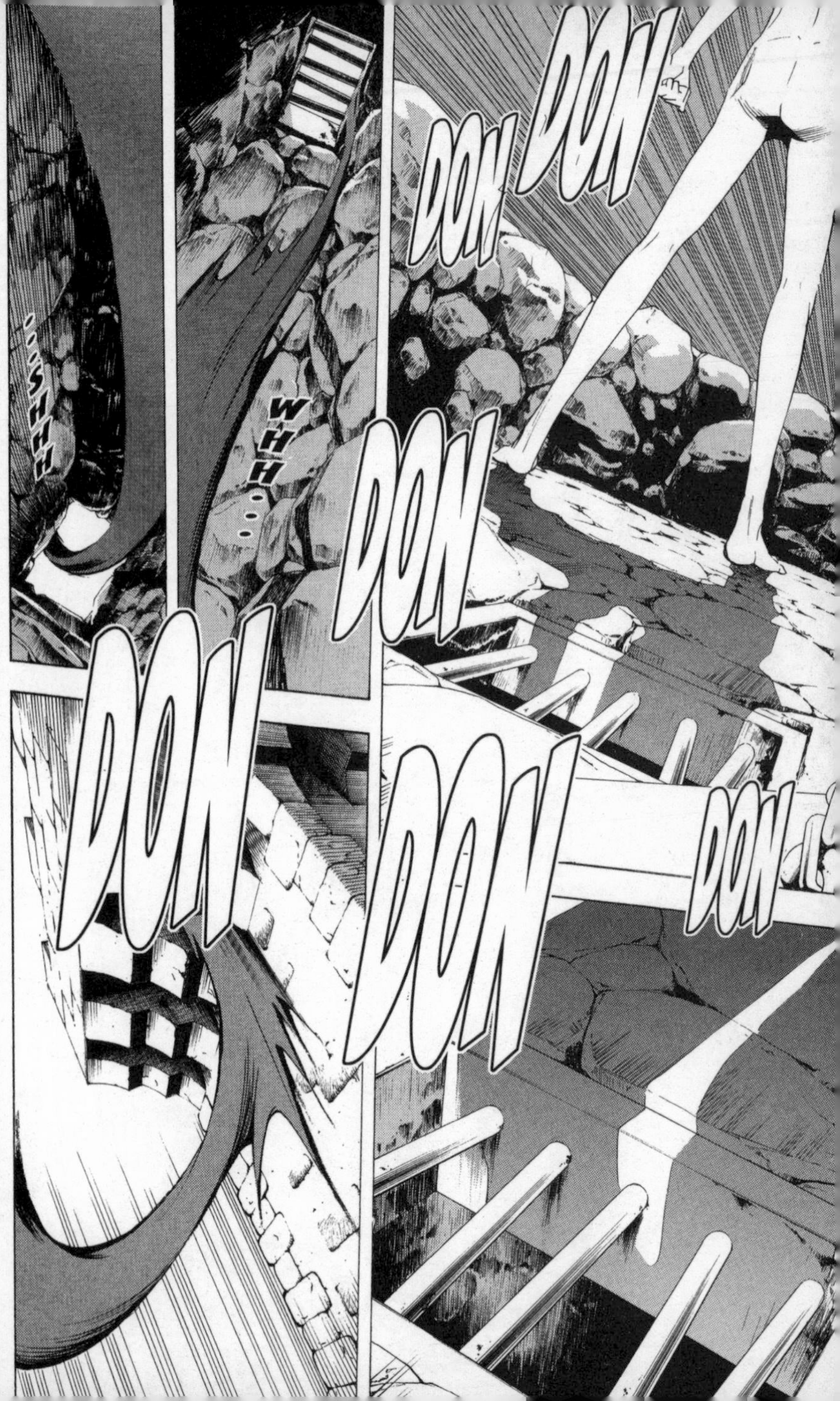
DON DON
DON DON
WHHH...
...SHHH
DON
DON DON
DON

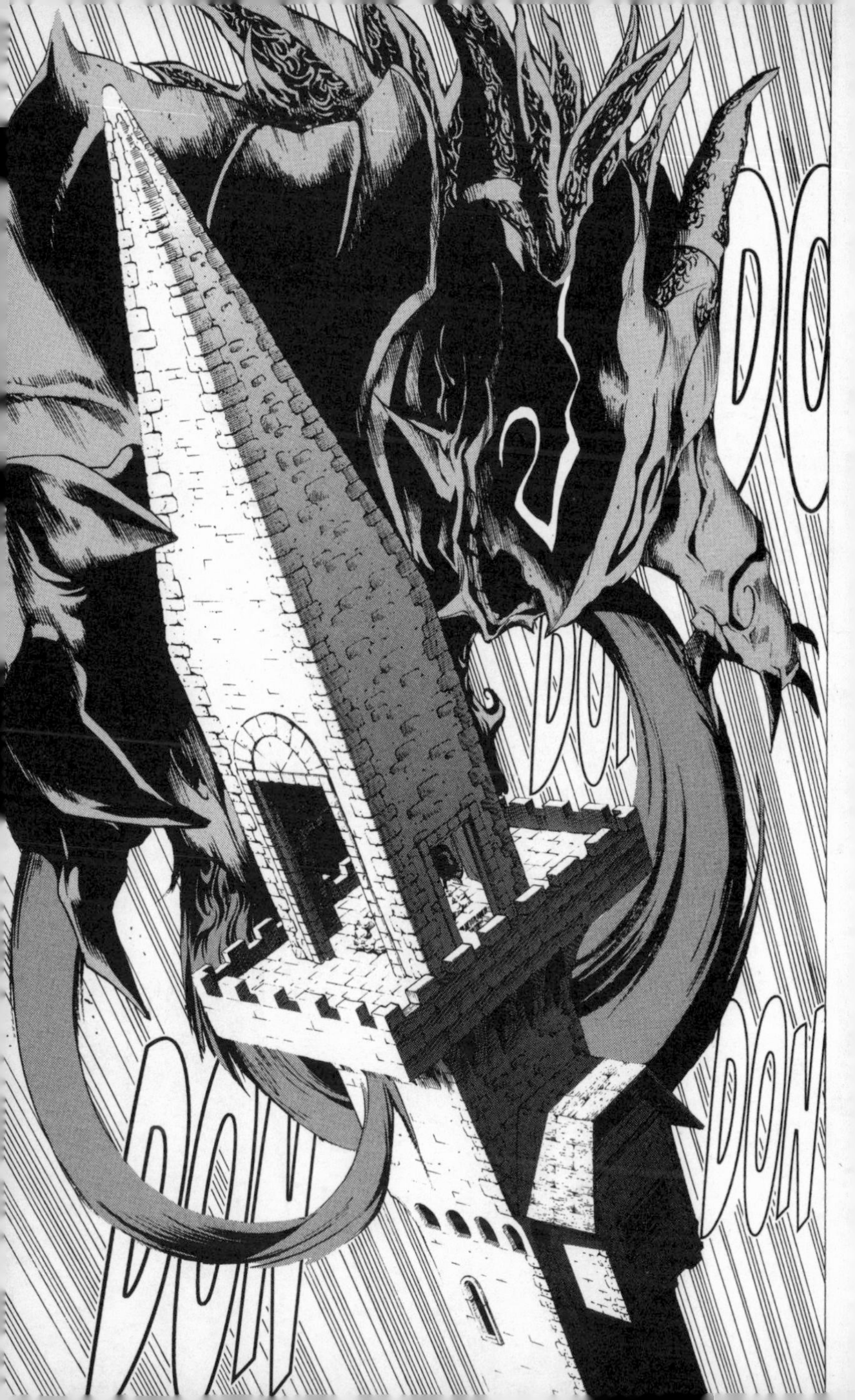
DO
DOM
DOM
DOM

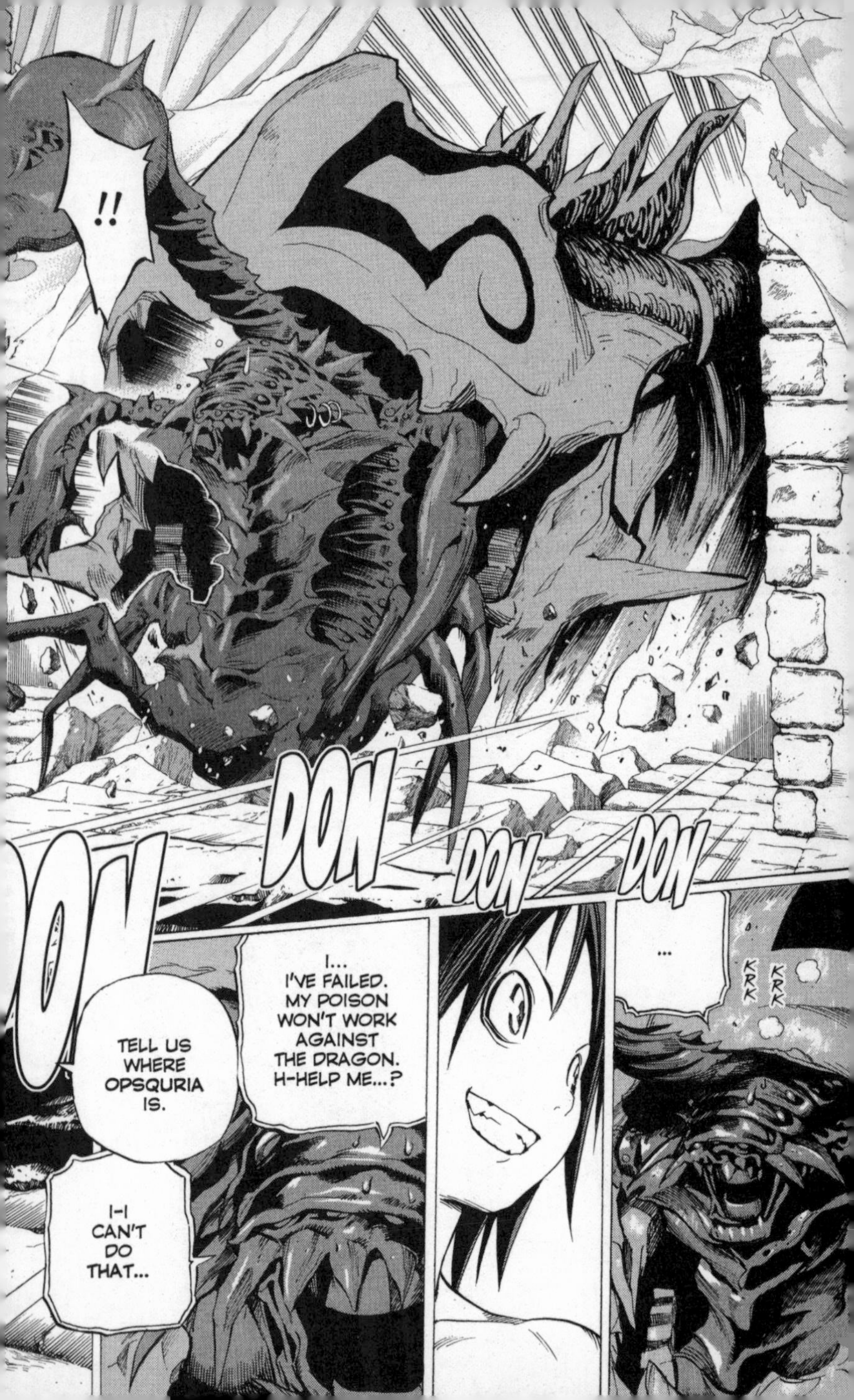
!!
DON
DON
DON
...
KRK KRK
I... I'VE FAILED. MY POISON WON'T WORK AGAINST THE DRAGON. H-HELP ME...?
TELL US WHERE OPSQURIA IS.
I-I CAN'T DO THAT...

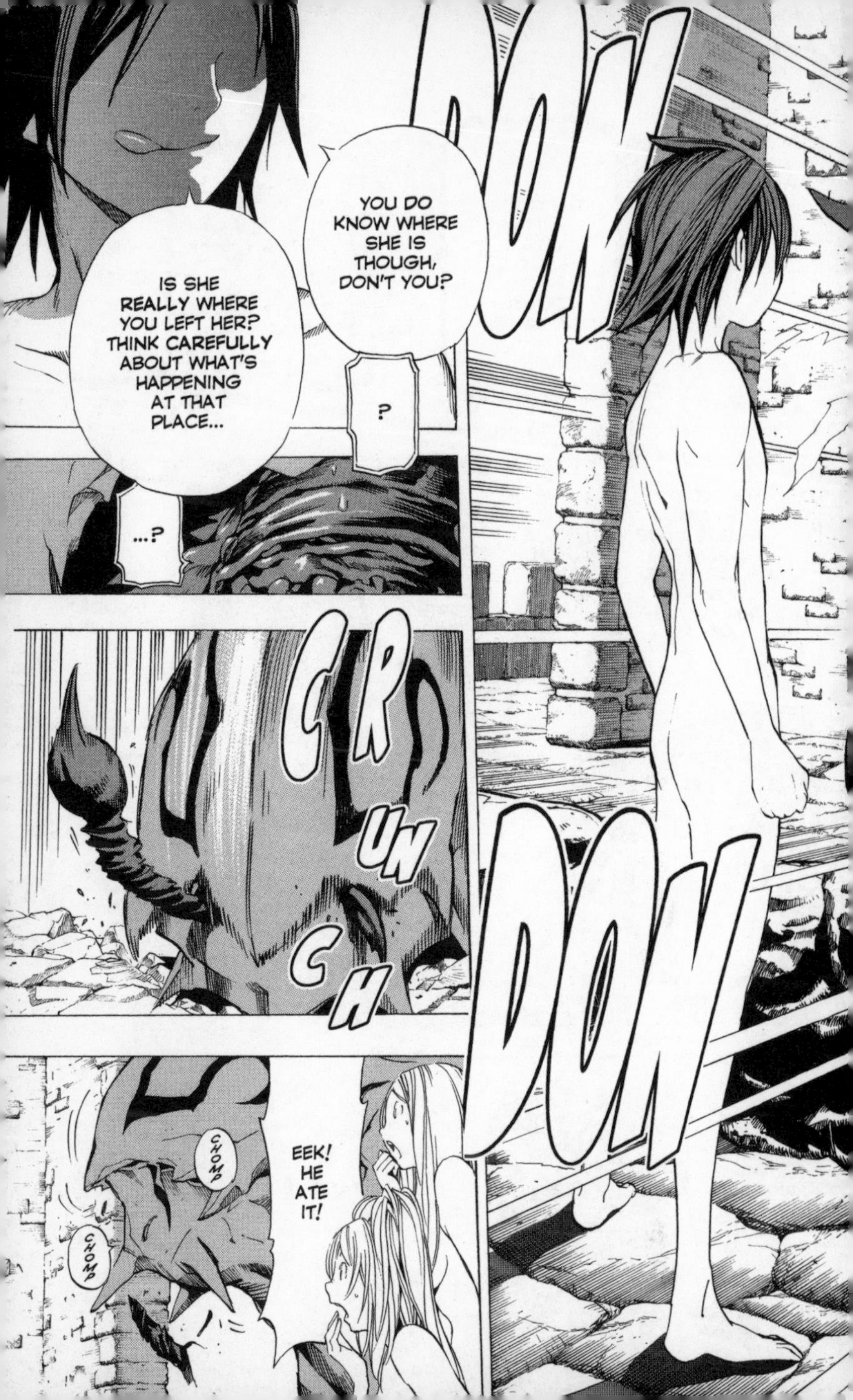
DOOM
DOOM
YOU DO KNOW WHERE SHE IS THOUGH, DON'T YOU?
IS SHE REALLY WHERE YOU LEFT HER? THINK CAREFULLY ABOUT WHAT'S HAPPENING AT THAT PLACE...
?
...?
CRUNCH
EEK! HE ATE IT!
CHOMP
CHOMP

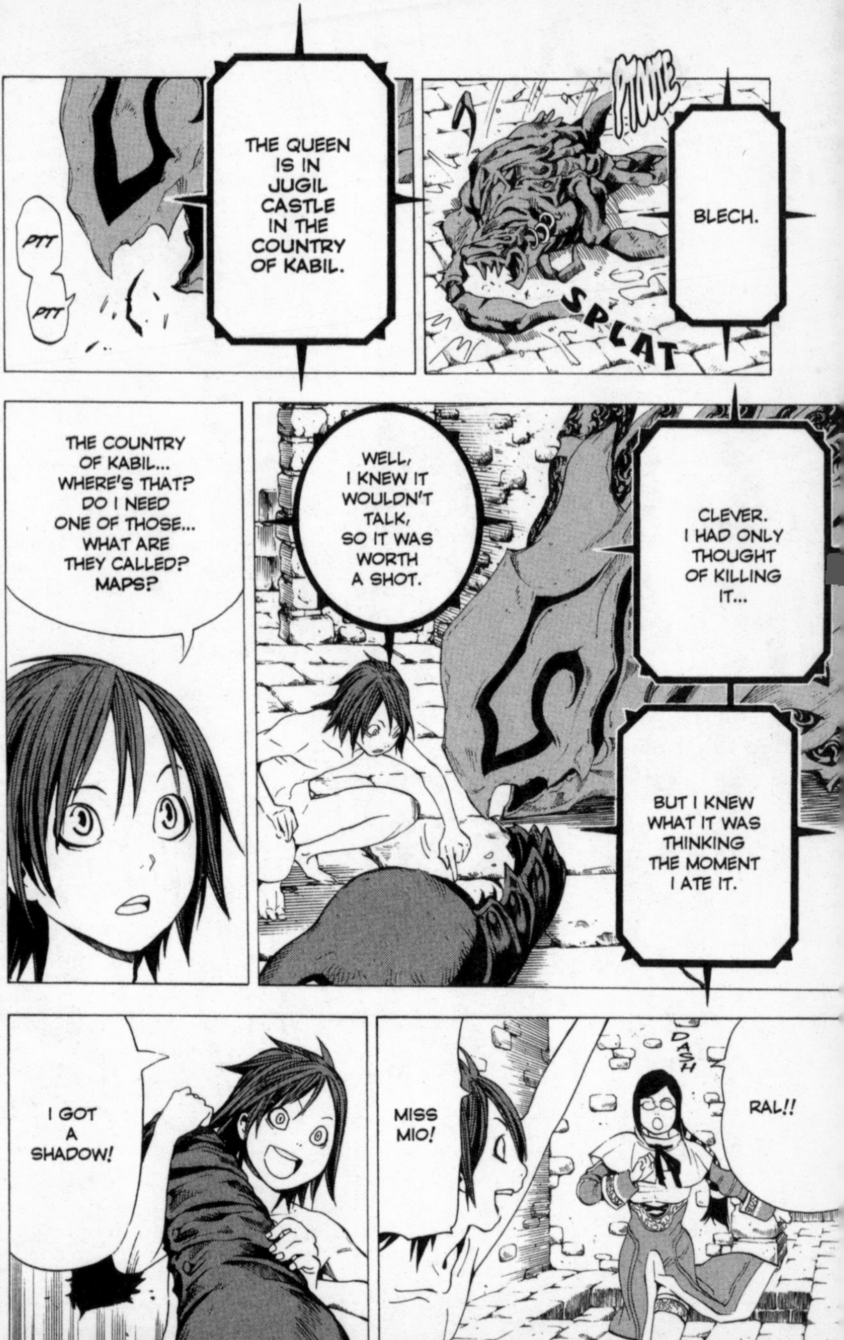
PTOOIE
BLECH.
SPLAT
THE QUEEN IS IN JUGIL CASTLE IN THE COUNTRY OF KABIL.
PTT
PTT
CLEVER. I HAD ONLY THOUGHT OF KILLING IT...
BUT I KNEW WHAT IT WAS THINKING THE MOMENT I ATE IT.
WELL, I KNEW IT WOULDN'T TALK, SO IT WAS WORTH A SHOT.
THE COUNTRY OF KABIL... WHERE'S THAT? DO I NEED ONE OF THOSE... WHAT ARE THEY CALLED? MAPS?
RAL!!
DASH
MISS MIO!
I GOT A SHADOW!

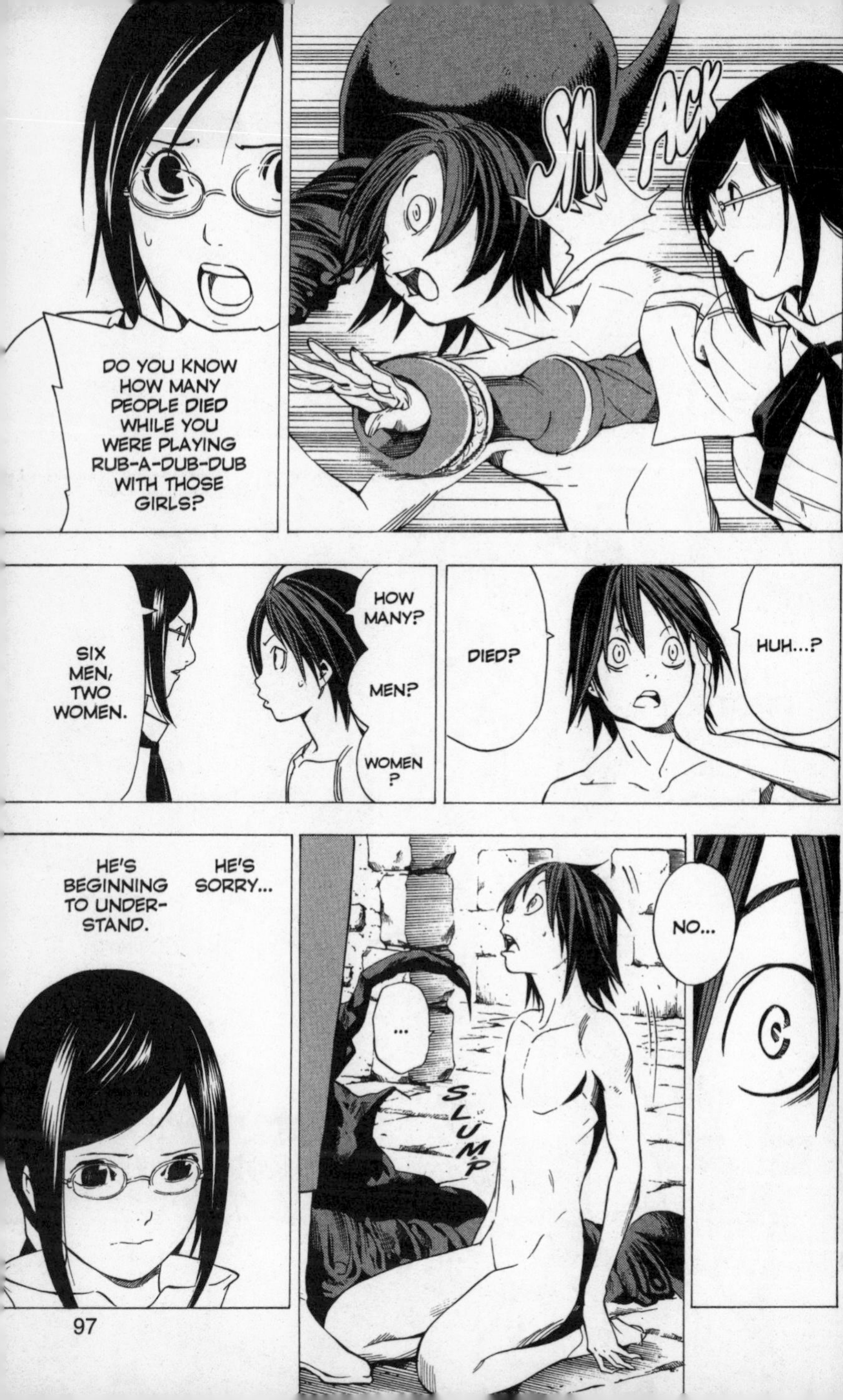
SMACK
DO YOU KNOW HOW MANY PEOPLE DIED WHILE YOU WERE PLAYING RUB-A-DUB-DUB WITH THOSE GIRLS?
HUH...?
DIED?
HOW MANY?
MEN?
WOMEN?
SIX MEN, TWO WOMEN.
NO...
...
SLUMP
HE'S SORRY...
HE'S BEGINNING TO UNDER-STAND.

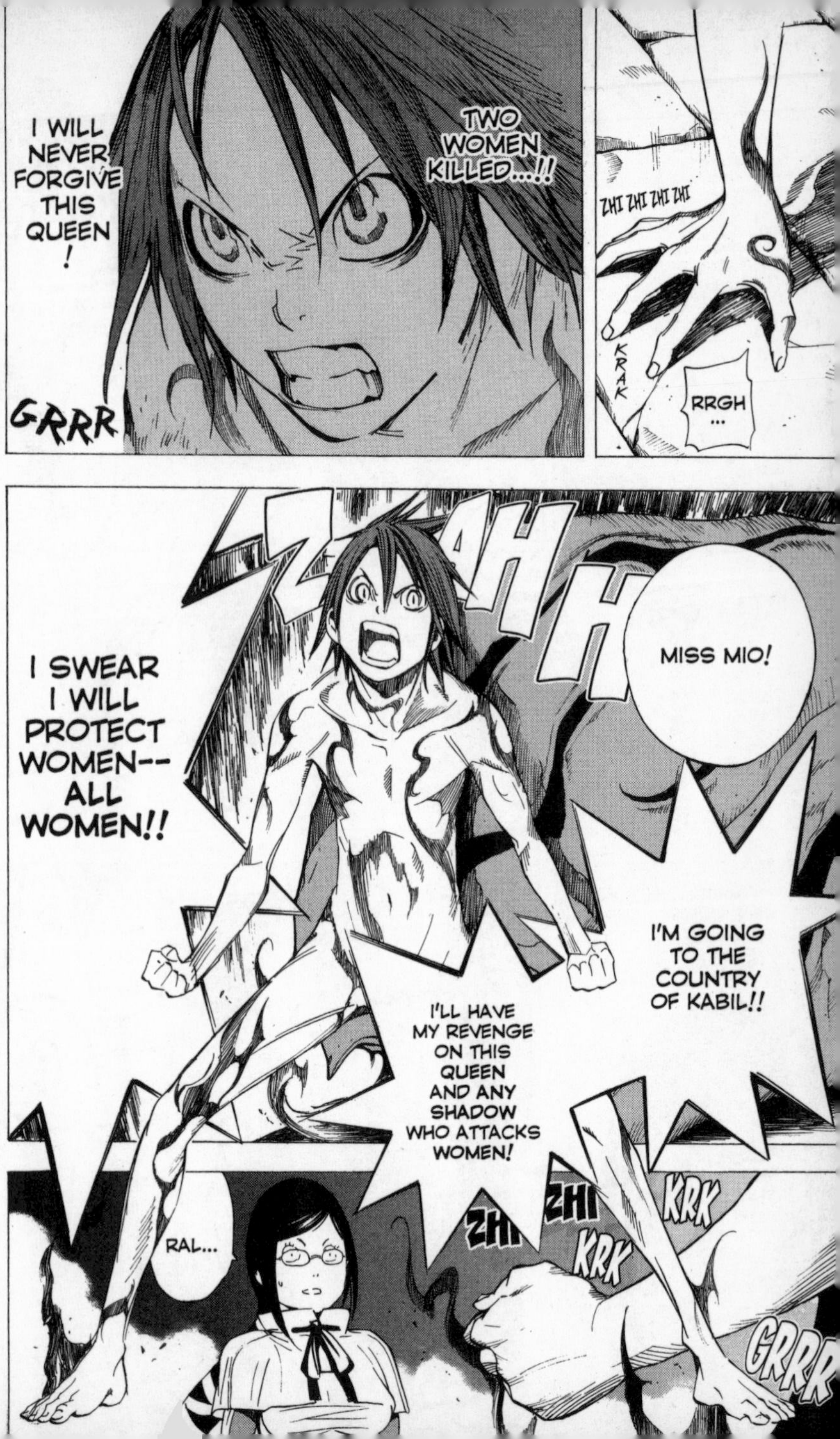
ZHI ZHI ZHI ZHI
KRAK
RRGH ...
TWO WOMEN KILLED...!!
I WILL NEVER FORGIVE THIS QUEEN!
GRRR
ZAHHH
MISS MIO!
I SWEAR I WILL PROTECT WOMEN-- ALL WOMEN!!
I'M GOING TO THE COUNTRY OF KABIL!!
I'LL HAVE MY REVENGE ON THIS QUEEN AND ANY SHADOW WHO ATTACKS WOMEN!
KRK
ZHI
ZHI
KRK
GRRR
RAL...

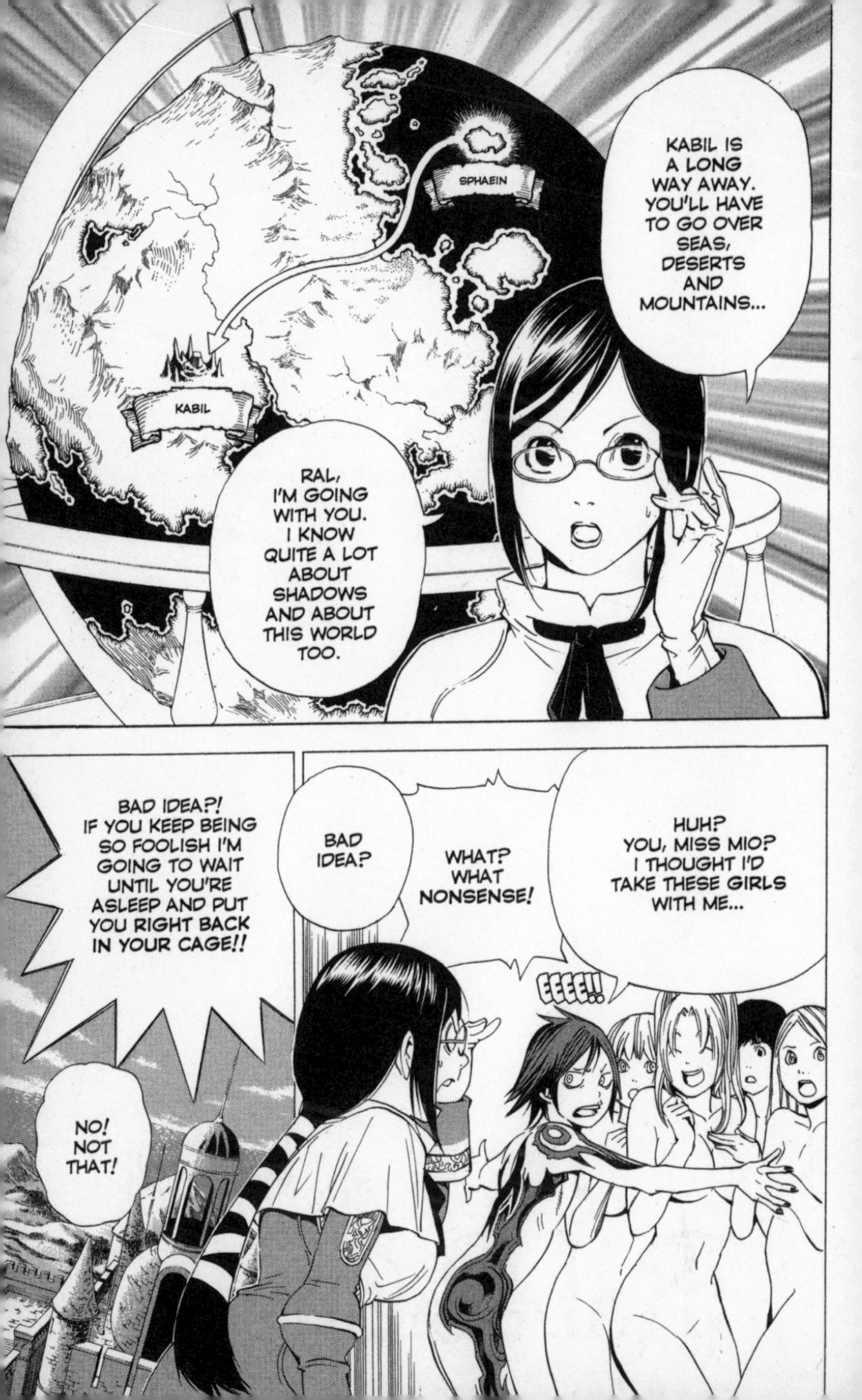
KABIL IS A LONG WAY AWAY. YOU'LL HAVE TO GO OVER SEAS, DESERTS AND MOUNTAINS...
SPHAEIN
KABIL
RAL, I'M GOING WITH YOU. I KNOW QUITE A LOT ABOUT SHADOWS AND ABOUT THIS WORLD TOO.
HUH? YOU, MISS MIO? I THOUGHT I'D TAKE THESE GIRLS WITH ME...
EEEE!!
WHAT? WHAT NONSENSE!
BAD IDEA?
BAD IDEA?! IF YOU KEEP BEING SO FOOLISH I'M GOING TO WAIT UNTIL YOU'RE ASLEEP AND PUT YOU RIGHT BACK IN YOUR CAGE!!
NO! NOT THAT!

RalΩGrad

TALE 3 Ready

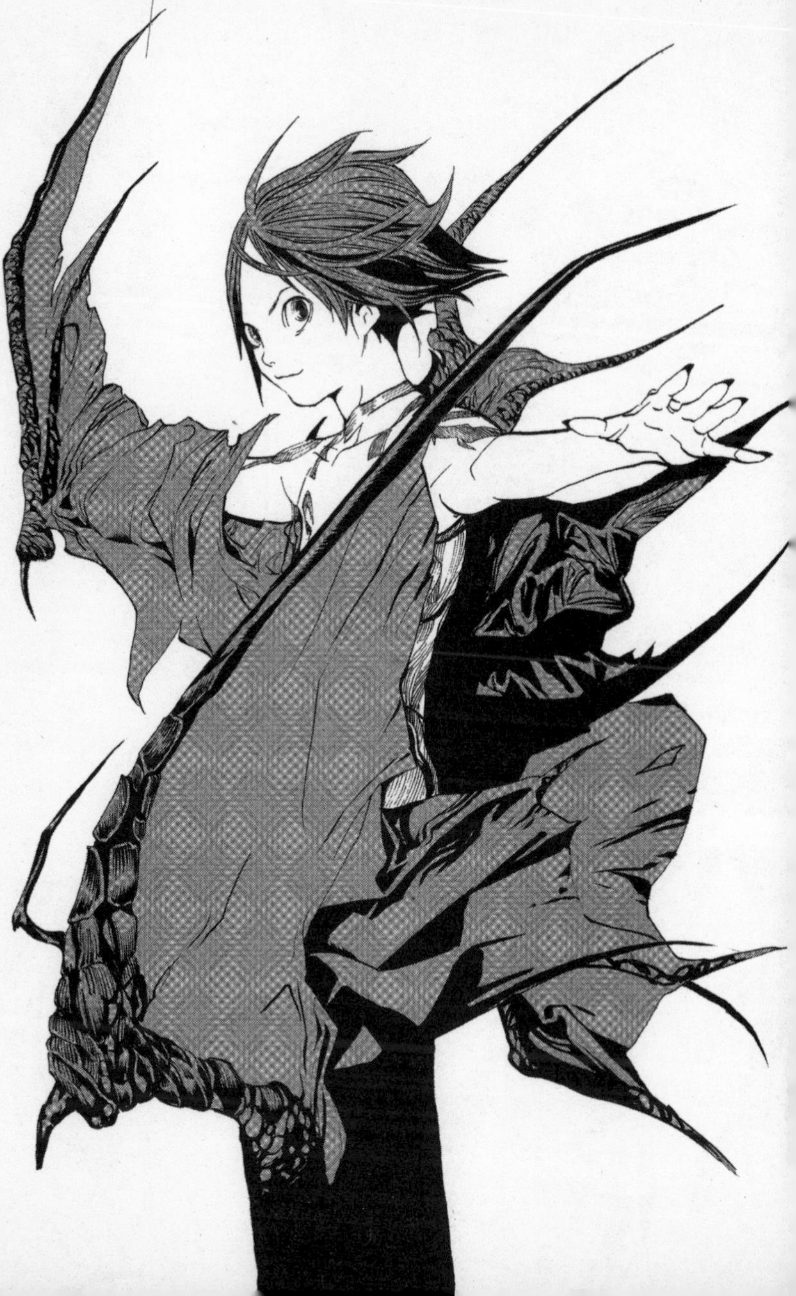

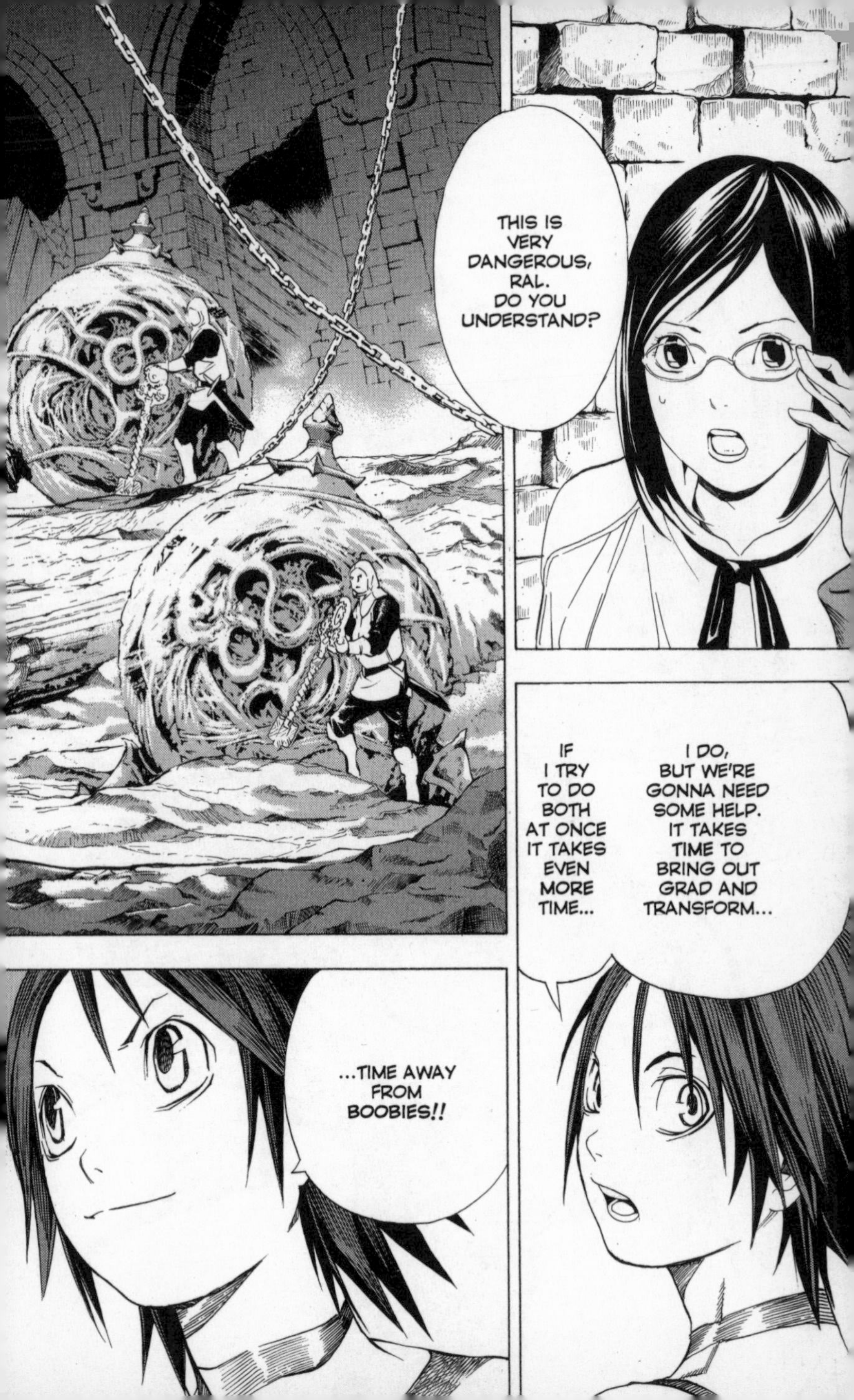
THIS IS VERY DANGEROUS, RAL. DO YOU UNDERSTAND?
I DO, BUT WE'RE GONNA NEED SOME HELP. IT TAKES TIME TO BRING OUT GRAD AND TRANSFORM...
IF I TRY TO DO BOTH AT ONCE IT TAKES EVEN MORE TIME...
...TIME AWAY FROM BOOBIES!!

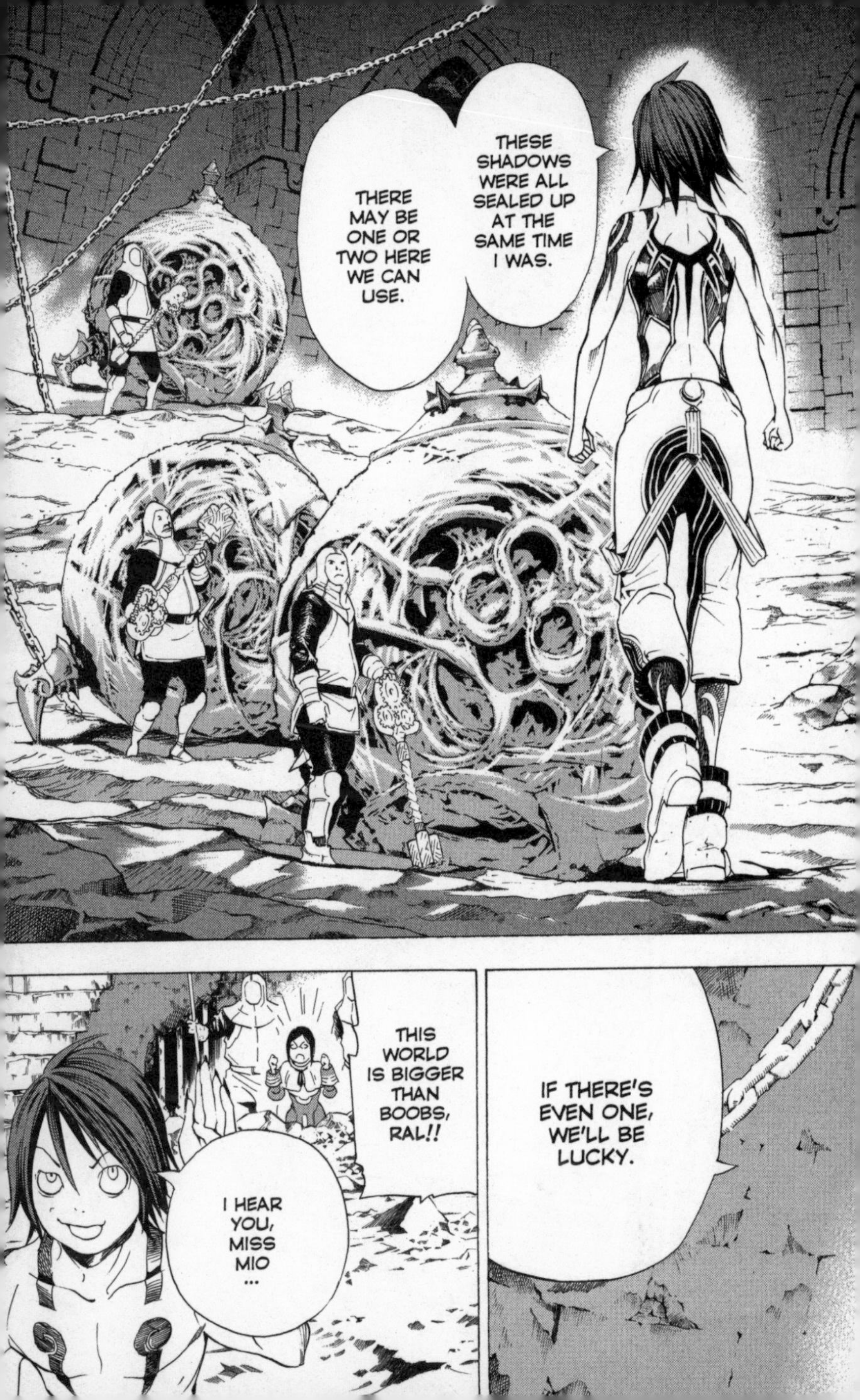
THESE SHADOWS WERE ALL SEALED UP AT THE SAME TIME I WAS.
THERE MAY BE ONE OR TWO HERE WE CAN USE.
IF THERE'S EVEN ONE, WE'LL BE LUCKY.
THIS WORLD IS BIGGER THAN BOOBS, RAL!!
I HEAR YOU, MISS MIO ...

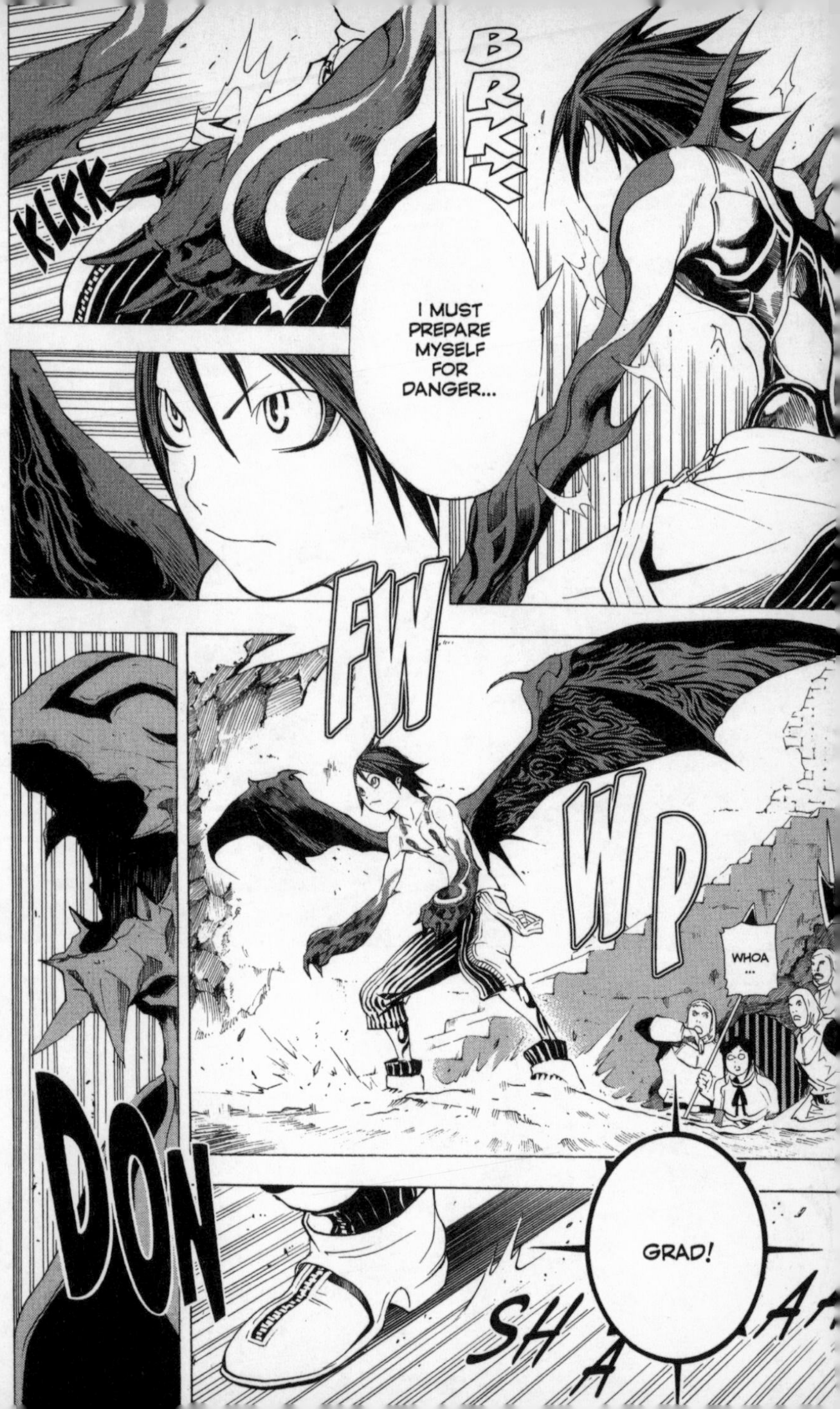
BRKK
I MUST PREPARE MYSELF FOR DANGER...
KLKK
FW
WP
WHOA ...
DON
GRAD!
SHA A

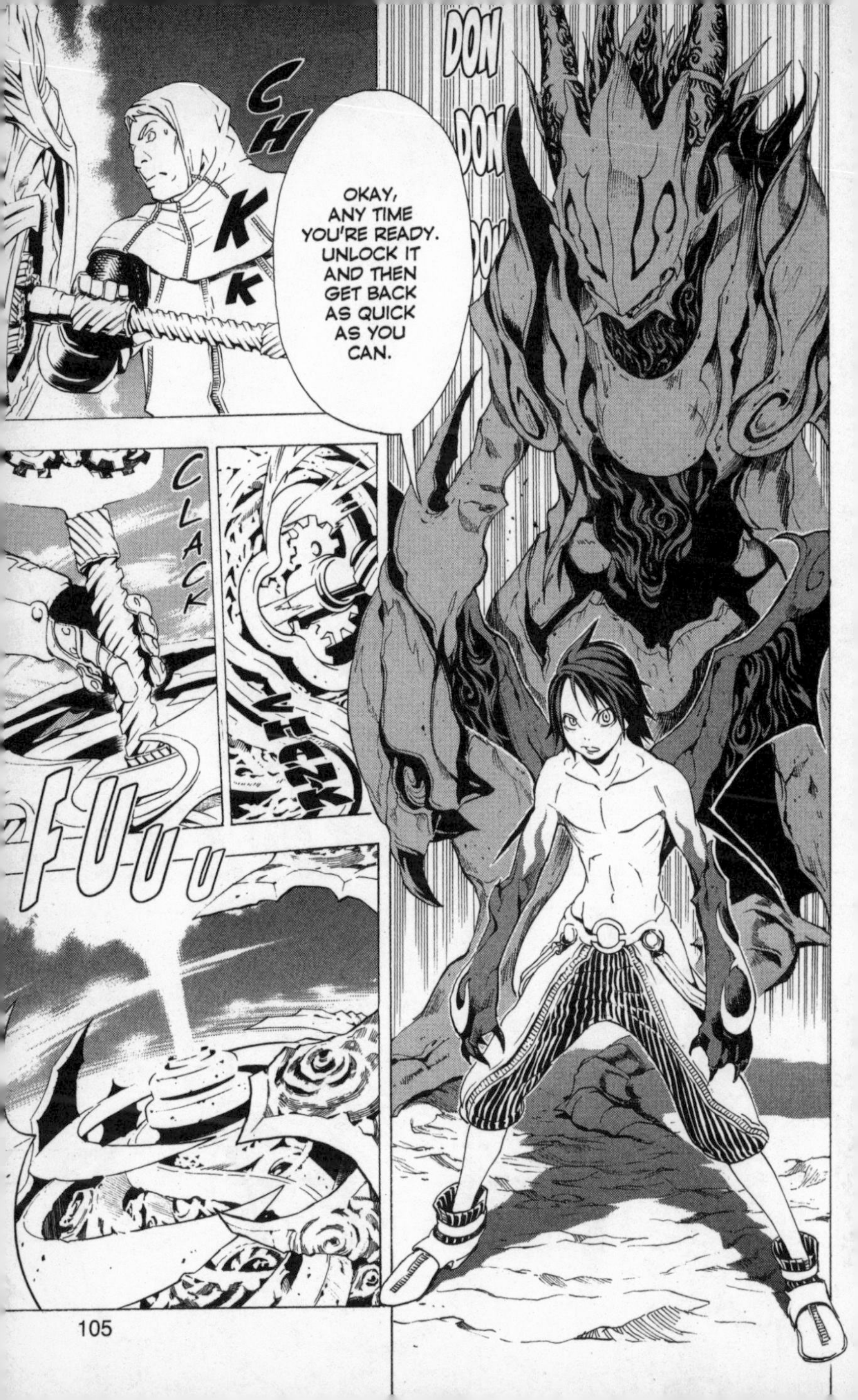
DON
DON
CHKK
OKAY, ANY TIME YOU'RE READY. UNLOCK IT AND THEN GET BACK AS QUICK AS YOU CAN.
CLACK
FUUU

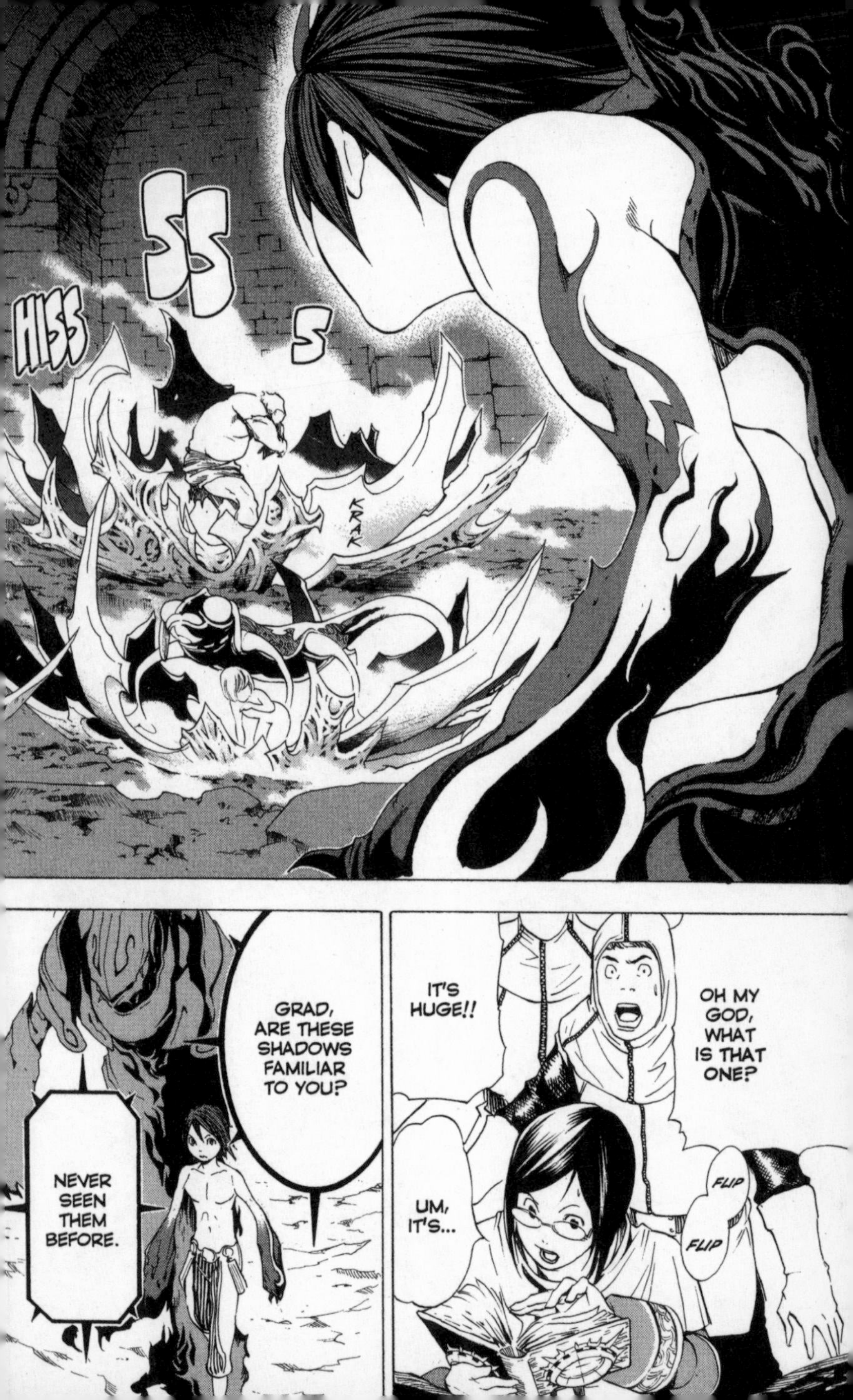
HISS
SS
S
KRAK
OH MY GOD, WHAT IS THAT ONE?
IT'S HUGE!!
FLIP
FLIP
UM, IT'S...
GRAD, ARE THESE SHADOWS FAMILIAR TO YOU?
NEVER SEEN THEM BEFORE.

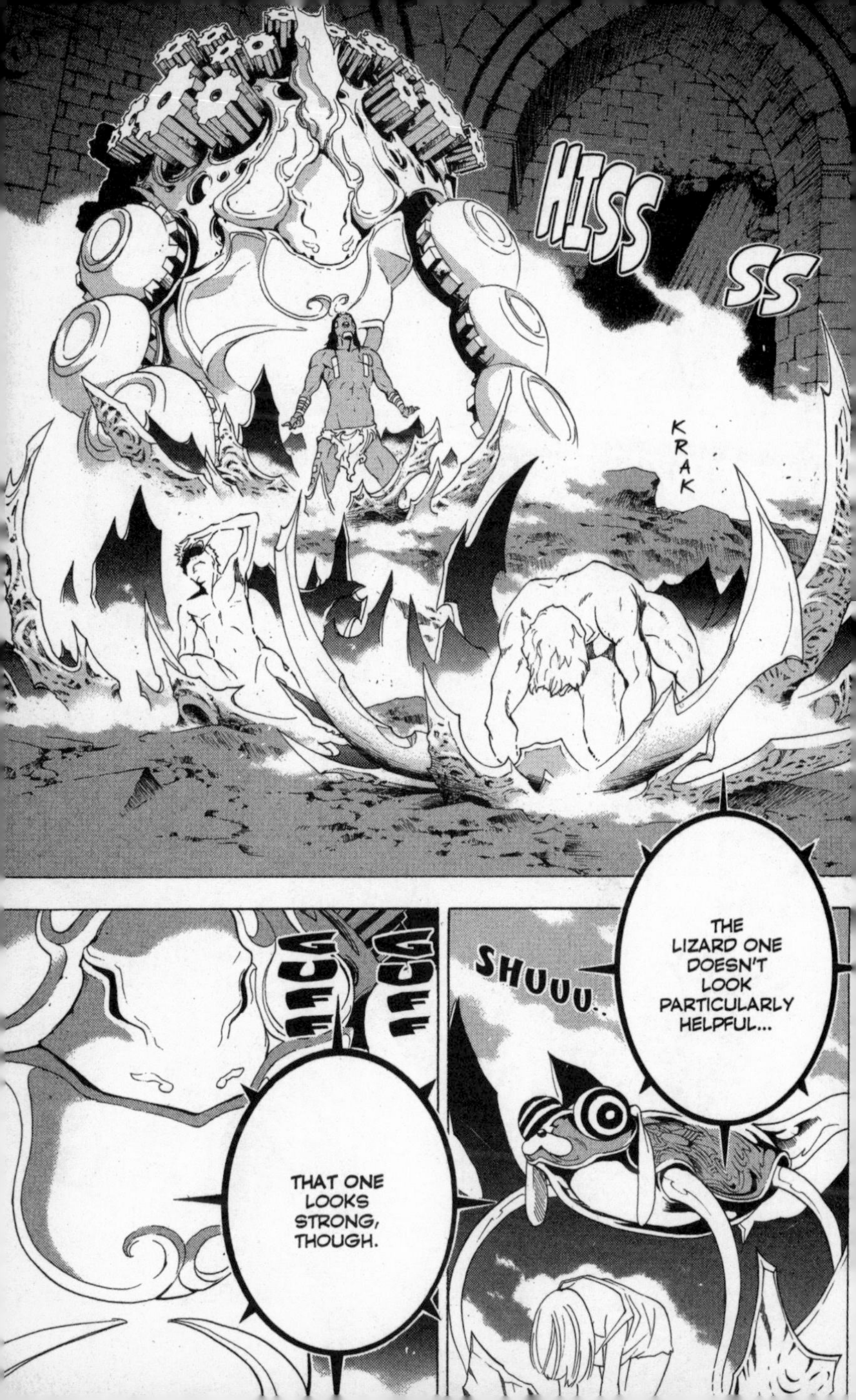
HISS
SS
KRAK
SHUUU...
THE LIZARD ONE DOESN'T LOOK PARTICULARLY HELPFUL...
GUFF
GUFF
THAT ONE LOOKS STRONG, THOUGH.

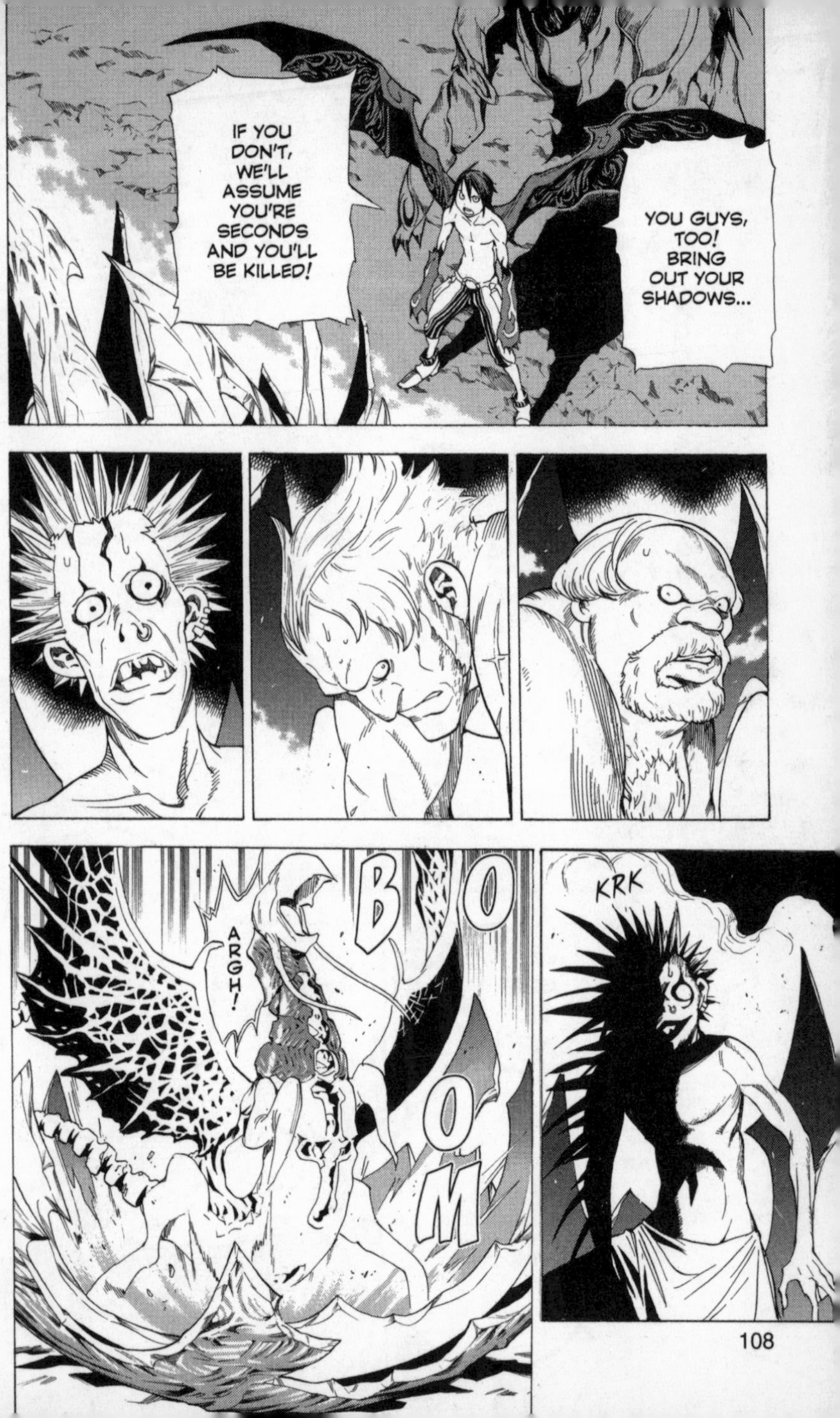
YOU GUYS, TOO! BRING OUT YOUR SHADOWS...
IF YOU DON'T, WE'LL ASSUME YOU'RE SECONDS AND YOU'LL BE KILLED!
KRK
BOOM
ARGH!

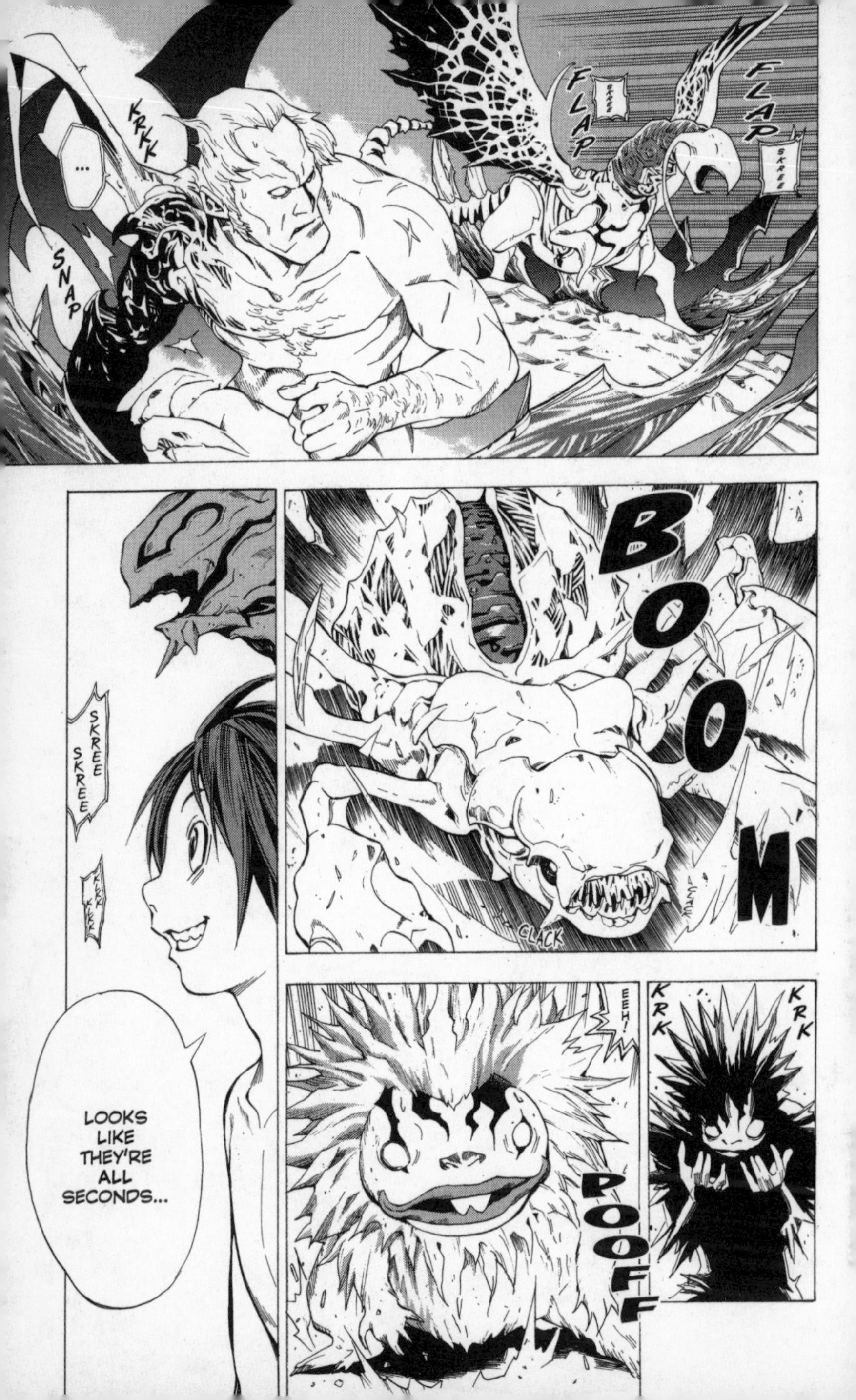
FLAP
SKREE
FLAP
SKREE
KRKK
...
SNAP
BOOM
CLACK
KRK KRK
EEH!
POOFF
SKREE SKREE
LOOKS LIKE THEY'RE ALL SECONDS...

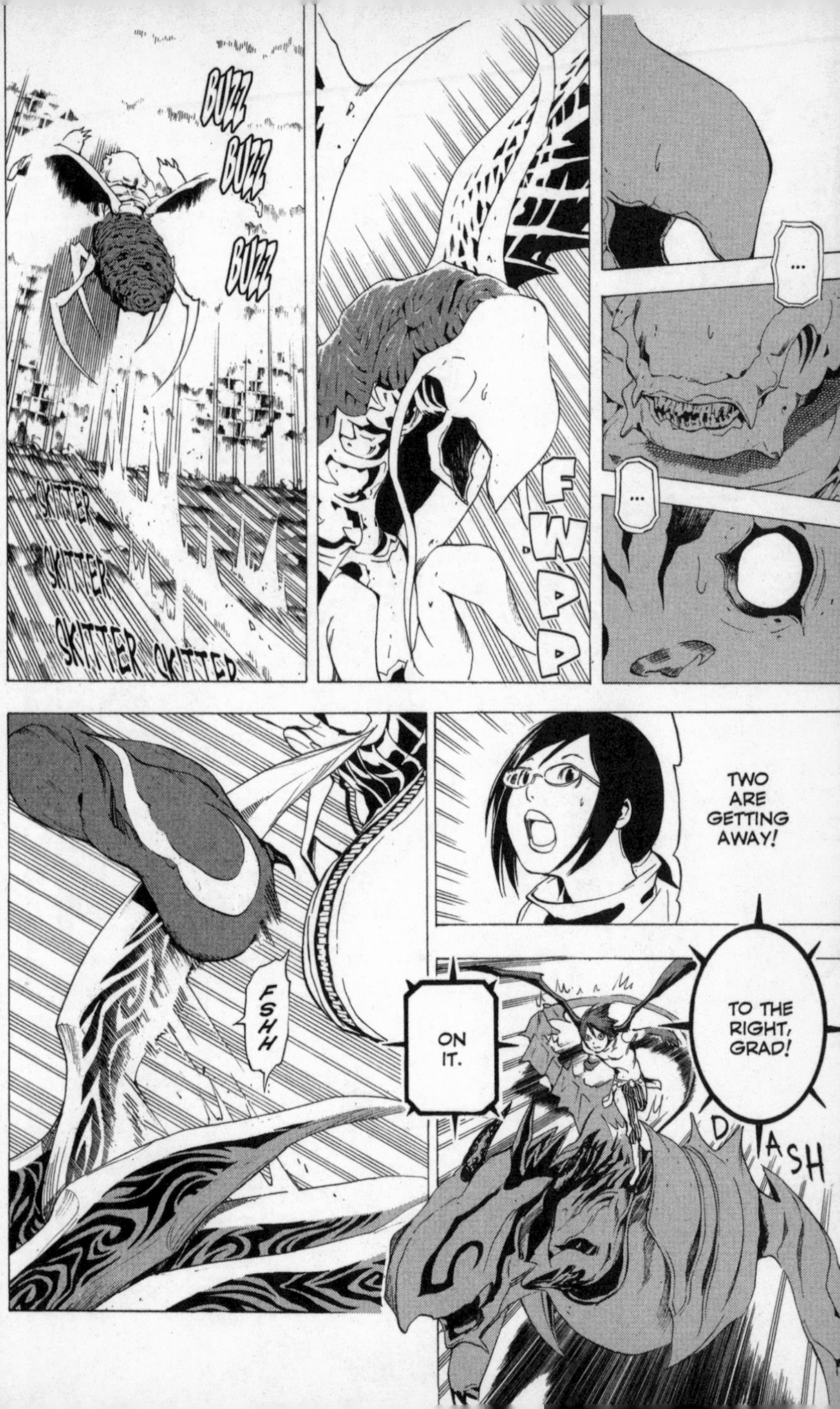
...
...
FWPP
BUZZ
BUZZ
BUZZ
SKITTER
SKITTER
SKITTER SKITTER
TWO ARE GETTING AWAY!
TO THE RIGHT, GRAD!
ON IT.
DASH
FSHH

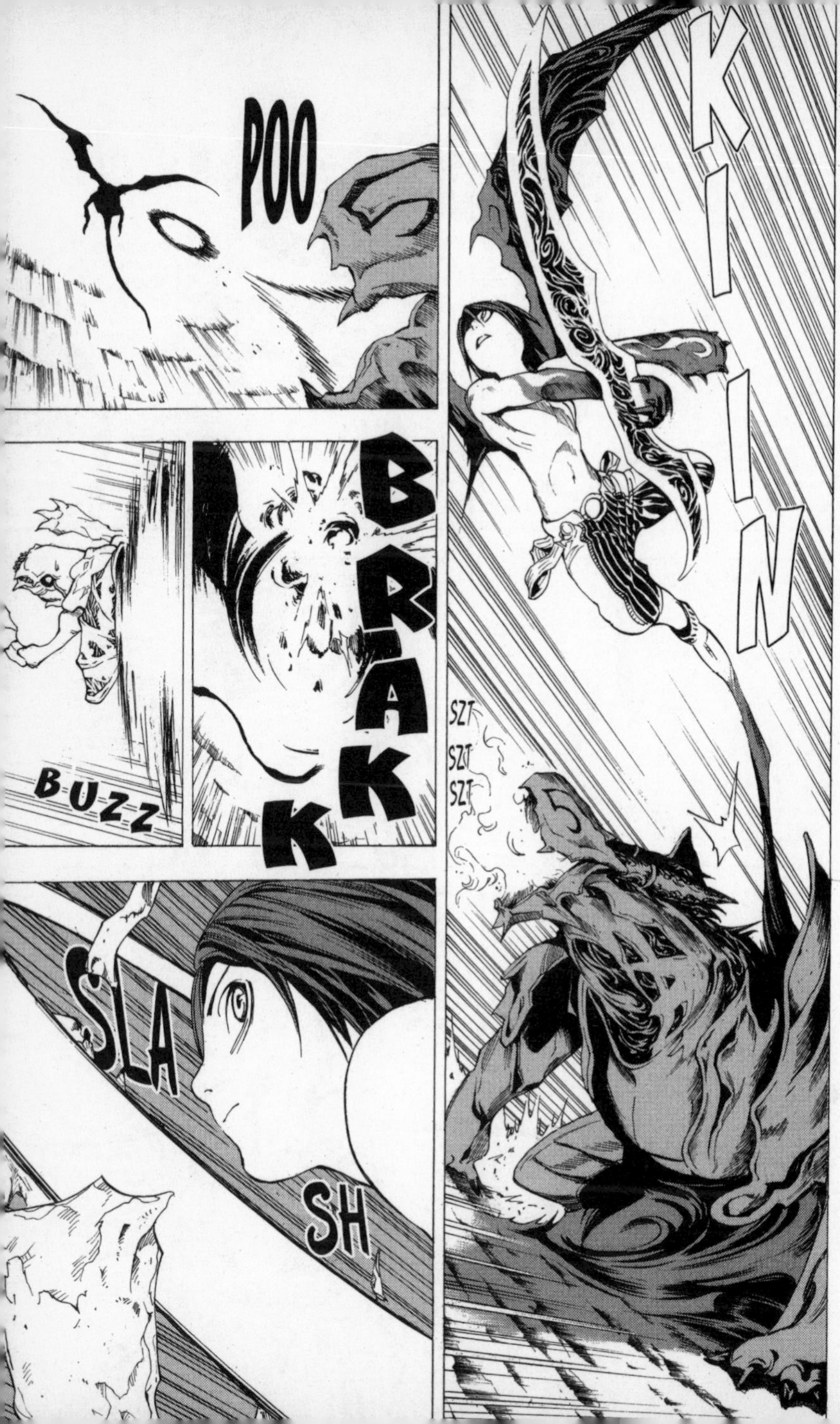
KIIN
SZT SZT SZT
POO
BRAKK
BUZZ
SLASH

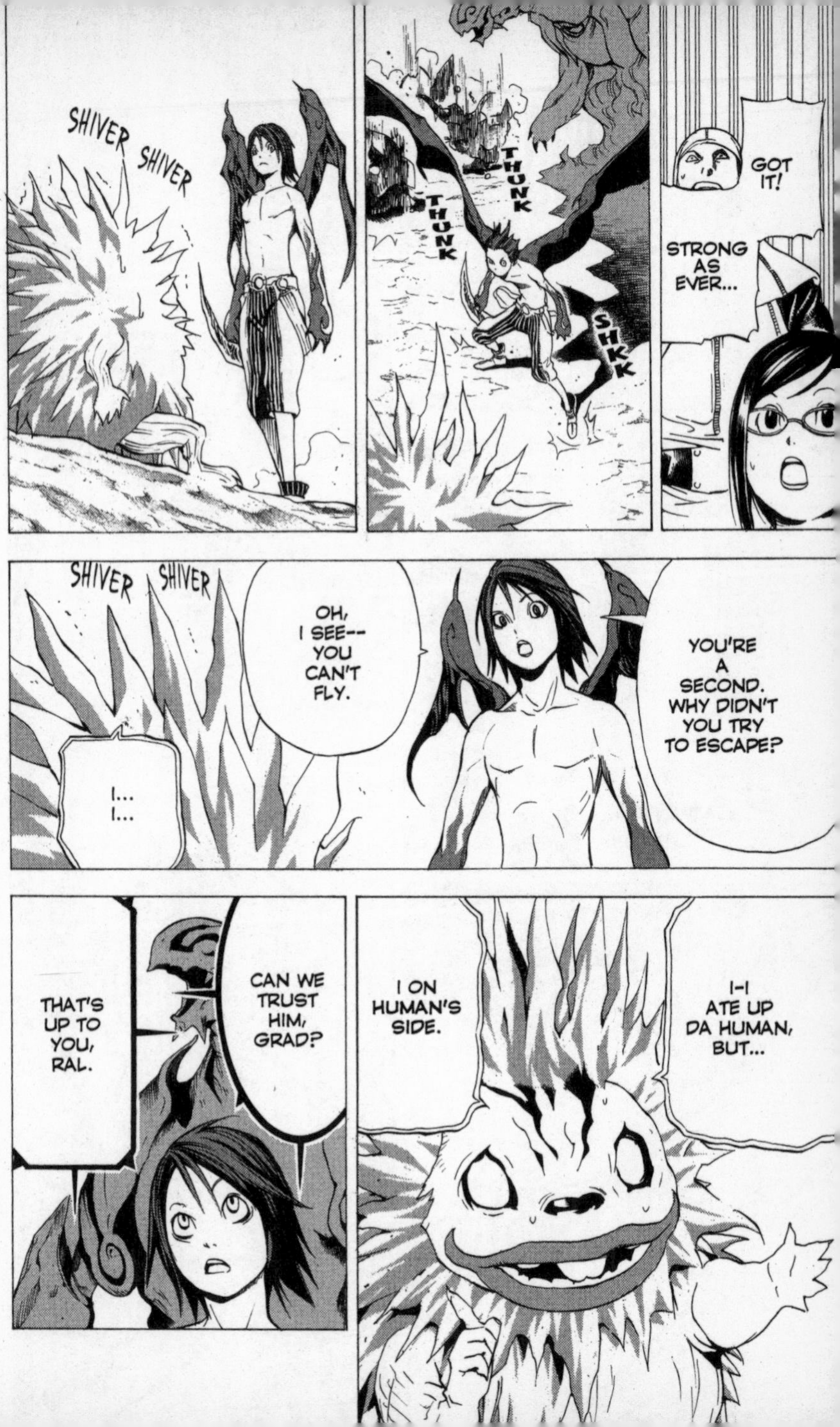
GOT IT!
STRONG AS EVER...
THUNK
THUNK
SHKK
SHIVER SHIVER
YOU'RE A SECOND. WHY DIDN'T YOU TRY TO ESCAPE?
OH, I SEE-- YOU CAN'T FLY.
SHIVER SHIVER
I... I...
I-I ATE UP DA HUMAN, BUT...
I ON HUMAN'S SIDE.
CAN WE TRUST HIM, GRAD?
THAT'S UP TO YOU, RAL.

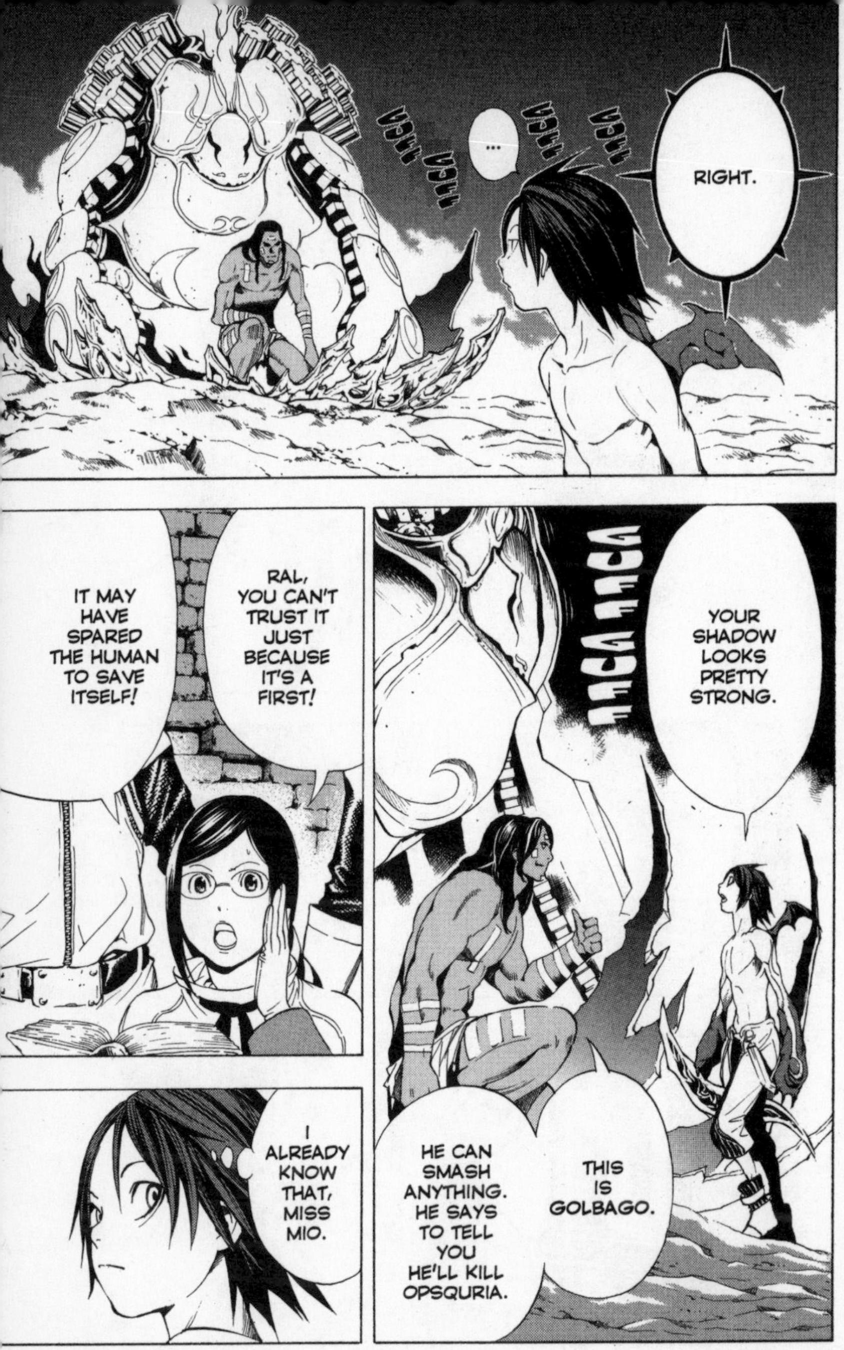
RIGHT.
VUFF VUFF
VUFF VUFF
...
VUFF VUFF
YOUR SHADOW LOOKS PRETTY STRONG.
VUFF VUFF
THIS IS GOLBAGO.
HE CAN SMASH ANYTHING. HE SAYS TO TELL YOU HE'LL KILL OPSQURIA.
RAL, YOU CAN'T TRUST IT JUST BECAUSE IT'S A FIRST!
IT MAY HAVE SPARED THE HUMAN TO SAVE ITSELF!
I ALREADY KNOW THAT, MISS MIO.

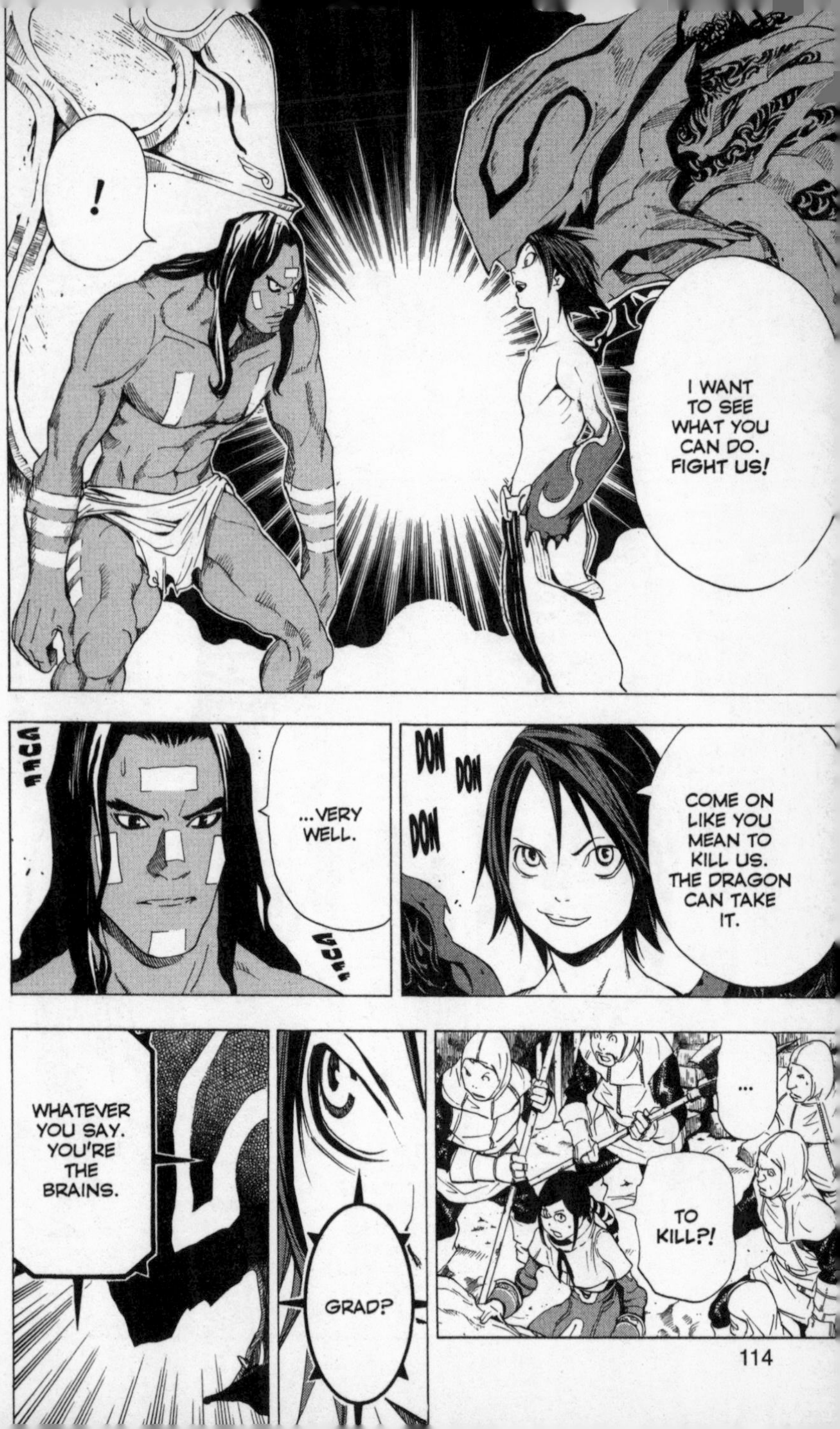
I WANT TO SEE WHAT YOU CAN DO. FIGHT US!
!
DON
DON
DON
COME ON LIKE YOU MEAN TO KILL US. THE DRAGON CAN TAKE IT.
GUFF
...VERY WELL.
GUFF
...
TO KILL?!
GRAD?
WHATEVER YOU SAY. YOU'RE THE BRAINS.

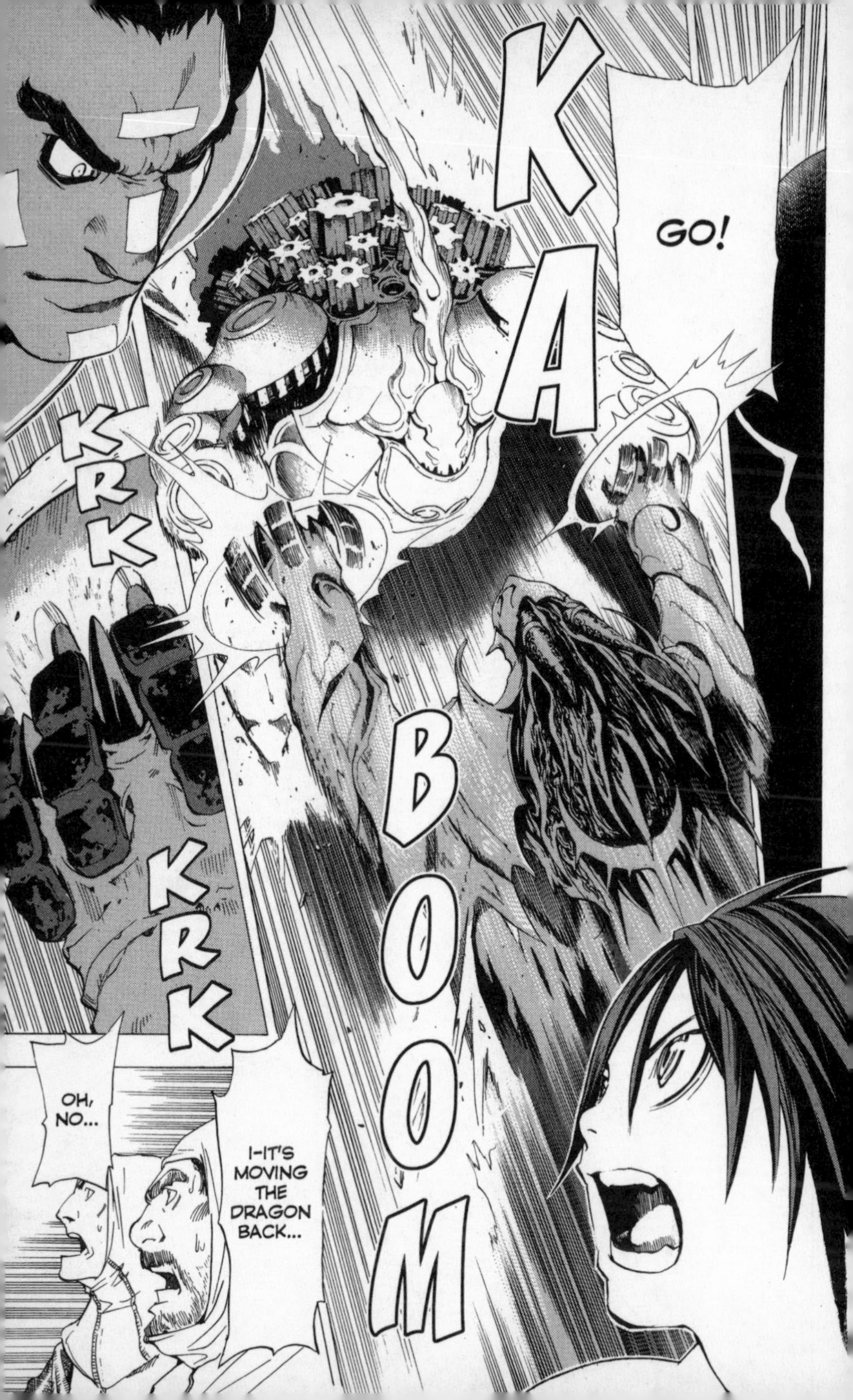
GO!
KABOOM
KRK
KRK
OH, NO...
I-IT'S MOVING THE DRAGON BACK...

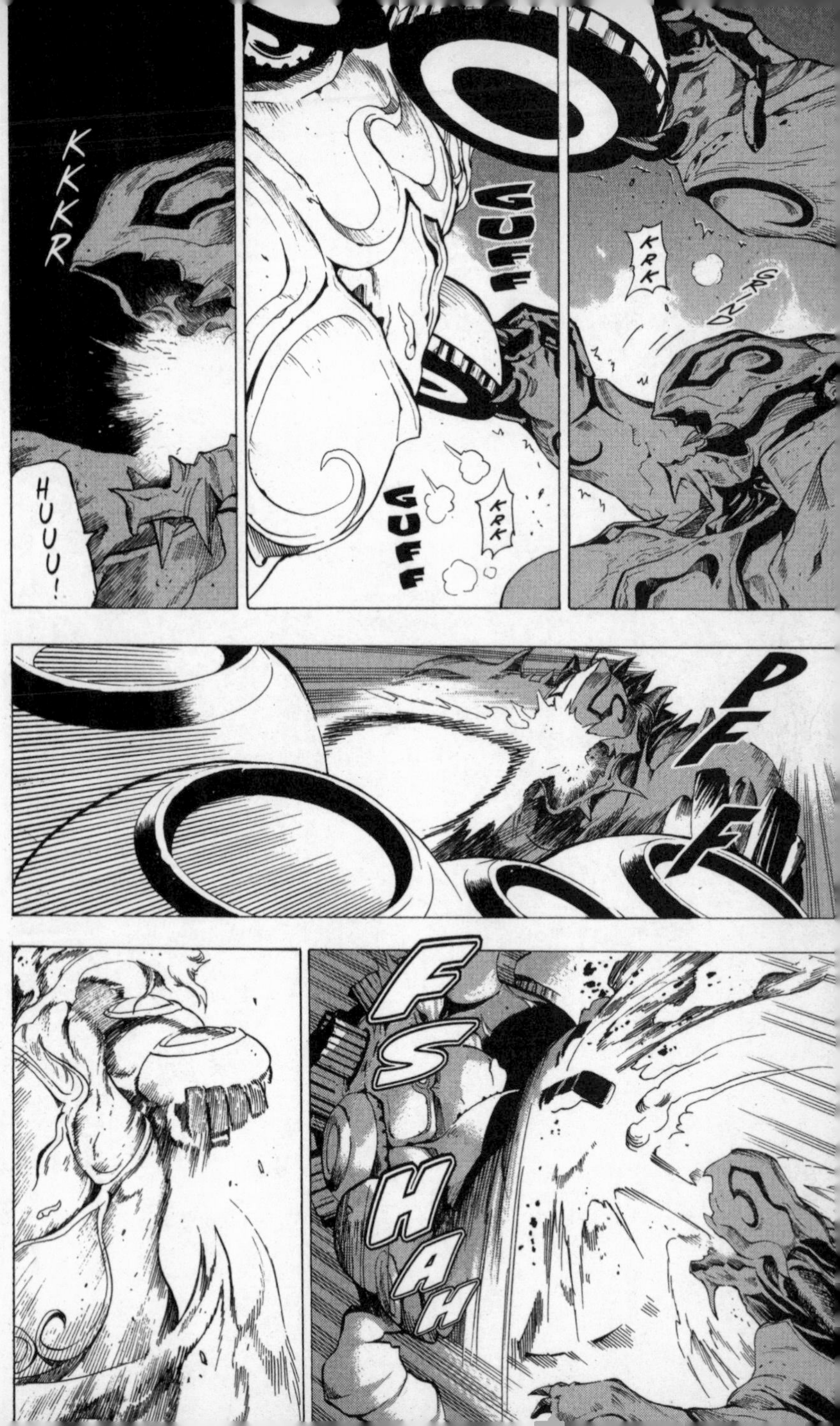
KRK
GRIND
GUFF
KRK
GUFF
KKKR
HUUU!
PFF
FSHHAH

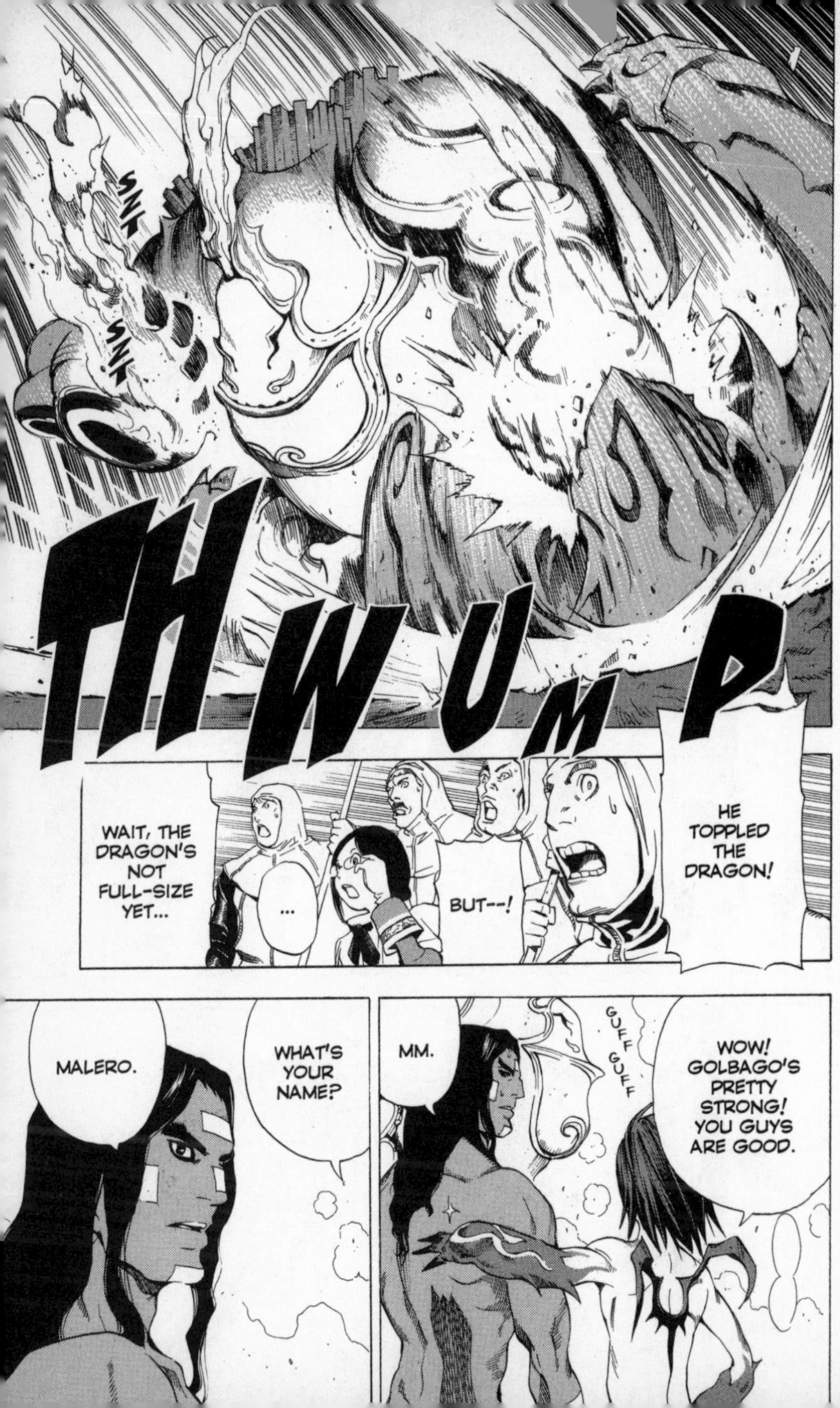
SNK
SNK
THWUMP
HE TOPPLED THE DRAGON!
BUT--!
...
WAIT, THE DRAGON'S NOT FULL-SIZE YET...
WOW! GOLBAGO'S PRETTY STRONG! YOU GUYS ARE GOOD.
GUFF GUFF
MM.
WHAT'S YOUR NAME?
MALERO.

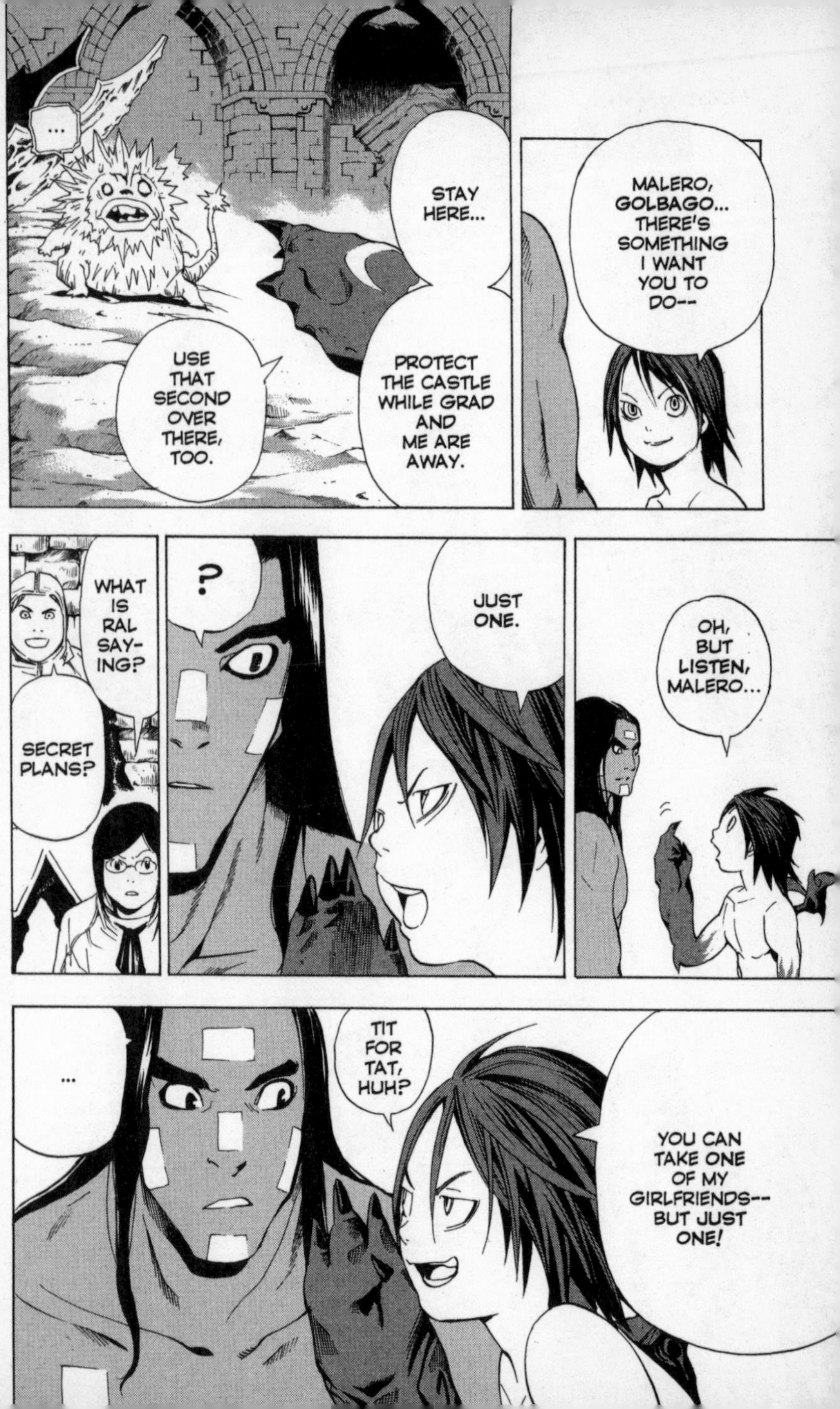
MALERO, GOLBAGO... THERE'S SOMETHING I WANT YOU TO DO--
STAY HERE...
PROTECT THE CASTLE WHILE GRAD AND ME ARE AWAY.
USE THAT SECOND OVER THERE, TOO.
...
OH, BUT LISTEN, MALERO...
JUST ONE.
?
WHAT IS RAL SAYING?
SECRET PLANS?
YOU CAN TAKE ONE OF MY GIRLFRIENDS-- BUT JUST ONE!
TIT FOR TAT, HUH?
...

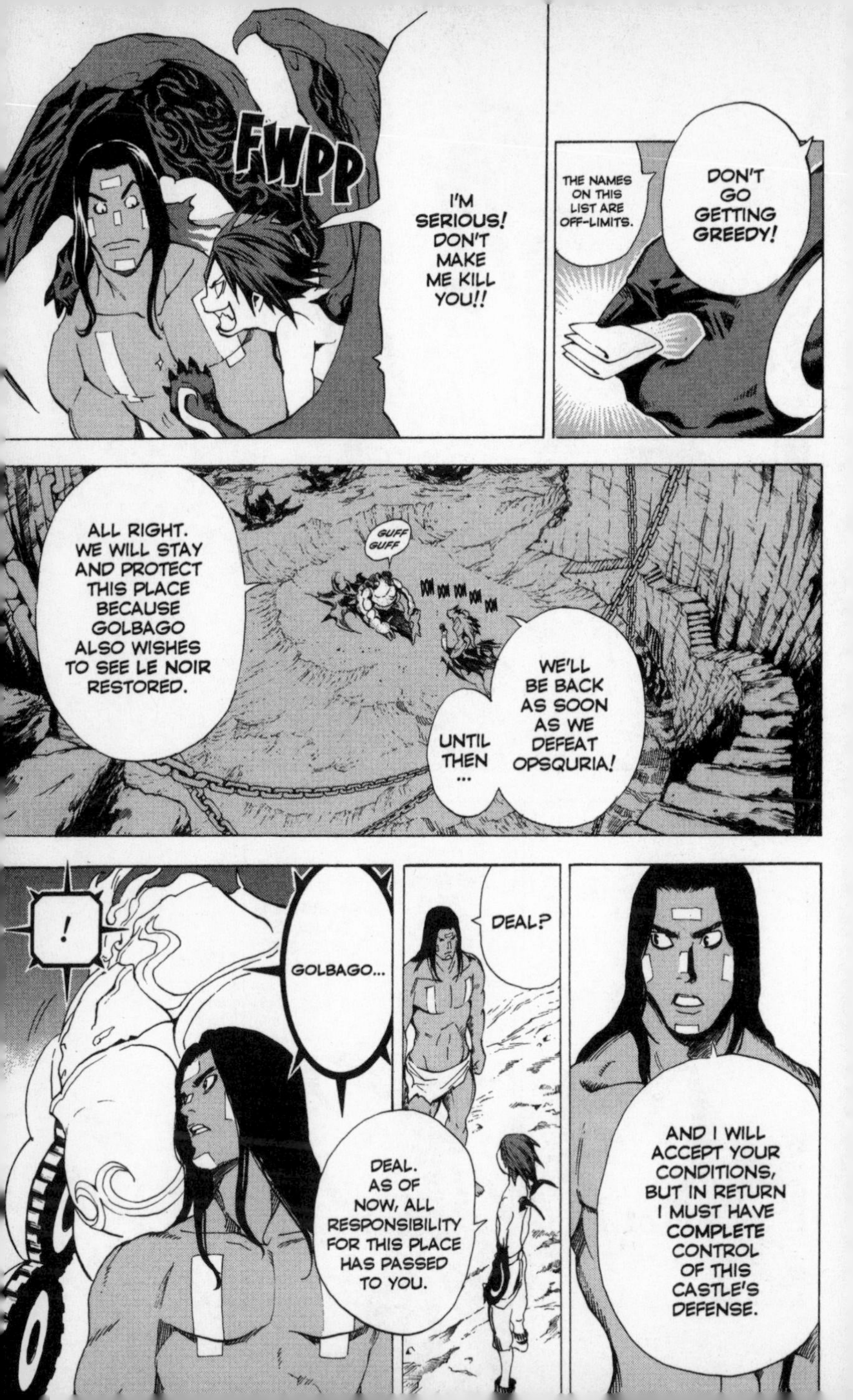
DON'T GO GETTING GREEDY!
THE NAMES ON THIS LIST ARE OFF-LIMITS.
FWPP
I'M SERIOUS! DON'T MAKE ME KILL YOU!!
DOM DOM DOM DOM DOM DOM
GUFF GUFF
WE'LL BE BACK AS SOON AS WE DEFEAT OPSQURIA!
UNTIL THEN...
ALL RIGHT. WE WILL STAY AND PROTECT THIS PLACE BECAUSE GOLBAGO ALSO WISHES TO SEE LE NOIR RESTORED.
AND I WILL ACCEPT YOUR CONDITIONS, BUT IN RETURN I MUST HAVE COMPLETE CONTROL OF THIS CASTLE'S DEFENSE.
DEAL?
DEAL. AS OF NOW, ALL RESPONSIBILITY FOR THIS PLACE HAS PASSED TO YOU.
GOLBAGO...
!

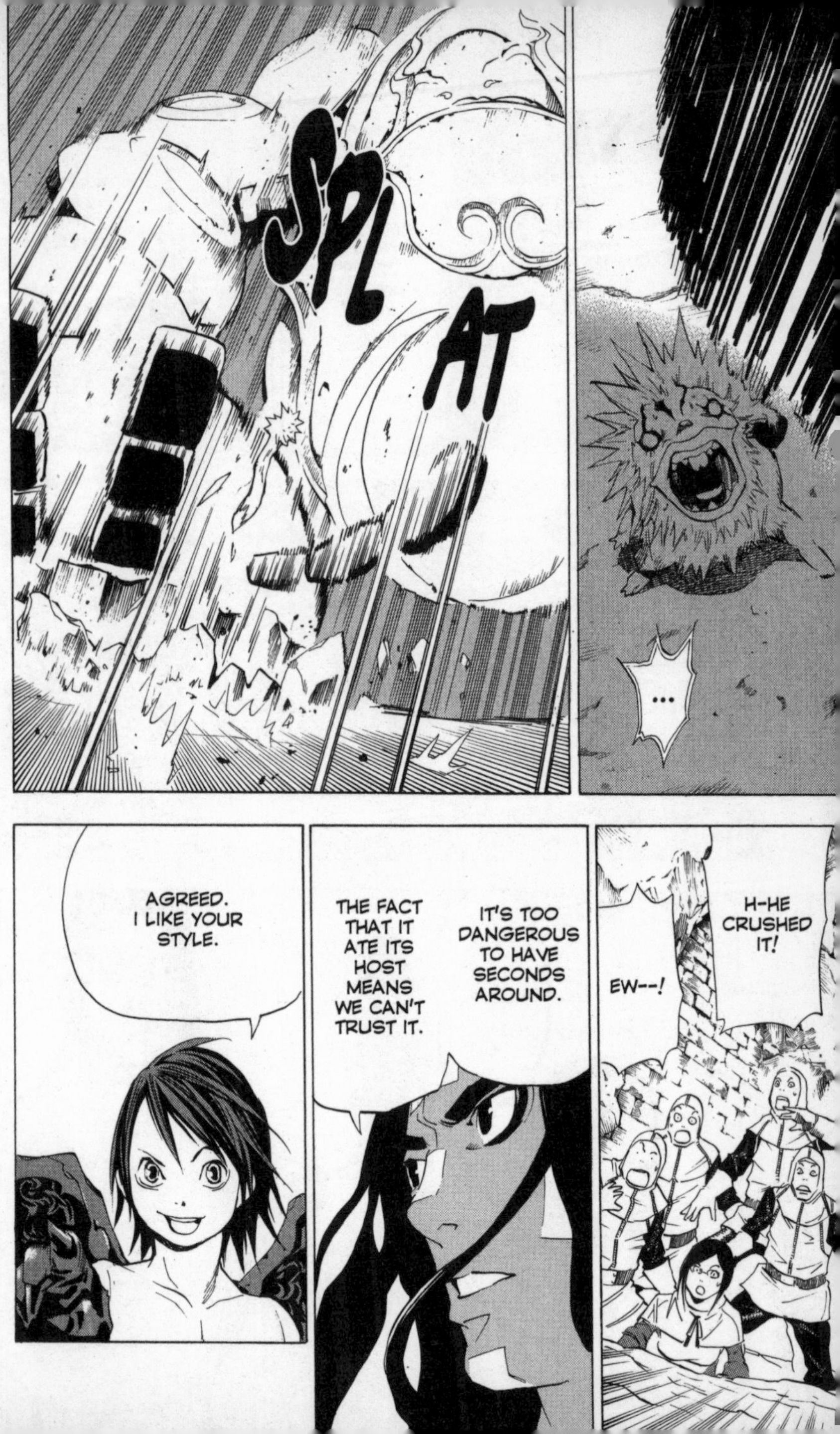
...
SPLAT
H-HE CRUSHED IT!
EW--!
IT'S TOO DANGEROUS TO HAVE SECONDS AROUND.
THE FACT THAT IT ATE ITS HOST MEANS WE CAN'T TRUST IT.
AGREED. I LIKE YOUR STYLE.

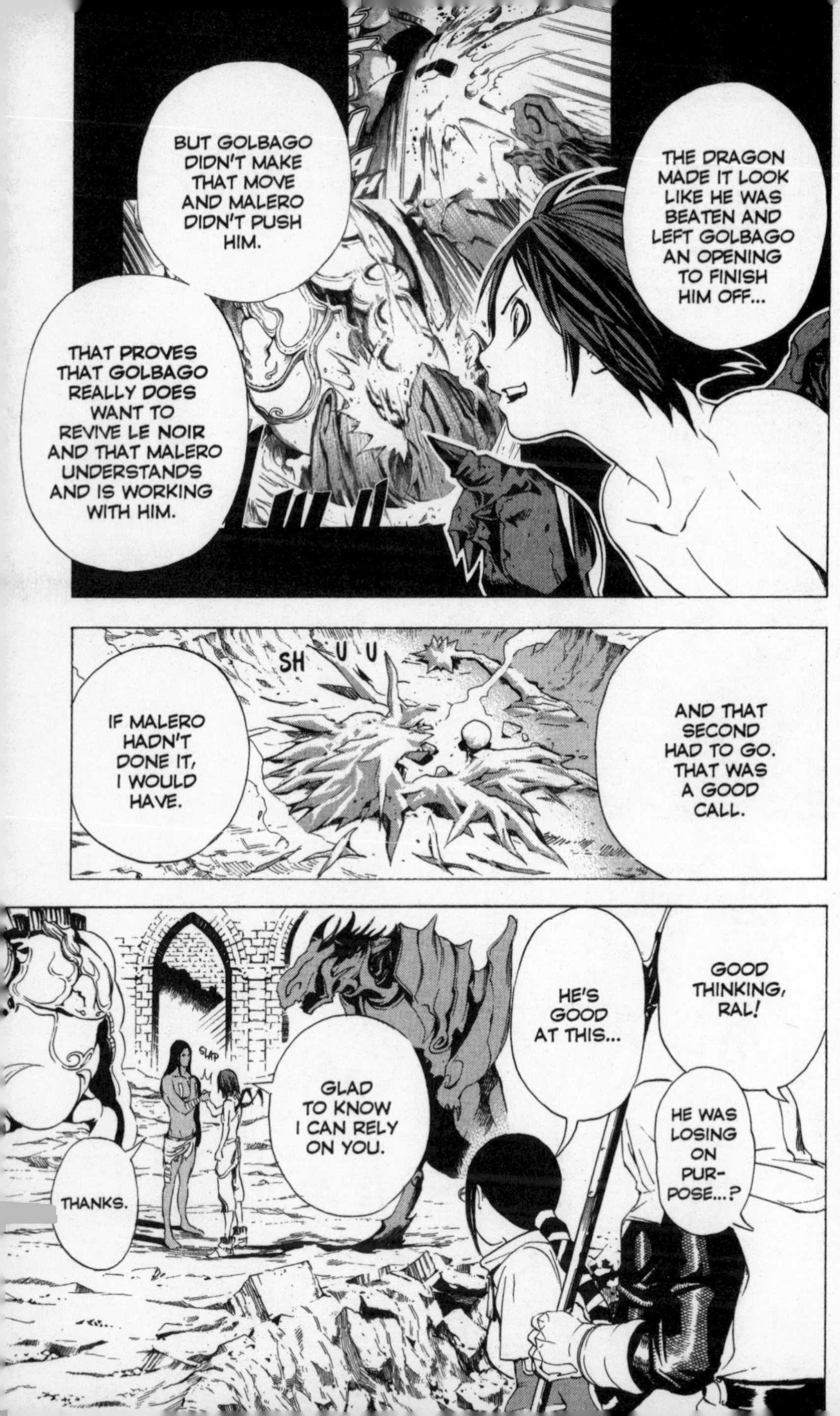
THE DRAGON MADE IT LOOK LIKE HE WAS BEATEN AND LEFT GOLBAGO AN OPENING TO FINISH HIM OFF...
BUT GOLBAGO DIDN'T MAKE THAT MOVE AND MALERO DIDN'T PUSH HIM.
THAT PROVES THAT GOLBAGO REALLY DOES WANT TO REVIVE LE NOIR AND THAT MALERO UNDERSTANDS AND IS WORKING WITH HIM.
AND THAT SECOND HAD TO GO. THAT WAS A GOOD CALL.
SH U U
IF MALERO HADN'T DONE IT, I WOULD HAVE.
GOOD THINKING, RAL!
HE'S GOOD AT THIS...
HE WAS LOSING ON PUR-POSE...?
GLAD TO KNOW I CAN RELY ON YOU.
SLAP
THANKS.

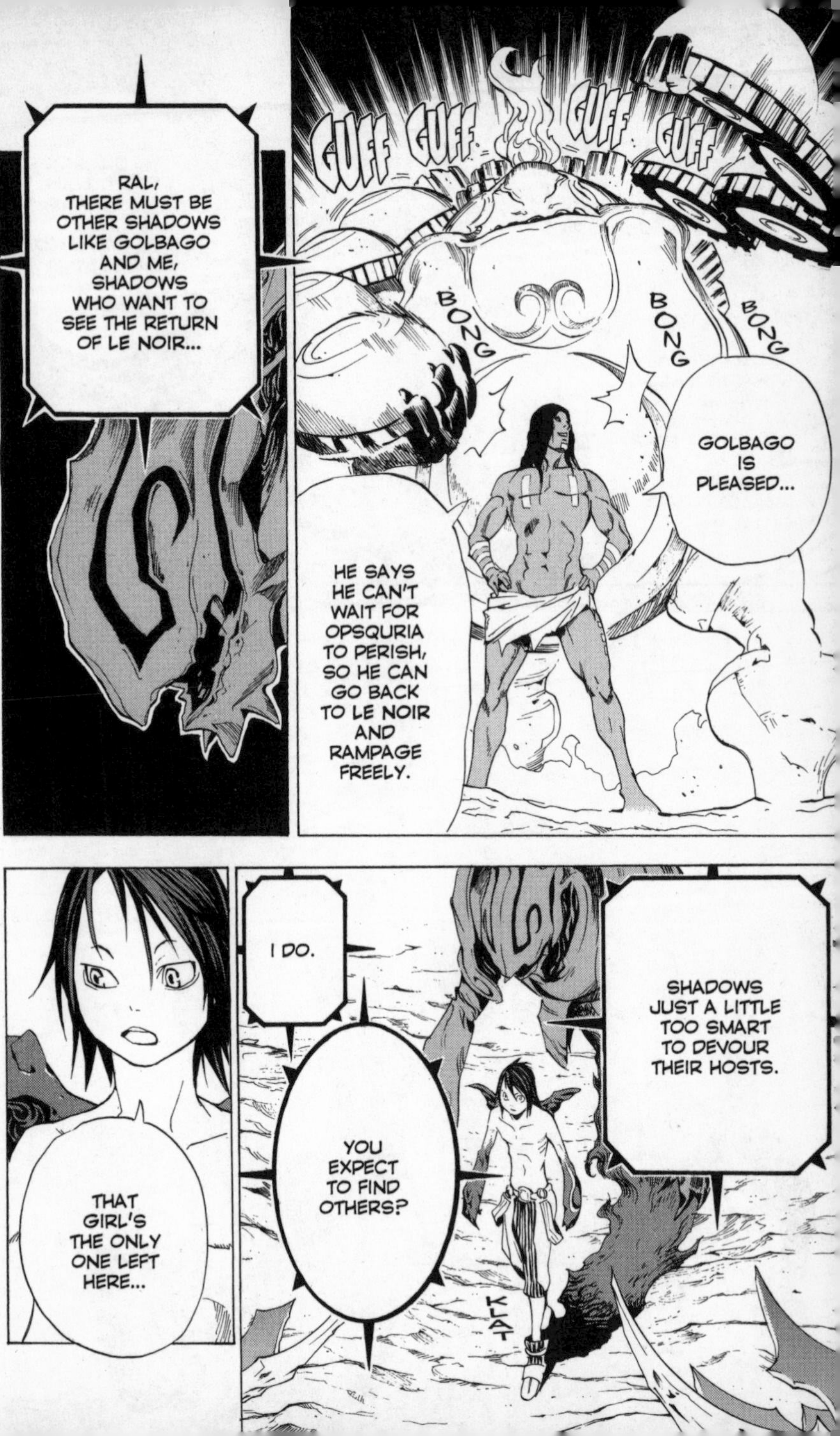
GUFF GUFF GUFF GUFF
BONG BONG BONG
GOLBAGO IS PLEASED...
HE SAYS HE CAN'T WAIT FOR OPSQURIA TO PERISH, SO HE CAN GO BACK TO LE NOIR AND RAMPAGE FREELY.
RAL, THERE MUST BE OTHER SHADOWS LIKE GOLBAGO AND ME, SHADOWS WHO WANT TO SEE THE RETURN OF LE NOIR...
SHADOWS JUST A LITTLE TOO SMART TO DEVOUR THEIR HOSTS.
I DO.
YOU EXPECT TO FIND OTHERS?
KLAT
THAT GIRL'S THE ONLY ONE LEFT HERE...

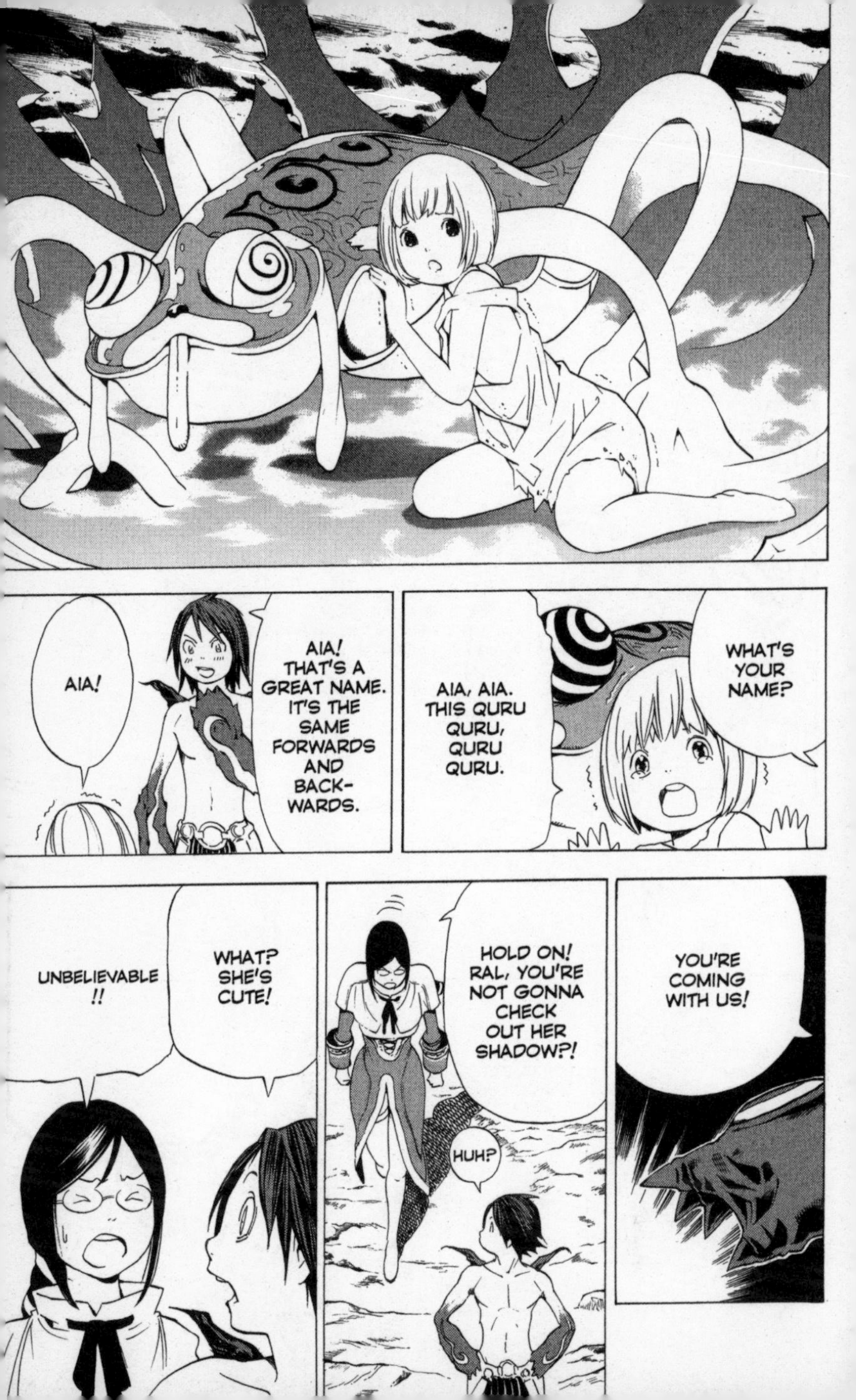
WHAT'S YOUR NAME?
AIA, AIA. THIS QURU QURU, QURU QURU.
AIA! THAT'S A GREAT NAME. IT'S THE SAME FORWARDS AND BACK-WARDS.
AIA!
YOU'RE COMING WITH US!
HOLD ON! RAL, YOU'RE NOT GONNA CHECK OUT HER SHADOW?!
HUH?
WHAT? SHE'S CUTE!
UNBELIEVABLE!!

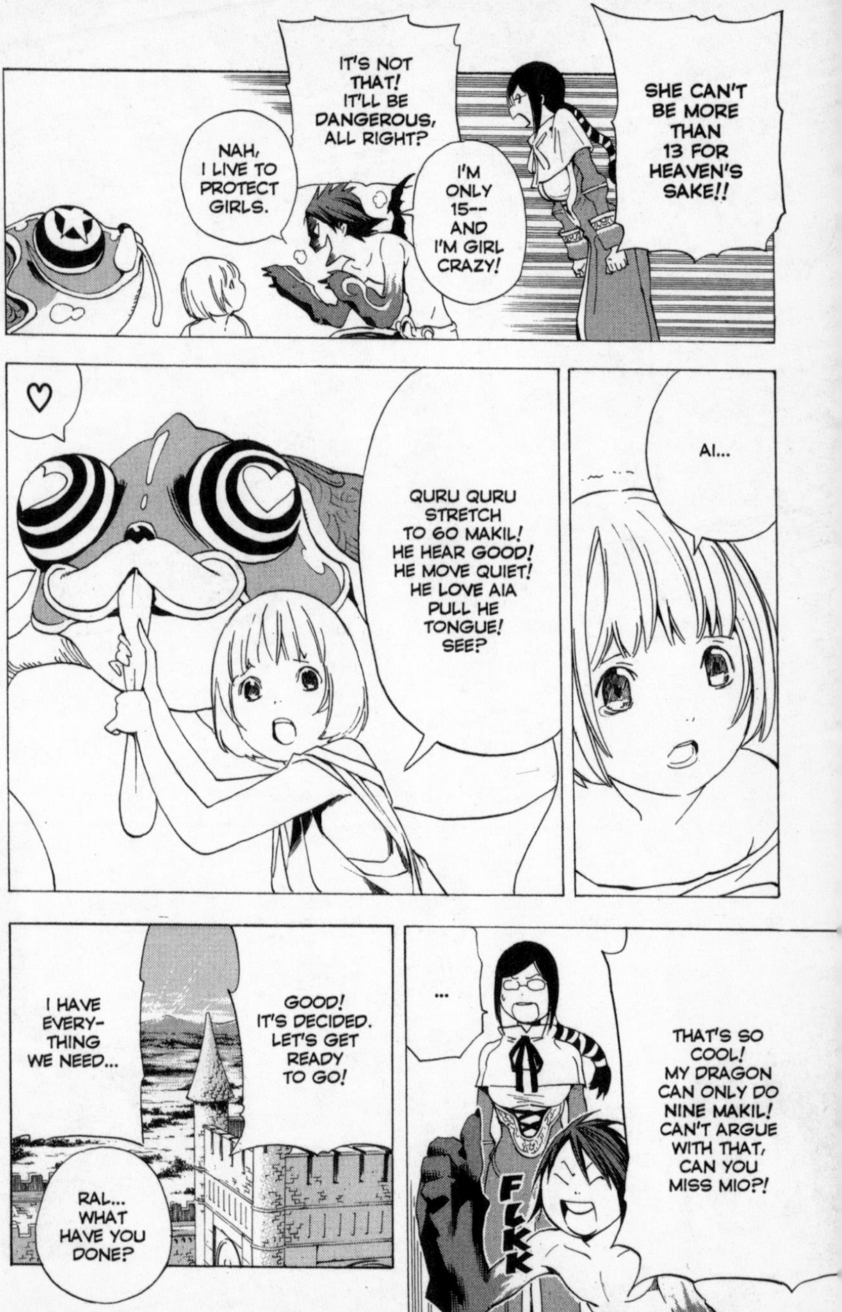
SHE CAN'T BE MORE THAN 13 FOR HEAVEN'S SAKE!!
IT'S NOT THAT! IT'LL BE DANGEROUS, ALL RIGHT?
I'M ONLY 15-- AND I'M GIRL CRAZY!
NAH, I LIVE TO PROTECT GIRLS.
AI...
QURU QURU STRETCH TO 60 MAKIL! HE HEAR GOOD! HE MOVE QUIET! HE LOVE AIA PULL HE TONGUE! SEE?
♡
THAT'S SO COOL! MY DRAGON CAN ONLY DO NINE MAKIL! CAN'T ARGUE WITH THAT, CAN YOU MISS MIO?!
FLKK
...
GOOD! IT'S DECIDED. LET'S GET READY TO GO!
I HAVE EVERY-THING WE NEED...
RAL... WHAT HAVE YOU DONE?

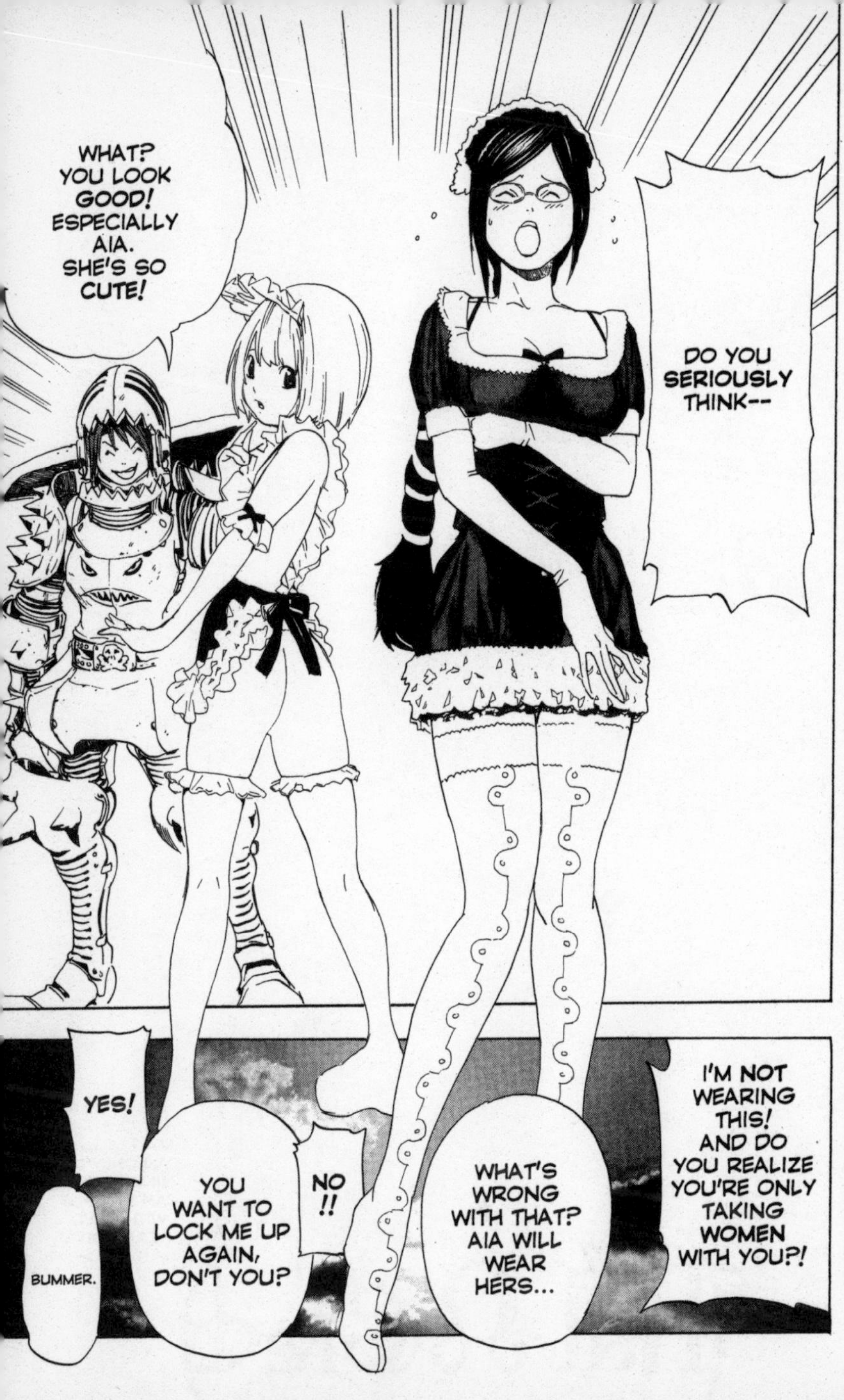
DO YOU SERIOUSLY THINK--
WHAT? YOU LOOK GOOD! ESPECIALLY AIA. SHE'S SO CUTE!
I'M NOT WEARING THIS! AND DO YOU REALIZE YOU'RE ONLY TAKING WOMEN WITH YOU?!
WHAT'S WRONG WITH THAT? AIA WILL WEAR HERS...
NO !!
YOU WANT TO LOCK ME UP AGAIN, DON'T YOU?
YES!
BUMMER.

Ral Ω Grad

TALE 4 Flower

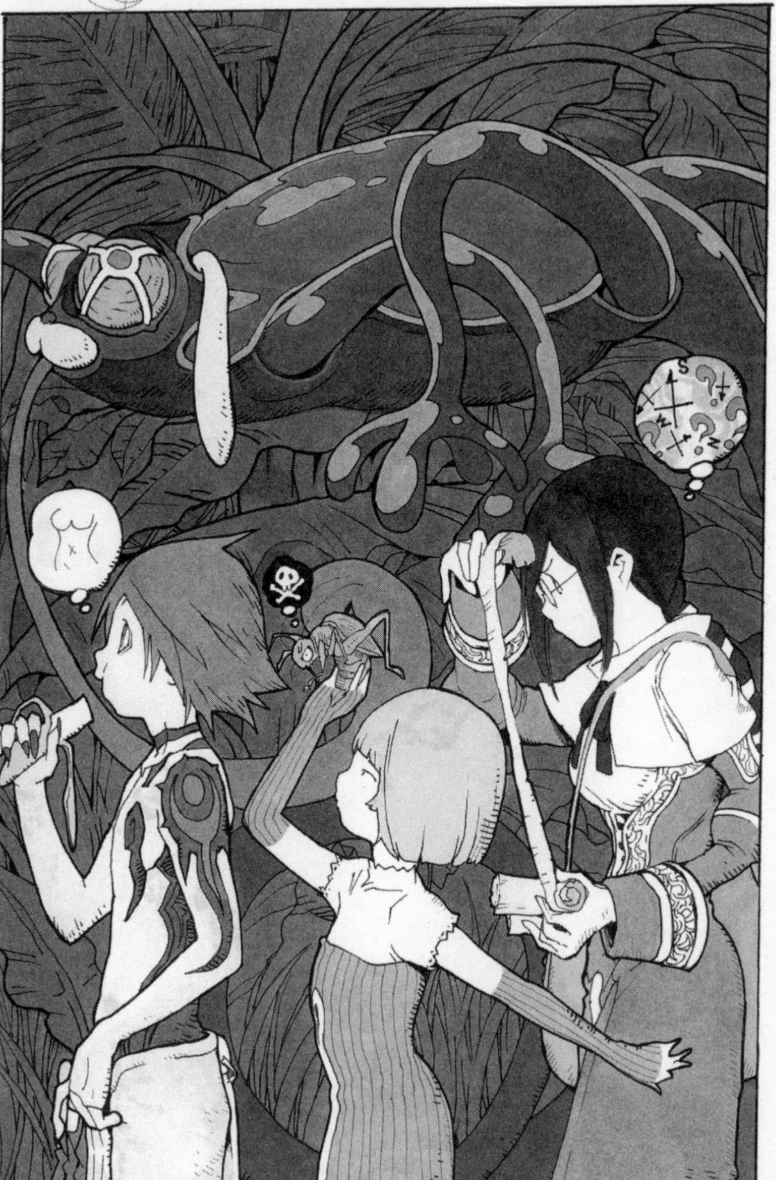

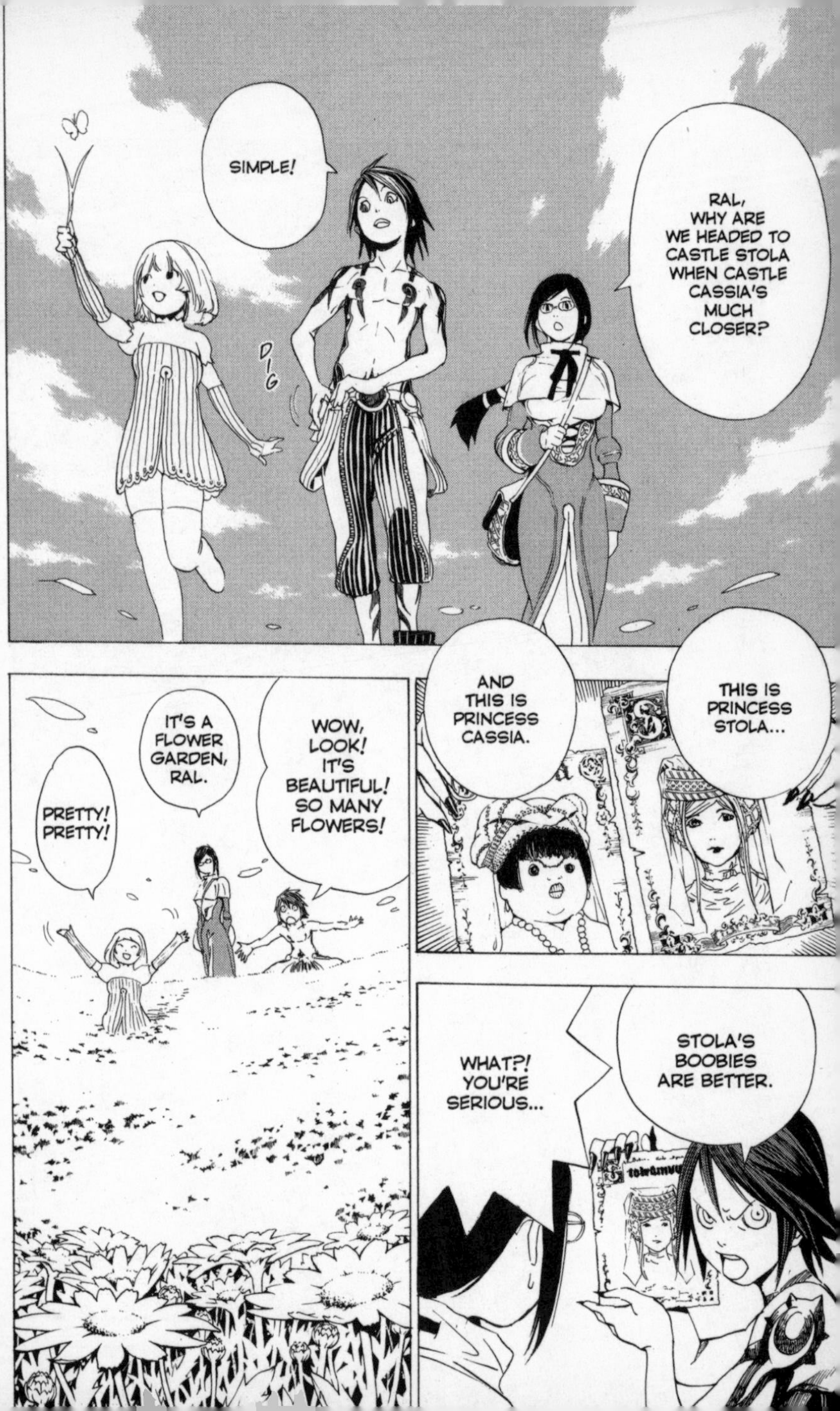
RAL, WHY ARE WE HEADED TO CASTLE STOLA WHEN CASTLE CASSIA'S MUCH CLOSER?
SIMPLE!
DIG
THIS IS PRINCESS STOLA...
AND THIS IS PRINCESS CASSIA.
STOLA'S BOOBIES ARE BETTER.
WHAT?! YOU'RE SERIOUS...
WOW, LOOK! IT'S BEAUTIFUL! SO MANY FLOWERS!
IT'S A FLOWER GARDEN, RAL.
PRETTY! PRETTY!

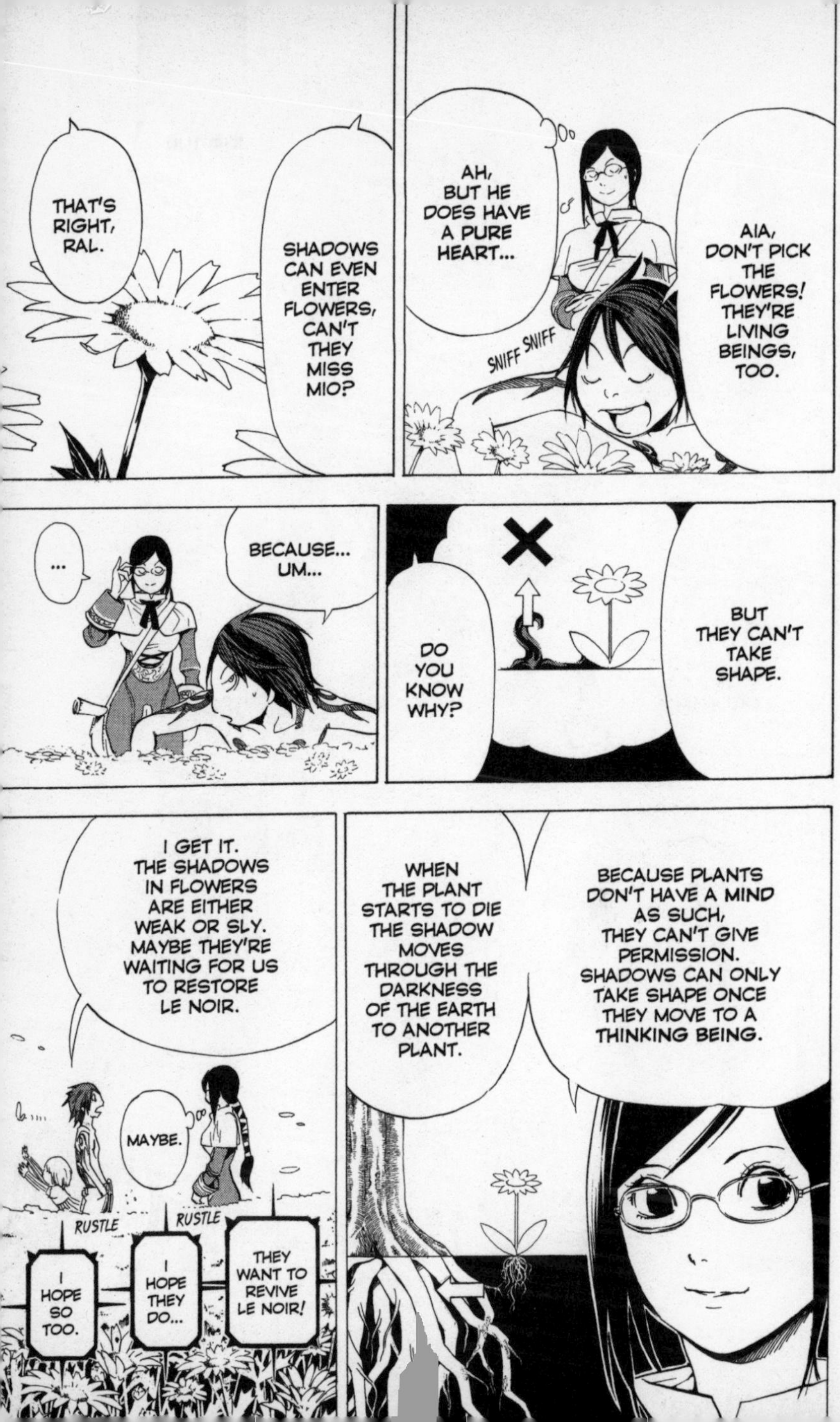
AIA, DON'T PICK THE FLOWERS! THEY'RE LIVING BEINGS, TOO.
SNIFF SNIFF
AH, BUT HE DOES HAVE A PURE HEART...
SHADOWS CAN EVEN ENTER FLOWERS, CAN'T THEY MISS MIO?
THAT'S RIGHT, RAL.
BUT THEY CAN'T TAKE SHAPE.
DO YOU KNOW WHY?
BECAUSE... UM...
...
BECAUSE PLANTS DON'T HAVE A MIND AS SUCH, THEY CAN'T GIVE PERMISSION. SHADOWS CAN ONLY TAKE SHAPE ONCE THEY MOVE TO A THINKING BEING.
WHEN THE PLANT STARTS TO DIE THE SHADOW MOVES THROUGH THE DARKNESS OF THE EARTH TO ANOTHER PLANT.
I GET IT. THE SHADOWS IN FLOWERS ARE EITHER WEAK OR SLY. MAYBE THEY'RE WAITING FOR US TO RESTORE LE NOIR.
MAYBE.
RUSTLE
RUSTLE
THEY WANT TO REVIVE LE NOIR!
I HOPE THEY DO...
I HOPE SO TOO.

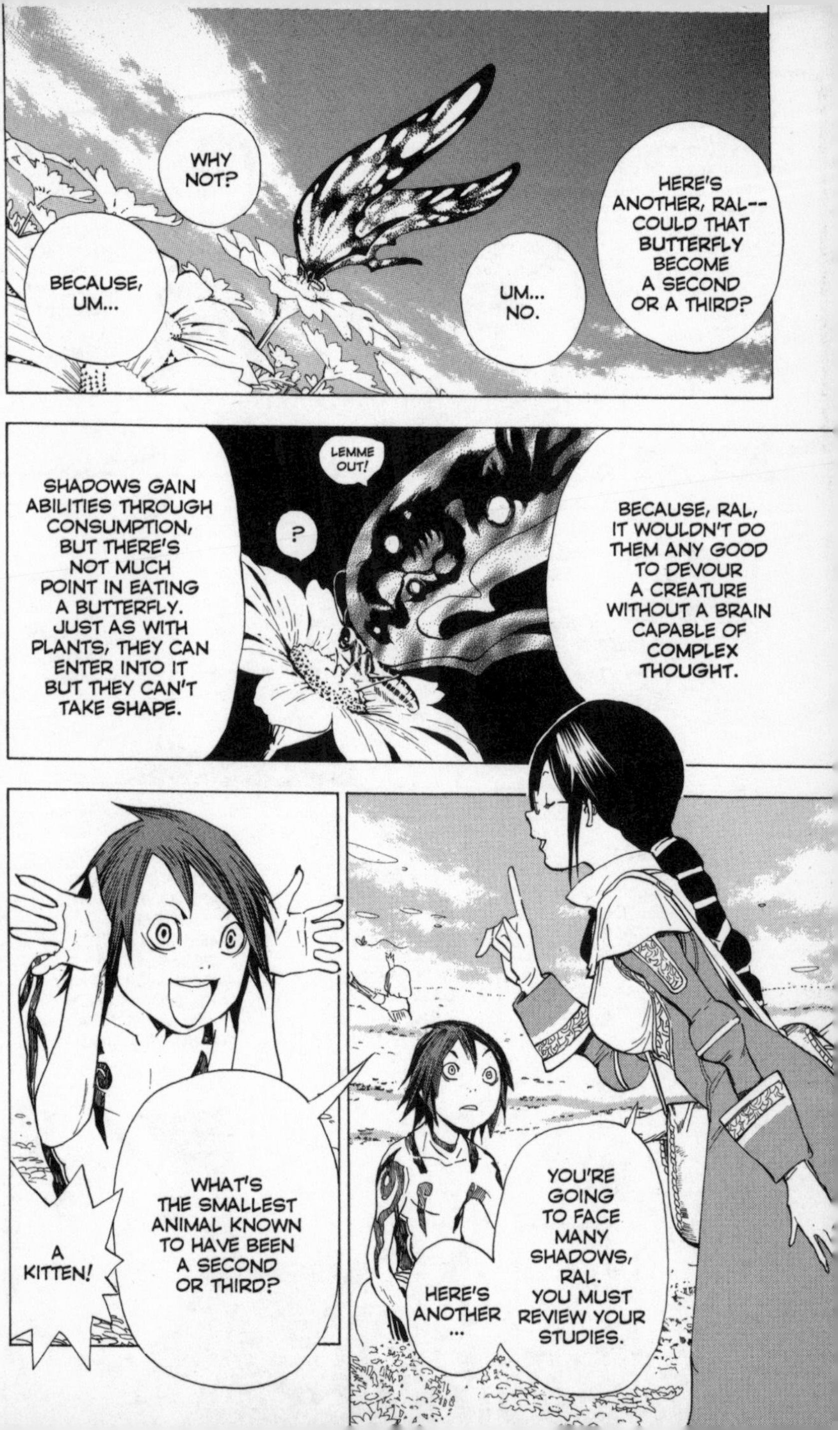
HERE'S ANOTHER, RAL-- COULD THAT BUTTERFLY BECOME A SECOND OR A THIRD?
UM... NO.
WHY NOT?
BECAUSE, UM...
BECAUSE, RAL, IT WOULDN'T DO THEM ANY GOOD TO DEVOUR A CREATURE WITHOUT A BRAIN CAPABLE OF COMPLEX THOUGHT.
LEMME OUT!
?
SHADOWS GAIN ABILITIES THROUGH CONSUMPTION, BUT THERE'S NOT MUCH POINT IN EATING A BUTTERFLY. JUST AS WITH PLANTS, THEY CAN ENTER INTO IT BUT THEY CAN'T TAKE SHAPE.
YOU'RE GOING TO FACE MANY SHADOWS, RAL. YOU MUST REVIEW YOUR STUDIES.
HERE'S ANOTHER ...
WHAT'S THE SMALLEST ANIMAL KNOWN TO HAVE BEEN A SECOND OR THIRD?
A KITTEN!

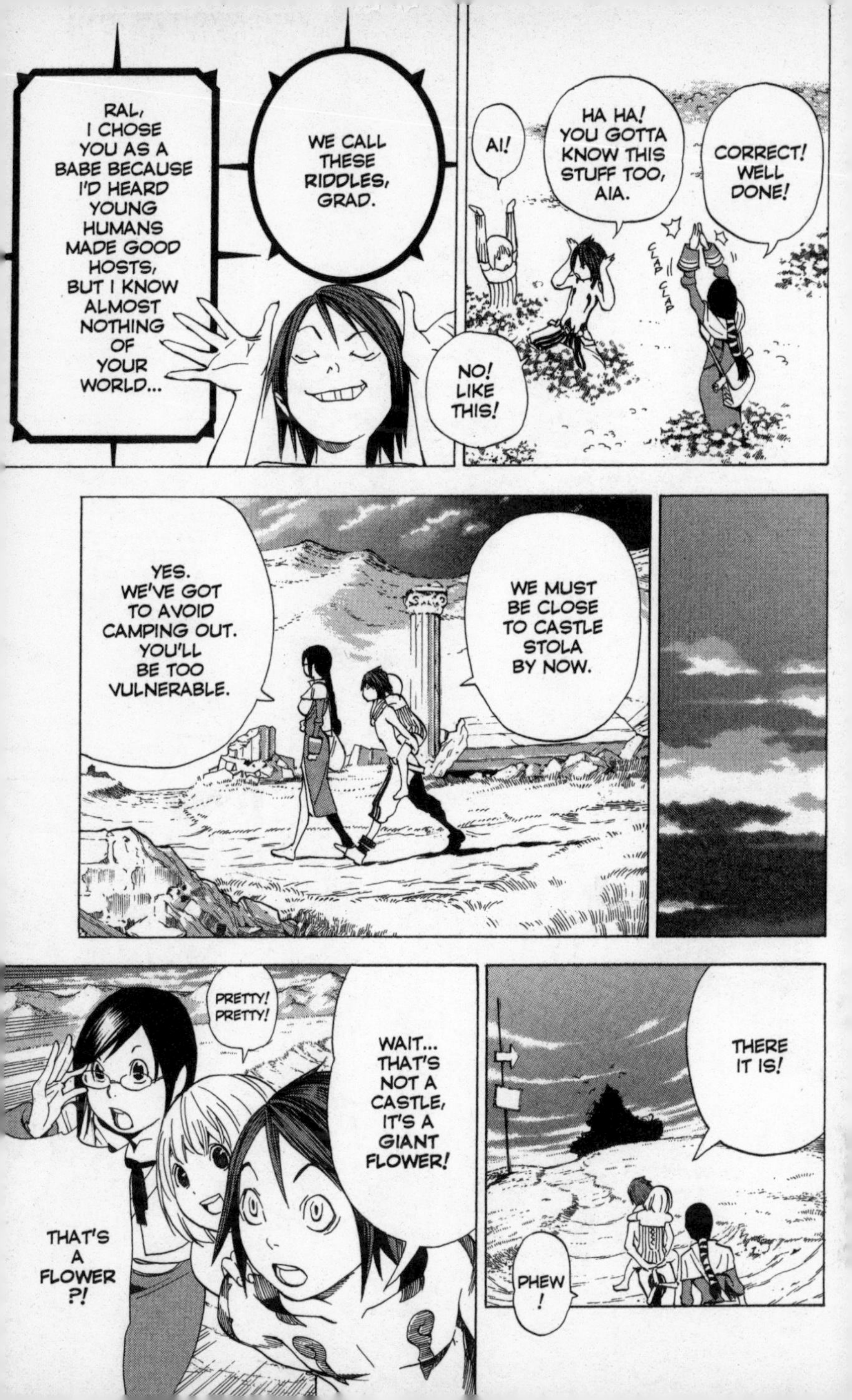
CORRECT! WELL DONE!
HA HA! YOU GOTTA KNOW THIS STUFF TOO, AIA.
AI!
CLAP CLAP
NO! LIKE THIS!
WE CALL THESE RIDDLES, GRAD.
RAL, I CHOSE YOU AS A BABE BECAUSE I'D HEARD YOUNG HUMANS MADE GOOD HOSTS, BUT I KNOW ALMOST NOTHING OF YOUR WORLD...
WE MUST BE CLOSE TO CASTLE STOLA BY NOW.
YES. WE'VE GOT TO AVOID CAMPING OUT. YOU'LL BE TOO VULNERABLE.
THERE IT IS!
PHEW!
WAIT... THAT'S NOT A CASTLE, IT'S A GIANT FLOWER!
PRETTY! PRETTY!
THAT'S A FLOWER?!

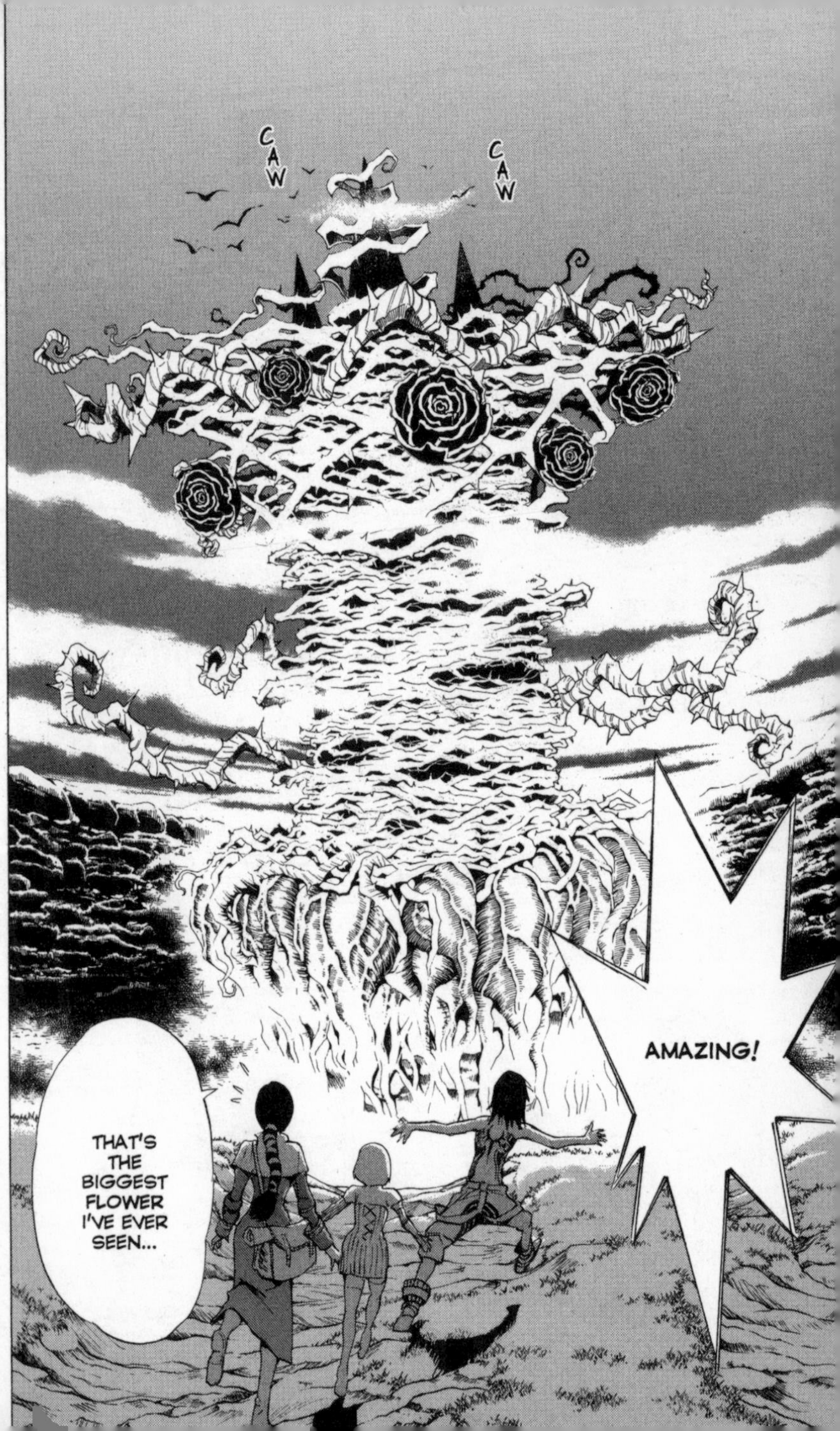
CAW
CAW
AMAZING!
THAT'S THE BIGGEST FLOWER I'VE EVER SEEN...

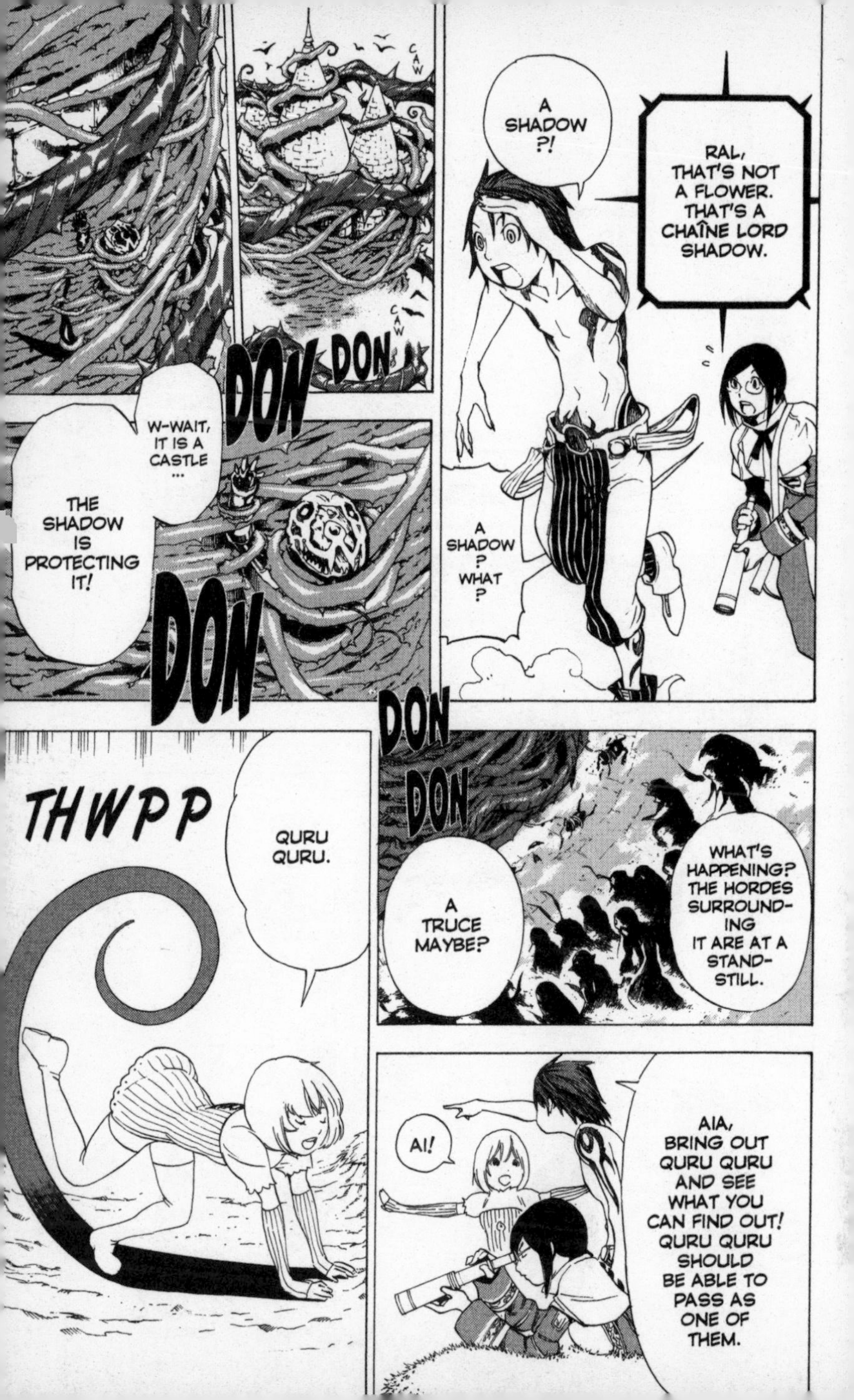

RAL, THAT'S NOT A FLOWER. THAT'S A CHAÎNE LORD SHADOW.
A SHADOW ?!
A SHADOW ? WHAT ?
CAW
CAW
DON DON
W-WAIT, IT IS A CASTLE ...
THE SHADOW IS PROTECTING IT!
DON
DON
DON DON
WHAT'S HAPPENING? THE HORDES SURROUNDING IT ARE AT A STANDSTILL.
A TRUCE MAYBE?
AIA, BRING OUT QURU QURU AND SEE WHAT YOU CAN FIND OUT! QURU QURU SHOULD BE ABLE TO PASS AS ONE OF THEM.
AI!
QURU QURU.
THWPP

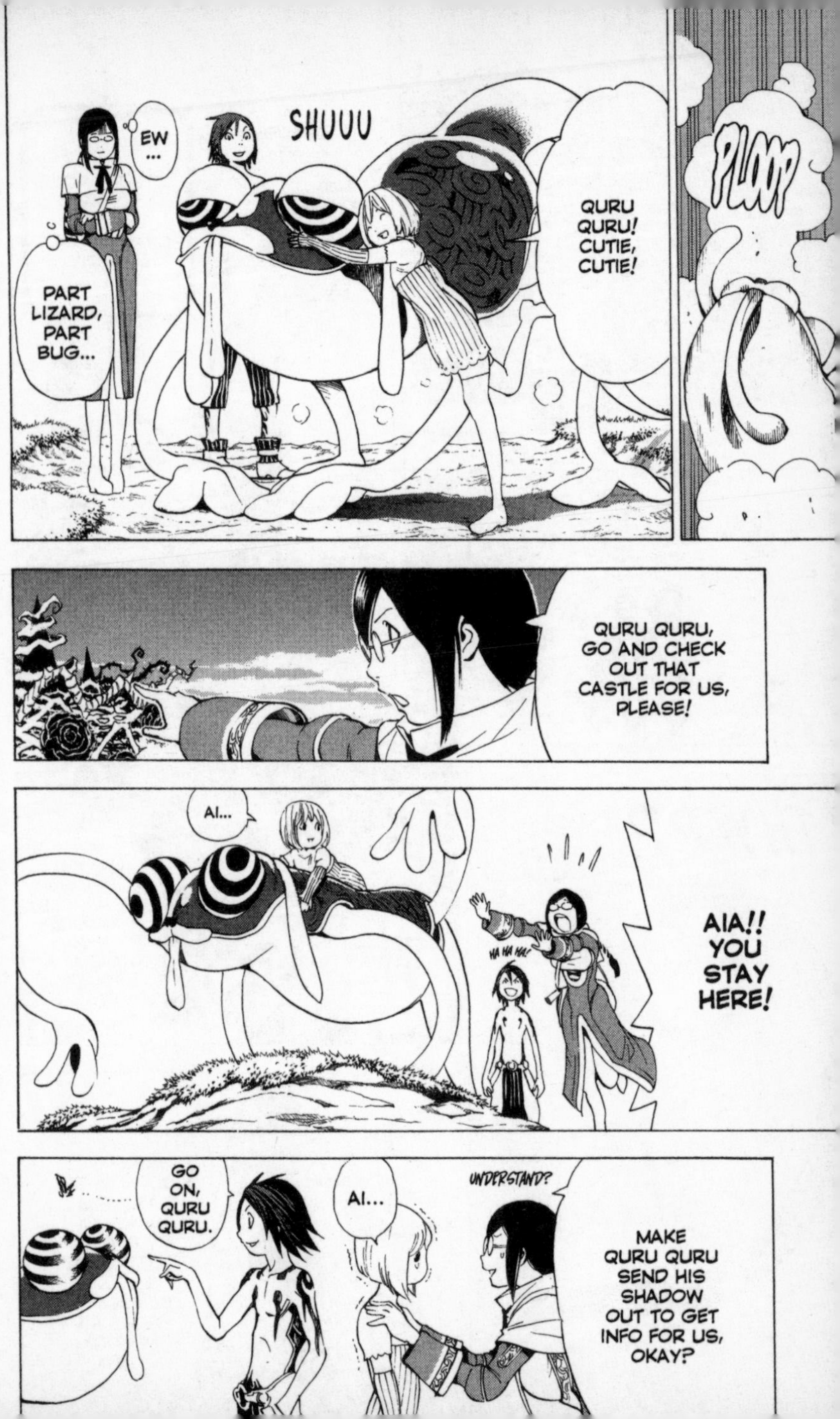
PLOOP
QURU QURU! CUTIE, CUTIE!
SHUUU
EW ...
PART LIZARD, PART BUG...
QURU QURU, GO AND CHECK OUT THAT CASTLE FOR US, PLEASE!
AIA!! YOU STAY HERE!
HA HA HA!
AI...
MAKE QURU QURU SEND HIS SHADOW OUT TO GET INFO FOR US, OKAY?
UNDERSTAND?
AI...
GO ON, QURU QURU.
......

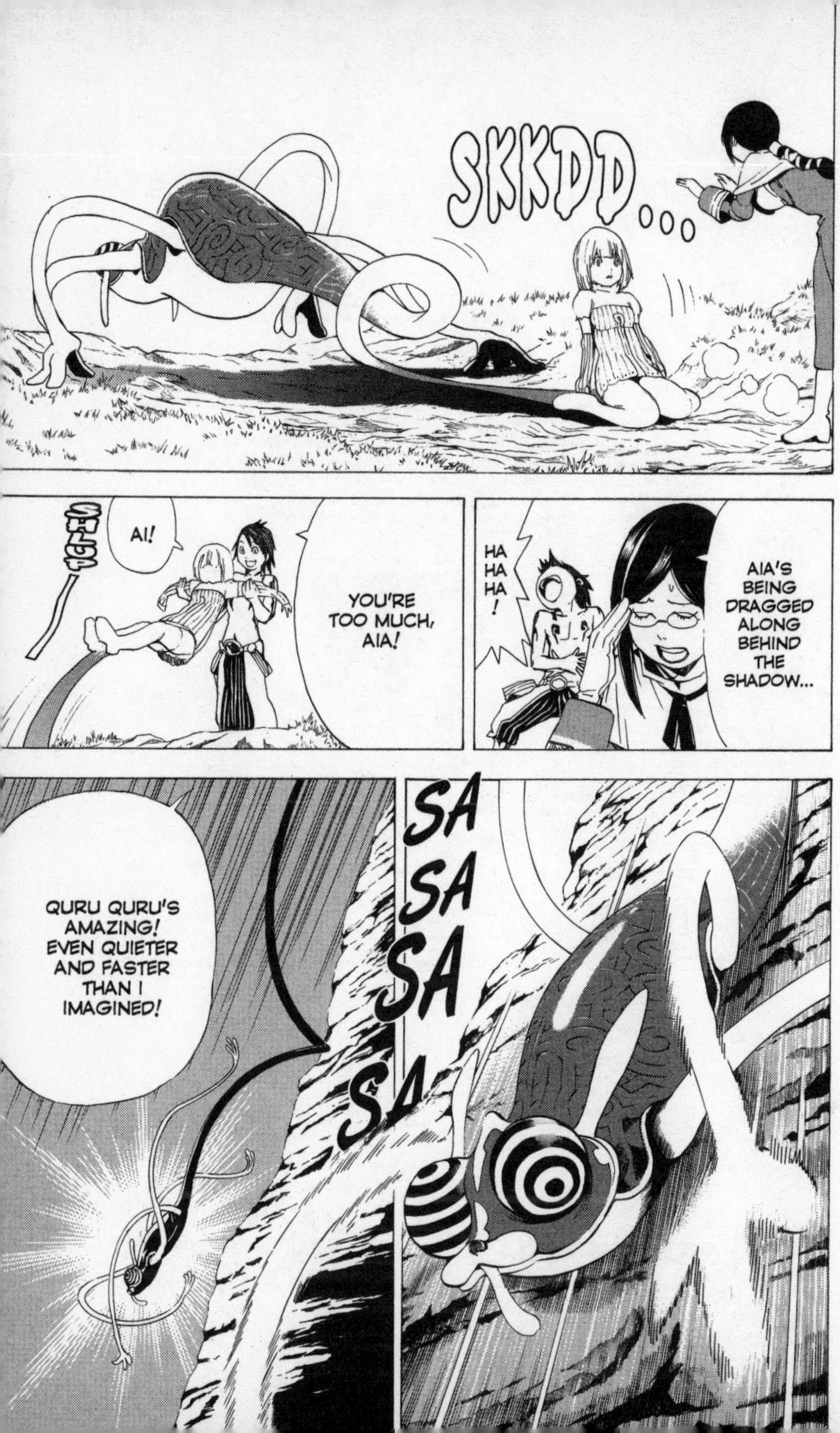
SKKDD...
AIA'S BEING DRAGGED ALONG BEHIND THE SHADOW...
HA HA HA!
YOU'RE TOO MUCH, AIA!
AI!
SHUP
SA SA SA SA
QURU QURU'S AMAZING! EVEN QUIETER AND FASTER THAN I IMAGINED!

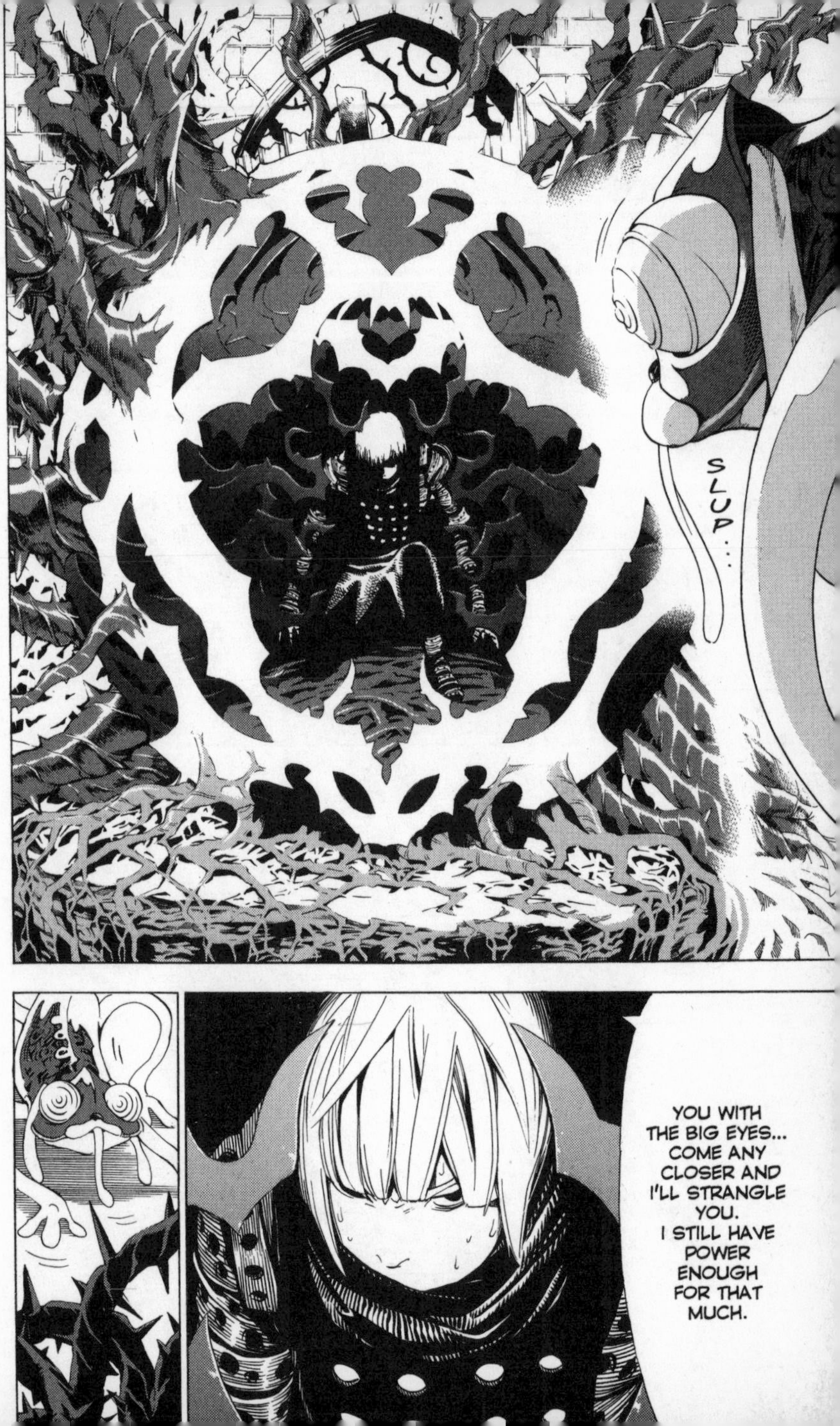
SLUP...
YOU WITH THE BIG EYES... COME ANY CLOSER AND I'LL STRANGLE YOU. I STILL HAVE POWER ENOUGH FOR THAT MUCH.

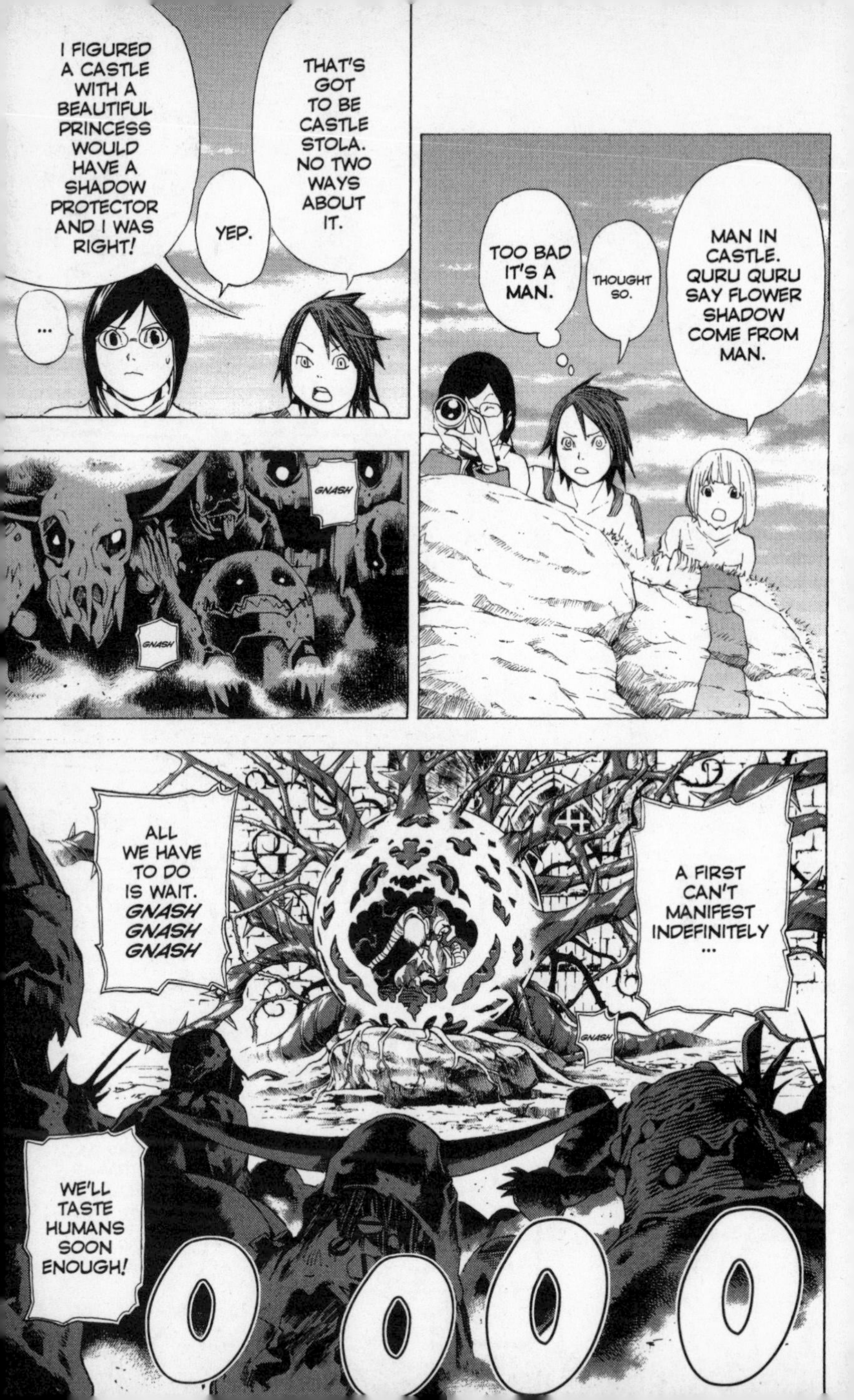

THAT'S GOT TO BE CASTLE STOLA. NO TWO WAYS ABOUT IT.
YEP.
I FIGURED A CASTLE WITH A BEAUTIFUL PRINCESS WOULD HAVE A SHADOW PROTECTOR AND I WAS RIGHT!
...
MAN IN CASTLE. QURU QURU SAY FLOWER SHADOW COME FROM MAN.
THOUGHT SO.
TOO BAD IT'S A MAN.
GNASH
GNASH
A FIRST CAN'T MANIFEST INDEFINITELY ...
GNASH
ALL WE HAVE TO DO IS WAIT. GNASH GNASH GNASH
WE'LL TASTE HUMANS SOON ENOUGH!

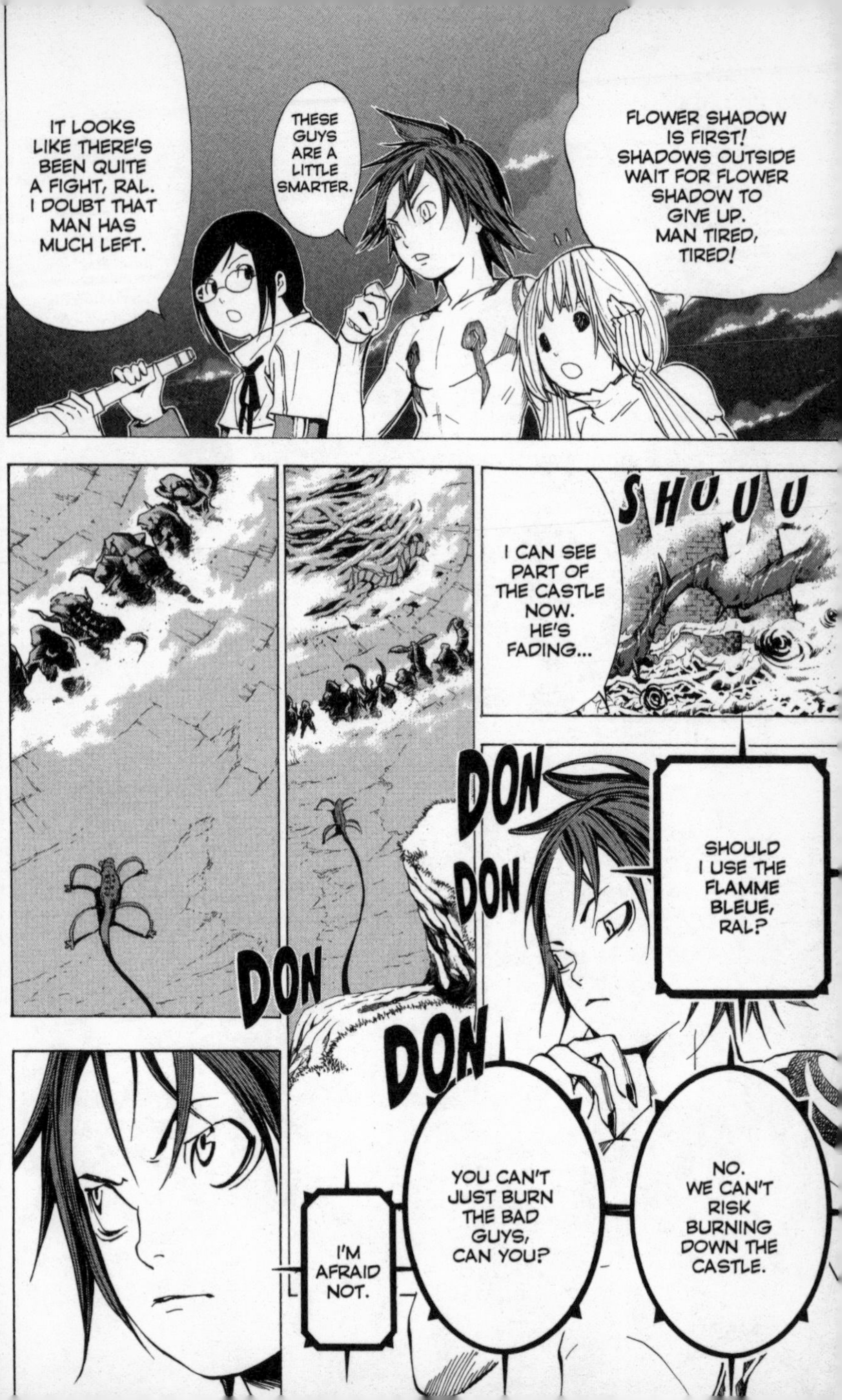
FLOWER SHADOW IS FIRST! SHADOWS OUTSIDE WAIT FOR FLOWER SHADOW TO GIVE UP. MAN TIRED, TIRED!
THESE GUYS ARE A LITTLE SMARTER.
IT LOOKS LIKE THERE'S BEEN QUITE A FIGHT, RAL. I DOUBT THAT MAN HAS MUCH LEFT.
SHUUU
I CAN SEE PART OF THE CASTLE NOW. HE'S FADING...
DON
DON
DON
DON
SHOULD I USE THE FLAMME BLEUE, RAL?
NO. WE CAN'T RISK BURNING DOWN THE CASTLE.
YOU CAN'T JUST BURN THE BAD GUYS, CAN YOU?
I'M AFRAID NOT.

READ THIS WAY

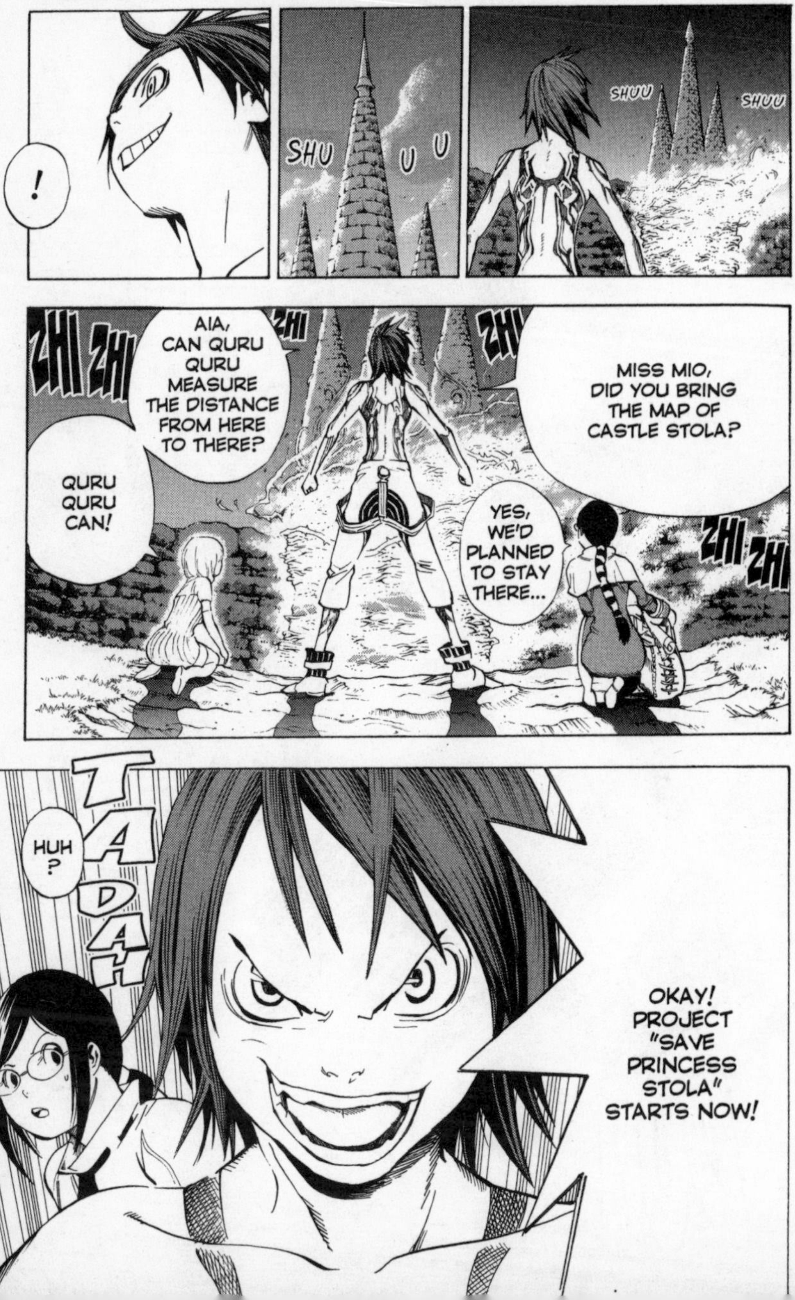
SHUU
SHUU
SHU U U
!
ZHI
MISS MIO, DID YOU BRING THE MAP OF CASTLE STOLA?
ZHI
AIA, CAN QURU QURU MEASURE THE DISTANCE FROM HERE TO THERE?
ZHI ZHI
ZHI ZHI
YES, WE'D PLANNED TO STAY THERE...
QURU QURU CAN!
OKAY! PROJECT "SAVE PRINCESS STOLA" STARTS NOW!
TADAH
HUH?

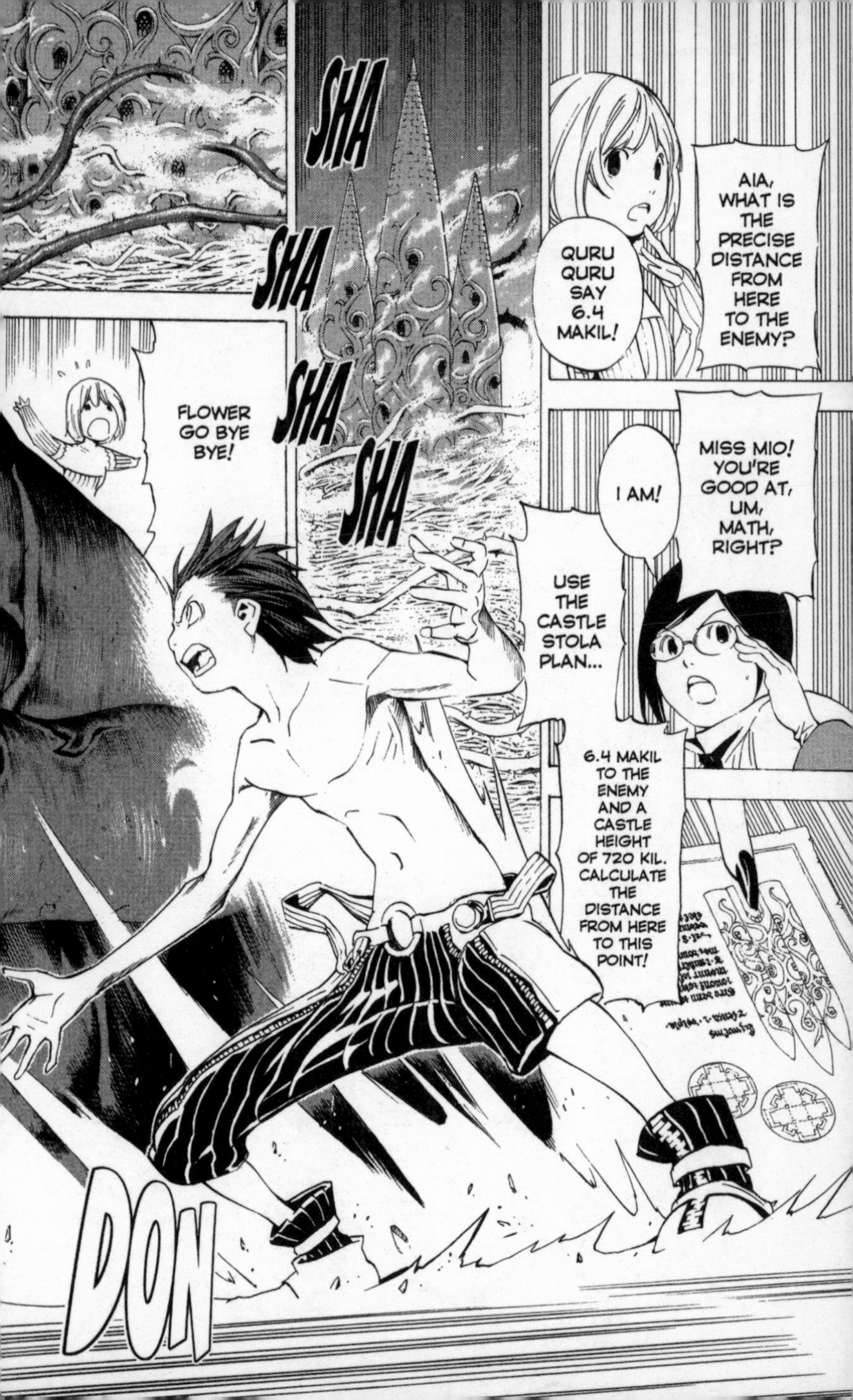
AIA, WHAT IS THE PRECISE DISTANCE FROM HERE TO THE ENEMY?
QURU QURU SAY 6.4 MAKIL!
MISS MIO! YOU'RE GOOD AT, UM, MATH, RIGHT?
I AM!
USE THE CASTLE STOLA PLAN...
6.4 MAKIL TO THE ENEMY AND A CASTLE HEIGHT OF 720 KIL. CALCULATE THE DISTANCE FROM HERE TO THIS POINT!
SHA
SHA
SHA
SHA
FLOWER GO BYE BYE!
DON

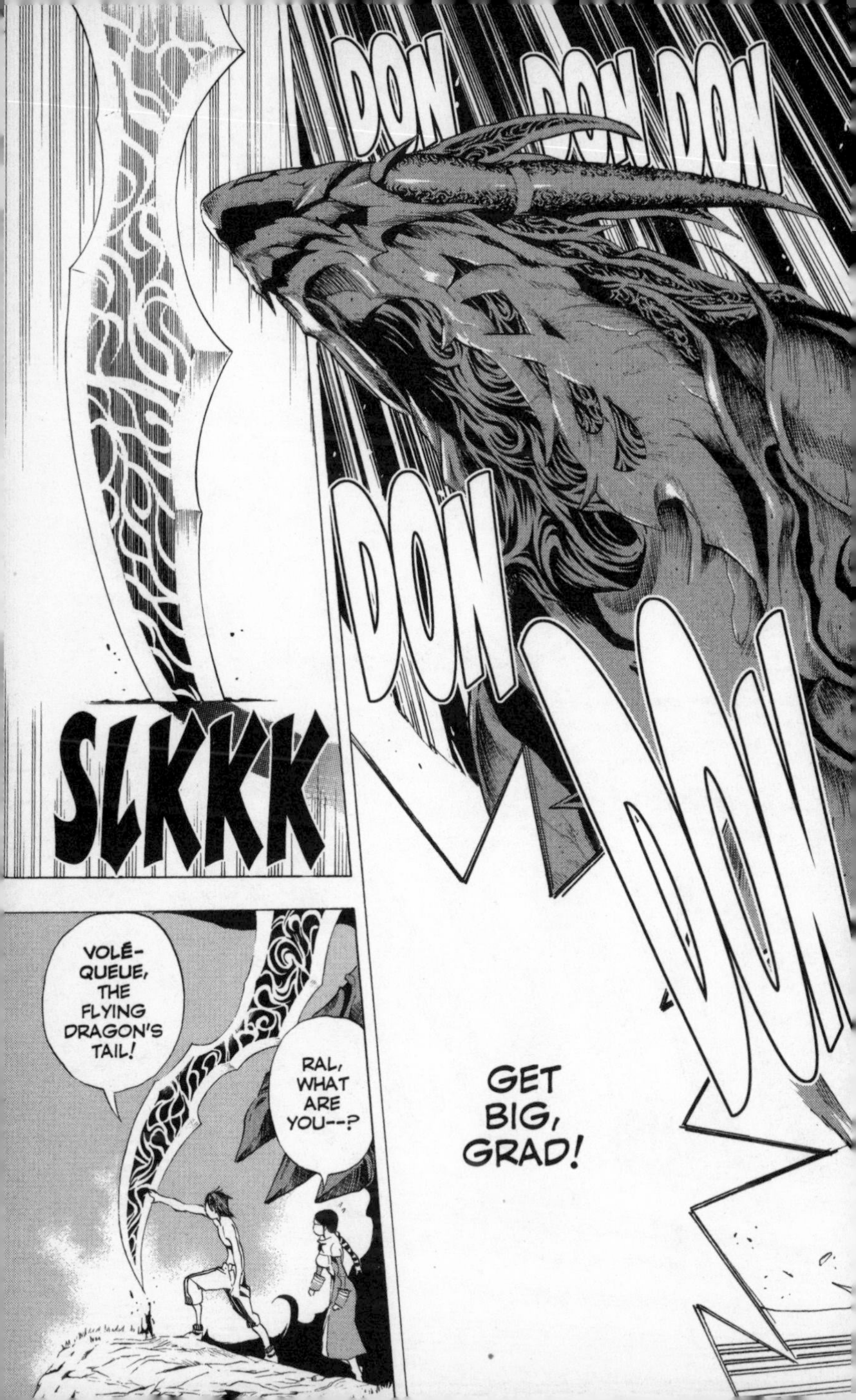
DON DON DON
DON
DON
GET BIG, GRAD!
SLKKK
VOLÉ-QUEUE, THE FLYING DRAGON'S TAIL!
RAL, WHAT ARE YOU--?

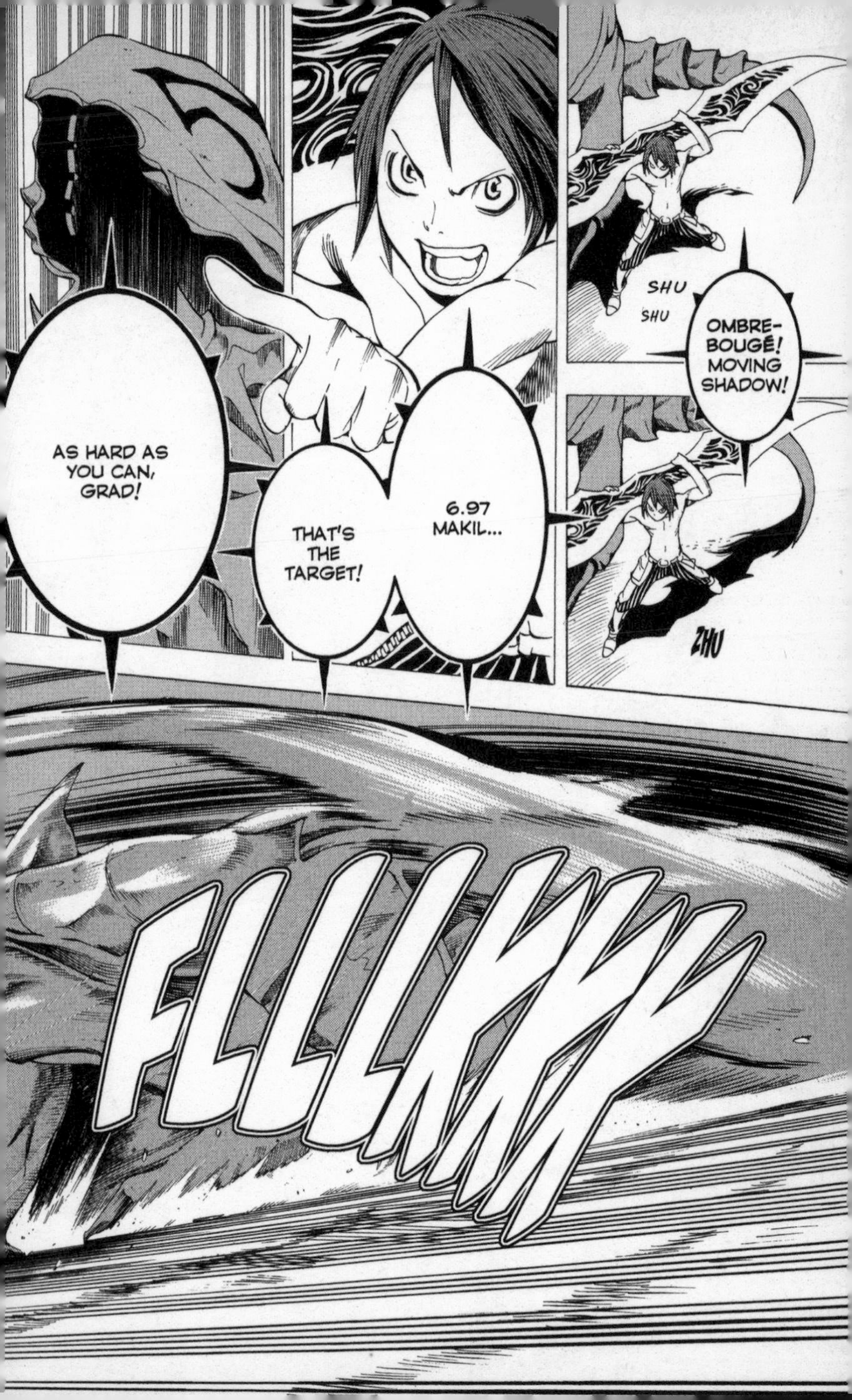
OMBRE-BOUGÉ! MOVING SHADOW!
SHU
SHU
ZHU
6.97 MAKIL...
THAT'S THE TARGET!
AS HARD AS YOU CAN, GRAD!

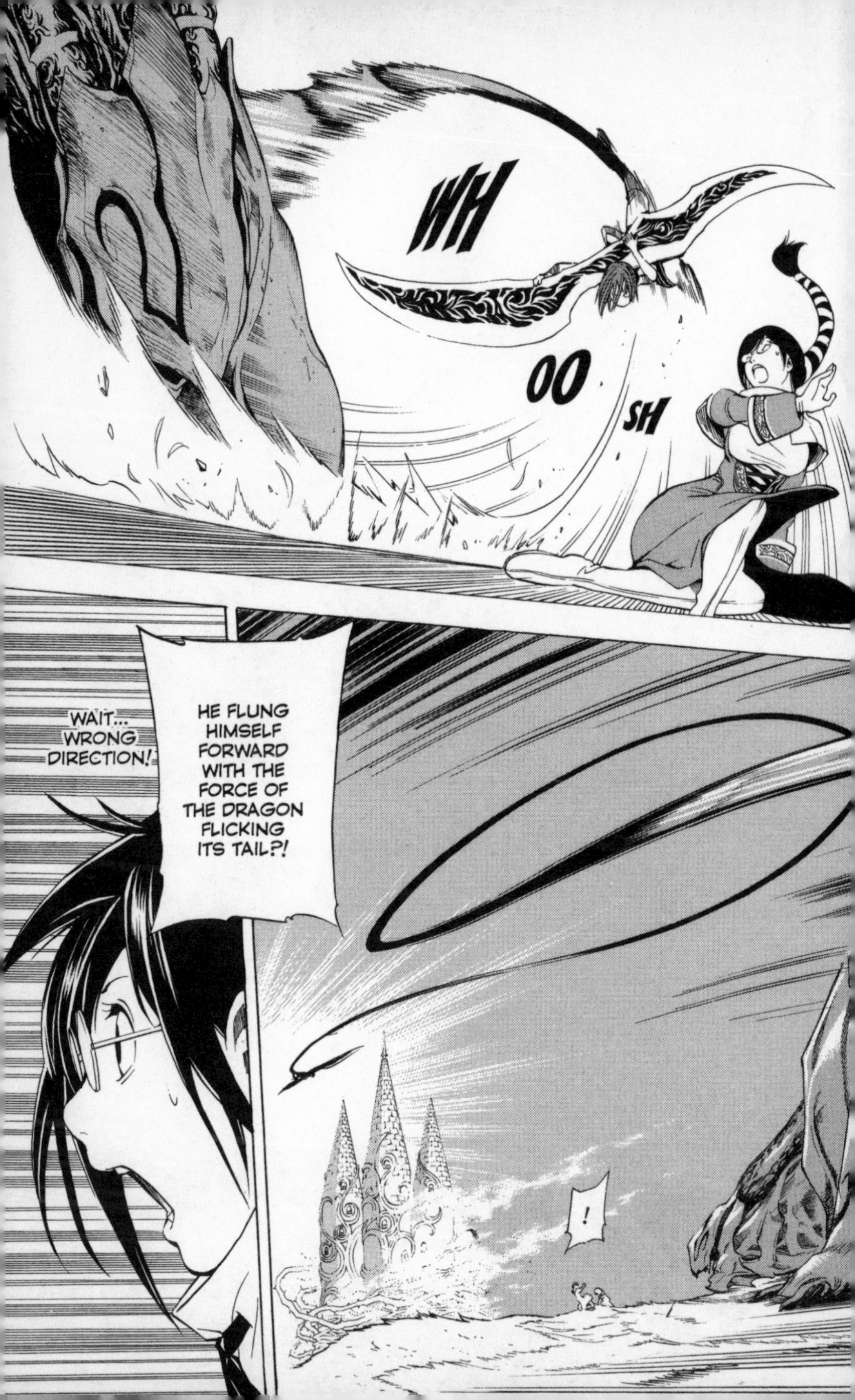
WHOOSH
!
HE FLUNG HIMSELF FORWARD WITH THE FORCE OF THE DRAGON FLICKING ITS TAIL?!
WAIT... WRONG DIRECTION!

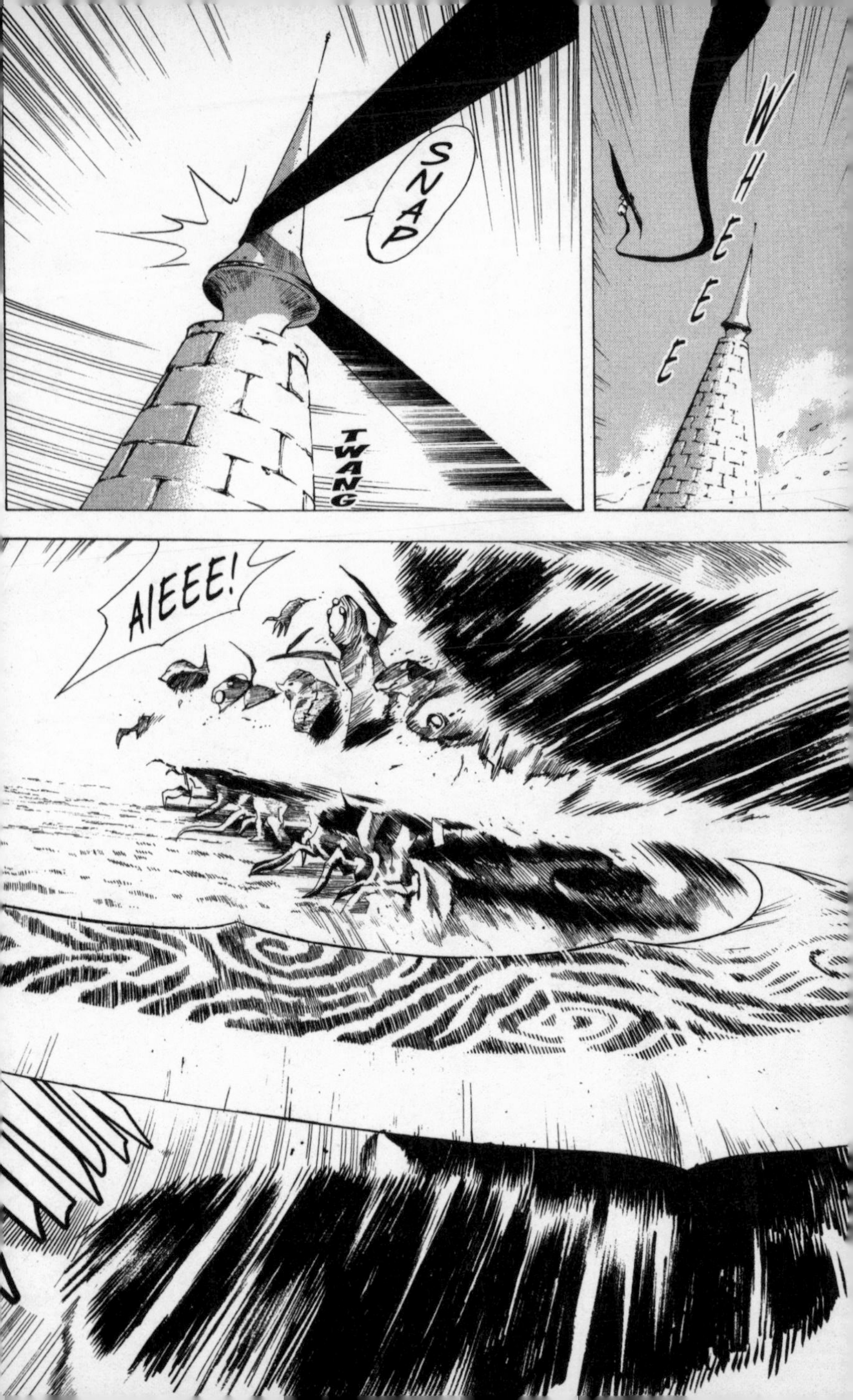
WHEEEE
SNAP
TWANG
AIEEE!

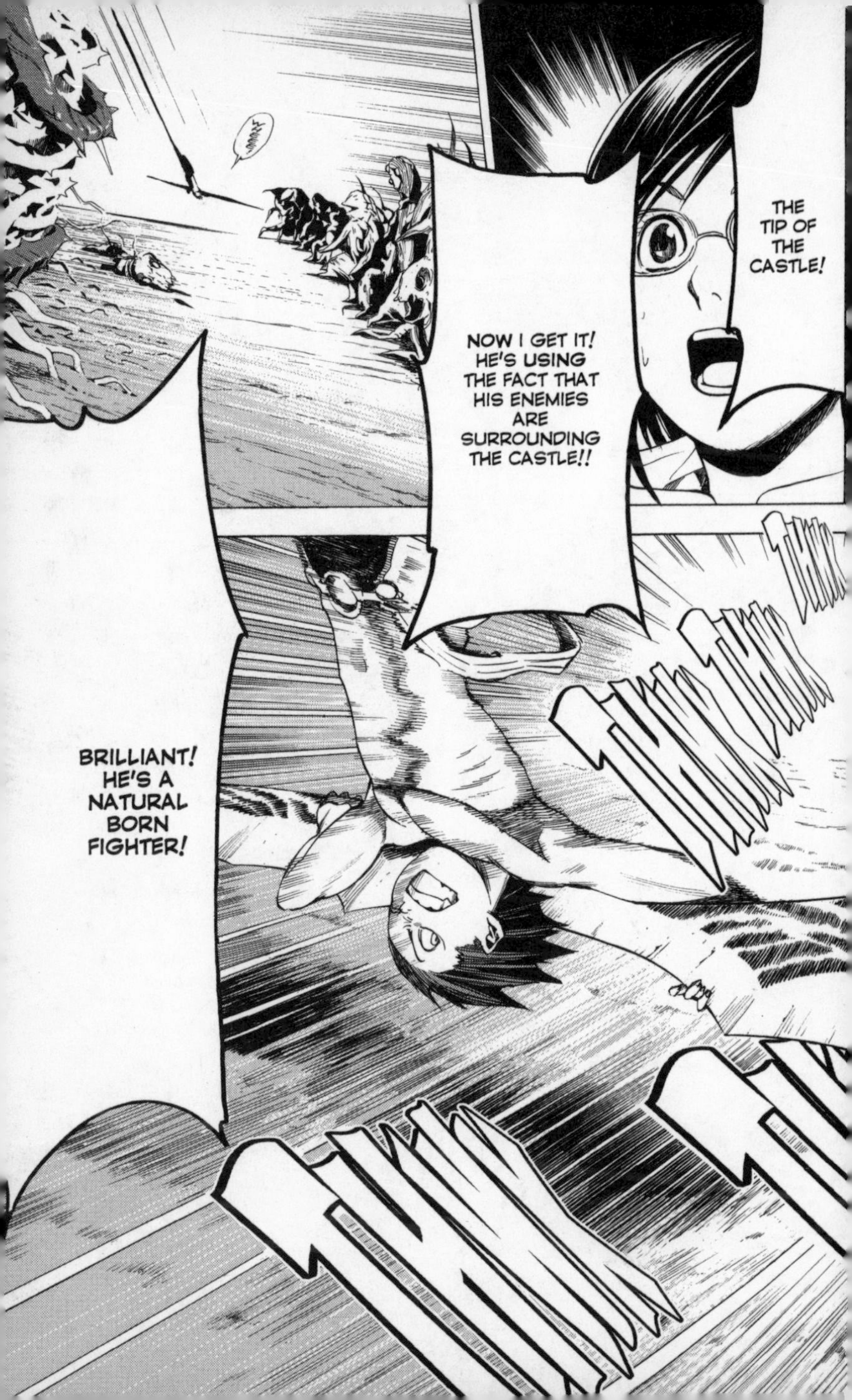
THE TIP OF THE CASTLE!
NOW I GET IT! HE'S USING THE FACT THAT HIS ENEMIES ARE SURROUNDING THE CASTLE!!
BRILLIANT! HE'S A NATURAL BORN FIGHTER!

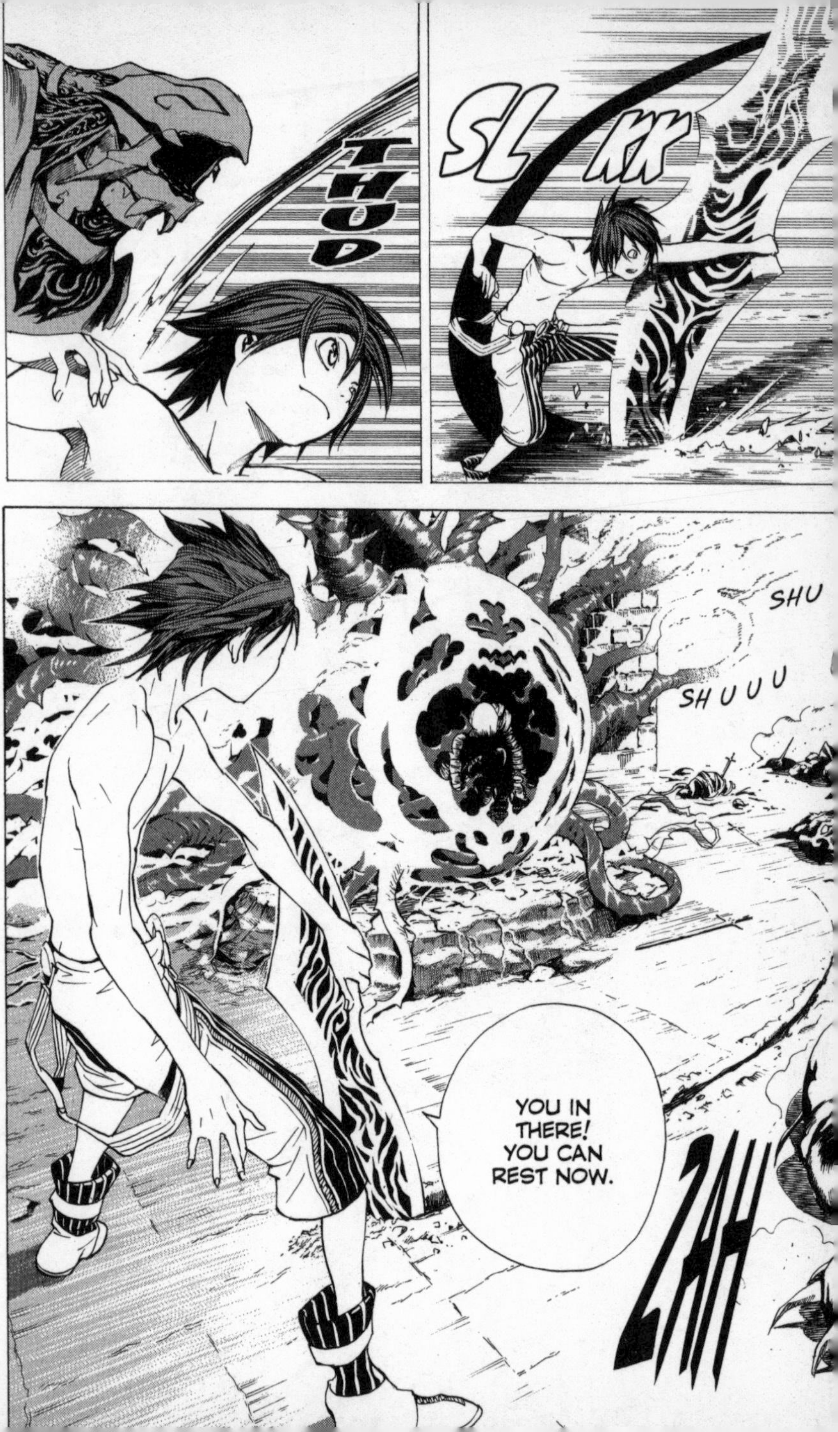
SL KK
THUD
SHU
SHUUU
YOU IN THERE! YOU CAN REST NOW.
ZAH

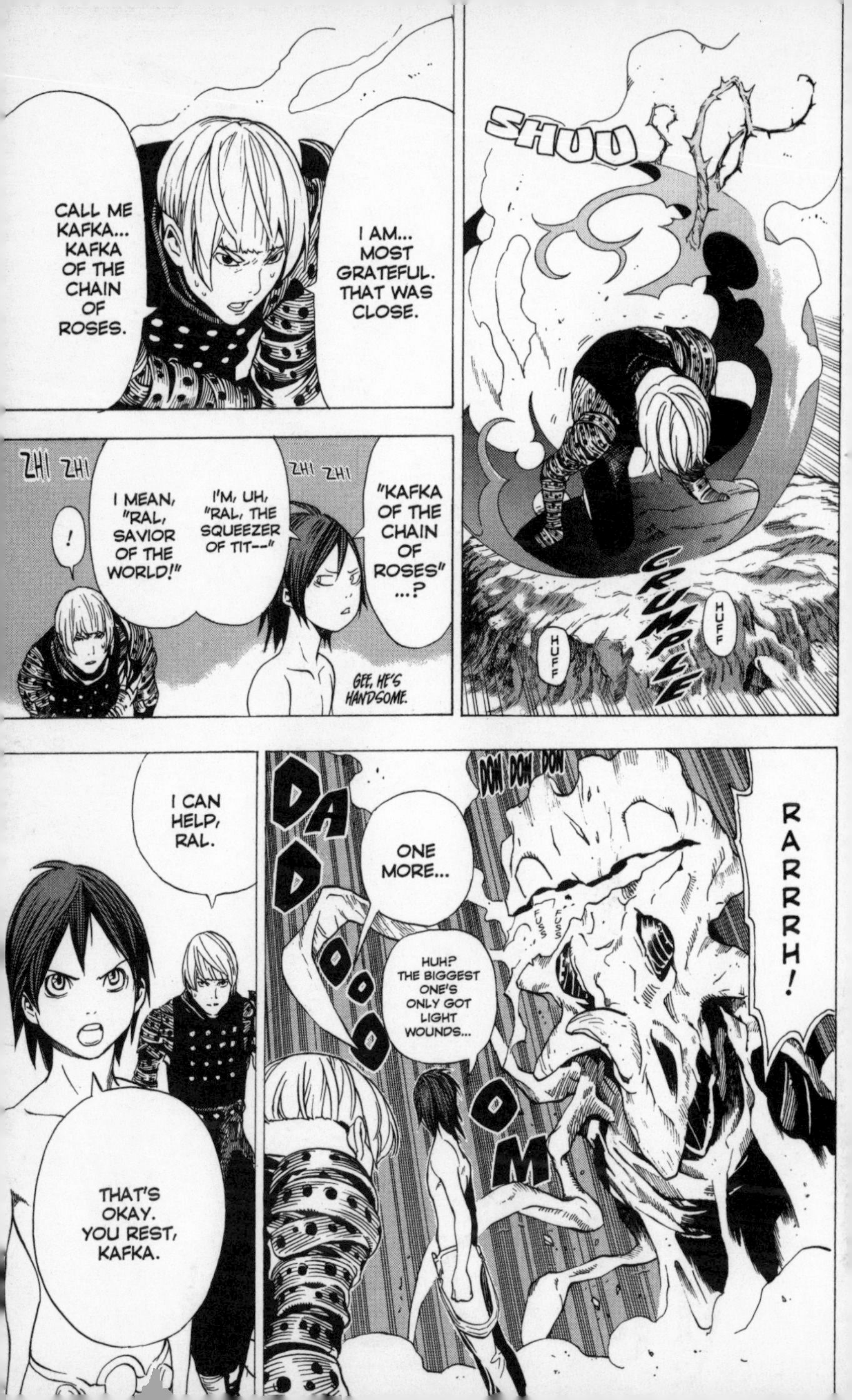
SHUU
HUFF
HUFF
CRUMPLE
I AM... MOST GRATEFUL. THAT WAS CLOSE.
CALL ME KAFKA... KAFKA OF THE CHAIN OF ROSES.
"KAFKA OF THE CHAIN OF ROSES" ...?
ZHI ZHI
I'M, UH, "RAL, THE SQUEEZER OF TIT--"
I MEAN, "RAL, SAVIOR OF THE WORLD!"
!
ZHI ZHI
GEE, HE'S HANDSOME.
RARRRH!
DOM DOM DOM
DADOOOOOM
ONE MORE...
FUSS FUSS
HUH? THE BIGGEST ONE'S ONLY GOT LIGHT WOUNDS...
I CAN HELP, RAL.
THAT'S OKAY. YOU REST, KAFKA.

Ral Ω Grad

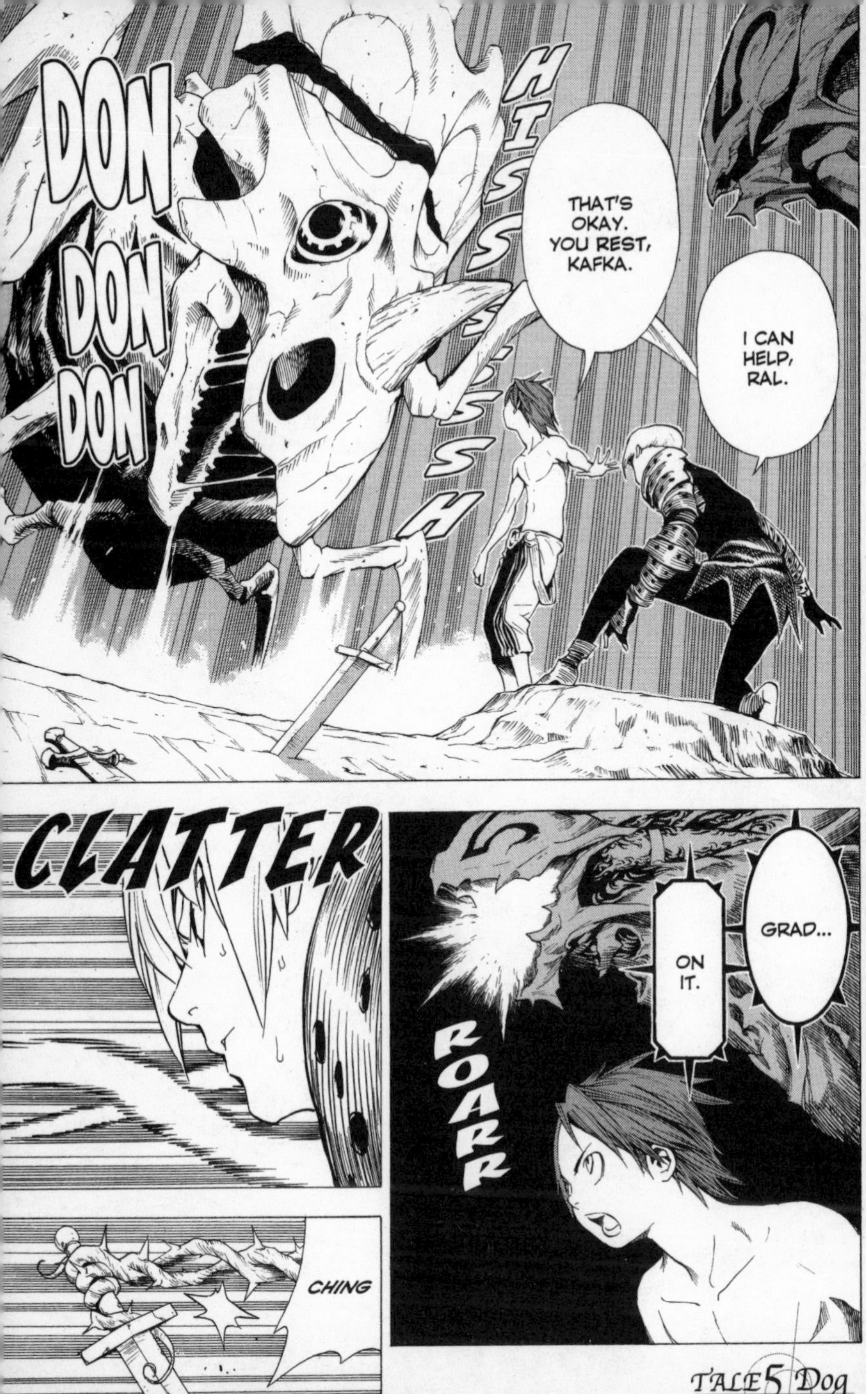
I CAN HELP, RAL.
THAT'S OKAY. YOU REST, KAFKA.
HISSSSSSH
DON DON DON DON
GRAD...
ON IT.
ROARR
CLATTER
CHING

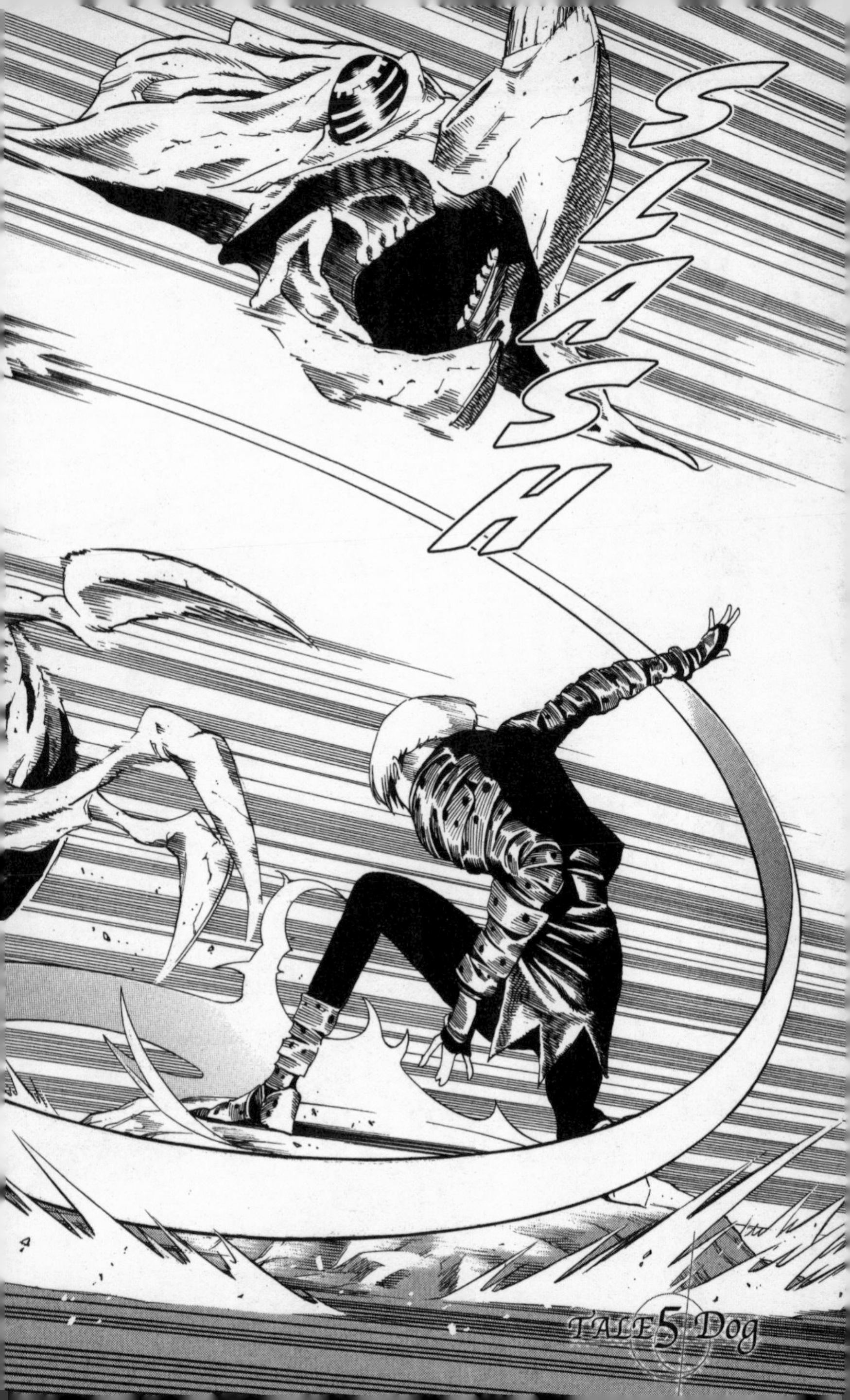
SLASH
TALE 5 Dog

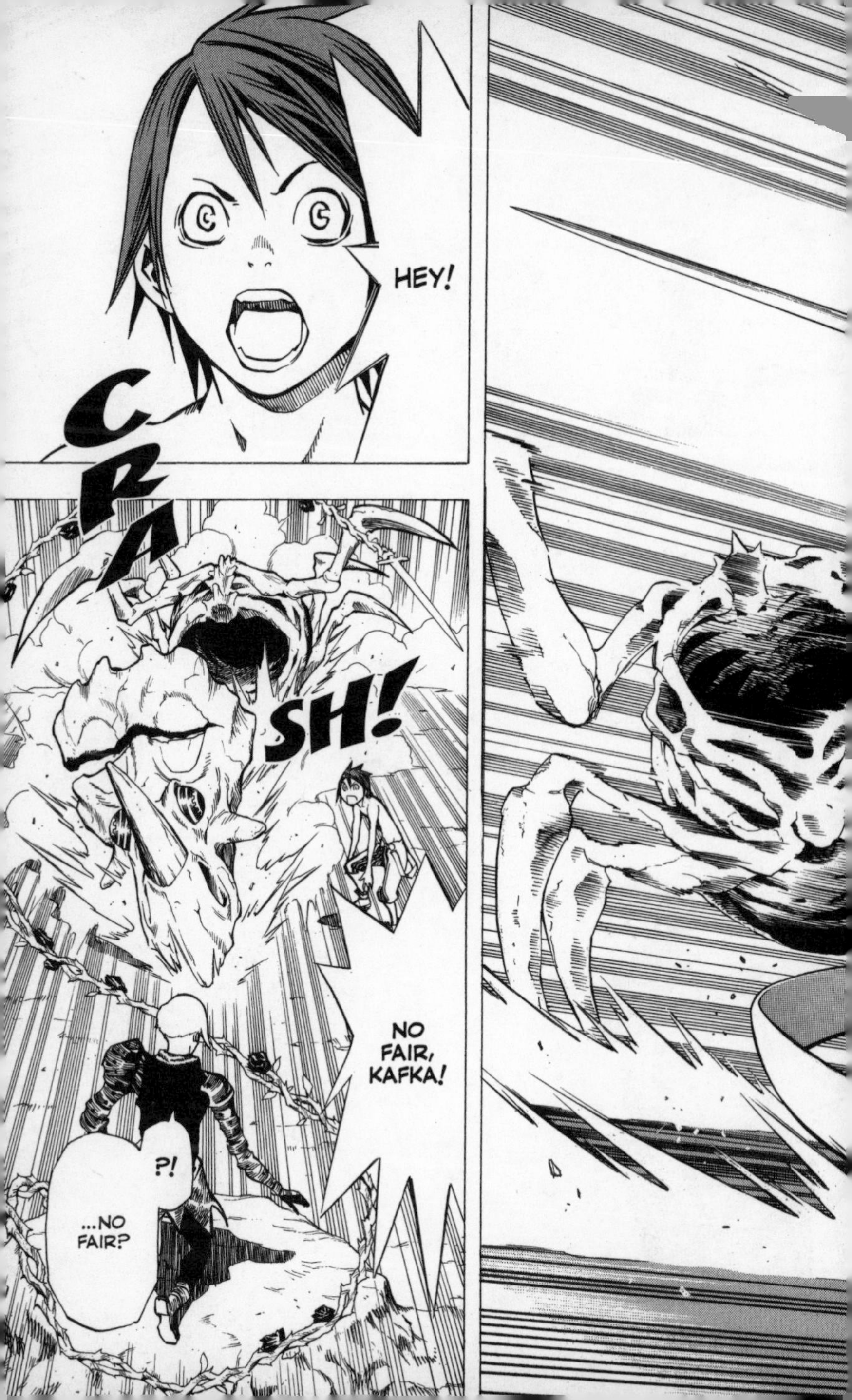
HEY!
CRASH!
NO FAIR, KAFKA!
?!
...NO FAIR?

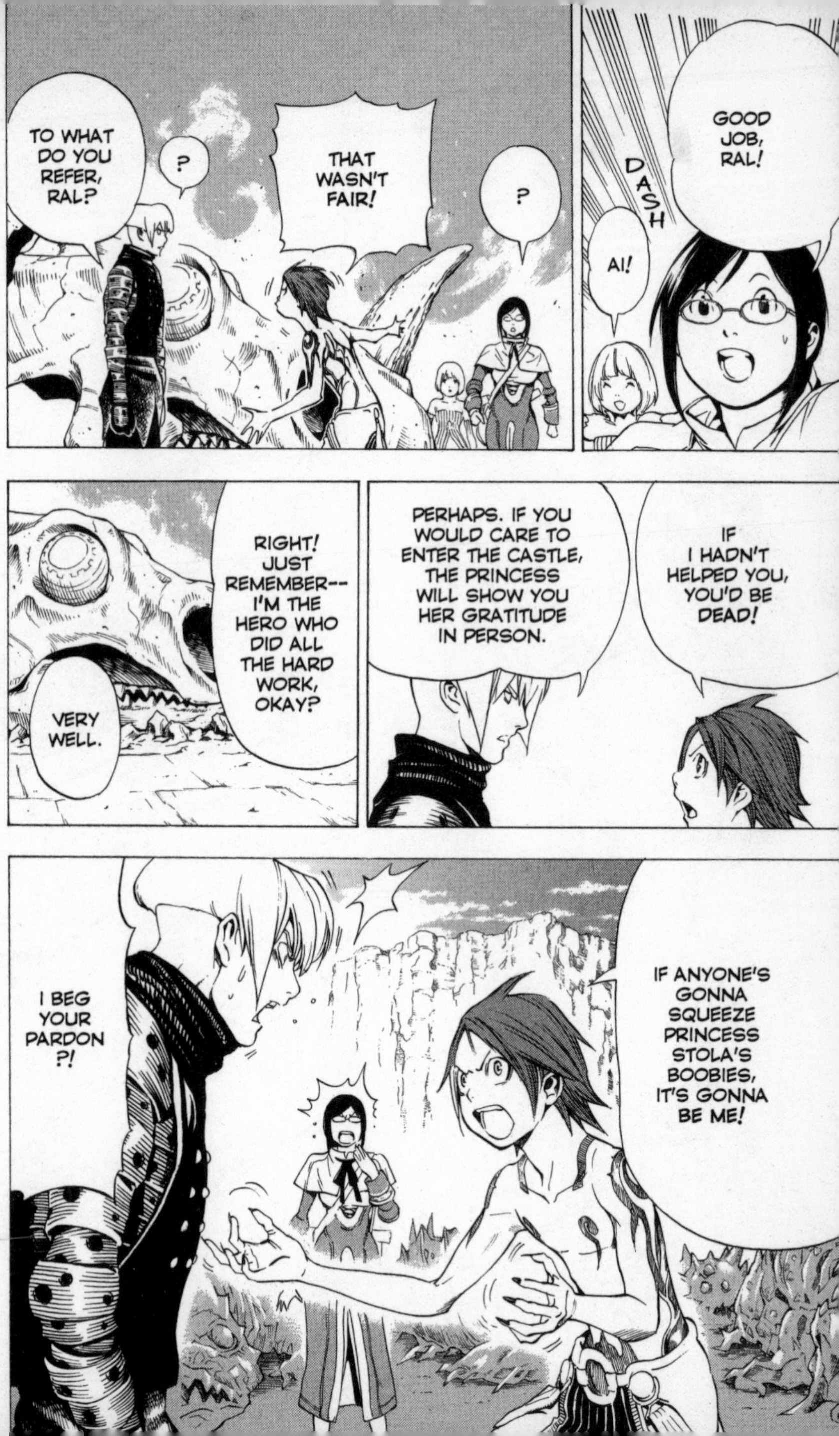
GOOD JOB, RAL!
DASH
AI!
?
THAT WASN'T FAIR!
?
TO WHAT DO YOU REFER, RAL?
IF I HADN'T HELPED YOU, YOU'D BE DEAD!
PERHAPS. IF YOU WOULD CARE TO ENTER THE CASTLE, THE PRINCESS WILL SHOW YOU HER GRATITUDE IN PERSON.
RIGHT! JUST REMEMBER-- I'M THE HERO WHO DID ALL THE HARD WORK, OKAY?
VERY WELL.
IF ANYONE'S GONNA SQUEEZE PRINCESS STOLA'S BOOBIES, IT'S GONNA BE ME!
I BEG YOUR PARDON?!

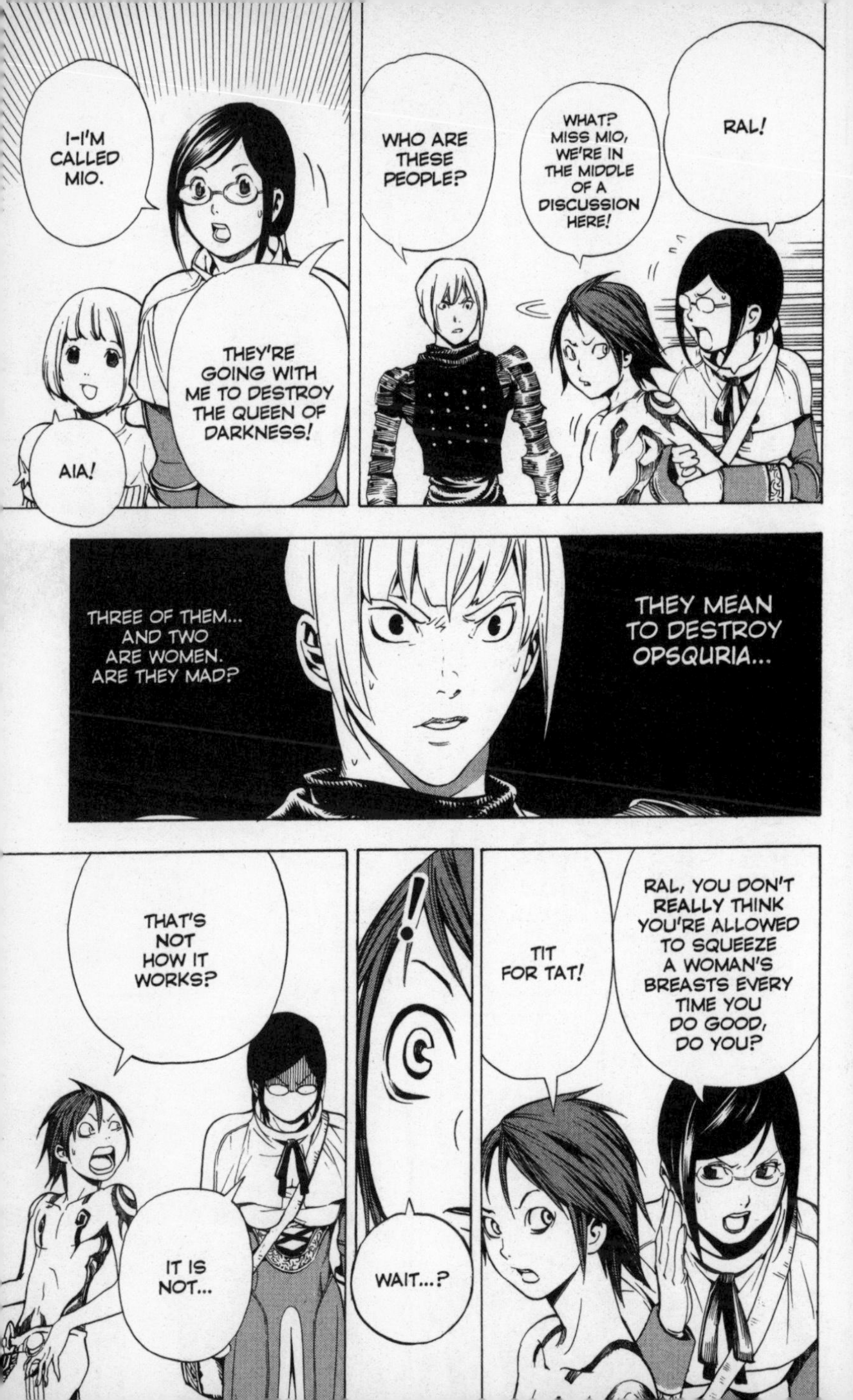
RAL!
WHAT? MISS MIO, WE'RE IN THE MIDDLE OF A DISCUSSION HERE!
WHO ARE THESE PEOPLE?
I-I'M CALLED MIO.
THEY'RE GOING WITH ME TO DESTROY THE QUEEN OF DARKNESS!
AIA!
THEY MEAN TO DESTROY OPSQURIA...
THREE OF THEM... AND TWO ARE WOMEN. ARE THEY MAD?
RAL, YOU DON'T REALLY THINK YOU'RE ALLOWED TO SQUEEZE A WOMAN'S BREASTS EVERY TIME YOU DO GOOD, DO YOU?
TIT FOR TAT!
!
WAIT...?
THAT'S NOT HOW IT WORKS?
IT IS NOT...

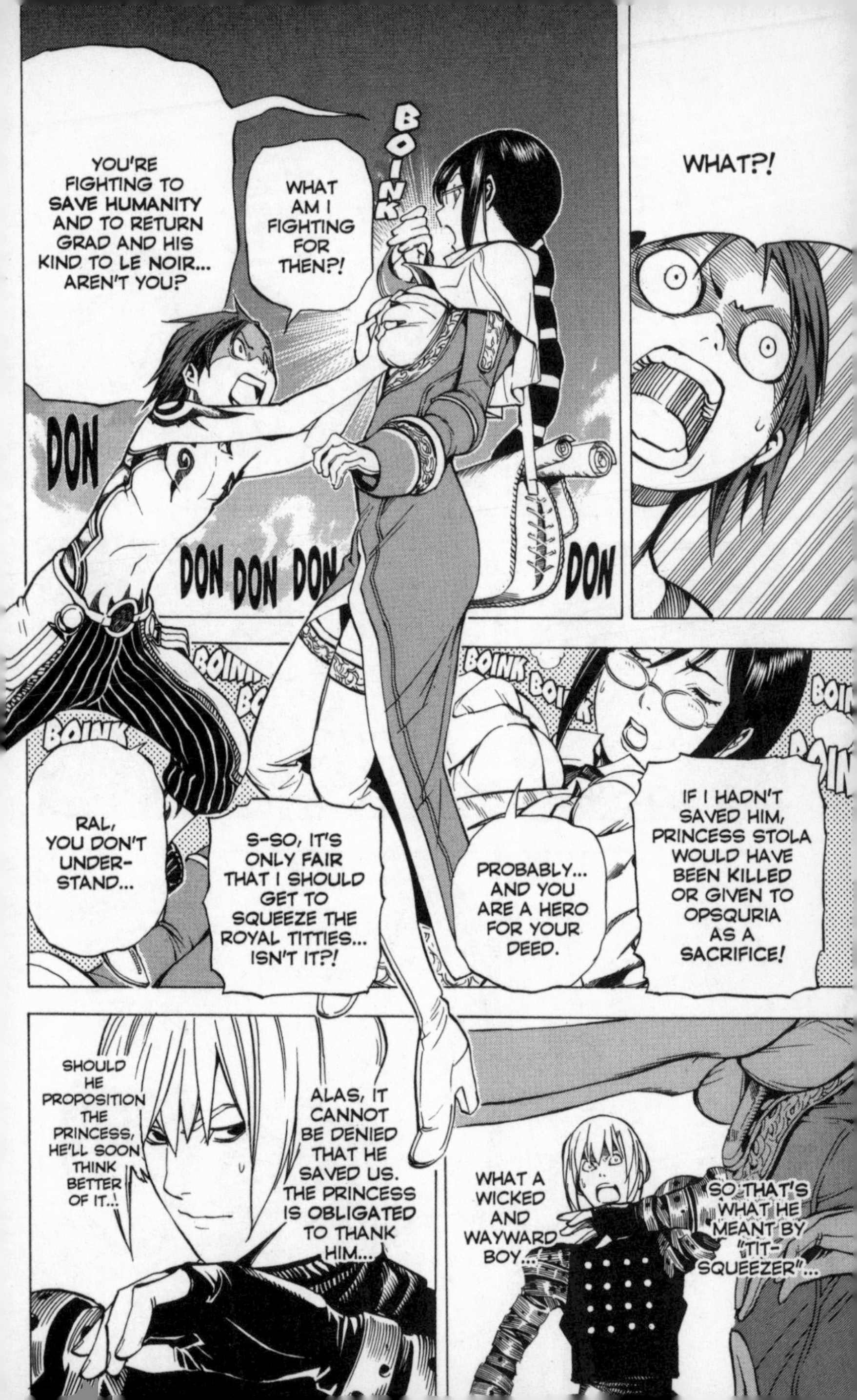
WHAT?!
BOINK
WHAT AM I FIGHTING FOR THEN?!
YOU'RE FIGHTING TO SAVE HUMANITY AND TO RETURN GRAD AND HIS KIND TO LE NOIR... AREN'T YOU?
DON
DON DON DON DON
DON
BOINK BOINK BOINK
IF I HADN'T SAVED HIM, PRINCESS STOLA WOULD HAVE BEEN KILLED OR GIVEN TO OPSQURIA AS A SACRIFICE!
PROBABLY... AND YOU ARE A HERO FOR YOUR DEED.
BOINK BOINK BOINK
S-SO, IT'S ONLY FAIR THAT I SHOULD GET TO SQUEEZE THE ROYAL TITTIES... ISN'T IT?!
RAL, YOU DON'T UNDER-STAND...
SO THAT'S WHAT HE MEANT BY "TIT-SQUEEZER"...
WHAT A WICKED AND WAYWARD BOY...
ALAS, IT CANNOT BE DENIED THAT HE SAVED US. THE PRINCESS IS OBLIGATED TO THANK HIM...
SHOULD HE PROPOSITION THE PRINCESS, HE'LL SOON THINK BETTER OF IT...

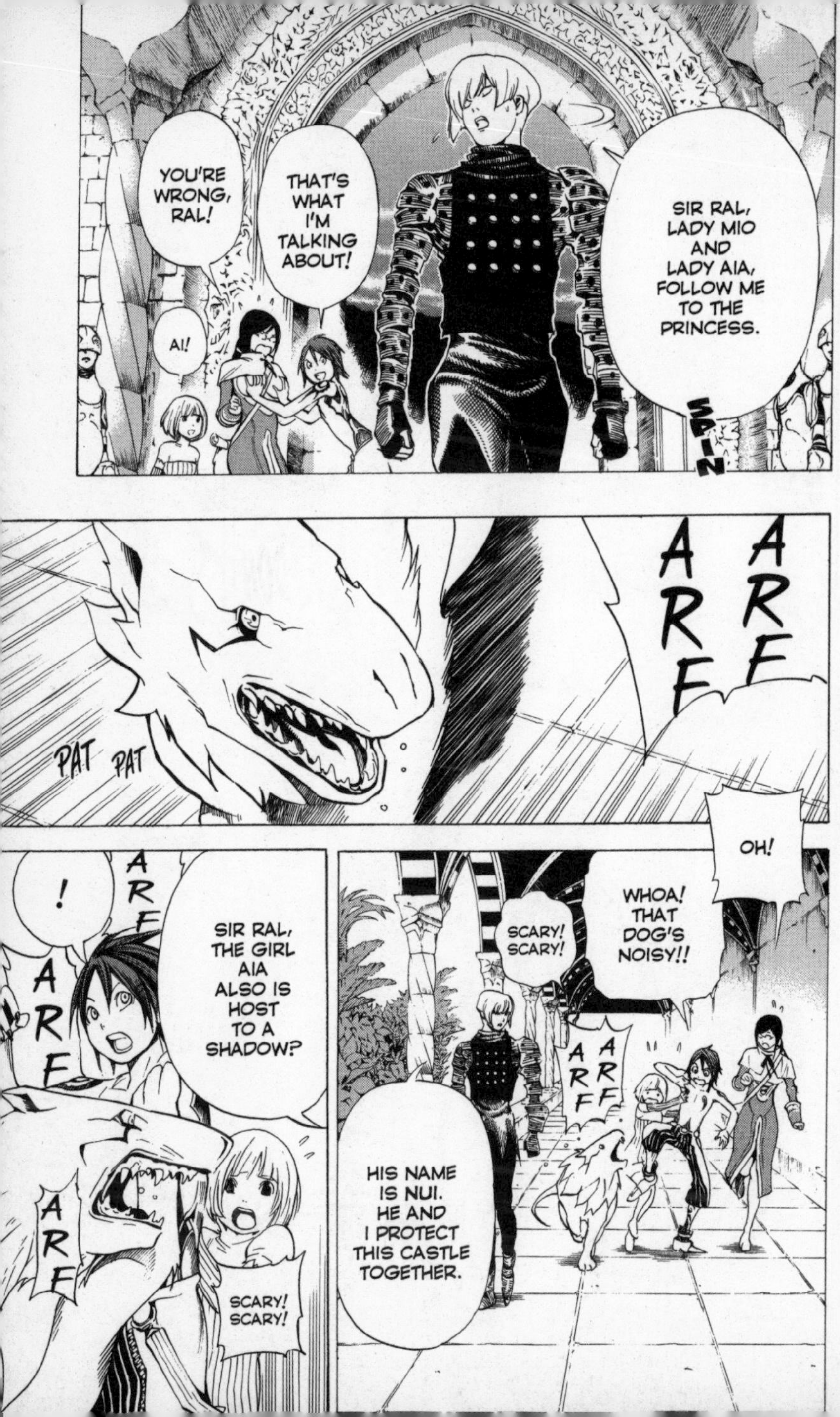
SIR RAL, LADY MIO AND LADY AIA, FOLLOW ME TO THE PRINCESS.
SPIN
THAT'S WHAT I'M TALKING ABOUT!
YOU'RE WRONG, RAL!
AI!
ARF ARF
PAT PAT
OH!
WHOA! THAT DOG'S NOISY!!
SCARY! SCARY!
ARF ARF
HIS NAME IS NUI. HE AND I PROTECT THIS CASTLE TOGETHER.
ARF
SIR RAL, THE GIRL AIA ALSO IS HOST TO A SHADOW?
!
ARF
ARF
SCARY! SCARY!

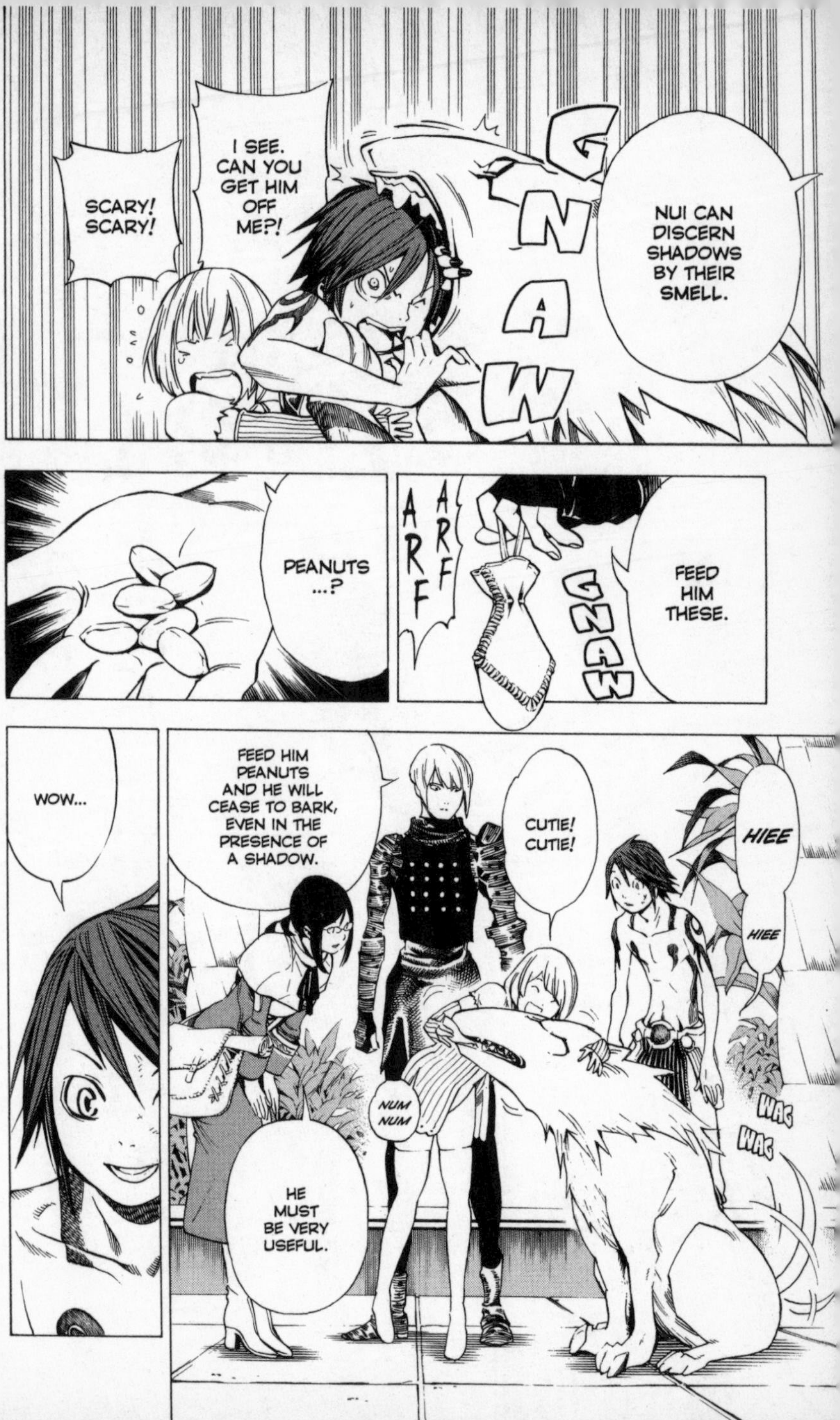
NUI CAN DISCERN SHADOWS BY THEIR SMELL.
GNAW
I SEE. CAN YOU GET HIM OFF ME?!
SCARY! SCARY!
FEED HIM THESE.
GNAW
ARF ARF
PEANUTS ...?
HIEE
HIEE
CUTIE! CUTIE!
WAG
WAG
FEED HIM PEANUTS AND HE WILL CEASE TO BARK, EVEN IN THE PRESENCE OF A SHADOW.
NUM NUM
HE MUST BE VERY USEFUL.
WOW...

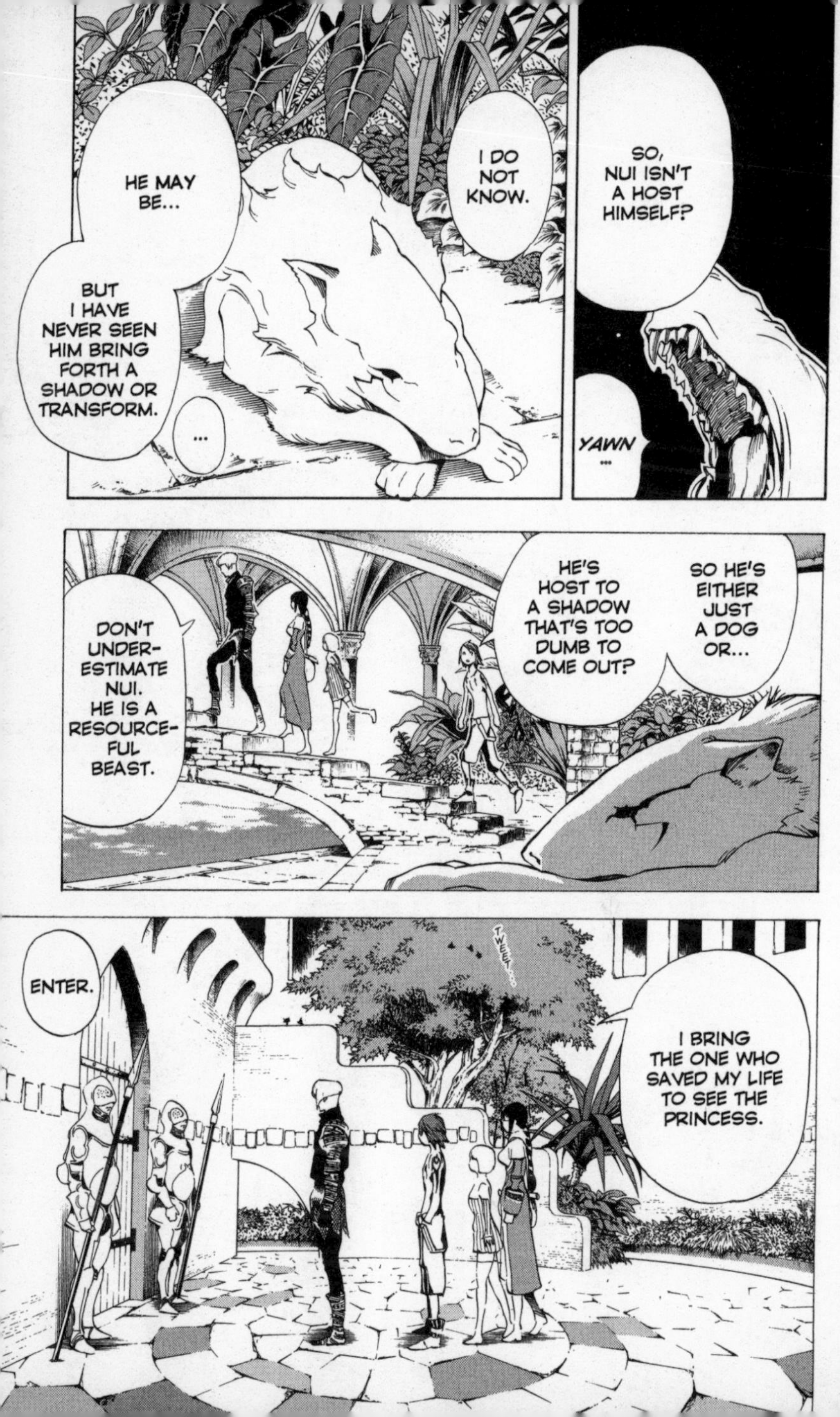
SO, NUI ISN'T A HOST HIMSELF?
YAWN...
I DO NOT KNOW.
HE MAY BE...
BUT I HAVE NEVER SEEN HIM BRING FORTH A SHADOW OR TRANSFORM.
...
SO HE'S EITHER JUST A DOG OR...
HE'S HOST TO A SHADOW THAT'S TOO DUMB TO COME OUT?
DON'T UNDER-ESTIMATE NUI. HE IS A RESOURCE-FUL BEAST.
TWEET...
I BRING THE ONE WHO SAVED MY LIFE TO SEE THE PRINCESS.
ENTER.

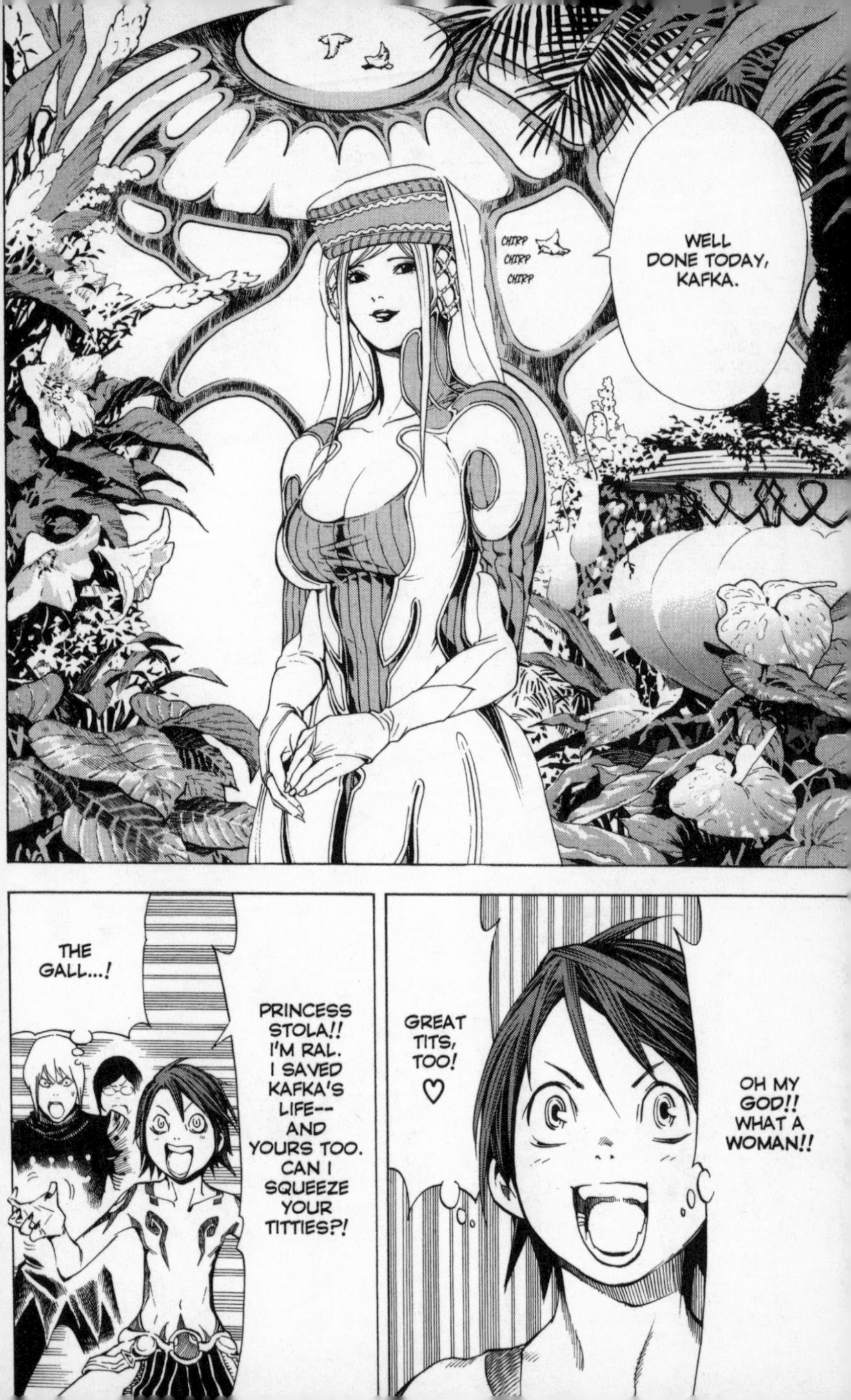
CHIRP CHIRP CHIRP
WELL DONE TODAY, KAFKA.
OH MY GOD!! WHAT A WOMAN!!
GREAT TITS, TOO! ♡
PRINCESS STOLA!! I'M RAL. I SAVED KAFKA'S LIFE-- AND YOURS TOO. CAN I SQUEEZE YOUR TITTIES?!
THE GALL...!

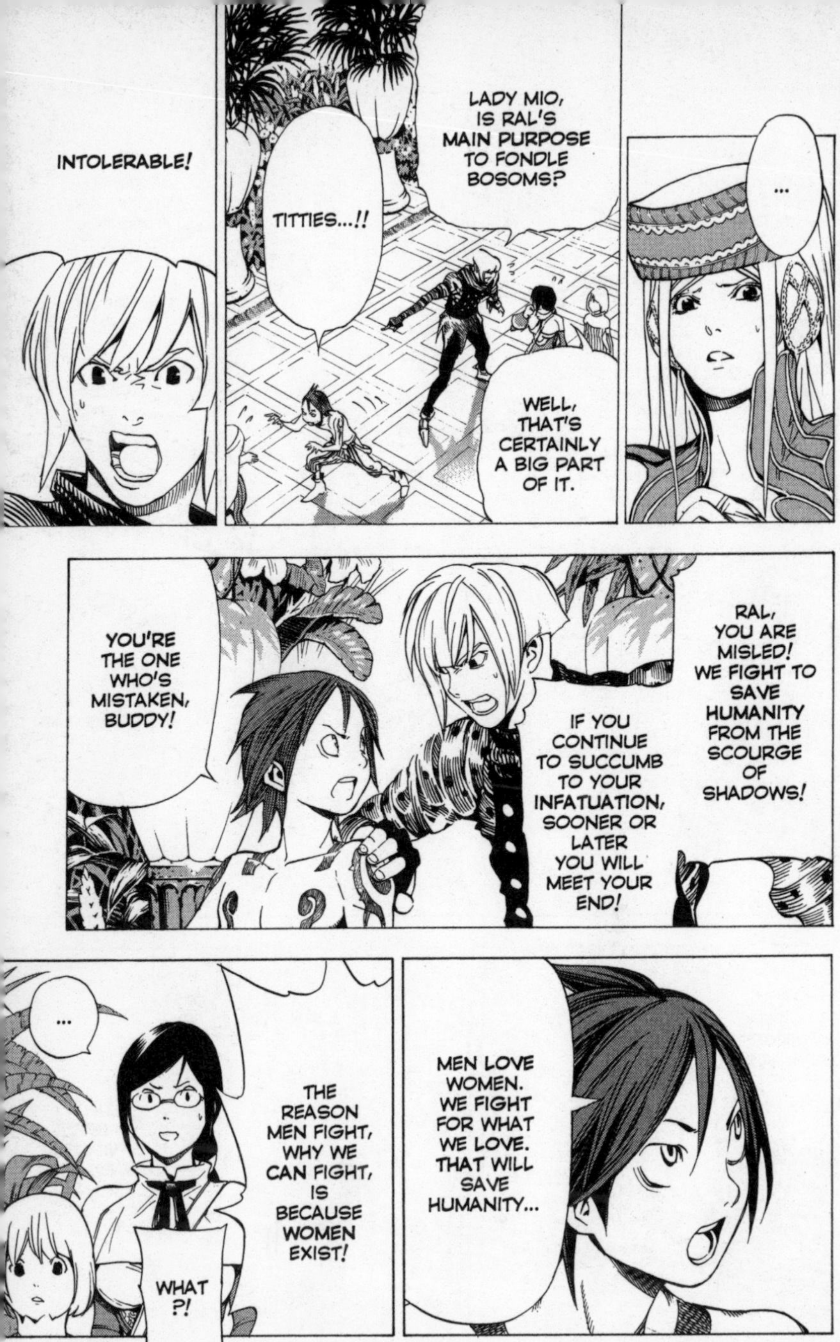
...
LADY MIO, IS RAL'S MAIN PURPOSE TO FONDLE BOSOMS?
WELL, THAT'S CERTAINLY A BIG PART OF IT.
TITTIES...!!
INTOLERABLE!
RAL, YOU ARE MISLED! WE FIGHT TO SAVE HUMANITY FROM THE SCOURGE OF SHADOWS!
IF YOU CONTINUE TO SUCCUMB TO YOUR INFATUATION, SOONER OR LATER YOU WILL MEET YOUR END!
YOU'RE THE ONE WHO'S MISTAKEN, BUDDY!
MEN LOVE WOMEN. WE FIGHT FOR WHAT WE LOVE. THAT WILL SAVE HUMANITY...
THE REASON MEN FIGHT, WHY WE CAN FIGHT, IS BECAUSE WOMEN EXIST!
...
WHAT?!

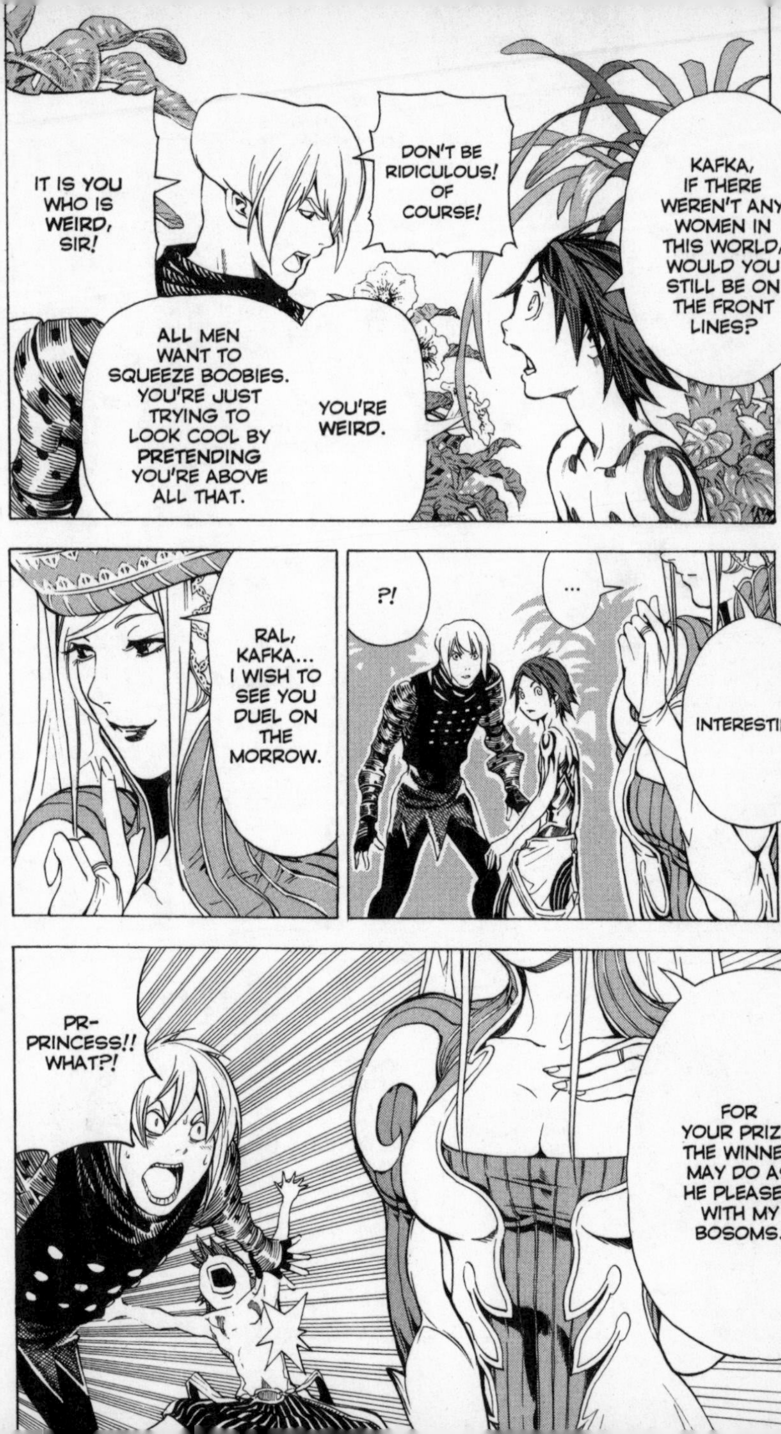
KAFKA, IF THERE WEREN'T ANY WOMEN IN THIS WORLD, WOULD YOU STILL BE ON THE FRONT LINES?
DON'T BE RIDICULOUS! OF COURSE!
YOU'RE WEIRD.
ALL MEN WANT TO SQUEEZE BOOBIES. YOU'RE JUST TRYING TO LOOK COOL BY PRETENDING YOU'RE ABOVE ALL THAT.
IT IS YOU WHO IS WEIRD, SIR!
INTERESTING.
...
?!
RAL, KAFKA... I WISH TO SEE YOU DUEL ON THE MORROW.
FOR YOUR PRIZE, THE WINNER MAY DO AS HE PLEASES WITH MY BOSOMS.
PR- PRINCESS!! WHAT?!

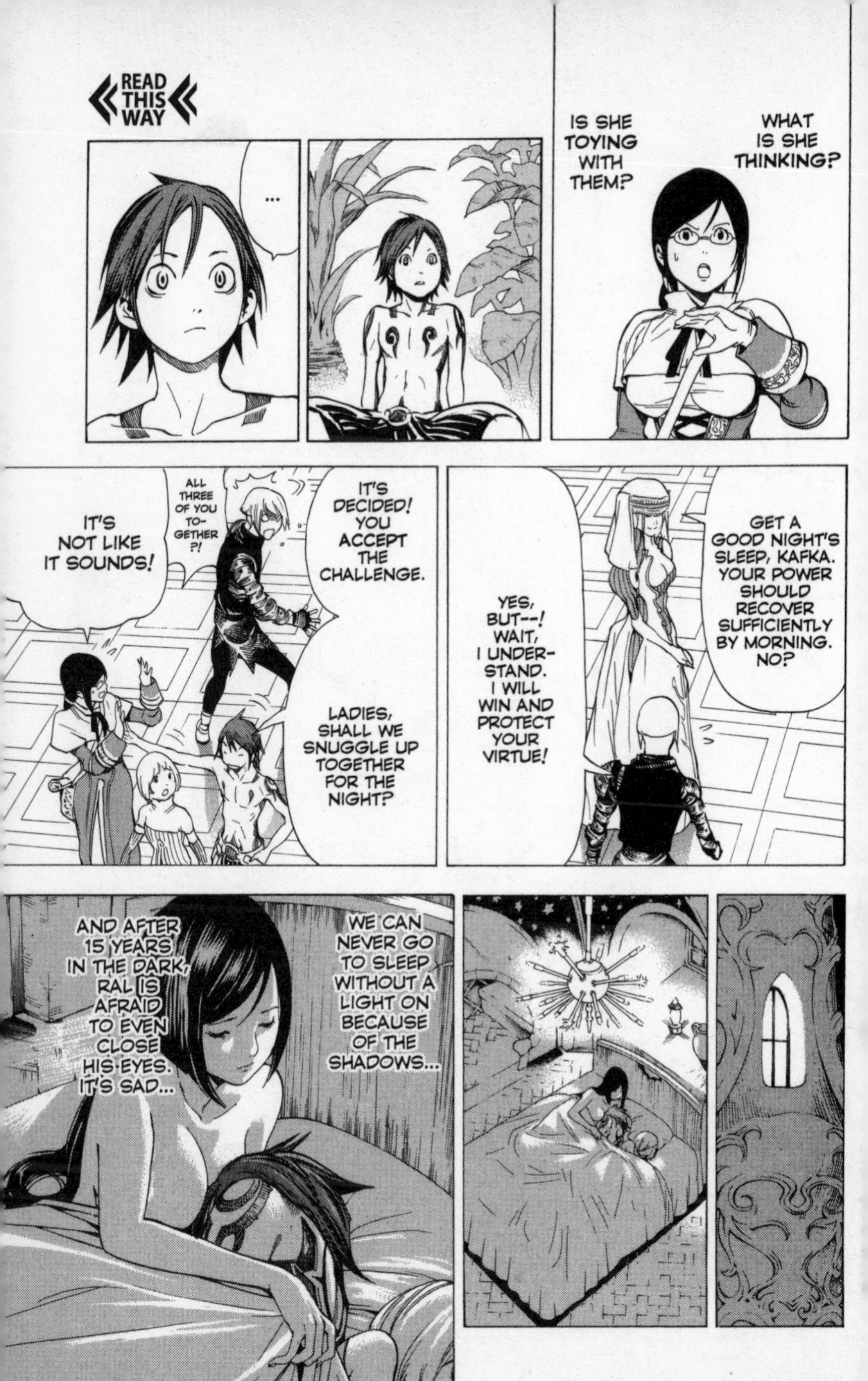
READ THIS WAY
WHAT IS SHE THINKING?
IS SHE TOYING WITH THEM?
...
GET A GOOD NIGHT'S SLEEP, KAFKA. YOUR POWER SHOULD RECOVER SUFFICIENTLY BY MORNING. NO?
YES, BUT--! WAIT, I UNDER-STAND. I WILL WIN AND PROTECT YOUR VIRTUE!
IT'S DECIDED! YOU ACCEPT THE CHALLENGE.
LADIES, SHALL WE SNUGGLE UP TOGETHER FOR THE NIGHT?
ALL THREE OF YOU TO-GETHER ?!
IT'S NOT LIKE IT SOUNDS!
WE CAN NEVER GO TO SLEEP WITHOUT A LIGHT ON BECAUSE OF THE SHADOWS...
AND AFTER 15 YEARS IN THE DARK, RAL IS AFRAID TO EVEN CLOSE HIS EYES. IT'S SAD...

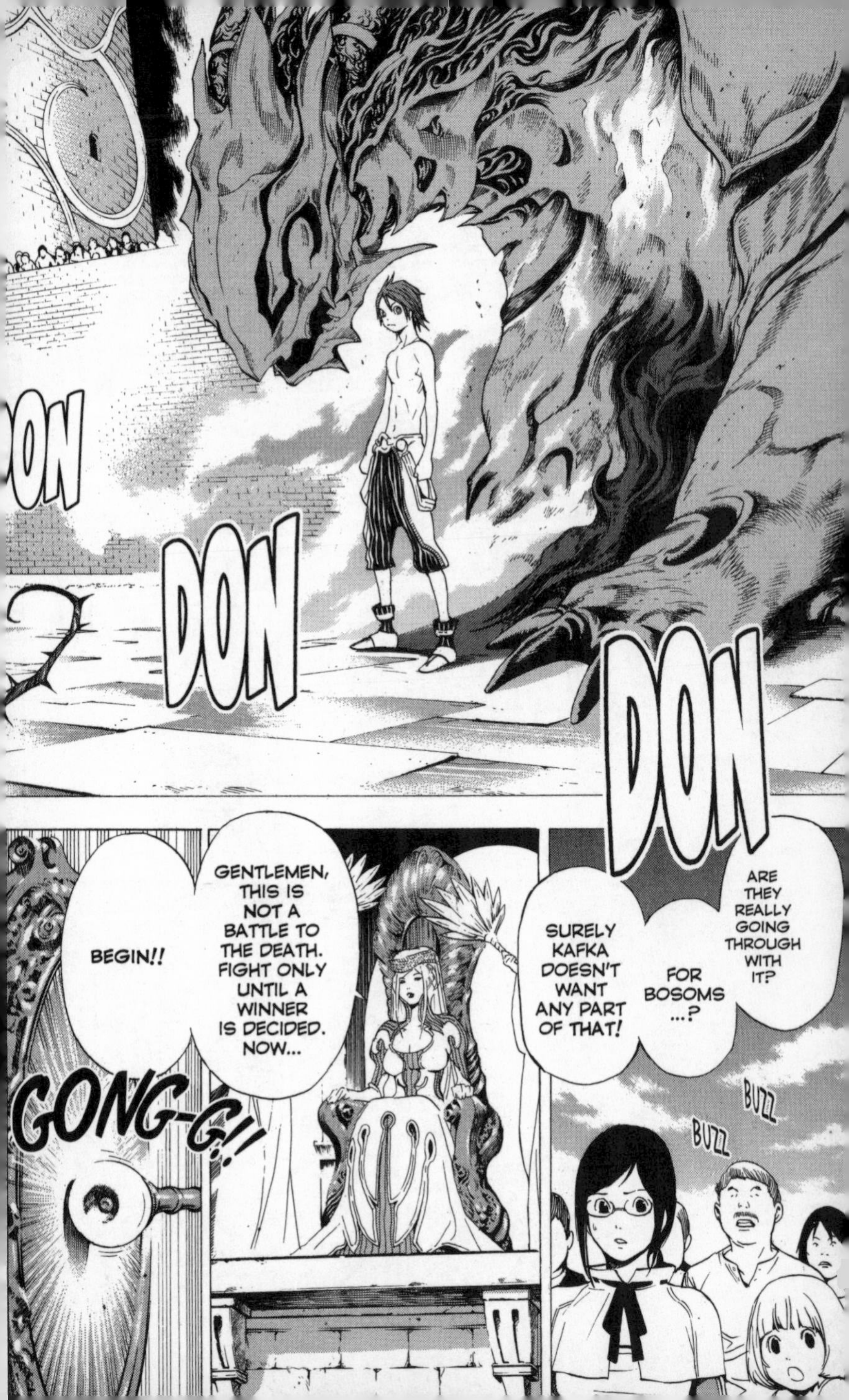
DON
DON
DON
ARE THEY REALLY GOING THROUGH WITH IT?
FOR BOSOMS ...?
SURELY KAFKA DOESN'T WANT ANY PART OF THAT!
BUZZ
BUZZ
GENTLEMEN, THIS IS NOT A BATTLE TO THE DEATH. FIGHT ONLY UNTIL A WINNER IS DECIDED. NOW...
BEGIN!!
GONG-G!!

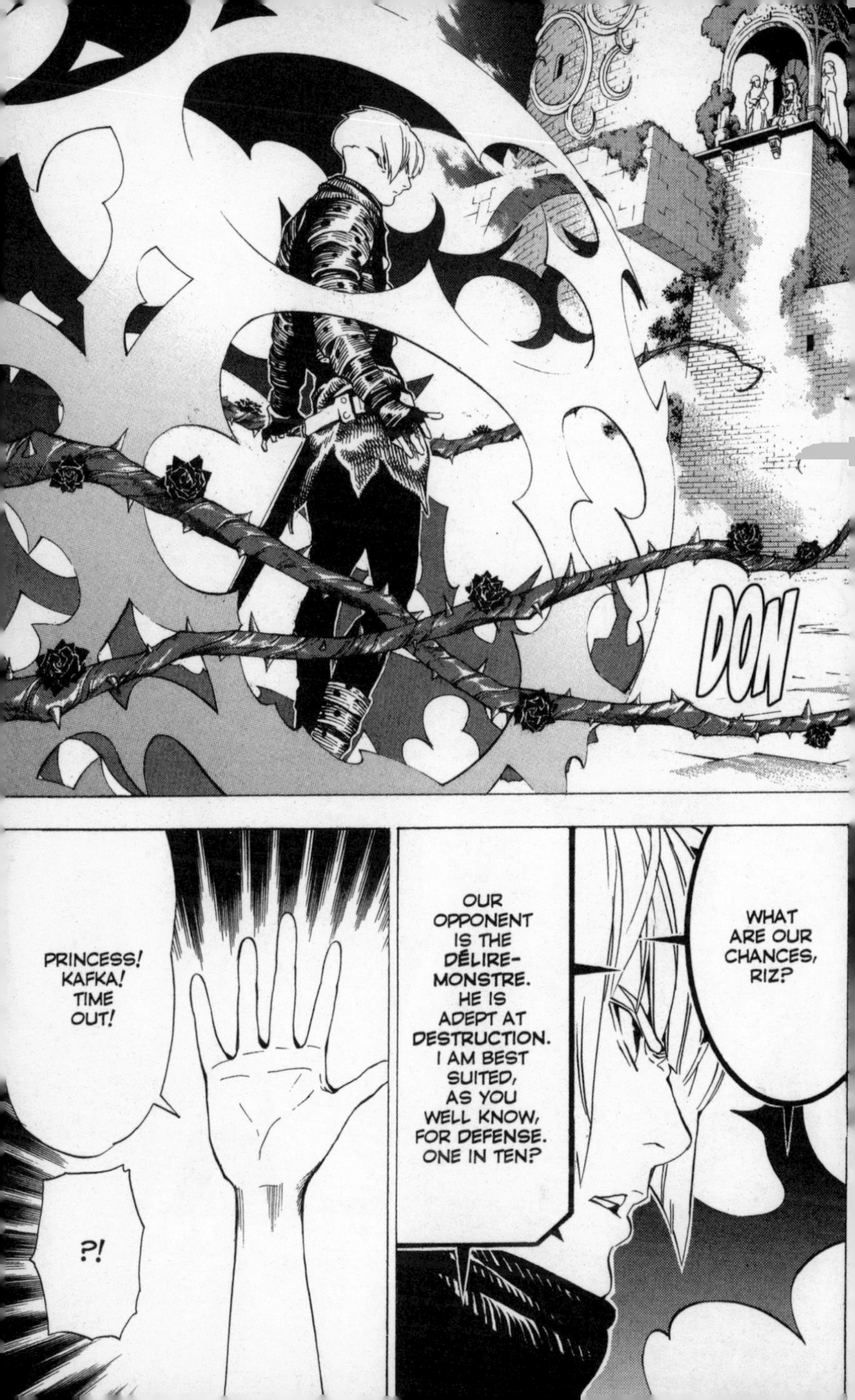
DON
WHAT ARE OUR CHANCES, RIZ?
OUR OPPONENT IS THE DÉLIRE-MONSTRE. HE IS ADEPT AT DESTRUCTION. I AM BEST SUITED, AS YOU WELL KNOW, FOR DEFENSE. ONE IN TEN?
PRINCESS! KAFKA! TIME OUT!
?!

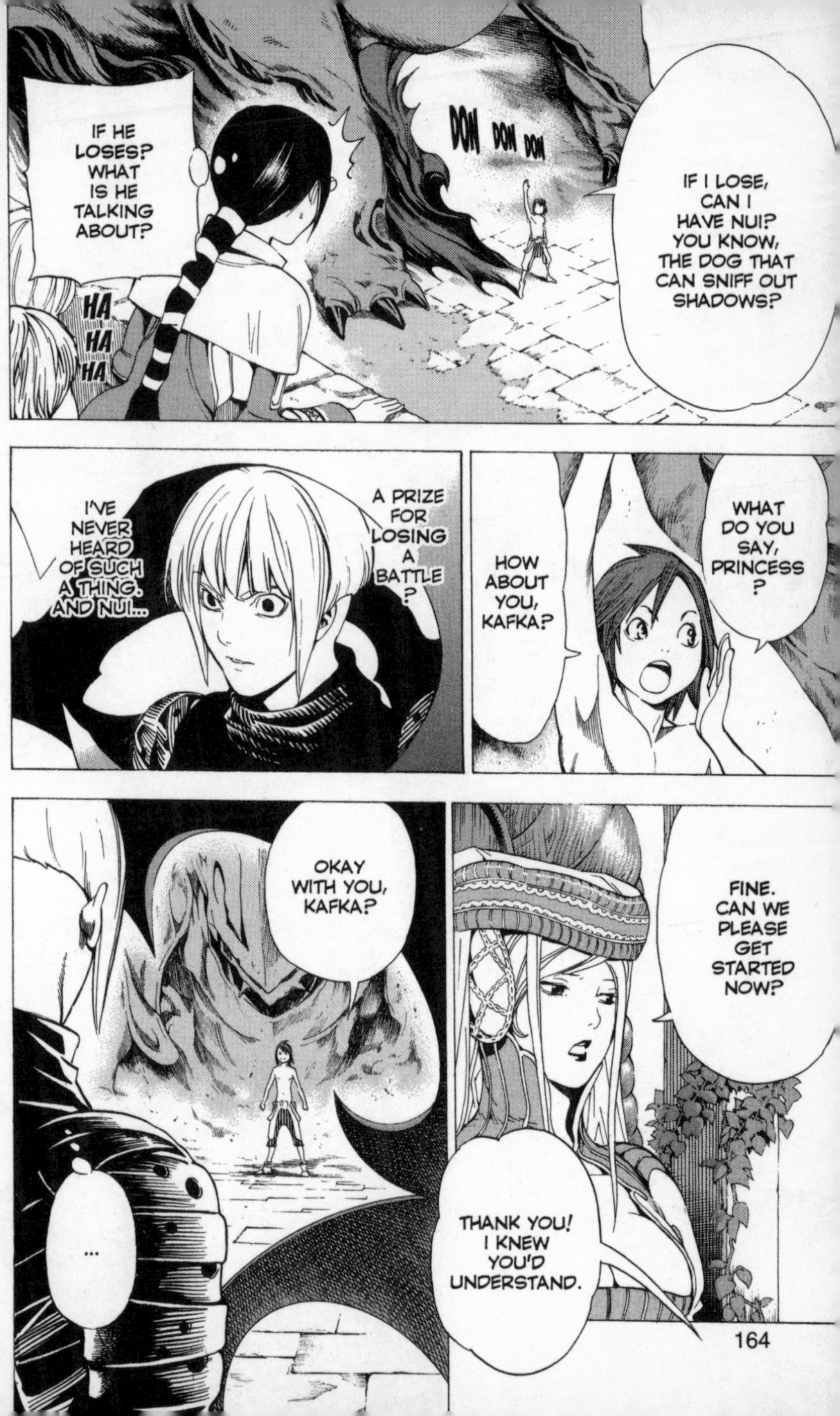
IF I LOSE, CAN I HAVE NUI? YOU KNOW, THE DOG THAT CAN SNIFF OUT SHADOWS?
DOM DOM DOM
IF HE LOSES? WHAT IS HE TALKING ABOUT?
HA HA HA
WHAT DO YOU SAY, PRINCESS?
HOW ABOUT YOU, KAFKA?
A PRIZE FOR LOSING A BATTLE?
I'VE NEVER HEARD OF SUCH A THING. AND NUI...
FINE. CAN WE PLEASE GET STARTED NOW?
THANK YOU! I KNEW YOU'D UNDERSTAND.
OKAY WITH YOU, KAFKA?
...

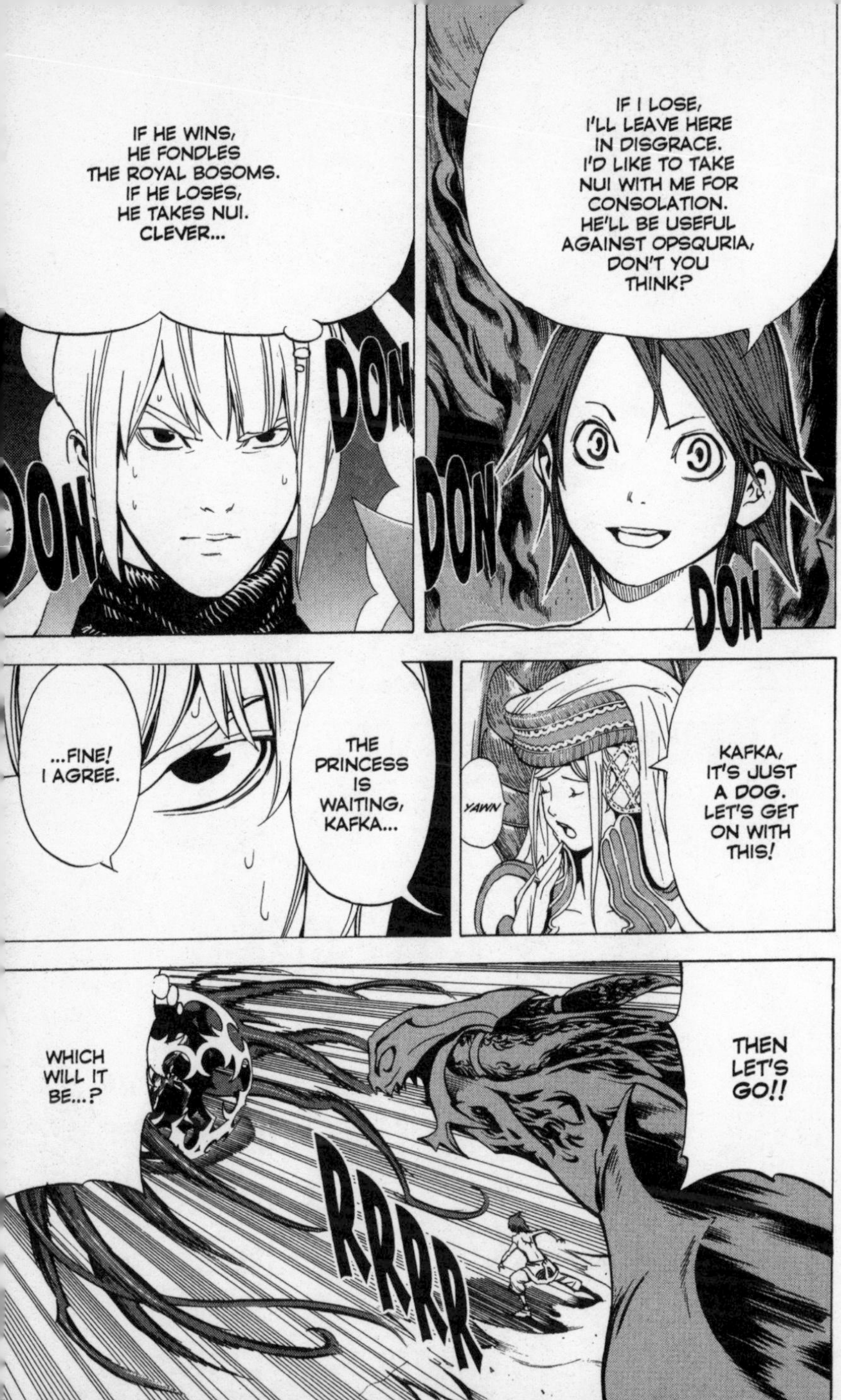
IF I LOSE, I'LL LEAVE HERE IN DISGRACE. I'D LIKE TO TAKE NUI WITH ME FOR CONSOLATION. HE'LL BE USEFUL AGAINST OPSQURIA, DON'T YOU THINK?
DON
DON
IF HE WINS, HE FONDLES THE ROYAL BOSOMS. IF HE LOSES, HE TAKES NUI. CLEVER...
DON
DON
KAFKA, IT'S JUST A DOG. LET'S GET ON WITH THIS!
YAWN
THE PRINCESS IS WAITING, KAFKA...
...FINE! I AGREE.
THEN LET'S GO!!
RRRR
WHICH WILL IT BE...?

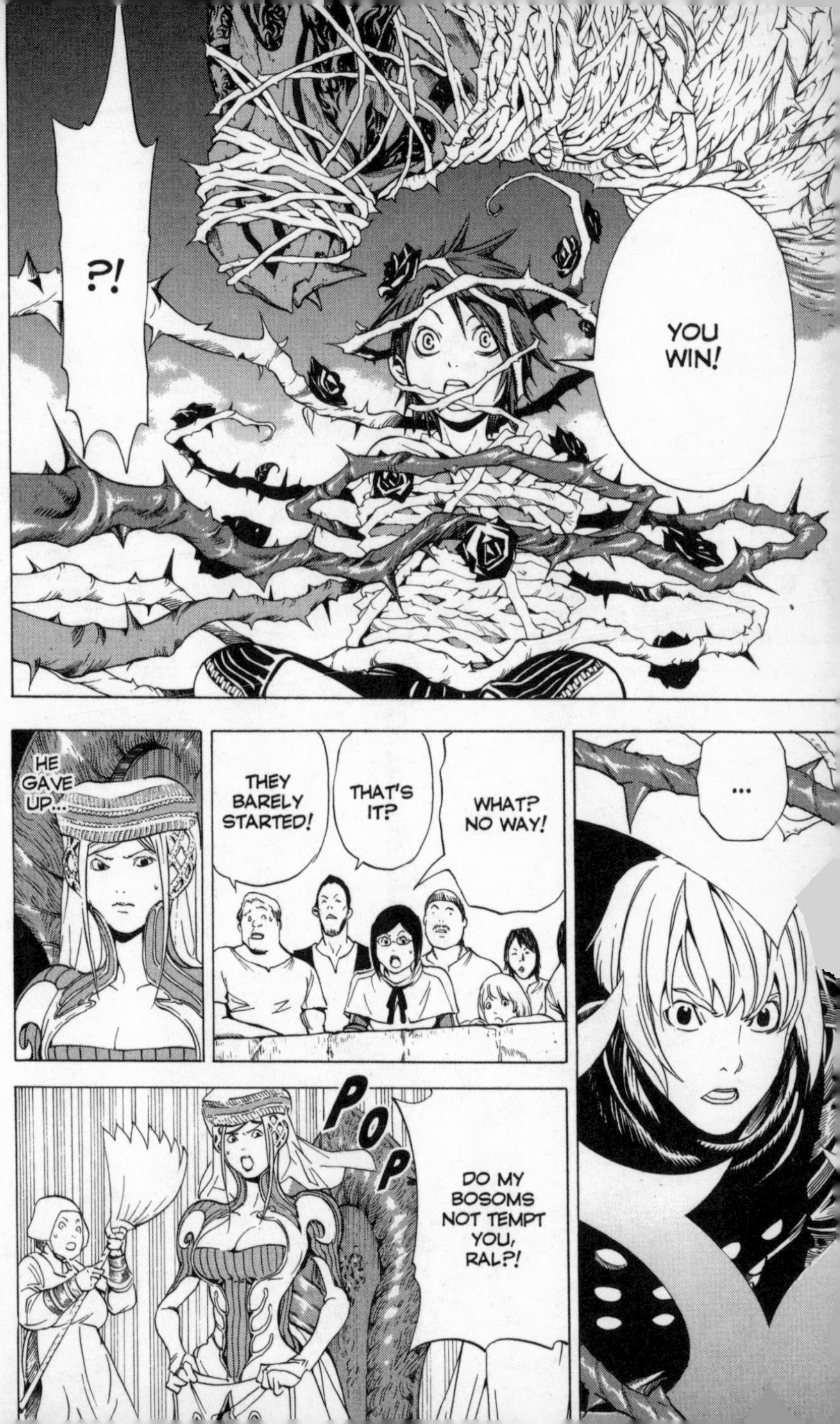
YOU WIN!
?!
...
WHAT? NO WAY!
THAT'S IT?
THEY BARELY STARTED!
HE GAVE UP...
POP
DO MY BOSOMS NOT TEMPT YOU, RAL?!

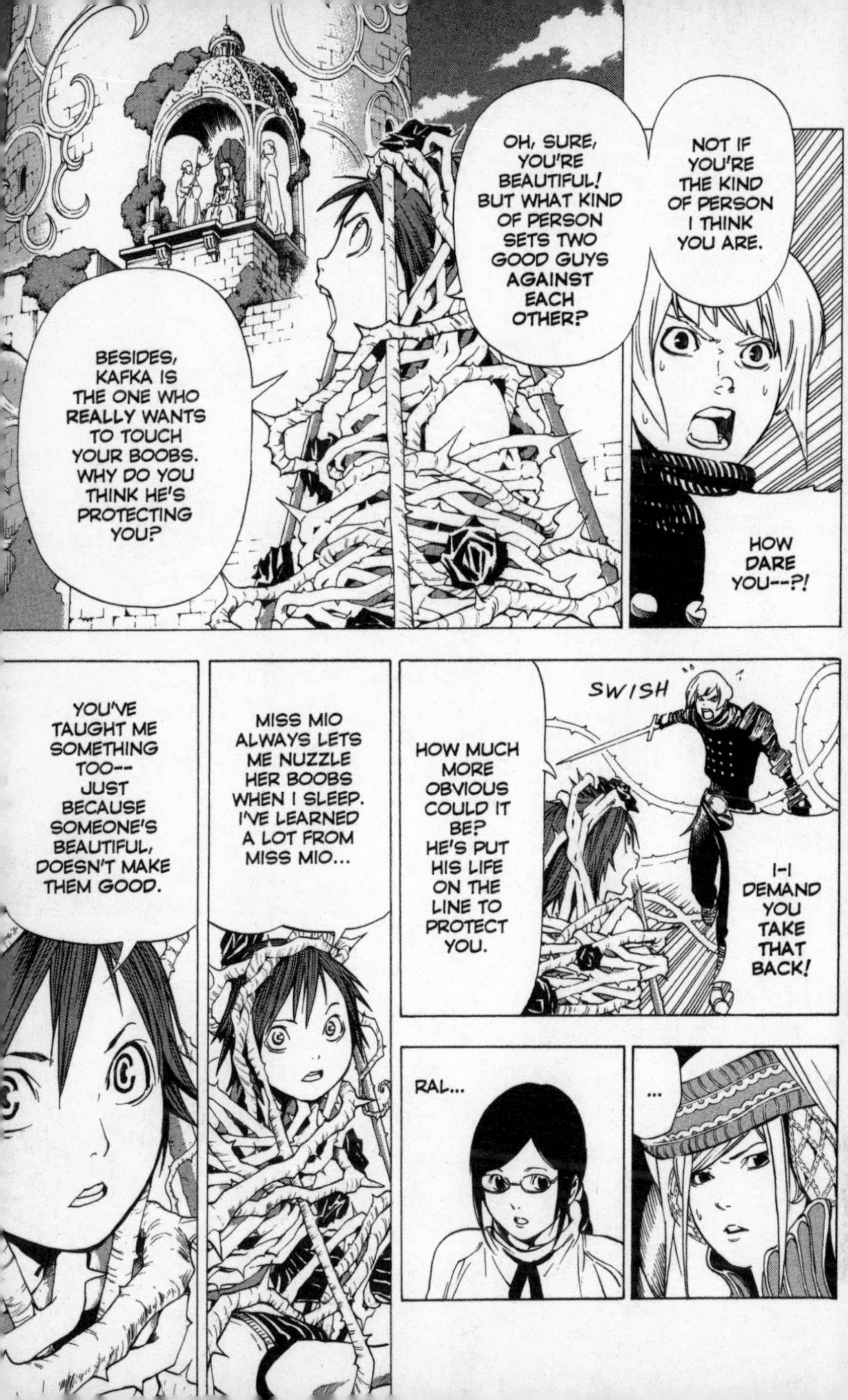
NOT IF YOU'RE THE KIND OF PERSON I THINK YOU ARE.
HOW DARE YOU--?!
OH, SURE, YOU'RE BEAUTIFUL! BUT WHAT KIND OF PERSON SETS TWO GOOD GUYS AGAINST EACH OTHER?
BESIDES, KAFKA IS THE ONE WHO REALLY WANTS TO TOUCH YOUR BOOBS. WHY DO YOU THINK HE'S PROTECTING YOU?
SWISH
I-I DEMAND YOU TAKE THAT BACK!
HOW MUCH MORE OBVIOUS COULD IT BE? HE'S PUT HIS LIFE ON THE LINE TO PROTECT YOU.
...
RAL...
MISS MIO ALWAYS LETS ME NUZZLE HER BOOBS WHEN I SLEEP. I'VE LEARNED A LOT FROM MISS MIO...
YOU'VE TAUGHT ME SOMETHING TOO-- JUST BECAUSE SOMEONE'S BEAUTIFUL, DOESN'T MAKE THEM GOOD.

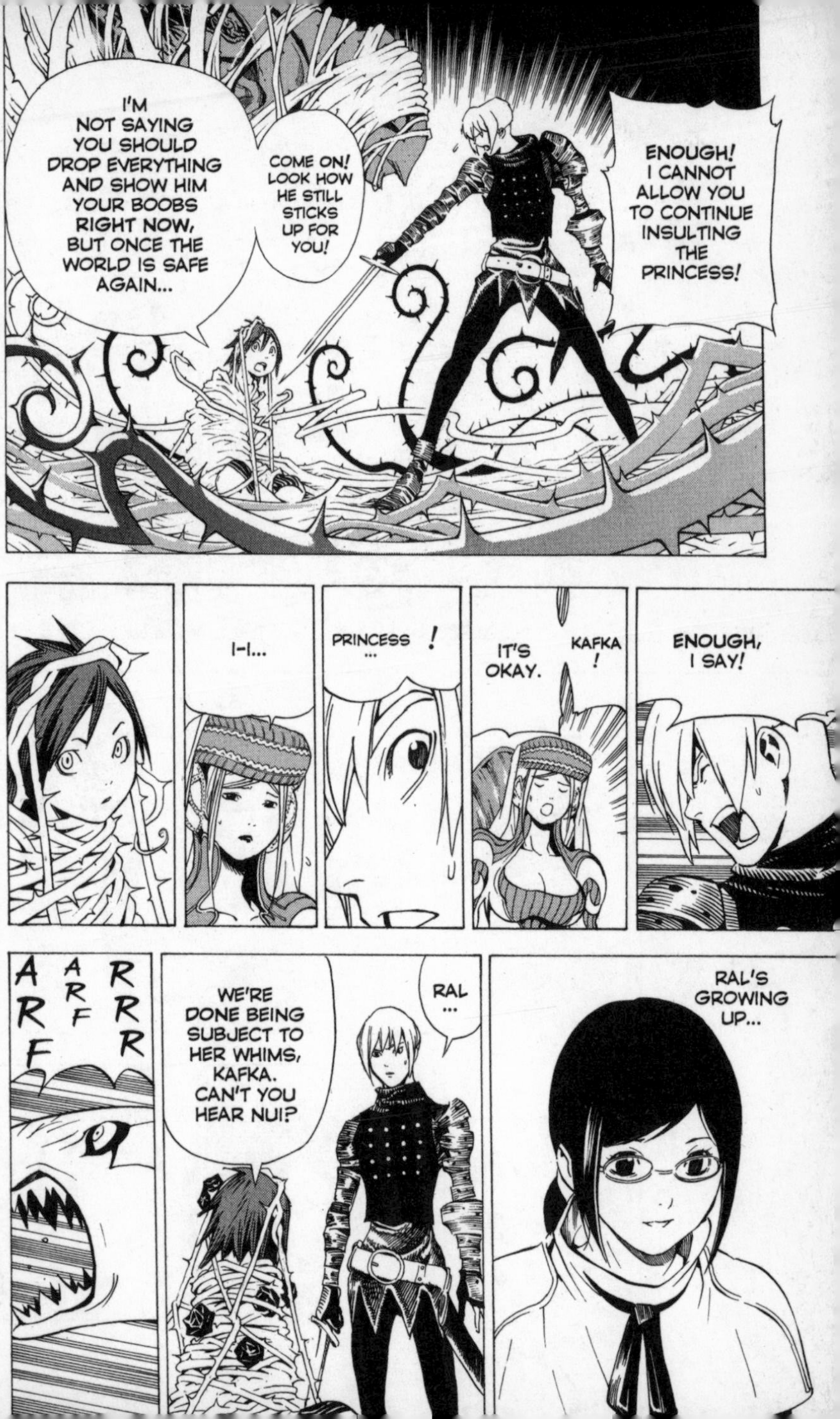
ENOUGH! I CANNOT ALLOW YOU TO CONTINUE INSULTING THE PRINCESS!
COME ON! LOOK HOW HE STILL STICKS UP FOR YOU!
I'M NOT SAYING YOU SHOULD DROP EVERYTHING AND SHOW HIM YOUR BOOBS RIGHT NOW, BUT ONCE THE WORLD IS SAFE AGAIN...
ENOUGH, I SAY!
KAFKA!
IT'S OKAY.
PRINCESS...!
I-I...
RAL'S GROWING UP...
RAL...
WE'RE DONE BEING SUBJECT TO HER WHIMS, KAFKA. CAN'T YOU HEAR NUI?
RRRR
ARF
ARF

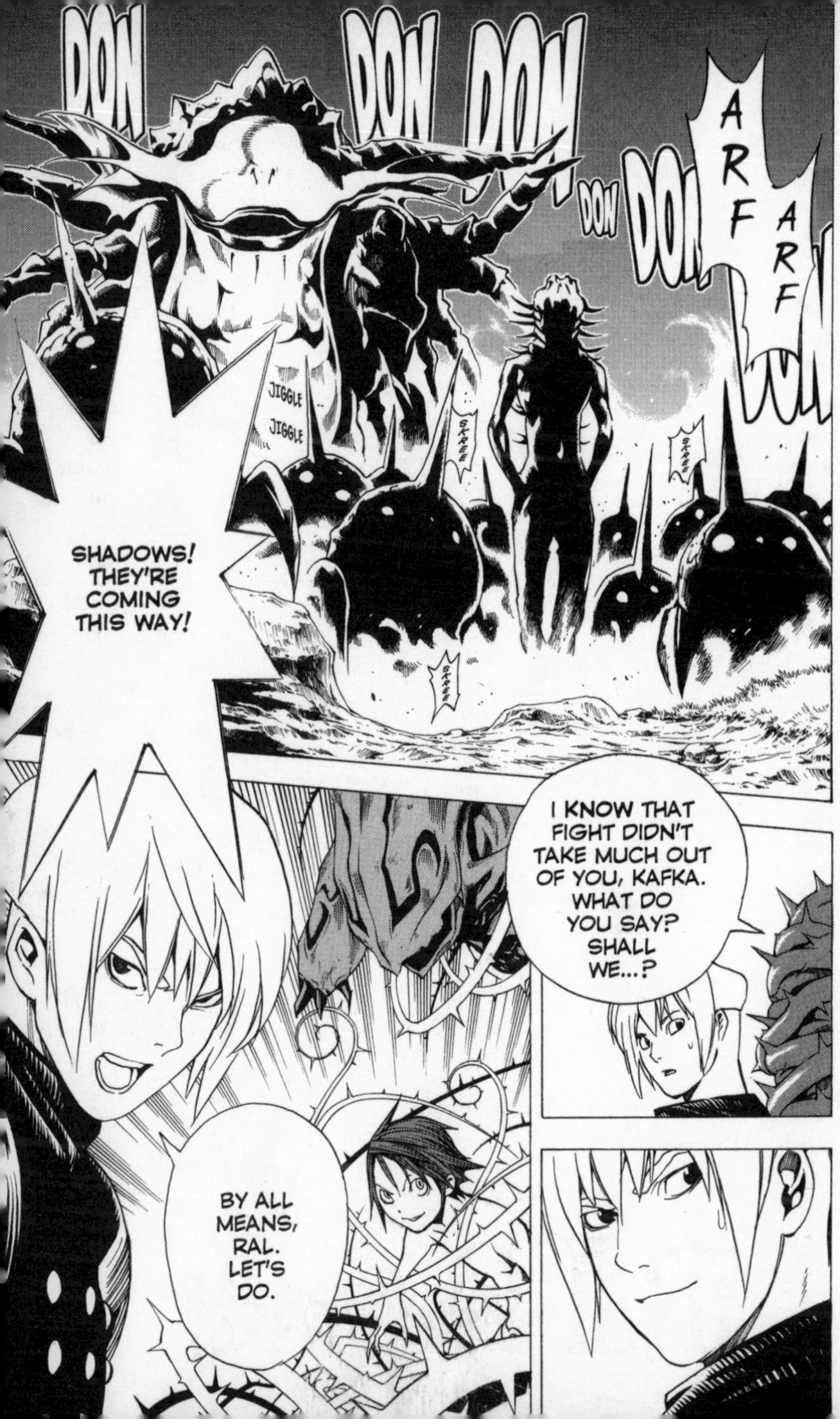

ARF ARF
ARF
DON DON DON DON DON DON DON
JIGGLE JIGGLE
SKREE
SKREE
SKREE
SHADOWS! THEY'RE COMING THIS WAY!
I KNOW THAT FIGHT DIDN'T TAKE MUCH OUT OF YOU, KAFKA. WHAT DO YOU SAY? SHALL WE...?
BY ALL MEANS, RAL. LET'S DO.

RalΩGrach

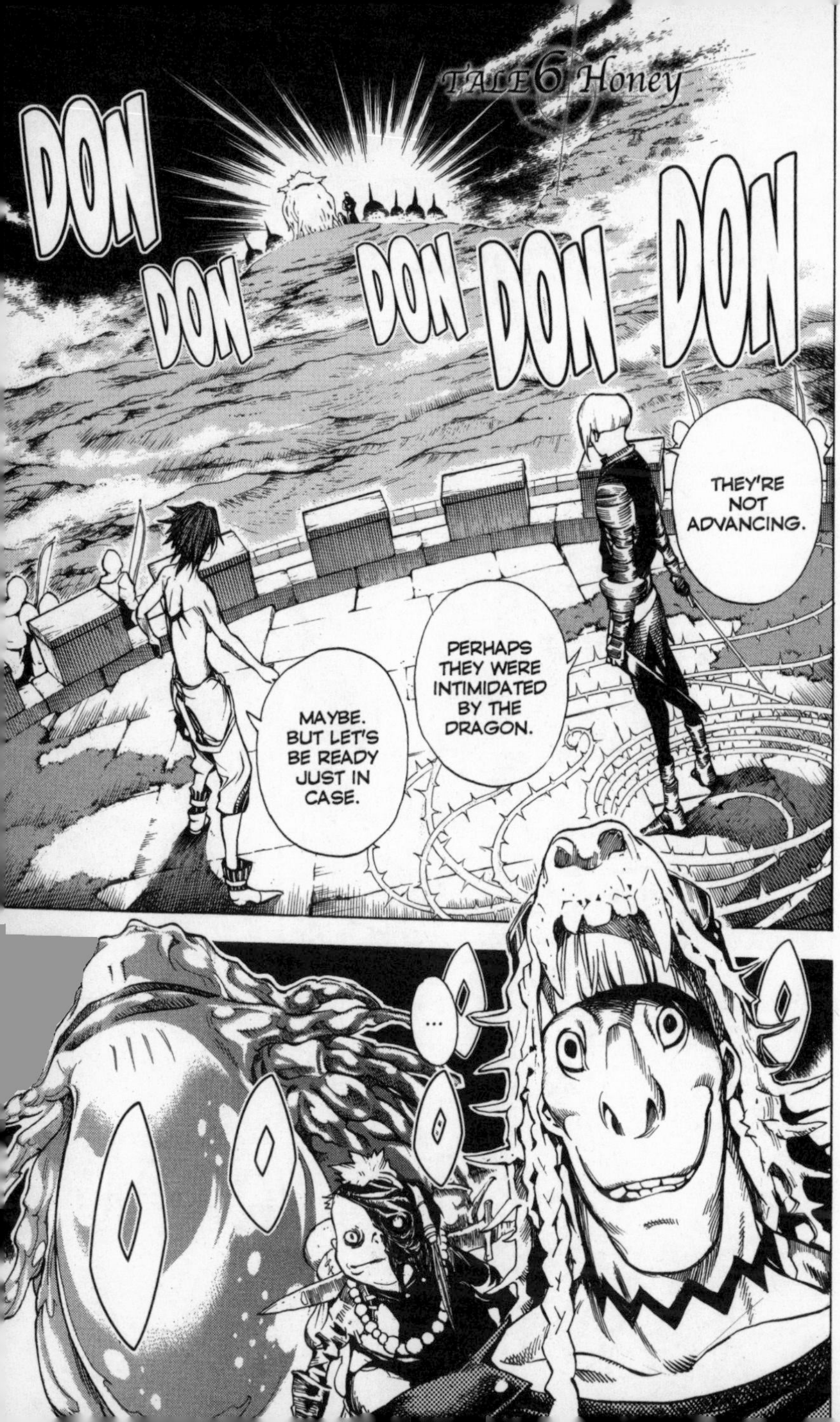
TALE 6 Honey
DON
DON
DON
DON
DON
THEY'RE NOT ADVANCING.
PERHAPS THEY WERE INTIMIDATED BY THE DRAGON.
MAYBE. BUT LET'S BE READY JUST IN CASE.
...

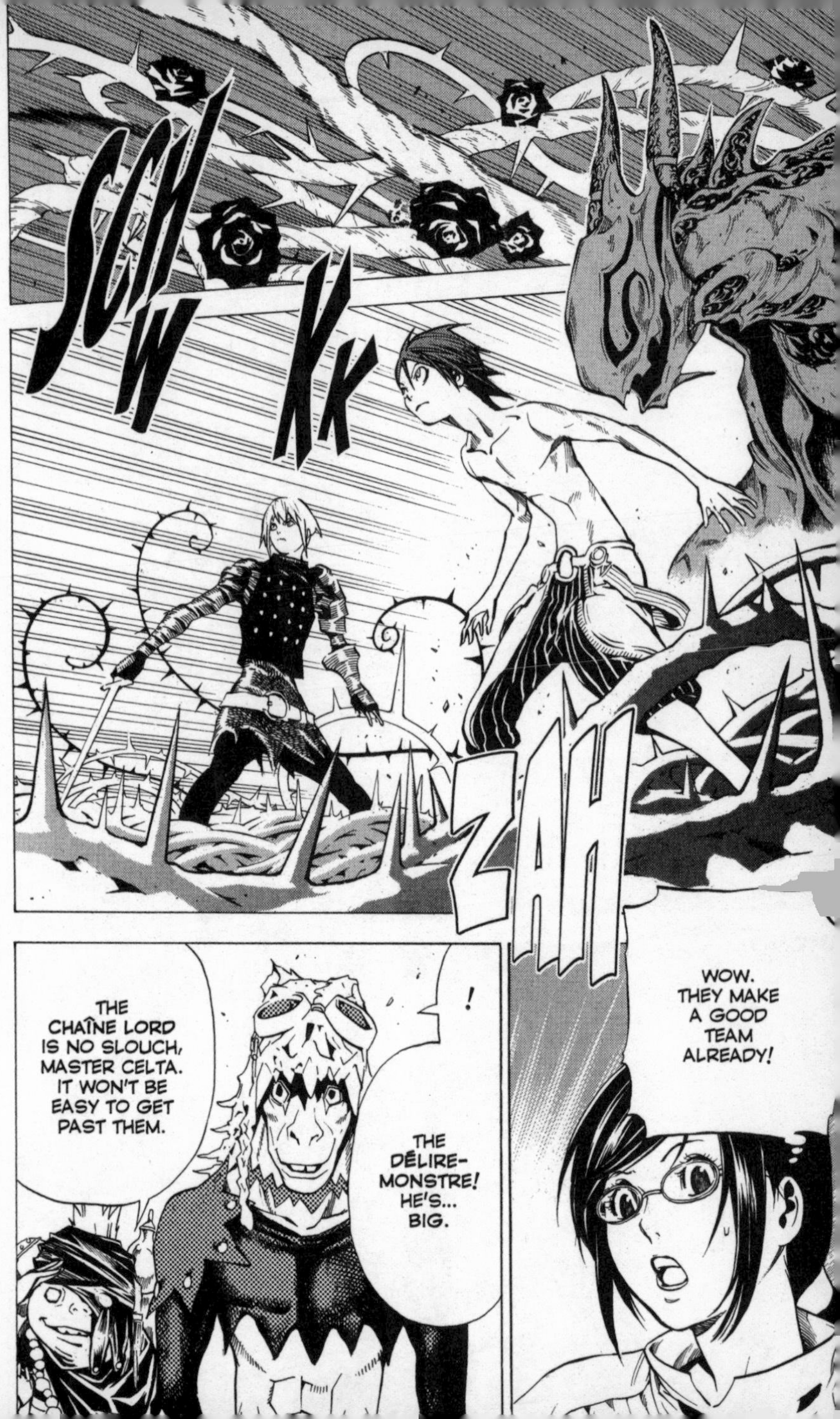
SCHWKK
ZAH
WOW. THEY MAKE A GOOD TEAM ALREADY!
!
THE DÉLIRE-MONSTRE! HE'S... BIG.
THE CHAÎNE LORD IS NO SLOUCH, MASTER CELTA. IT WON'T BE EASY TO GET PAST THEM.

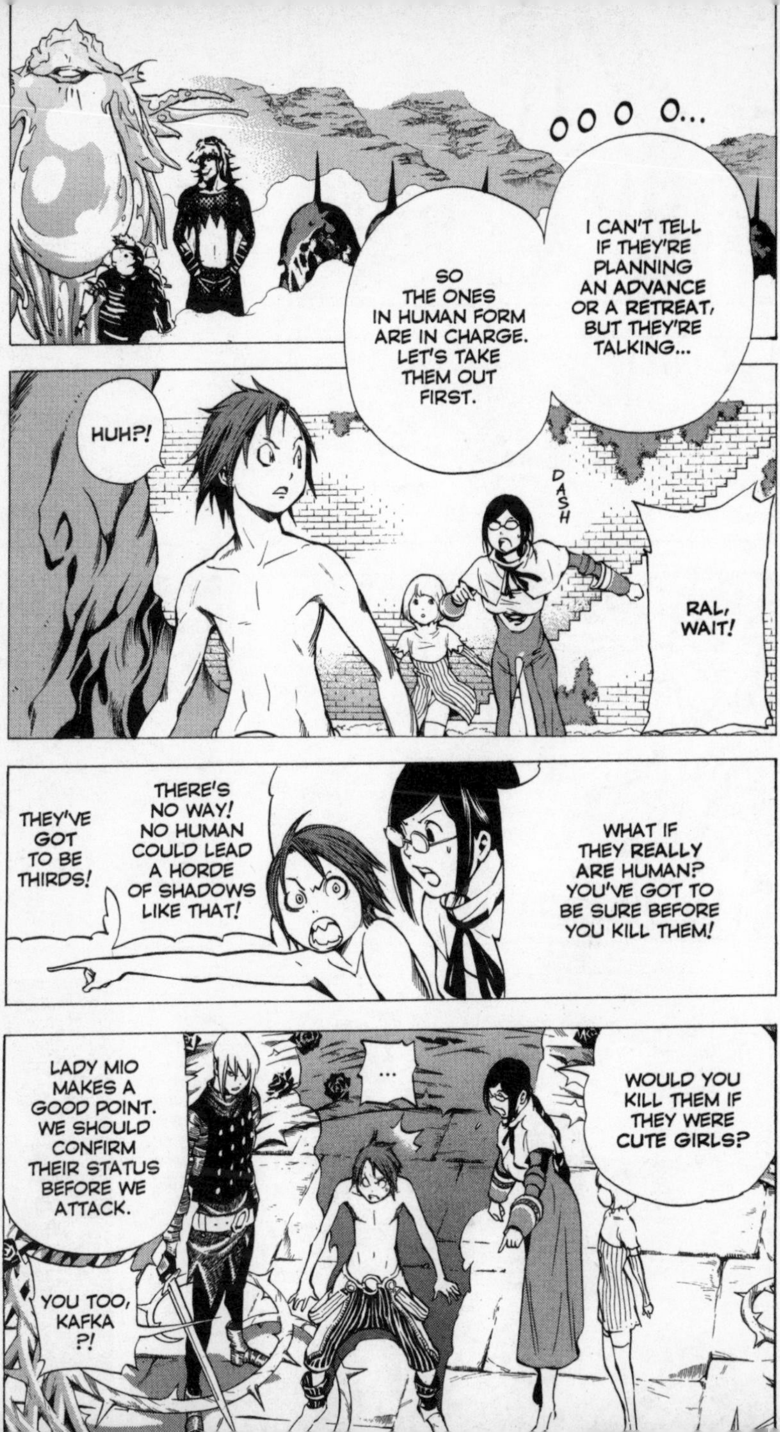
OO O O...
I CAN'T TELL IF THEY'RE PLANNING AN ADVANCE OR A RETREAT, BUT THEY'RE TALKING...
SO THE ONES IN HUMAN FORM ARE IN CHARGE. LET'S TAKE THEM OUT FIRST.
RAL, WAIT!
DASH
HUH?!
WHAT IF THEY REALLY ARE HUMAN? YOU'VE GOT TO BE SURE BEFORE YOU KILL THEM!
THERE'S NO WAY! NO HUMAN COULD LEAD A HORDE OF SHADOWS LIKE THAT!
THEY'VE GOT TO BE THIRDS!
WOULD YOU KILL THEM IF THEY WERE CUTE GIRLS?
...
LADY MIO MAKES A GOOD POINT. WE SHOULD CONFIRM THEIR STATUS BEFORE WE ATTACK.
YOU TOO, KAFKA?!

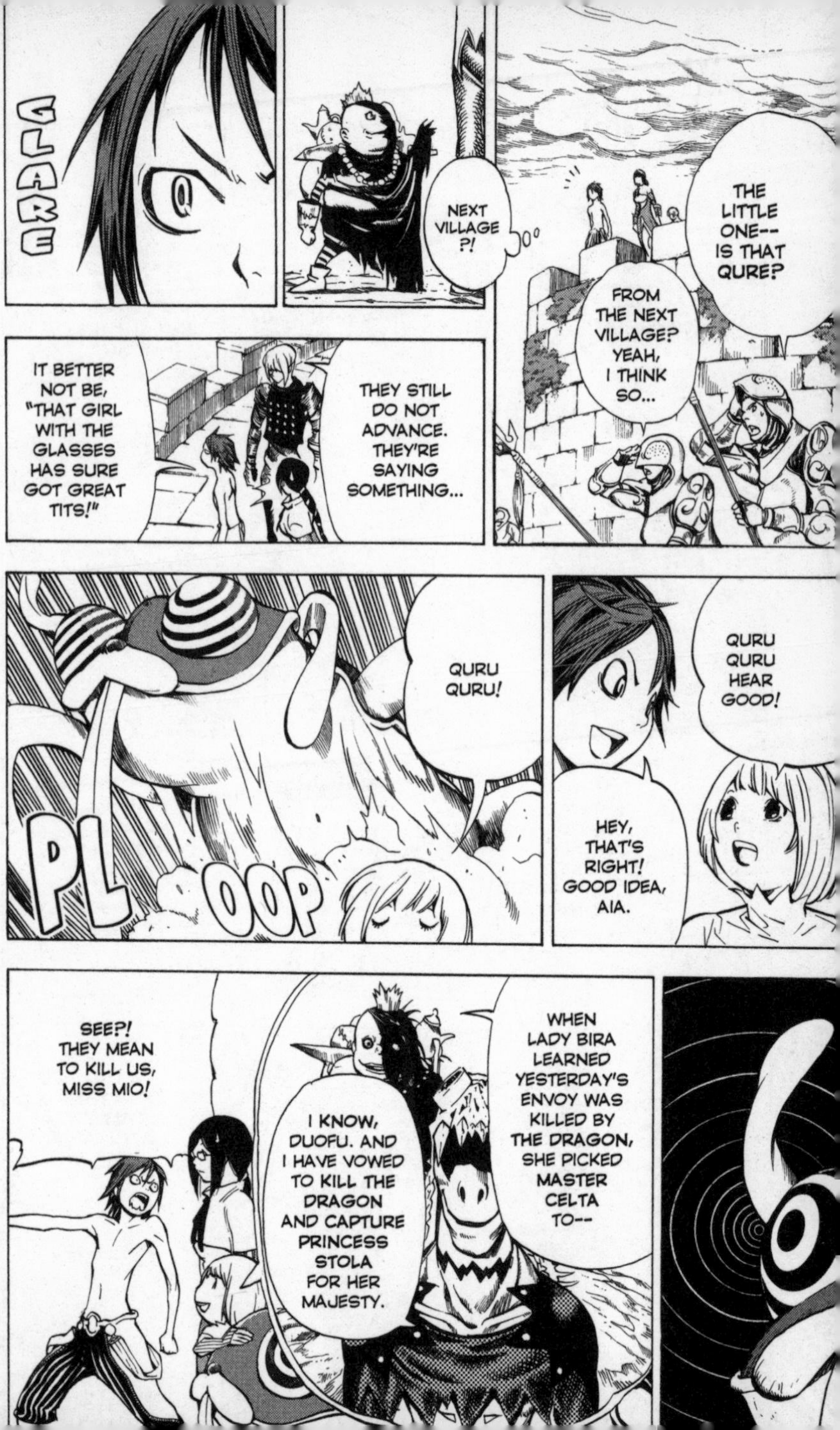
THE LITTLE ONE-- IS THAT QURE?
FROM THE NEXT VILLAGE? YEAH, I THINK SO...
NEXT VILLAGE?!
GLARE
THEY STILL DO NOT ADVANCE. THEY'RE SAYING SOMETHING...
IT BETTER NOT BE, "THAT GIRL WITH THE GLASSES HAS SURE GOT GREAT TITS!"
QURU QURU HEAR GOOD!
HEY, THAT'S RIGHT! GOOD IDEA, AIA.
QURU QURU!
PLOOP
WHEN LADY BIRA LEARNED YESTERDAY'S ENVOY WAS KILLED BY THE DRAGON, SHE PICKED MASTER CELTA TO--
I KNOW, DUOFU. AND I HAVE VOWED TO KILL THE DRAGON AND CAPTURE PRINCESS STOLA FOR HER MAJESTY.
SEE?! THEY MEAN TO KILL US, MISS MIO!

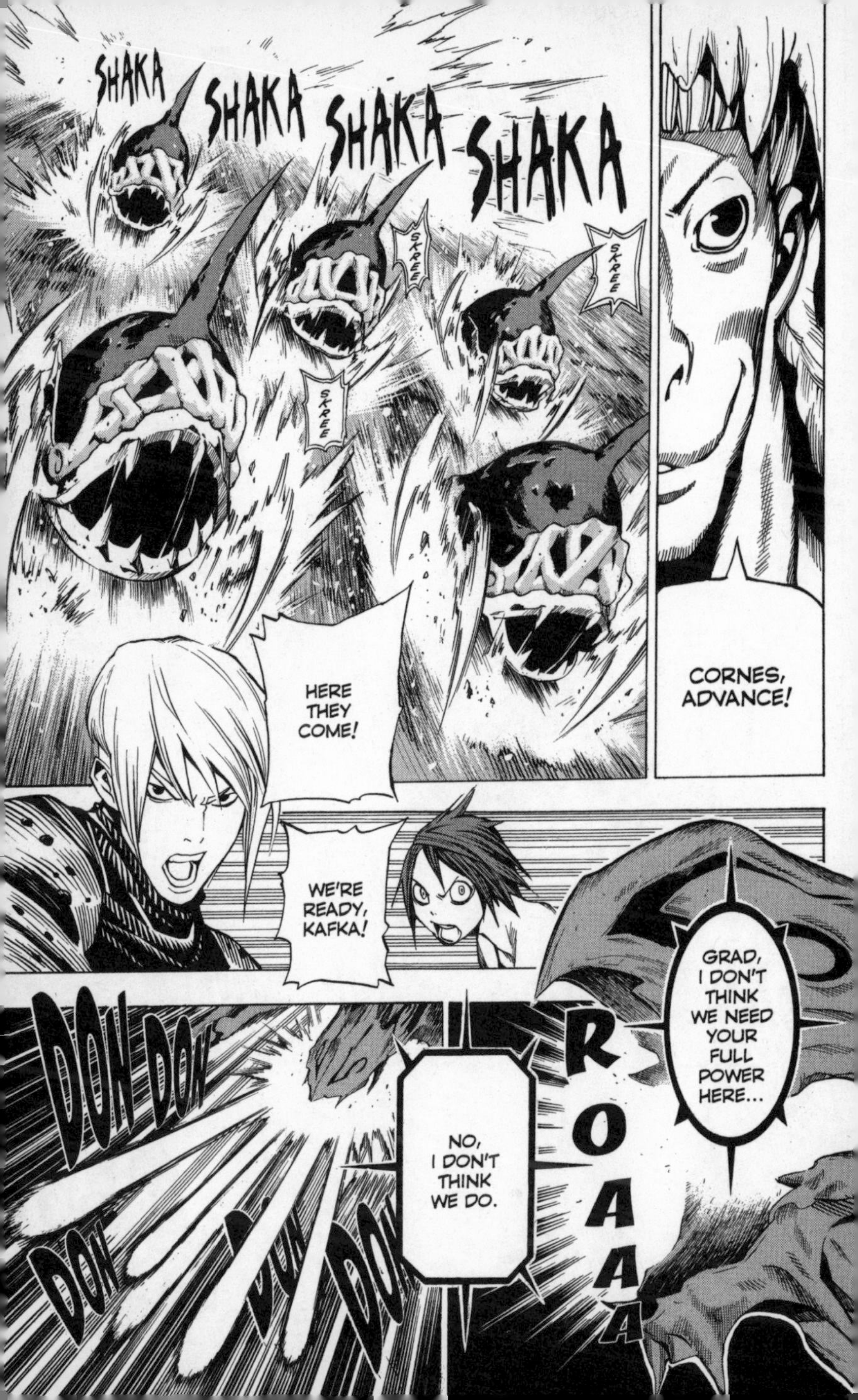
CORNES, ADVANCE!
SHAKA SHAKA SHAKA SHAKA
SKREE
SKREE
SKREE
HERE THEY COME!
WE'RE READY, KAFKA!
GRAD, I DON'T THINK WE NEED YOUR FULL POWER HERE...
ROAAAA
NO, I DON'T THINK WE DO.
DON DON
DON DON DON

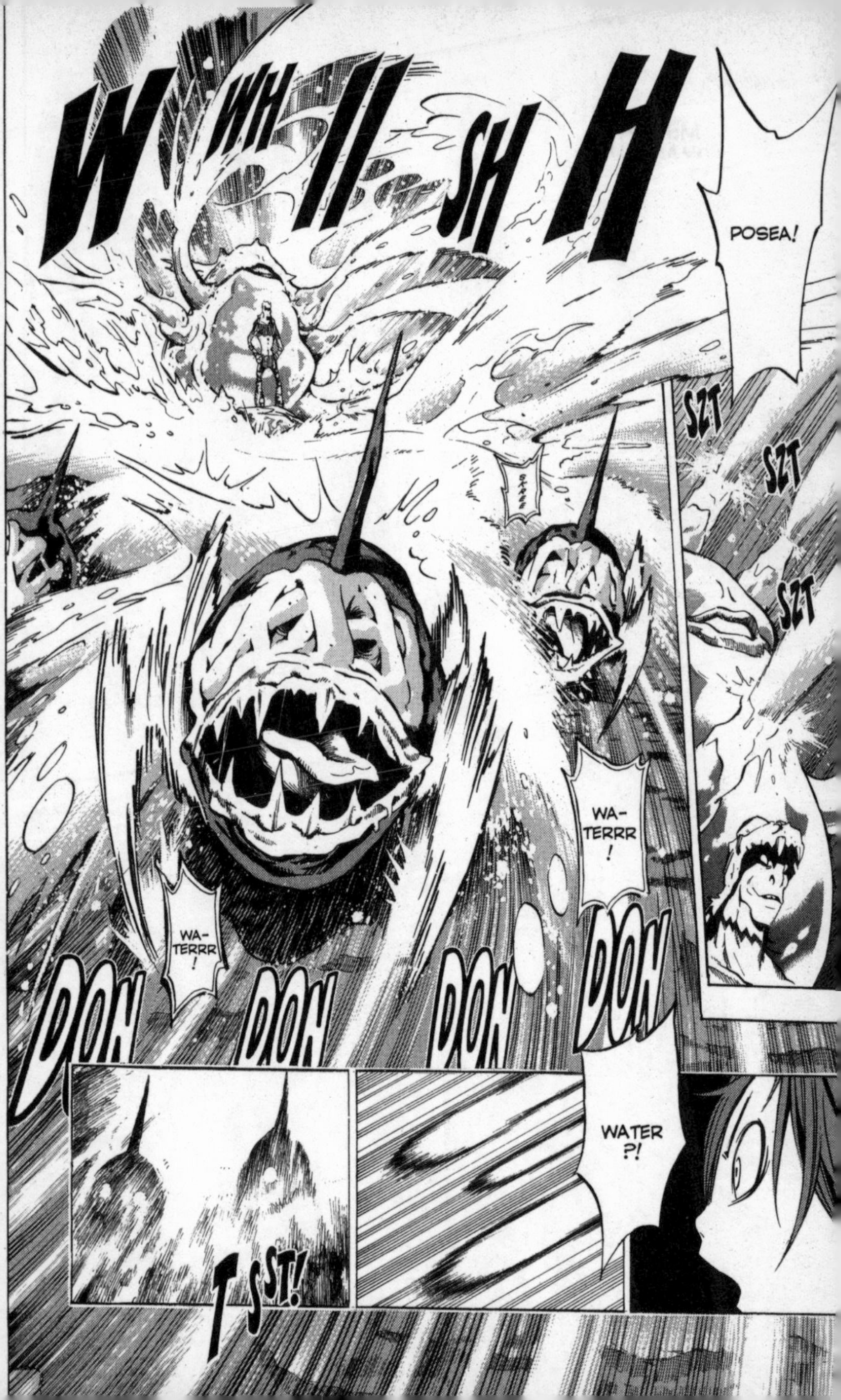
POSEA!
WWHIISHH
SZT
SZT
SZT
WA-TERRR!
WA-TERRR!
DOH DOH DOH DOH
WATER?!
TSST!

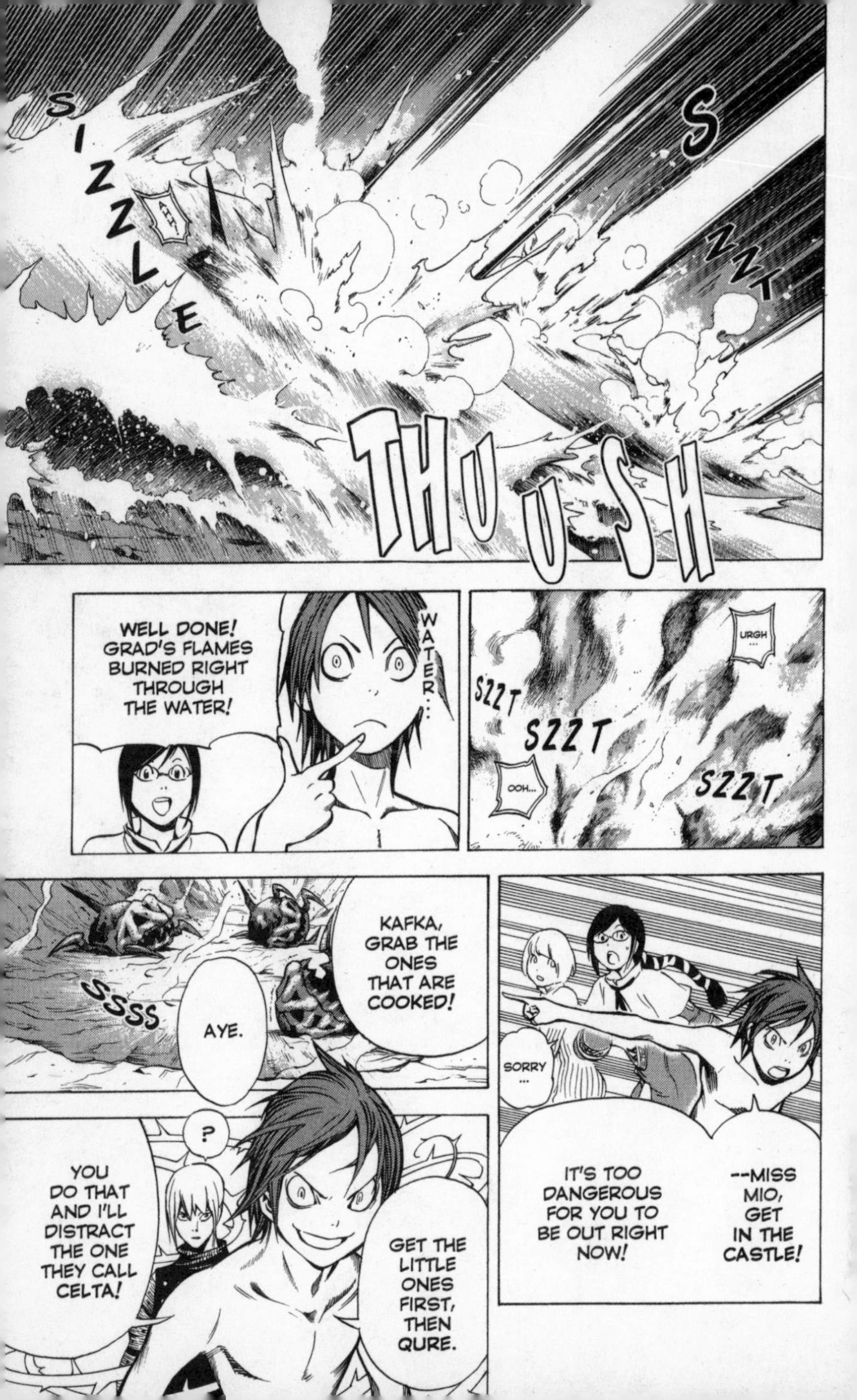
SZZT
SIZZLE
AHH!
THUUSH
URGH...
SZZT
SZZT
SZZT
OOH...
WATER...
WELL DONE! GRAD'S FLAMES BURNED RIGHT THROUGH THE WATER!
SORRY...
--MISS MIO, GET IN THE CASTLE!
IT'S TOO DANGEROUS FOR YOU TO BE OUT RIGHT NOW!
KAFKA, GRAB THE ONES THAT ARE COOKED!
AYE.
SSSS
GET THE LITTLE ONES FIRST, THEN QURE.
?
YOU DO THAT AND I'LL DISTRACT THE ONE THEY CALL CELTA!

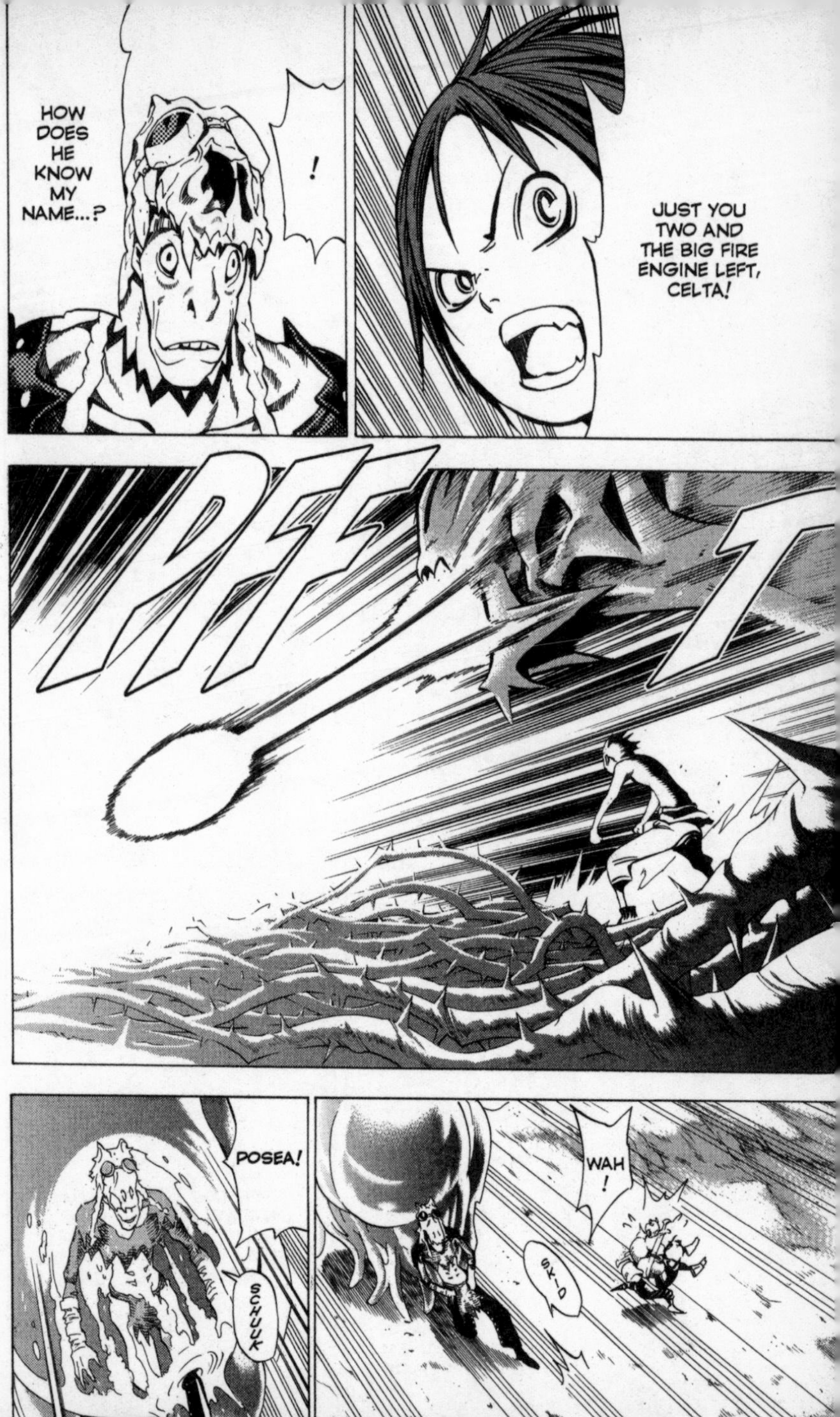
JUST YOU TWO AND THE BIG FIRE ENGINE LEFT, CELTA!
!
HOW DOES HE KNOW MY NAME...?
WAH!
SKID
POSEA!
SCHUUK

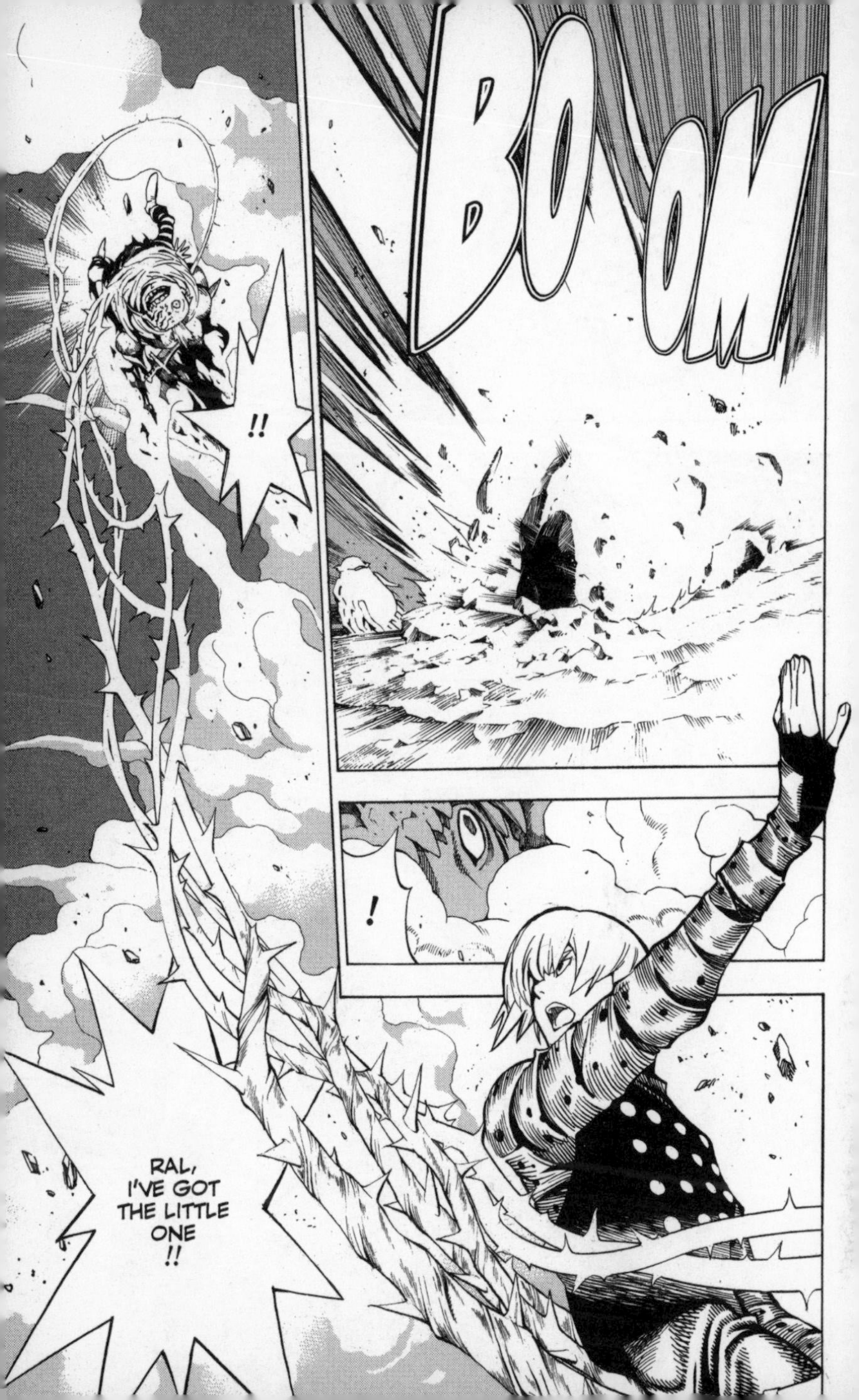
BOOM
!
!!
RAL, I'VE GOT THE LITTLE ONE !!

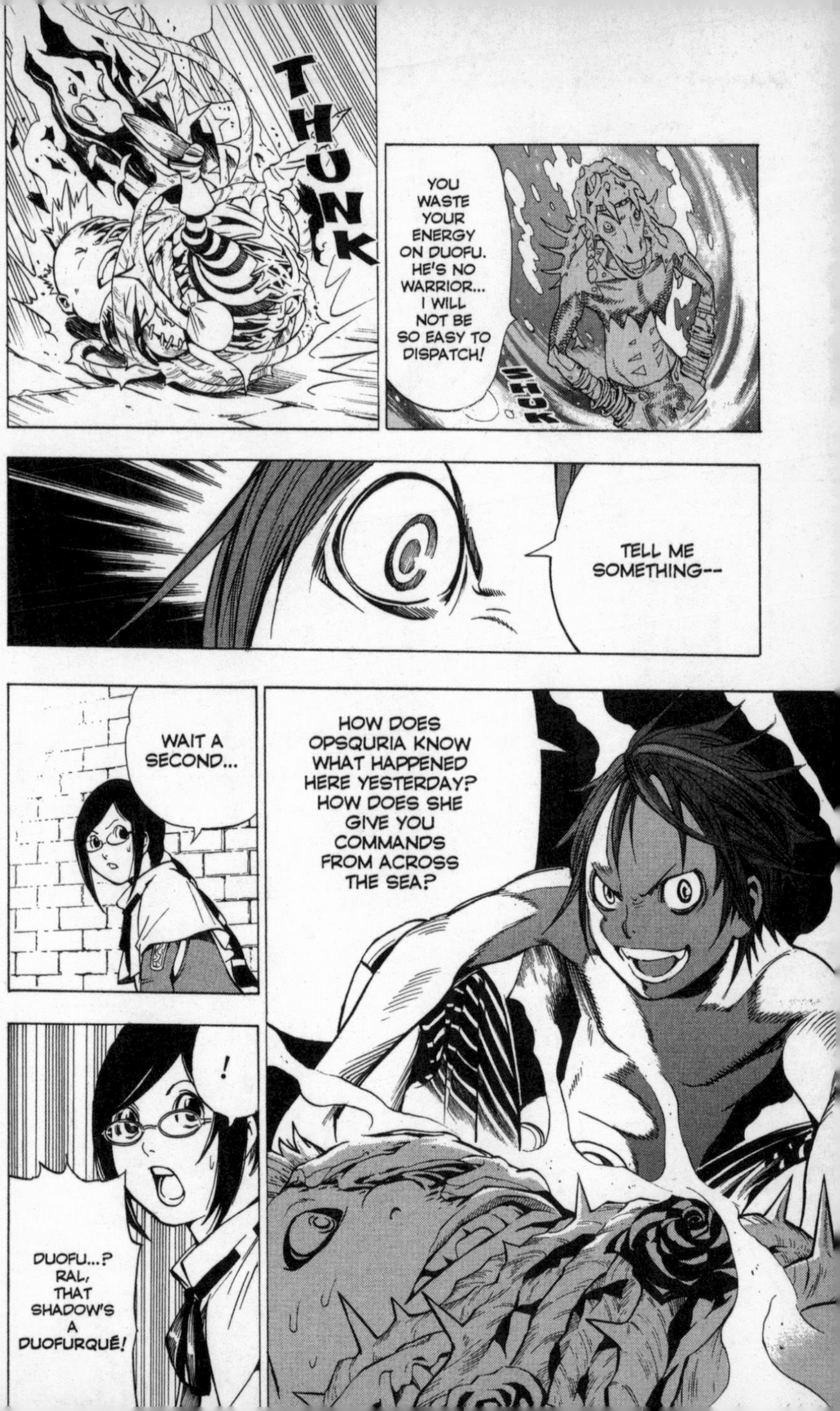
YOU WASTE YOUR ENERGY ON DUOFU. HE'S NO WARRIOR... I WILL NOT BE SO EASY TO DISPATCH!
THUNK
TELL ME SOMETHING--
HOW DOES OPSQURIA KNOW WHAT HAPPENED HERE YESTERDAY? HOW DOES SHE GIVE YOU COMMANDS FROM ACROSS THE SEA?
WAIT A SECOND...
!
DUOFU...? RAL, THAT SHADOW'S A DUOFURQUÉ!

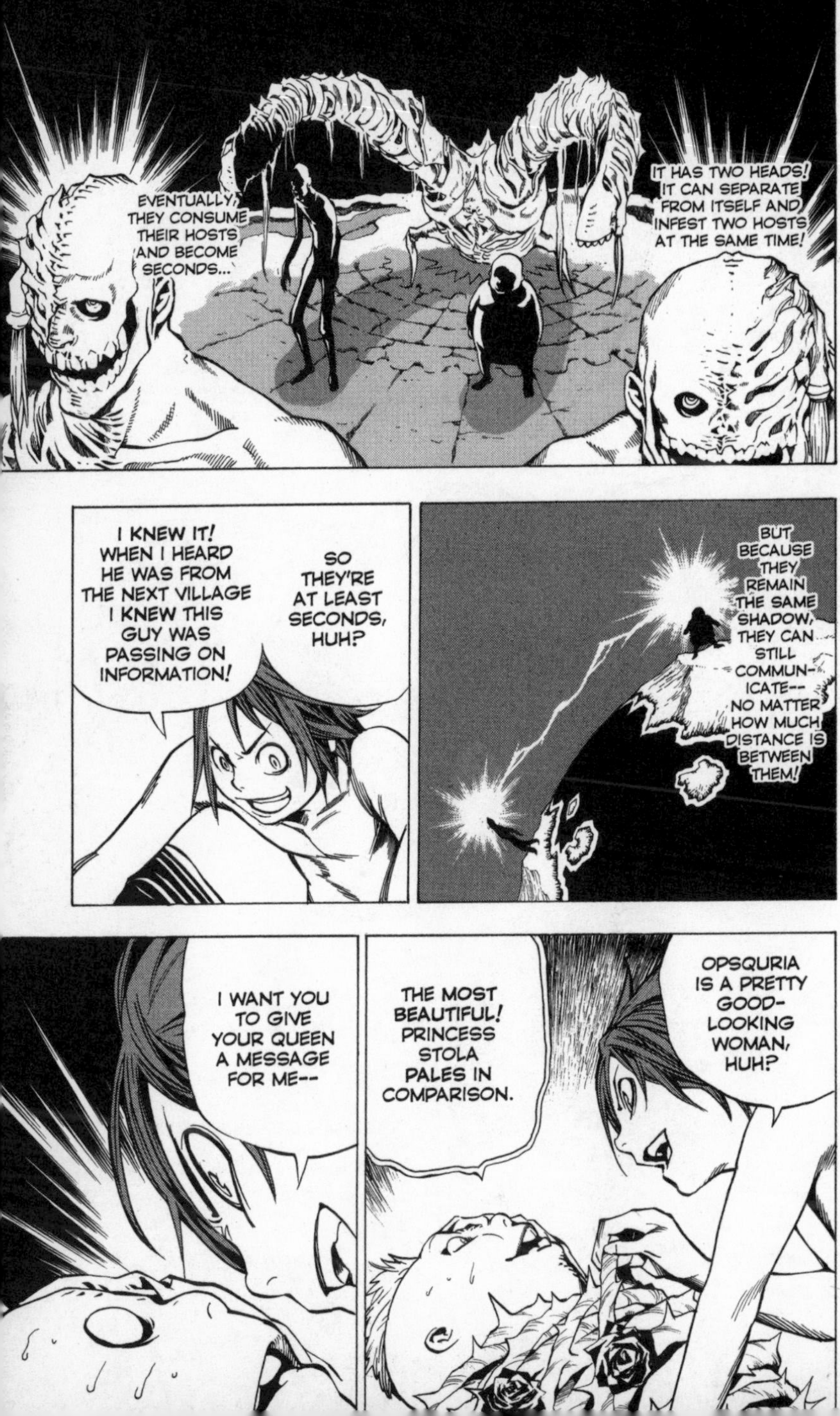
IT HAS TWO HEADS! IT CAN SEPARATE FROM ITSELF AND INFEST TWO HOSTS AT THE SAME TIME!
EVENTUALLY, THEY CONSUME THEIR HOSTS AND BECOME SECONDS...
BUT BECAUSE THEY REMAIN THE SAME SHADOW, THEY CAN STILL COMMUNICATE-- NO MATTER HOW MUCH DISTANCE IS BETWEEN THEM!
SO THEY'RE AT LEAST SECONDS, HUH?
I KNEW IT! WHEN I HEARD HE WAS FROM THE NEXT VILLAGE I KNEW THIS GUY WAS PASSING ON INFORMATION!
OPSQURIA IS A PRETTY GOOD-LOOKING WOMAN, HUH?
THE MOST BEAUTIFUL! PRINCESS STOLA PALES IN COMPARISON.
I WANT YOU TO GIVE YOUR QUEEN A MESSAGE FOR ME--

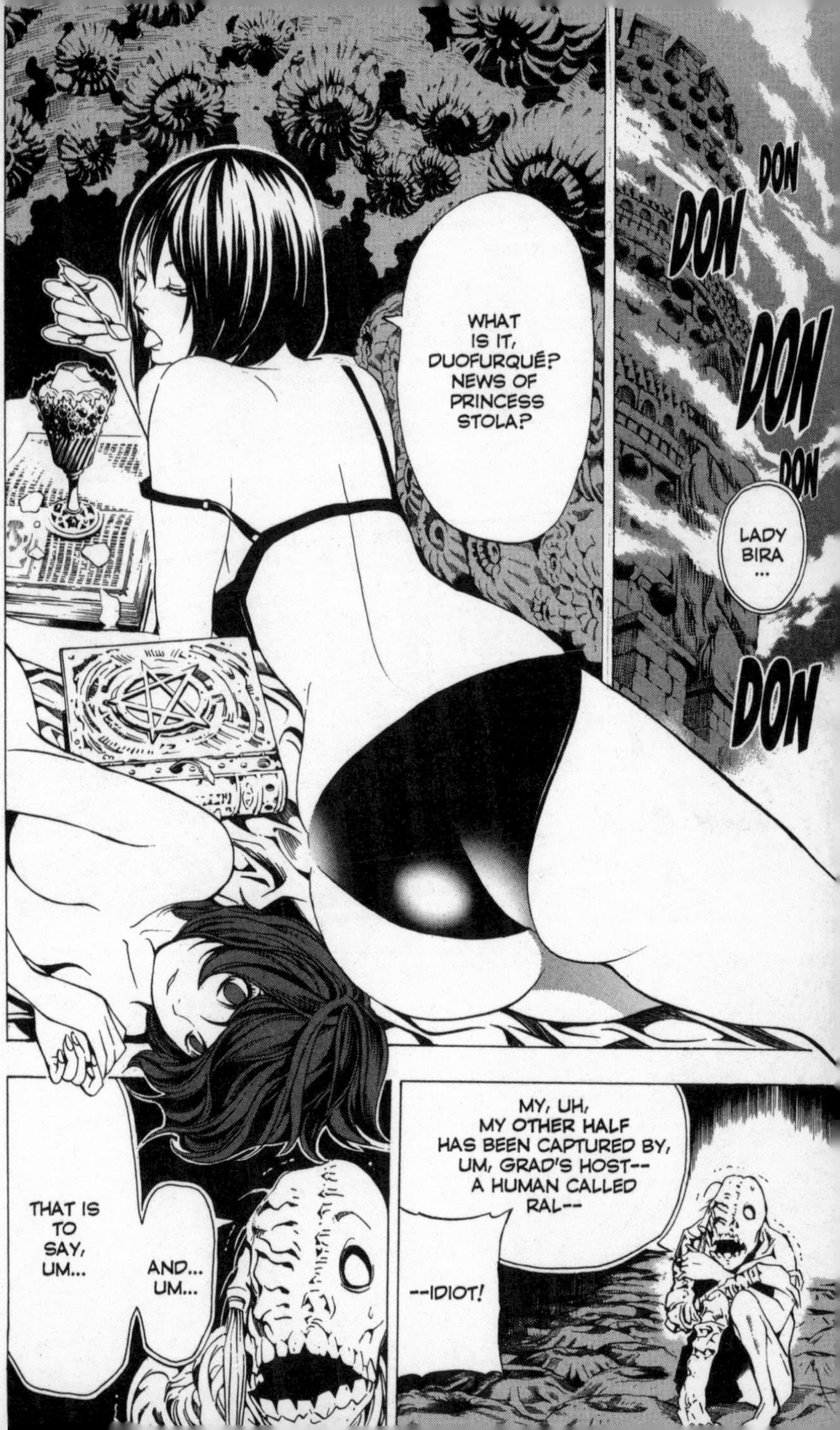
DON
DON
DON
DON
LADY BIRA...
DON
WHAT IS IT, DUOFURQUÉ? NEWS OF PRINCESS STOLA?
MY, UH, MY OTHER HALF HAS BEEN CAPTURED BY, UM, GRAD'S HOST-- A HUMAN CALLED RAL--
--IDIOT!
THAT IS TO SAY, UM...
AND... UM...

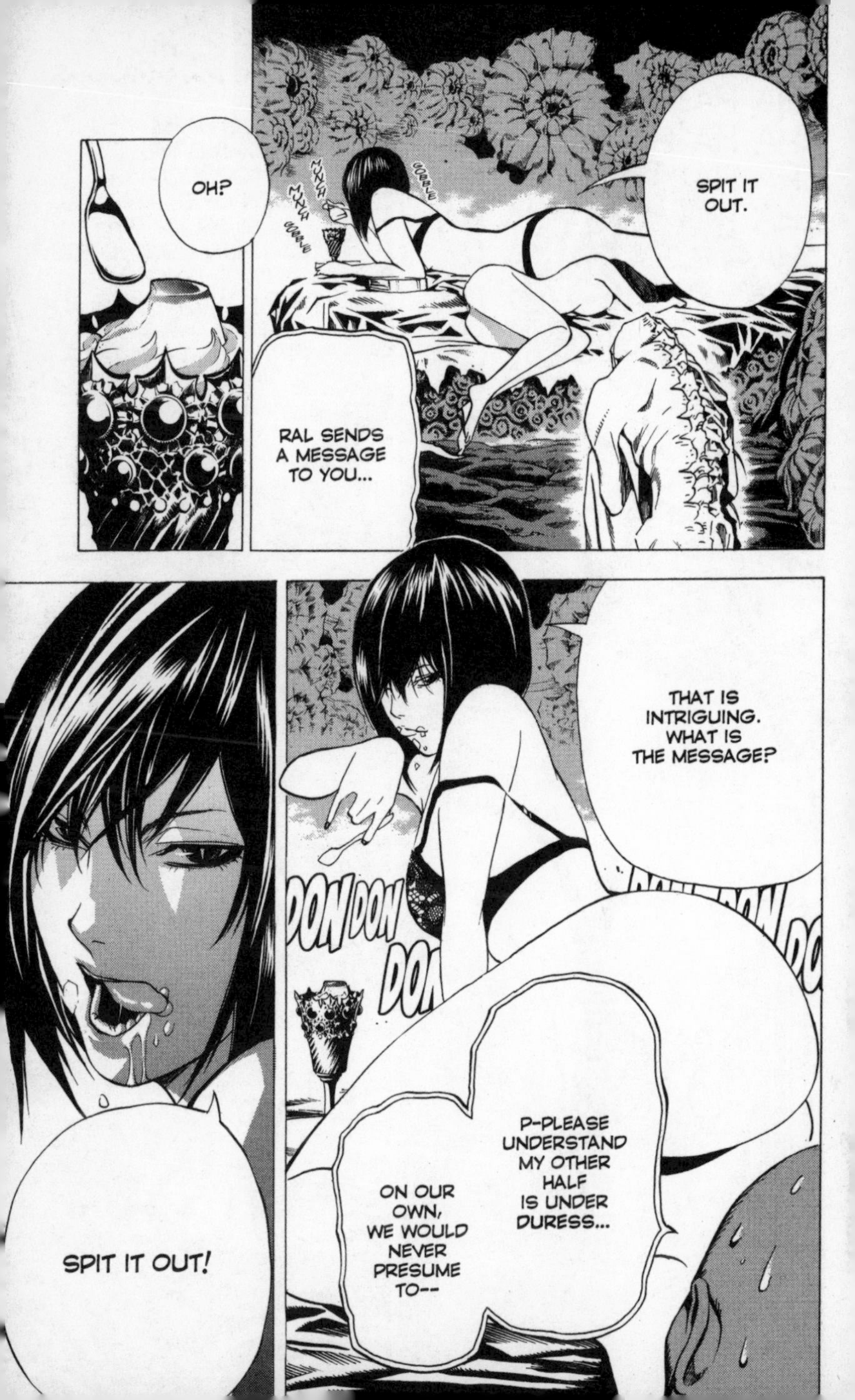
SPIT IT OUT.
GOBBLE
MUNCH
MUNCH
GOBBLE
RAL SENDS A MESSAGE TO YOU...
OH?
THAT IS INTRIGUING. WHAT IS THE MESSAGE?
DON DON DON
DON DON DON
P-PLEASE UNDERSTAND MY OTHER HALF IS UNDER DURESS...
ON OUR OWN, WE WOULD NEVER PRESUME TO--
SPIT IT OUT!

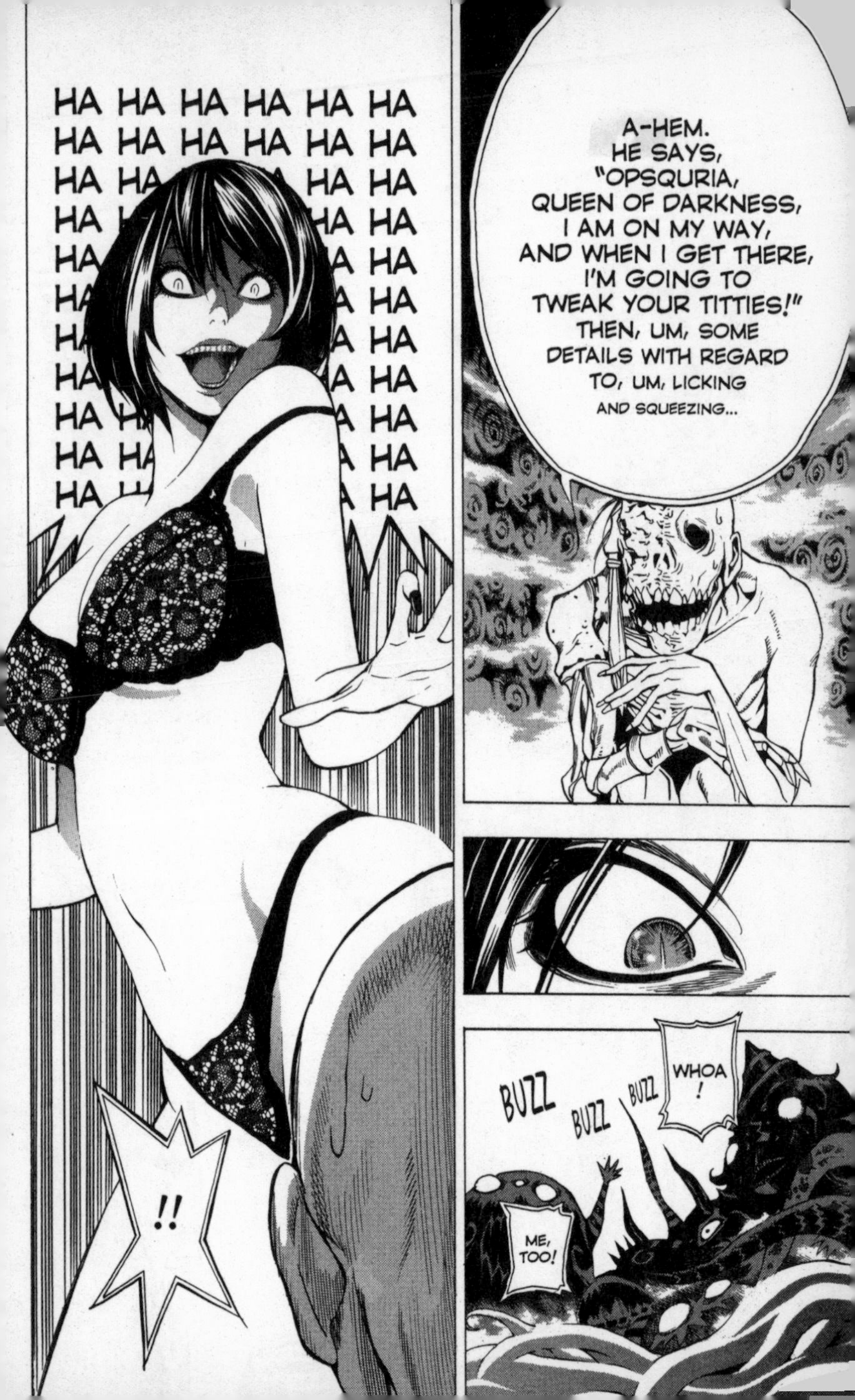
A-HEM. HE SAYS, "OPSQURIA, QUEEN OF DARKNESS, I AM ON MY WAY, AND WHEN I GET THERE, I'M GOING TO TWEAK YOUR TITTIES!" THEN, UM, SOME DETAILS WITH REGARD TO, UM, LICKING AND SQUEEZING...
BUZZ
BUZZ
BUZZ
WHOA!
ME, TOO!
HA HA HA HA HA HA
HA HA HA HA HA HA
HA HA HA HA
HA HA HA
HA HA
HA HA
HA HA
HA HA
HA HA
HA HA
HA HA
!!

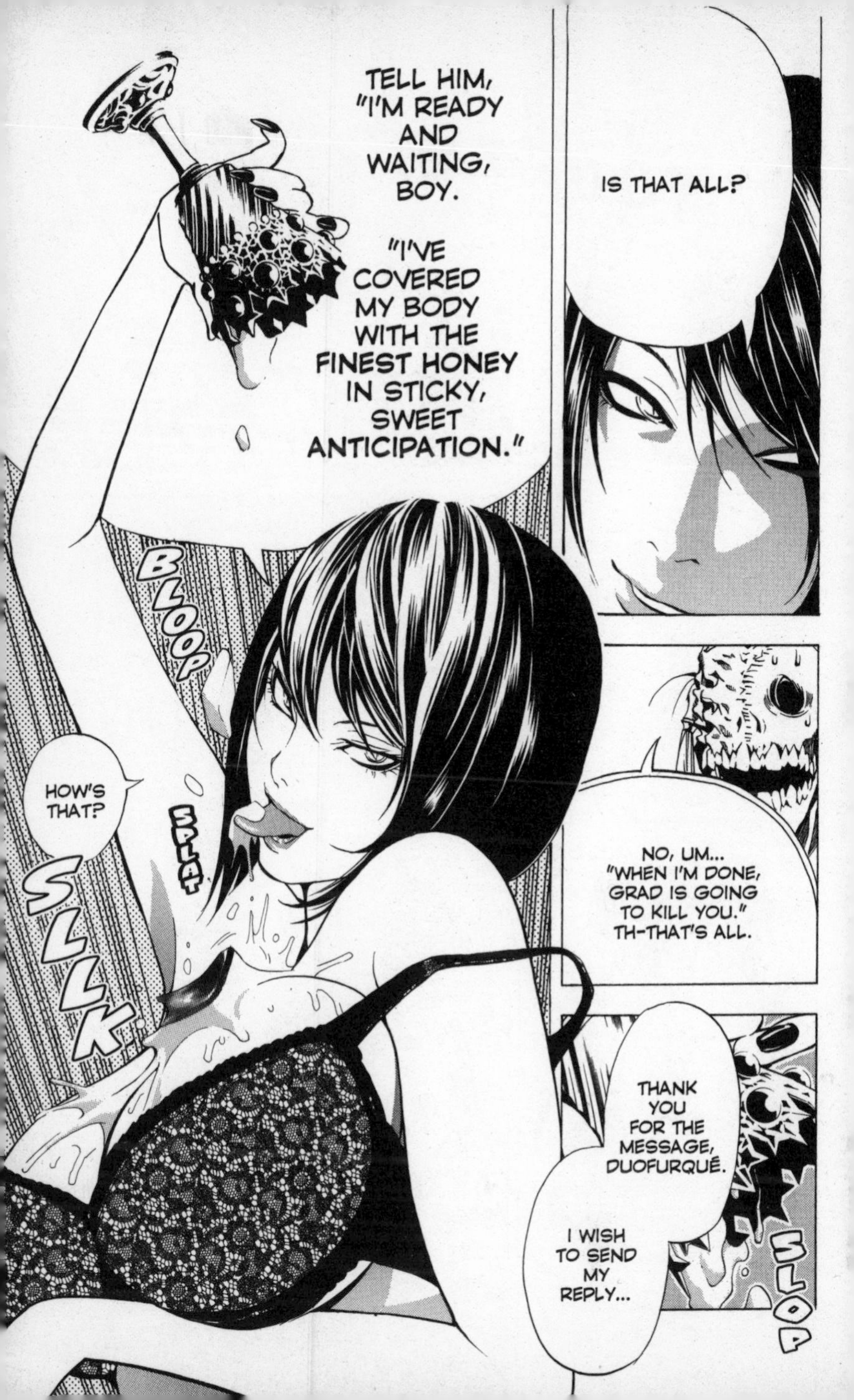
IS THAT ALL?
NO, UM... "WHEN I'M DONE, GRAD IS GOING TO KILL YOU." TH-THAT'S ALL.
THANK YOU FOR THE MESSAGE, DUOFURQUÉ.
I WISH TO SEND MY REPLY...
SLOP
TELL HIM, "I'M READY AND WAITING, BOY.
"I'VE COVERED MY BODY WITH THE FINEST HONEY IN STICKY, SWEET ANTICIPATION."
BLOOP
SPLAT
HOW'S THAT?
SLLK

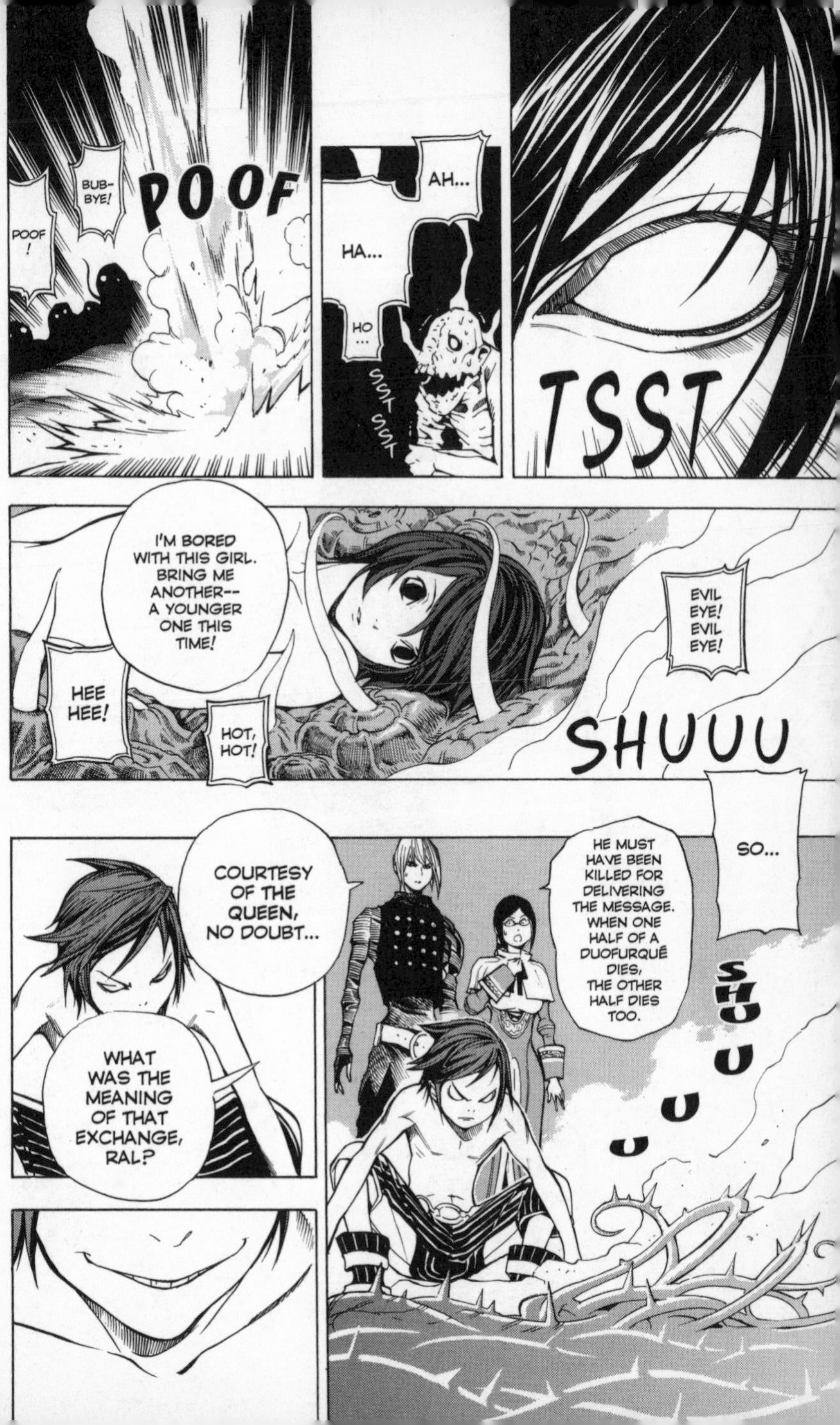
TSST
AH...
HA...
HO...
SST SST
POOF
BUB-BYE!
POOF!
EVIL EYE! EVIL EYE!
SHUUU
I'M BORED WITH THIS GIRL. BRING ME ANOTHER-- A YOUNGER ONE THIS TIME!
HOT, HOT!
HEE HEE!
SO...
HE MUST HAVE BEEN KILLED FOR DELIVERING THE MESSAGE. WHEN ONE HALF OF A DUOFURQUÉ DIES, THE OTHER HALF DIES TOO.
SHUUUU
COURTESY OF THE QUEEN, NO DOUBT...
WHAT WAS THE MEANING OF THAT EXCHANGE, RAL?

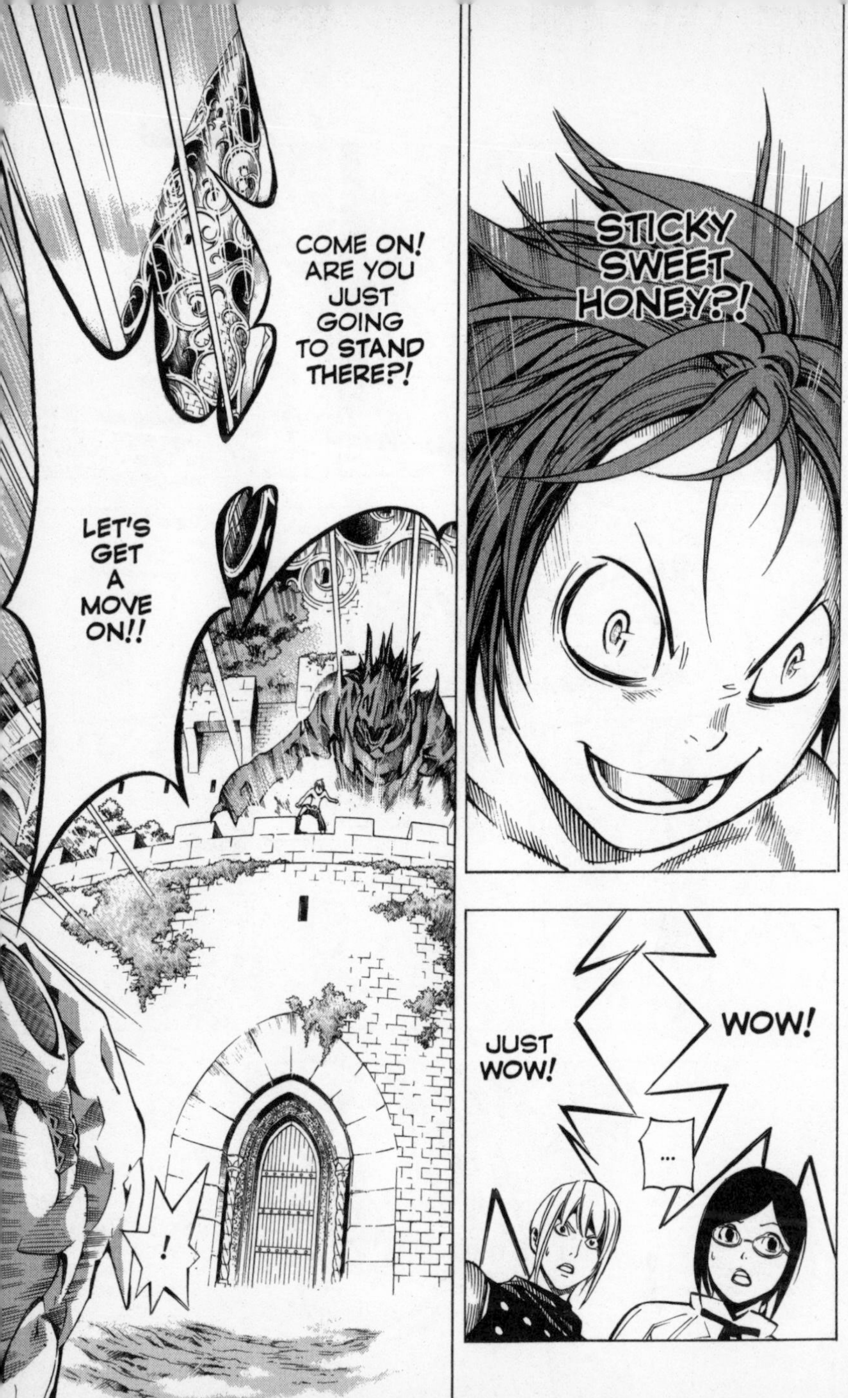
STICKY SWEET HONEY?!
WOW!
JUST WOW!
...
COME ON! ARE YOU JUST GOING TO STAND THERE?!
LET'S GET A MOVE ON!!
!

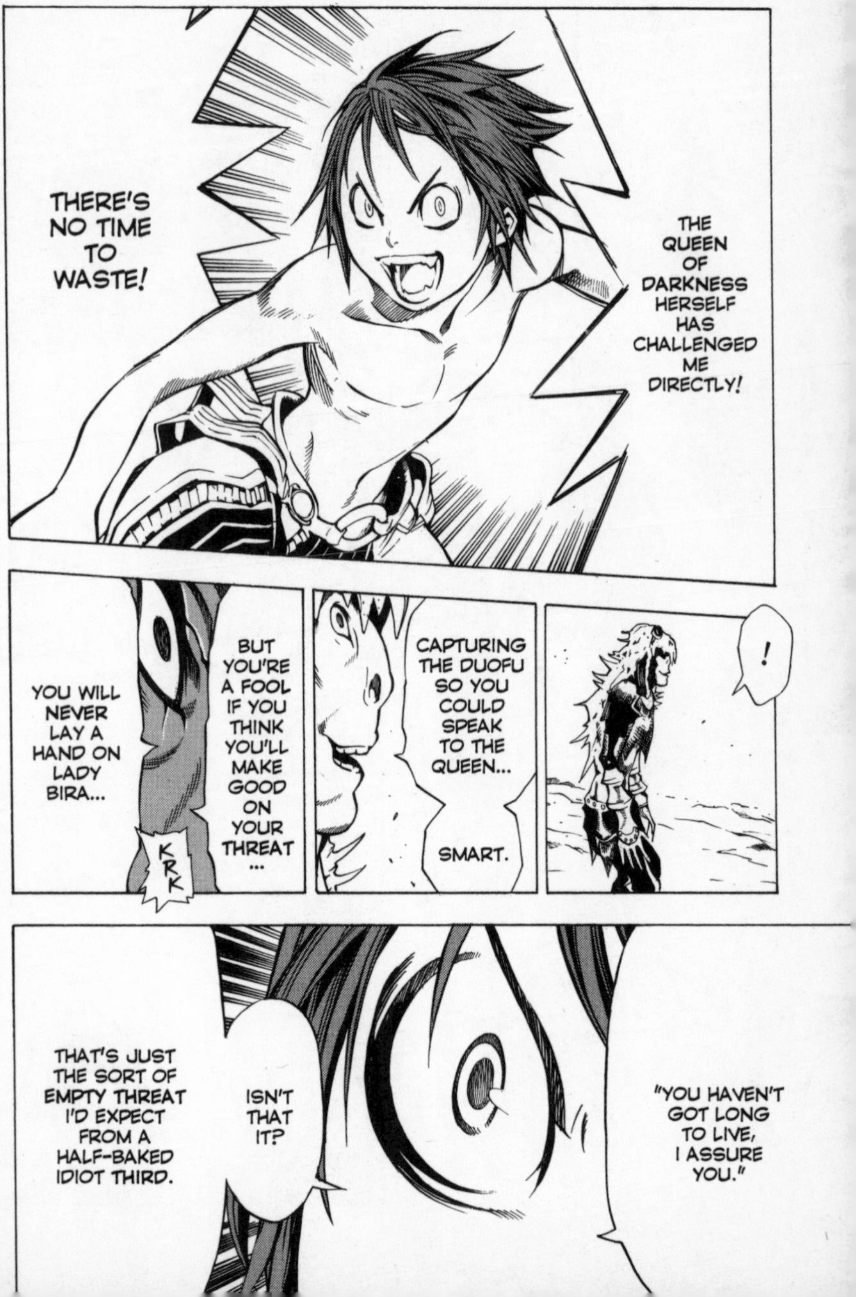
THE QUEEN OF DARKNESS HERSELF HAS CHALLENGED ME DIRECTLY!
THERE'S NO TIME TO WASTE!
!
CAPTURING THE DUOFU SO YOU COULD SPEAK TO THE QUEEN...
SMART.
BUT YOU'RE A FOOL IF YOU THINK YOU'LL MAKE GOOD ON YOUR THREAT...
YOU WILL NEVER LAY A HAND ON LADY BIRA...
KRK
"YOU HAVEN'T GOT LONG TO LIVE, I ASSURE YOU."
ISN'T THAT IT?
THAT'S JUST THE SORT OF EMPTY THREAT I'D EXPECT FROM A HALF-BAKED IDIOT THIRD.

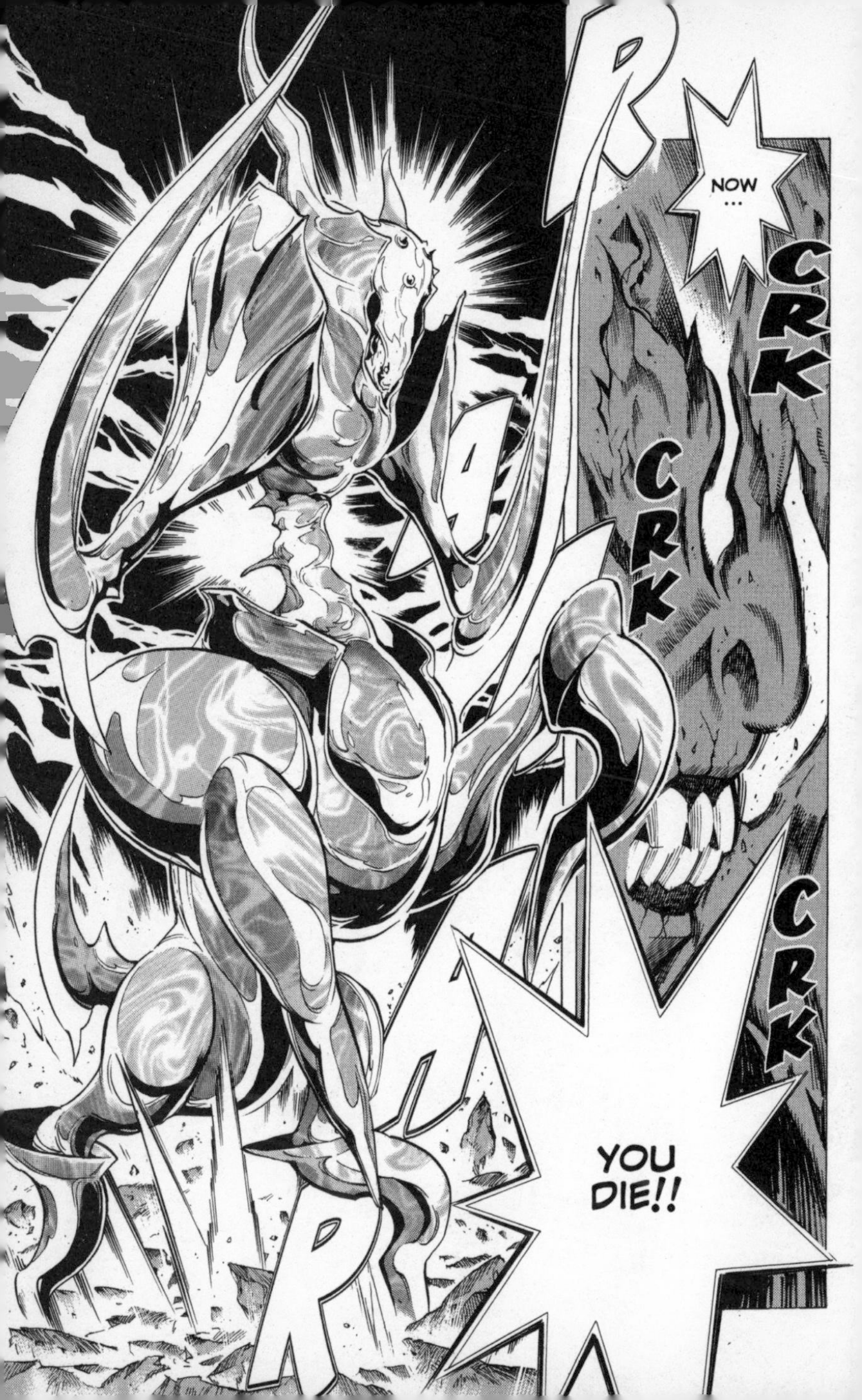
NOW ...
CRK CRK
CRK CRK
CRK CRK
YOU DIE!!

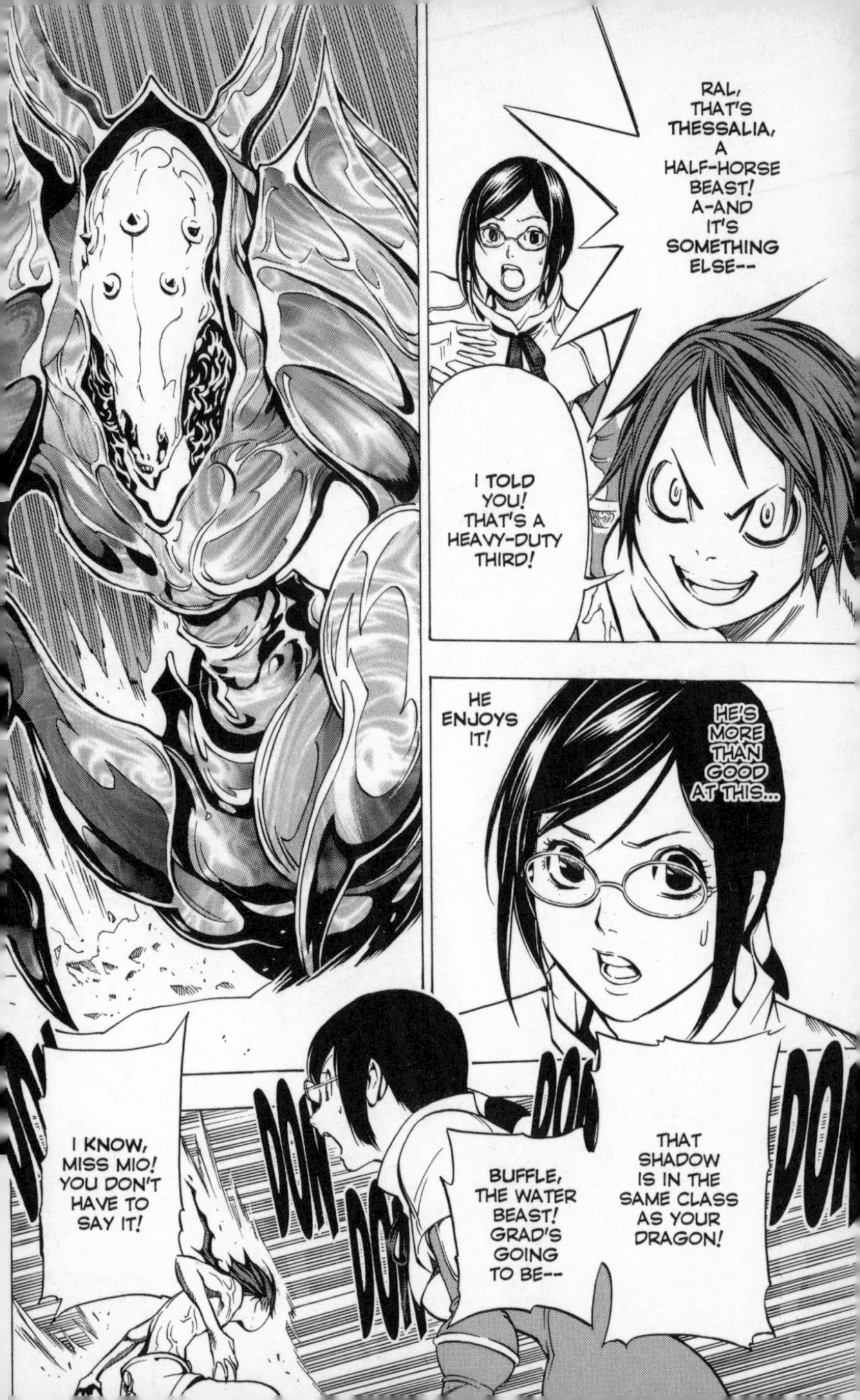

RAL, THAT'S THESSALIA, A HALF-HORSE BEAST! A-AND IT'S SOMETHING ELSE--
I TOLD YOU! THAT'S A HEAVY-DUTY THIRD!
HE'S MORE THAN GOOD AT THIS...
HE ENJOYS IT!
DON
THAT SHADOW IS IN THE SAME CLASS AS YOUR DRAGON!
DON
DON
BUFFLE, THE WATER BEAST! GRAD'S GOING TO BE--
DON
DON
I KNOW, MISS MIO! YOU DON'T HAVE TO SAY IT!

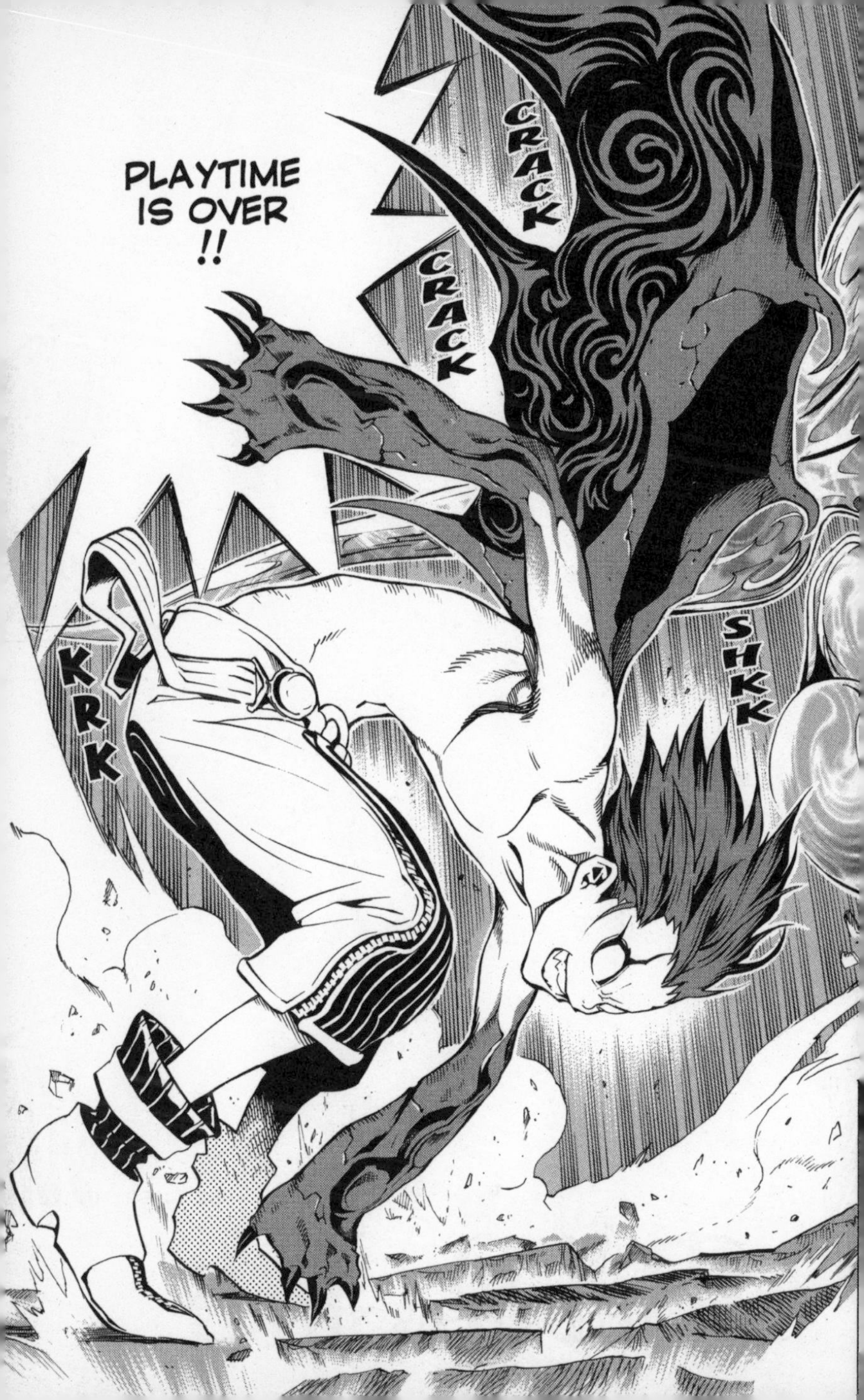
CRACK
CRACK
PLAYTIME IS OVER !!
SHKK
KRK

RalΩGrad

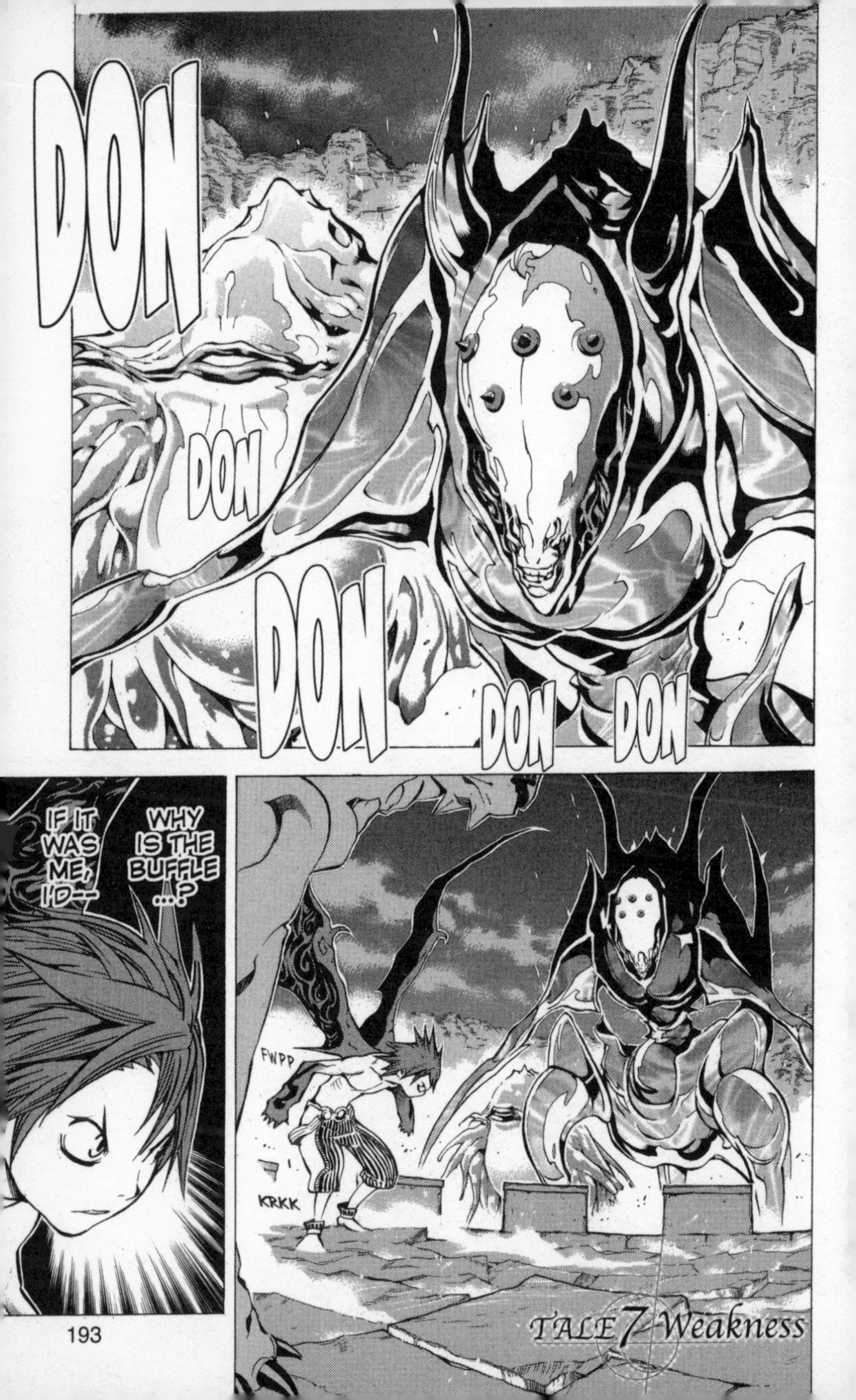
DON
DON
DON
DON
DON
FWPP
KRKK
WHY IS THE BUFFLE ...?
IF IT WAS ME, I'D--

TALE 7 Weakness

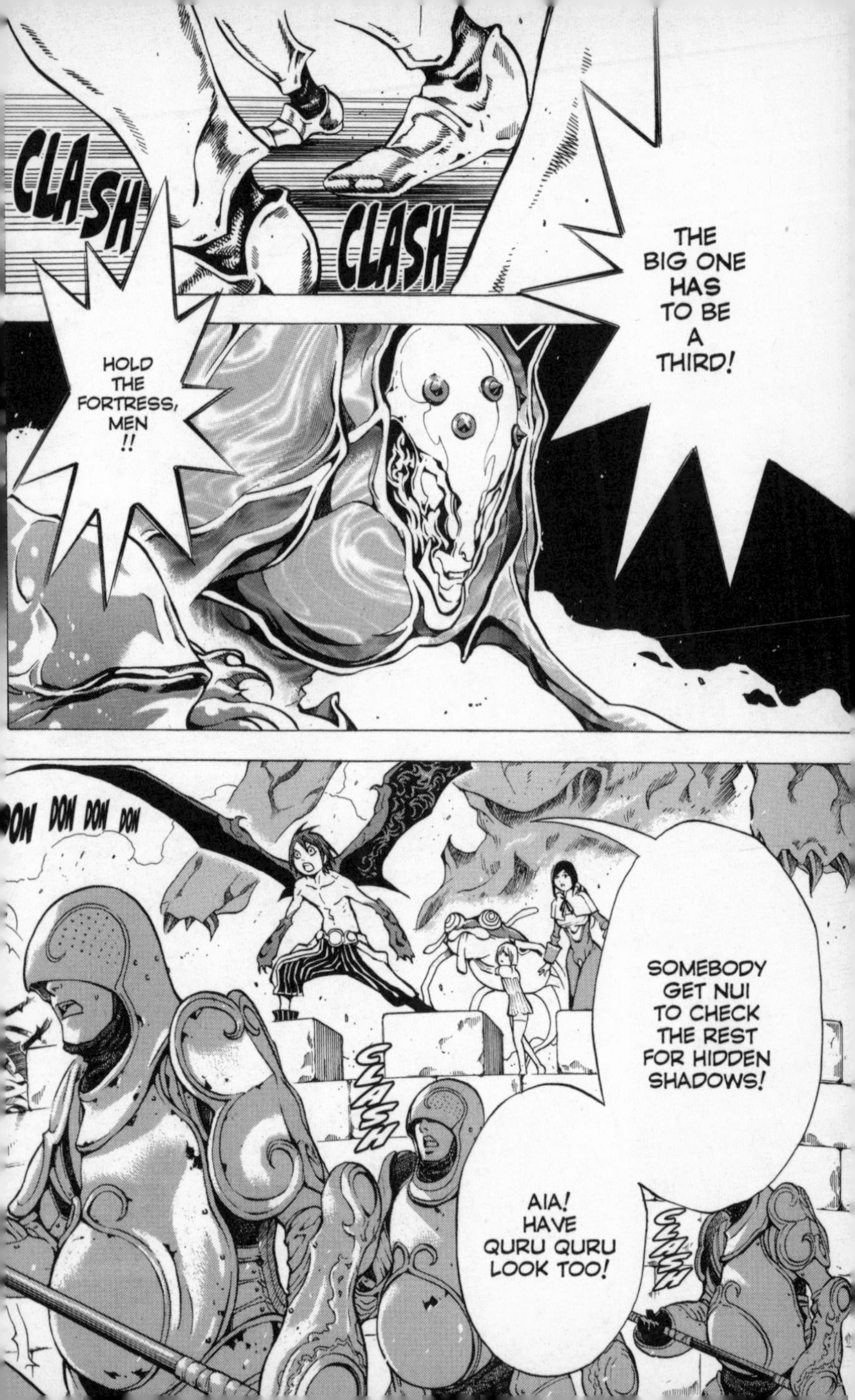

CLASH
CLASH
THE BIG ONE HAS TO BE A THIRD!
HOLD THE FORTRESS, MEN!!
DON DON DON DON
SOMEBODY GET NUI TO CHECK THE REST FOR HIDDEN SHADOWS!
AIA! HAVE QURU QURU LOOK TOO!

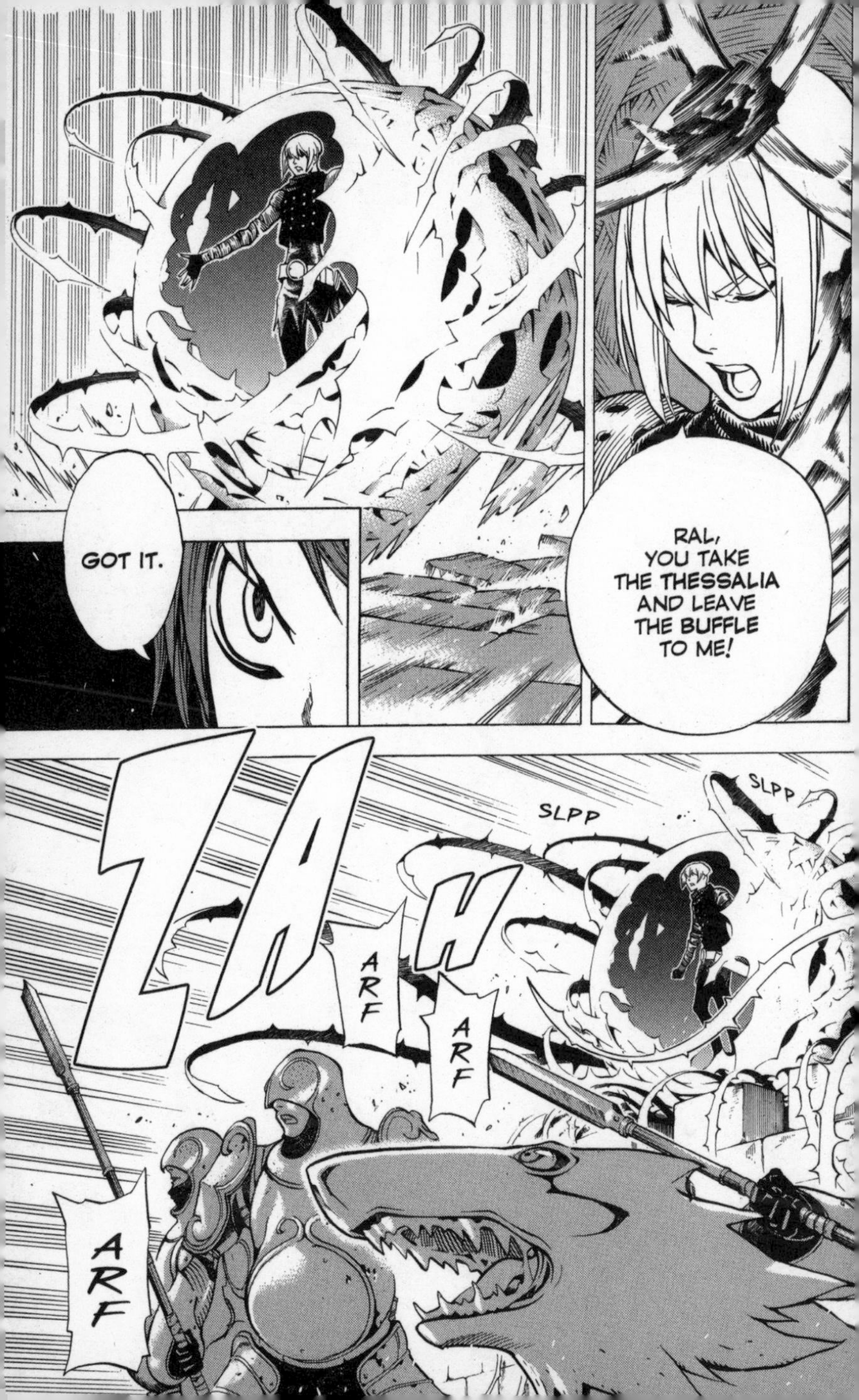
RAL, YOU TAKE THE THESSALIA AND LEAVE THE BUFFLE TO ME!
GOT IT.
SLPP
SLPP
ZAH
ARF
ARF
ARF

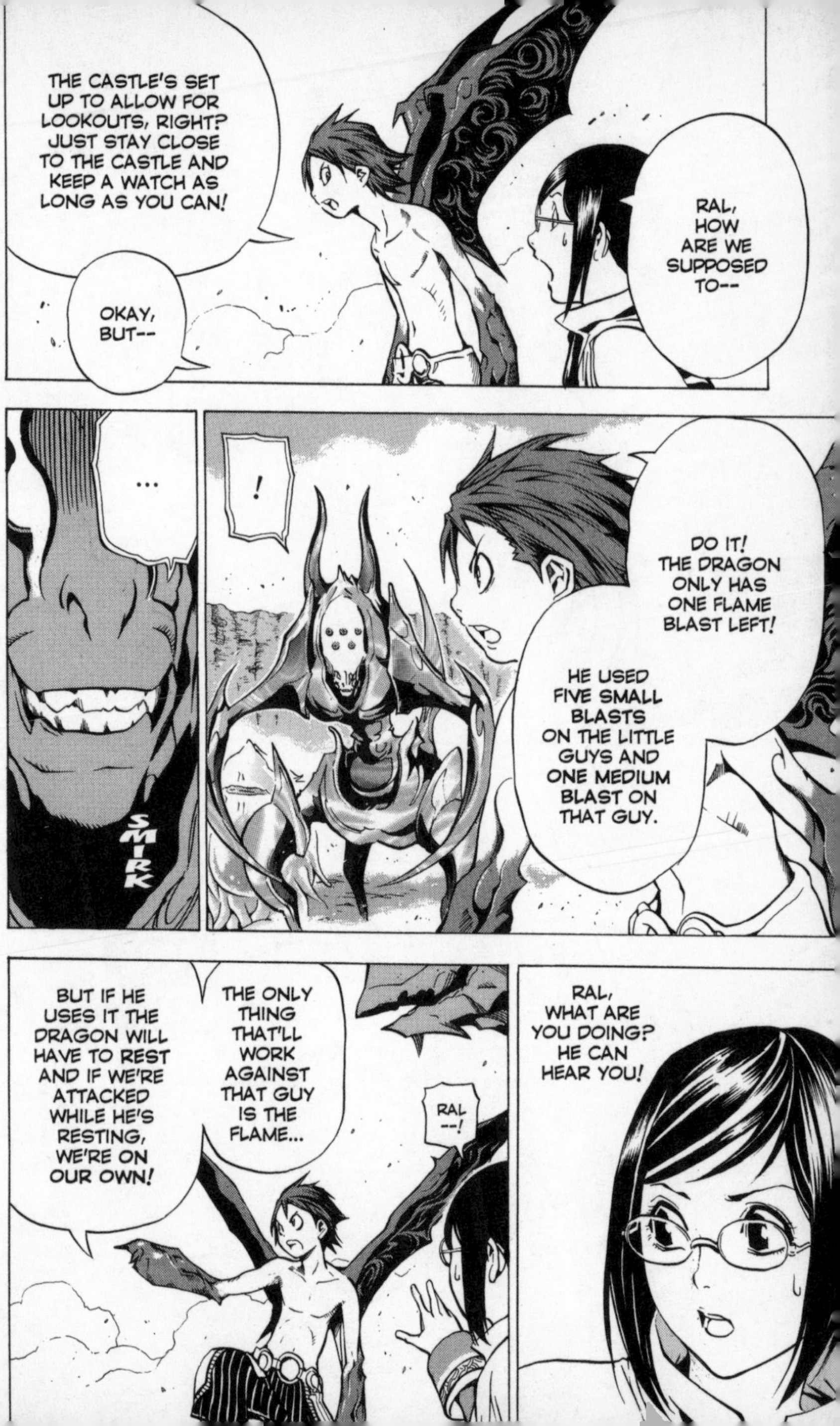
RAL, HOW ARE WE SUPPOSED TO--
THE CASTLE'S SET UP TO ALLOW FOR LOOKOUTS, RIGHT? JUST STAY CLOSE TO THE CASTLE AND KEEP A WATCH AS LONG AS YOU CAN!
OKAY, BUT--
DO IT! THE DRAGON ONLY HAS ONE FLAME BLAST LEFT!
HE USED FIVE SMALL BLASTS ON THE LITTLE GUYS AND ONE MEDIUM BLAST ON THAT GUY.
!
...
SMIRK
RAL, WHAT ARE YOU DOING? HE CAN HEAR YOU!
RAL --!
THE ONLY THING THAT'LL WORK AGAINST THAT GUY IS THE FLAME...
BUT IF HE USES IT THE DRAGON WILL HAVE TO REST AND IF WE'RE ATTACKED WHILE HE'S RESTING, WE'RE ON OUR OWN!

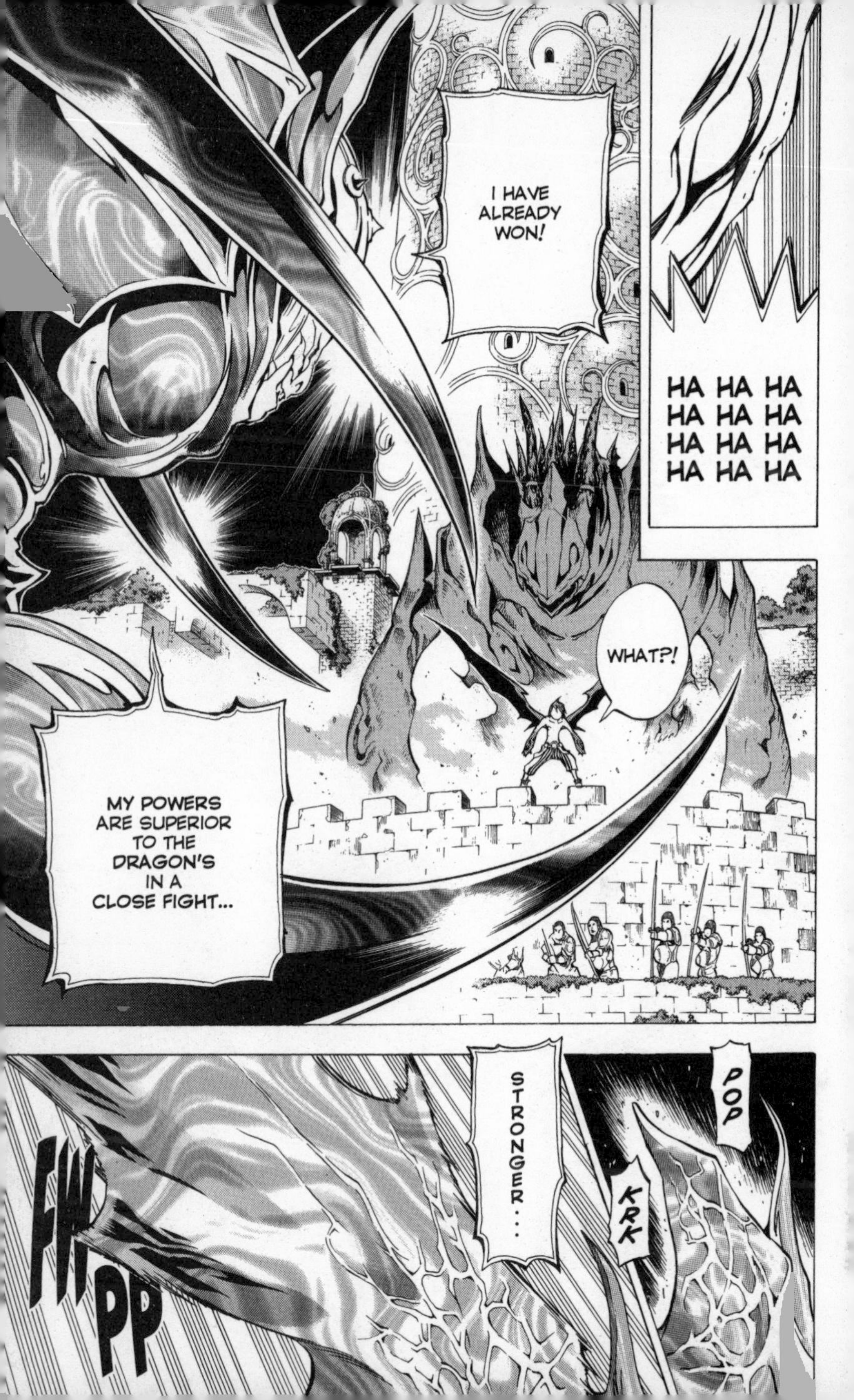
HA HA HA
HA HA HA
HA HA HA
HA HA HA
WHAT?!
I HAVE ALREADY WON!
MY POWERS ARE SUPERIOR TO THE DRAGON'S IN A CLOSE FIGHT...
POP
KRK
STRONGER...
FWIPP

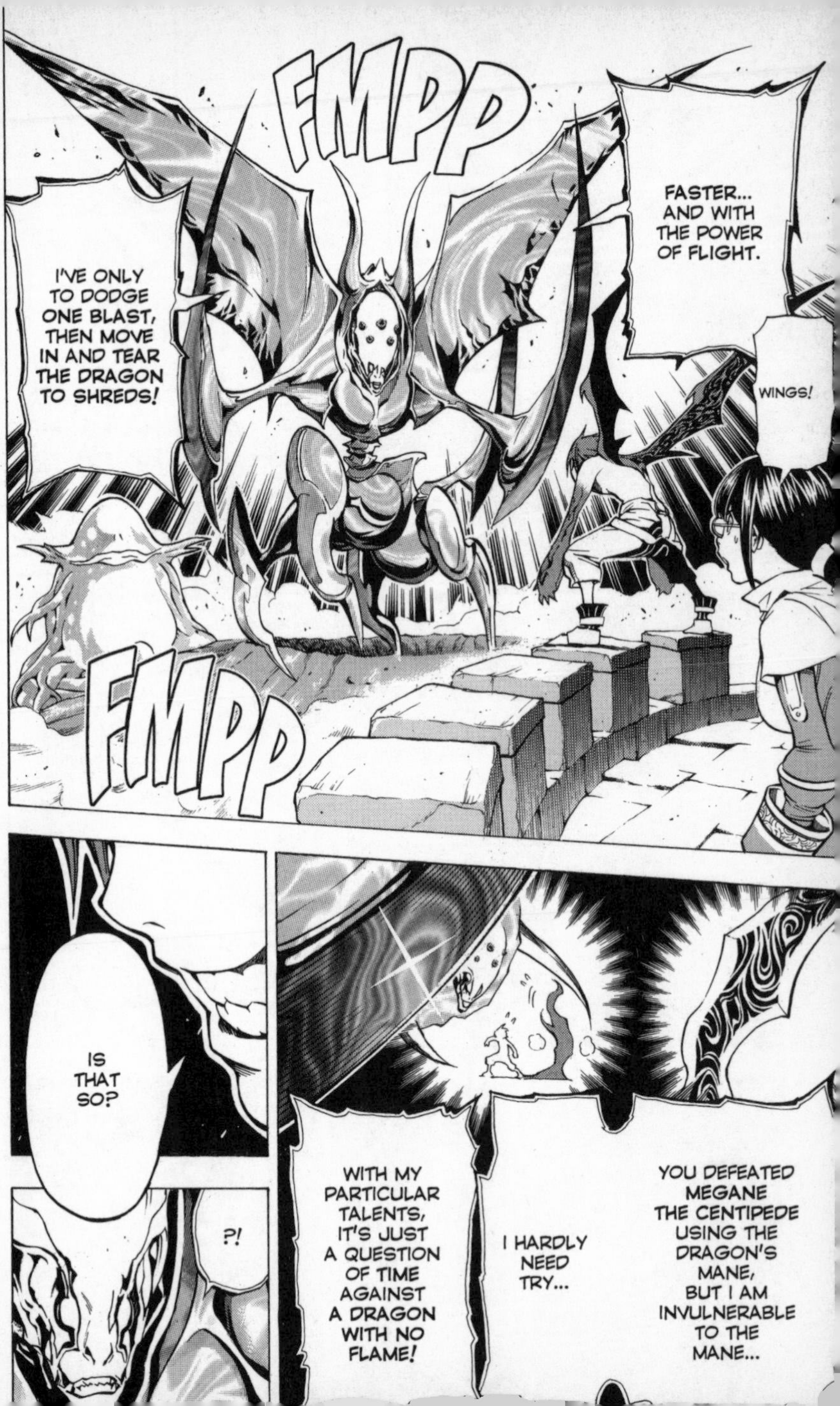
FASTER... AND WITH THE POWER OF FLIGHT.
WINGS!
FMPP
I'VE ONLY TO DODGE ONE BLAST, THEN MOVE IN AND TEAR THE DRAGON TO SHREDS!
FMPP
YOU DEFEATED MEGANE THE CENTIPEDE USING THE DRAGON'S MANE, BUT I AM INVULNERABLE TO THE MANE...
I HARDLY NEED TRY...
WITH MY PARTICULAR TALENTS, IT'S JUST A QUESTION OF TIME AGAINST A DRAGON WITH NO FLAME!
IS THAT SO?
?!

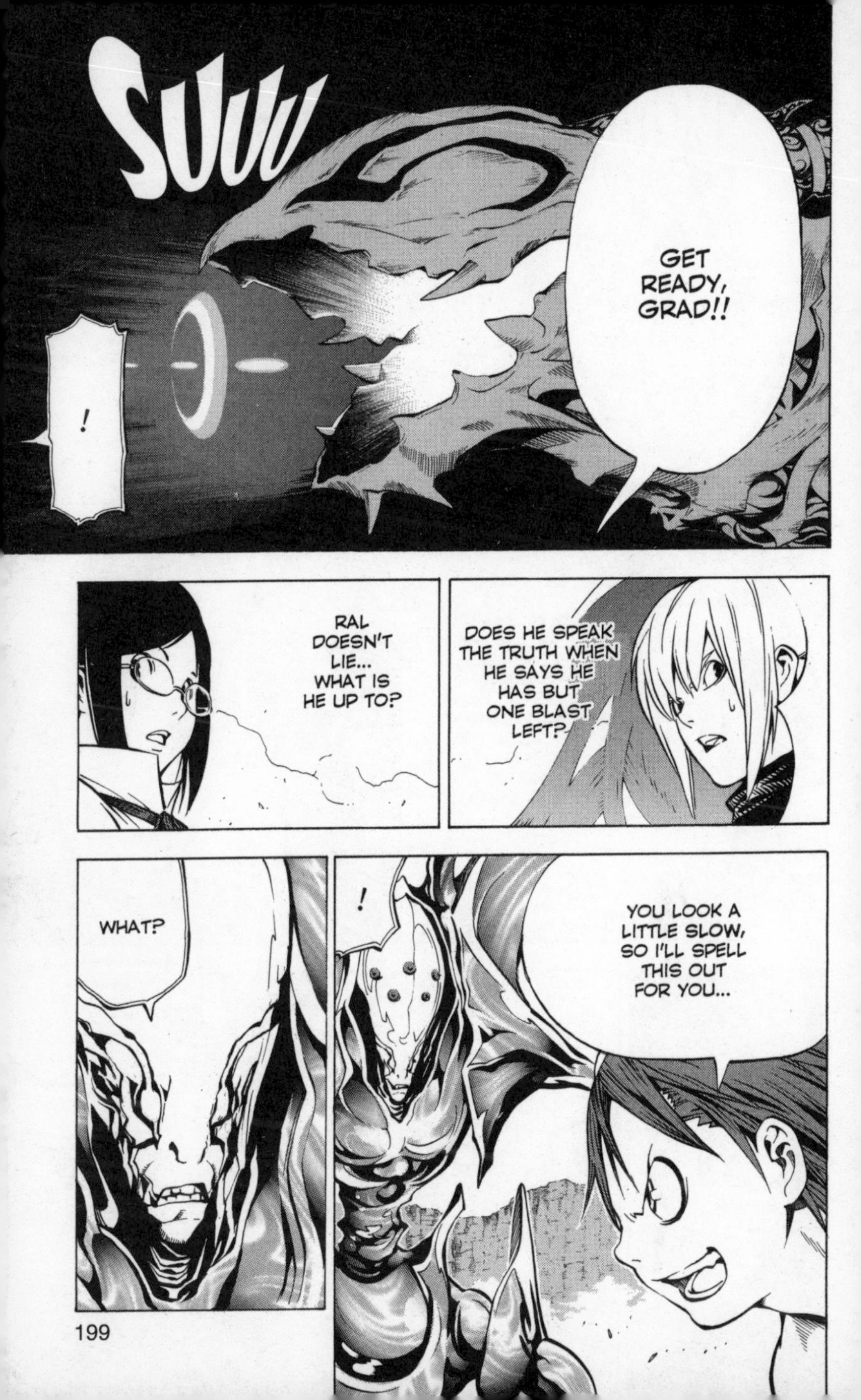
GET READY, GRAD!!
SUUU
!
DOES HE SPEAK THE TRUTH WHEN HE SAYS HE HAS BUT ONE BLAST LEFT?
RAL DOESN'T LIE... WHAT IS HE UP TO?
YOU LOOK A LITTLE SLOW, SO I'LL SPELL THIS OUT FOR YOU...
!
WHAT?

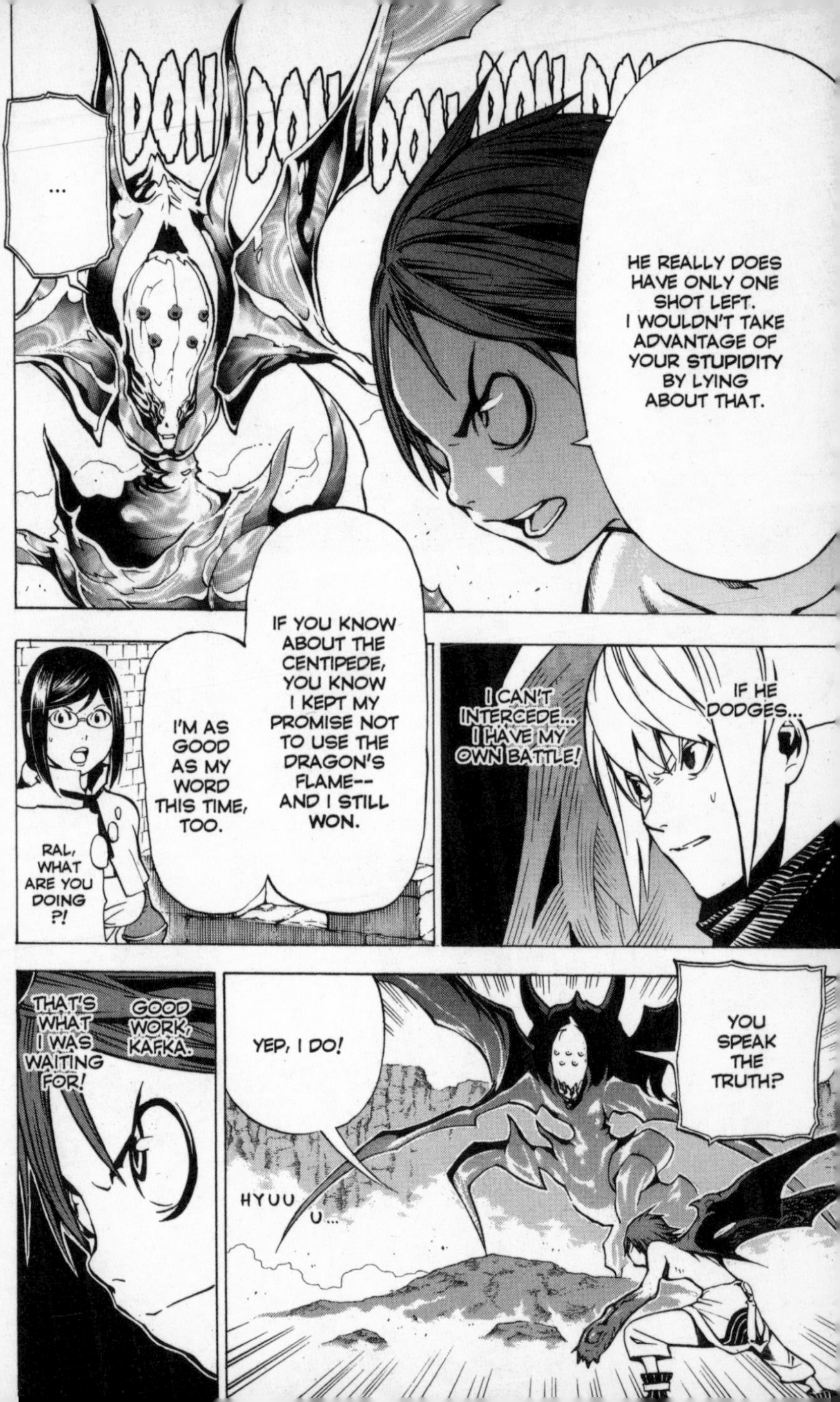

HE REALLY DOES HAVE ONLY ONE SHOT LEFT. I WOULDN'T TAKE ADVANTAGE OF YOUR STUPIDITY BY LYING ABOUT THAT.
DON DON DON DON
...
IF HE DODGES...
I CAN'T INTERCEDE... I HAVE MY OWN BATTLE!
IF YOU KNOW ABOUT THE CENTIPEDE, YOU KNOW I KEPT MY PROMISE NOT TO USE THE DRAGON'S FLAME--AND I STILL WON.
I'M AS GOOD AS MY WORD THIS TIME, TOO.
RAL, WHAT ARE YOU DOING?!
YOU SPEAK THE TRUTH?
YEP, I DO!
HYUUU...
GOOD WORK, KAFKA.
THAT'S WHAT I WAS WAITING FOR!

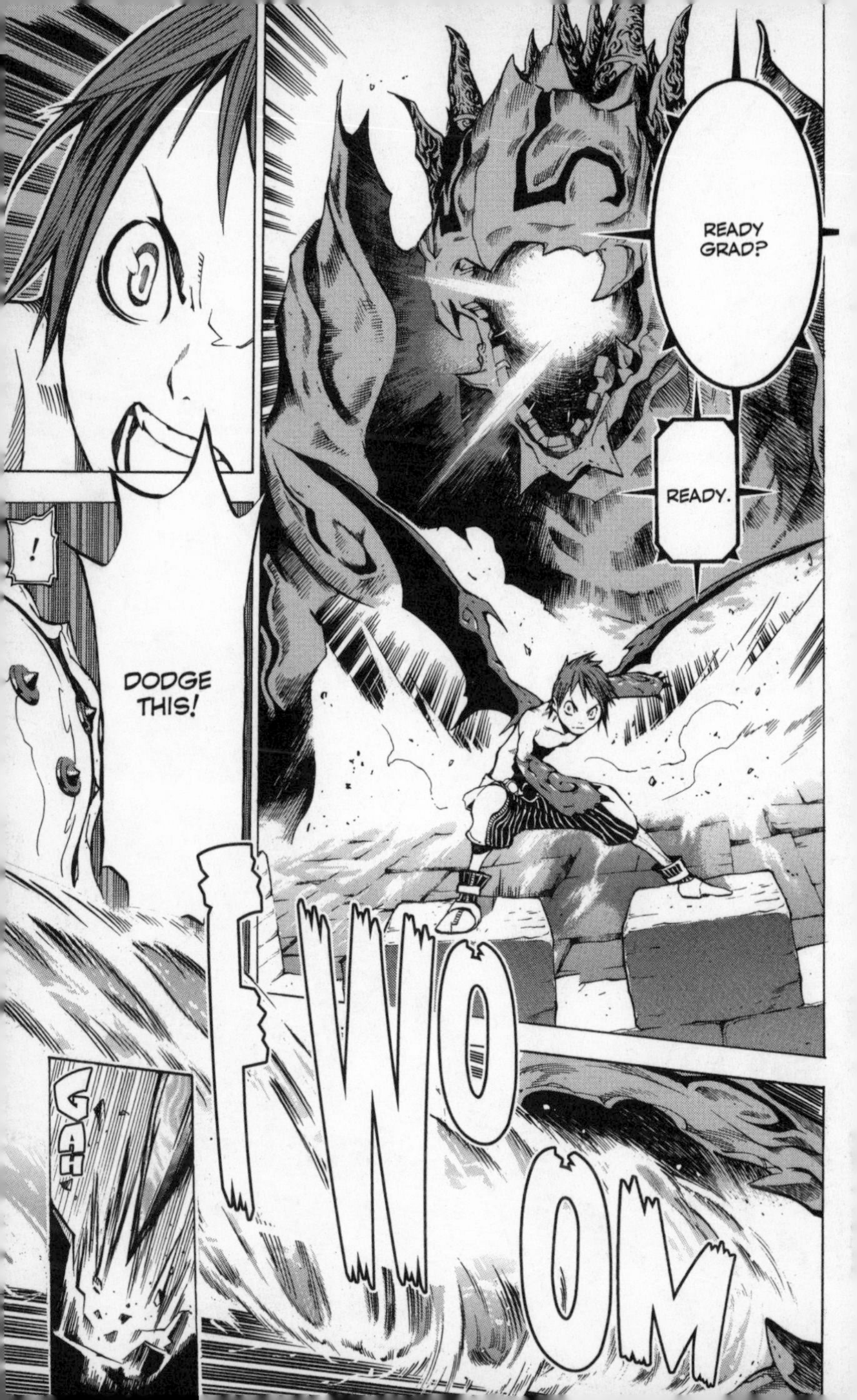
READY GRAD?
READY.
!
DODGE THIS!
FWOOM
GAH

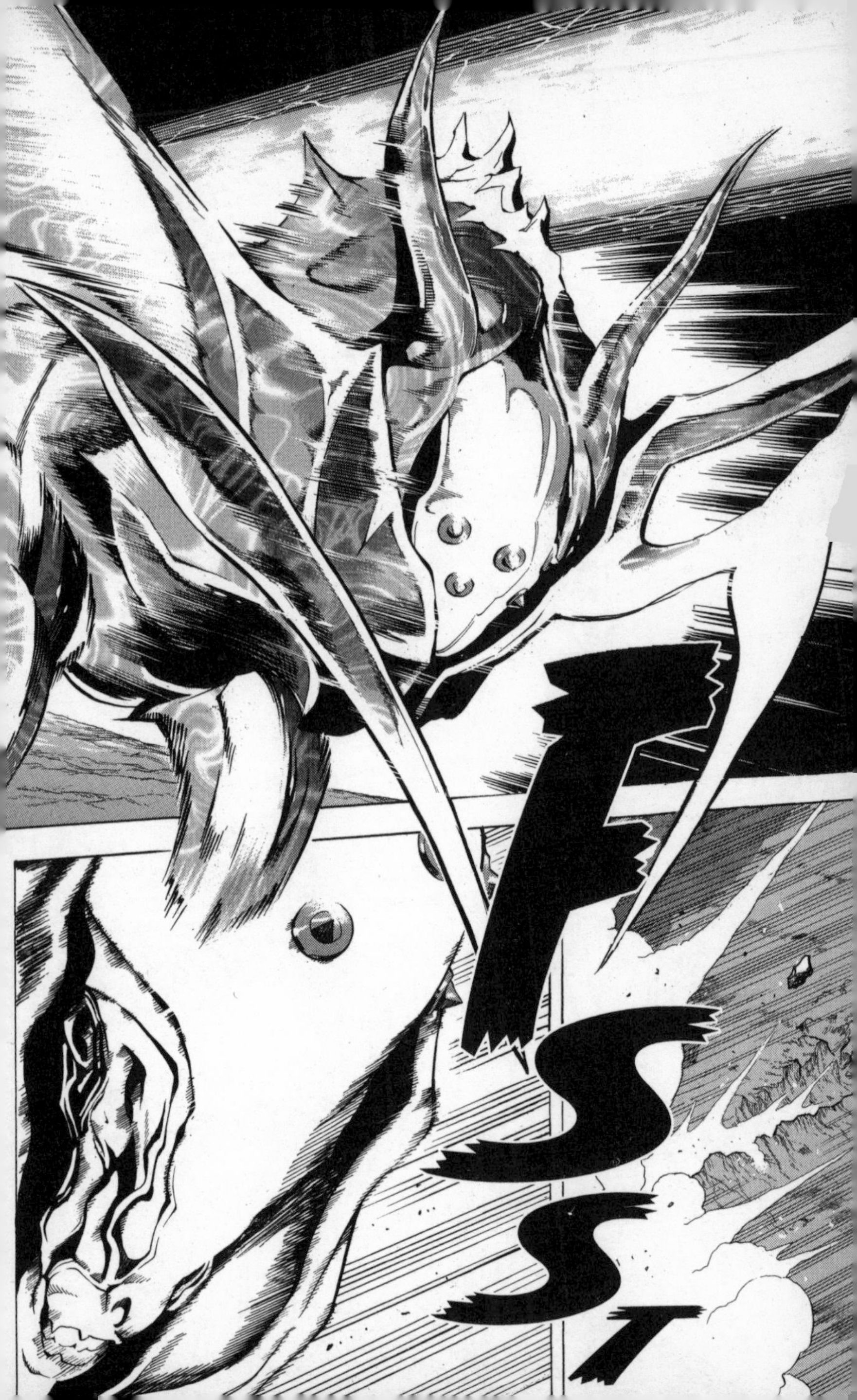
FSST

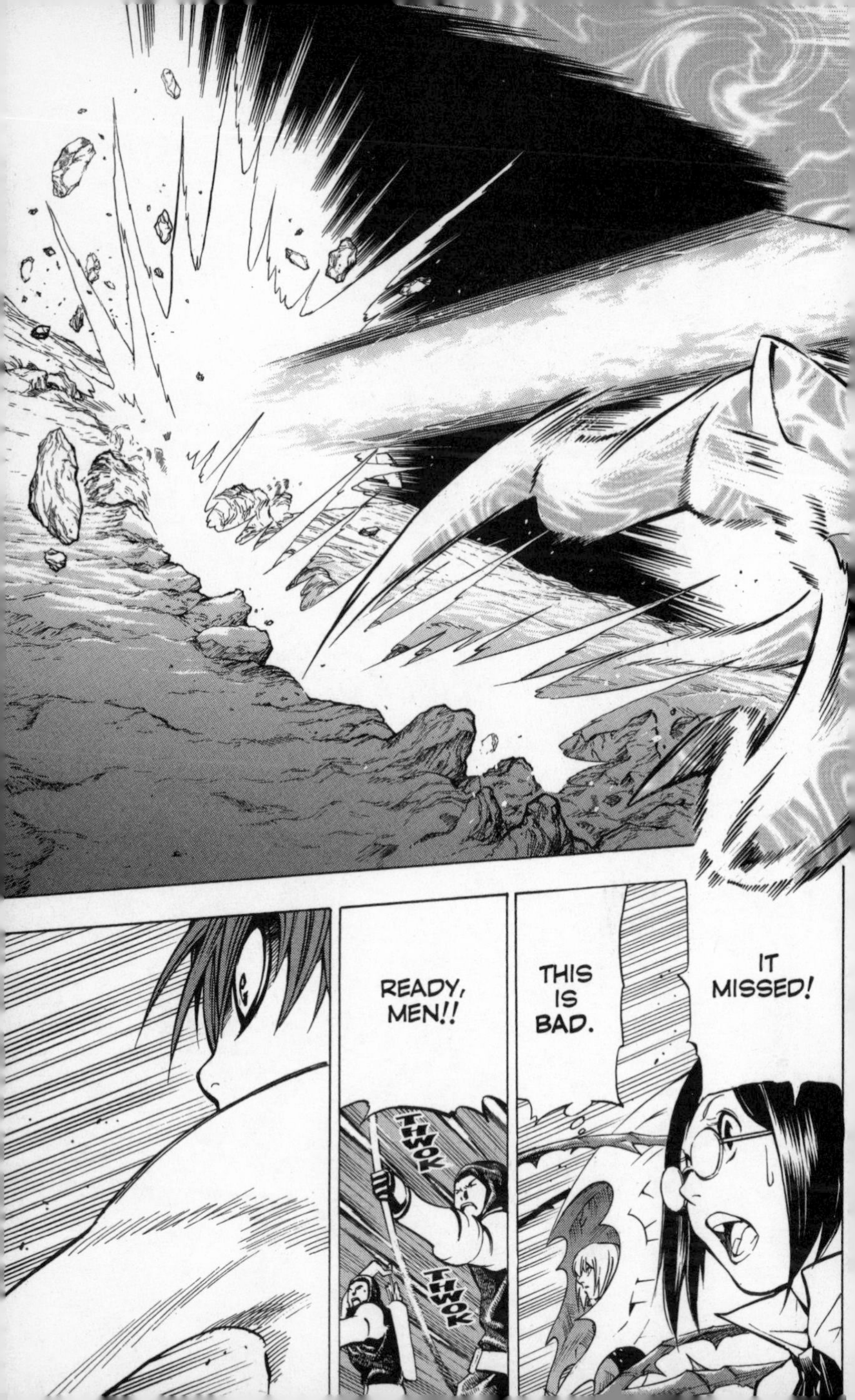
IT MISSED!
THIS IS BAD.
READY, MEN!!
THWOK
THWOK

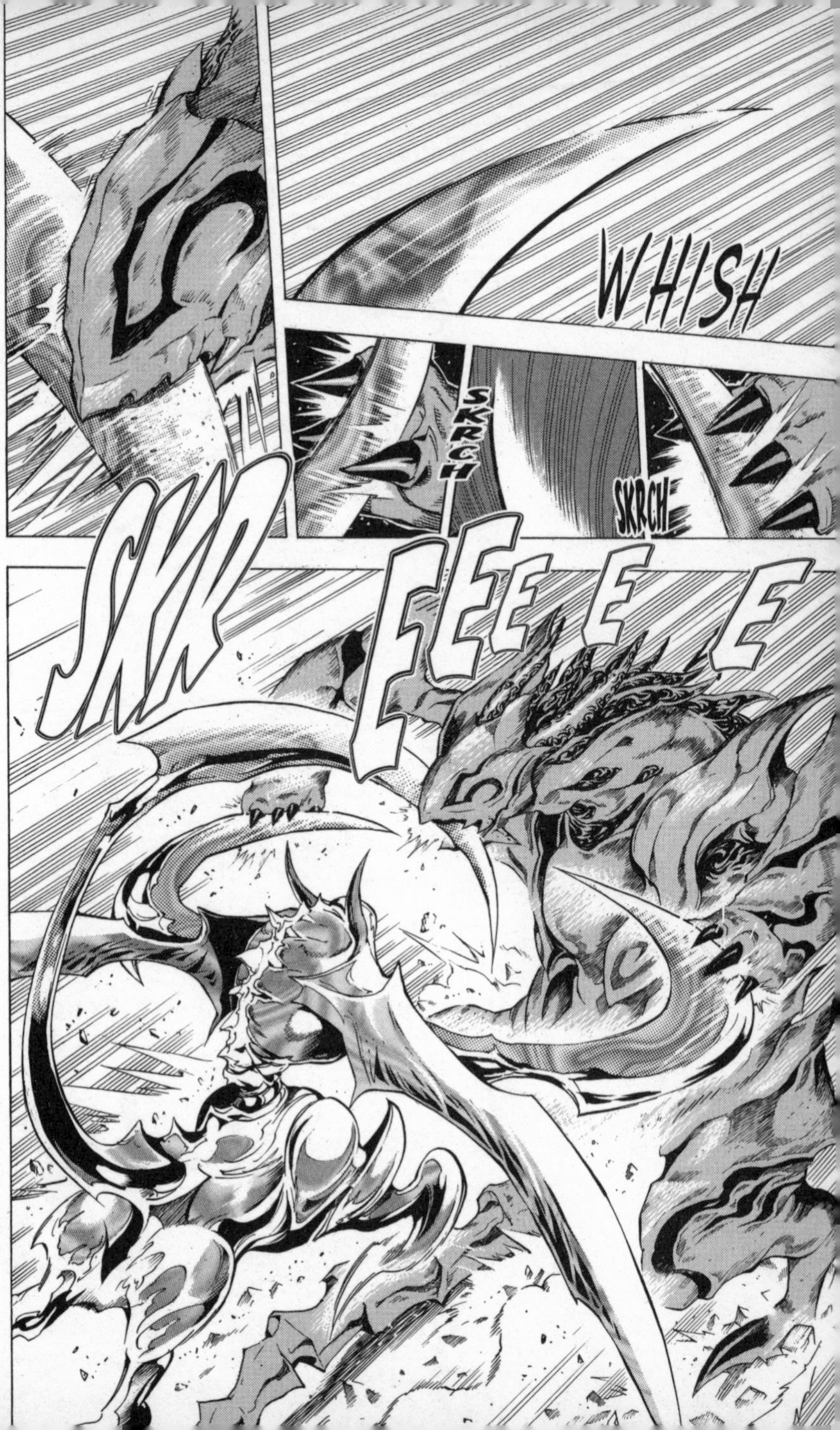
WHISH
SKRCH
SKRCH
SKREEEEE

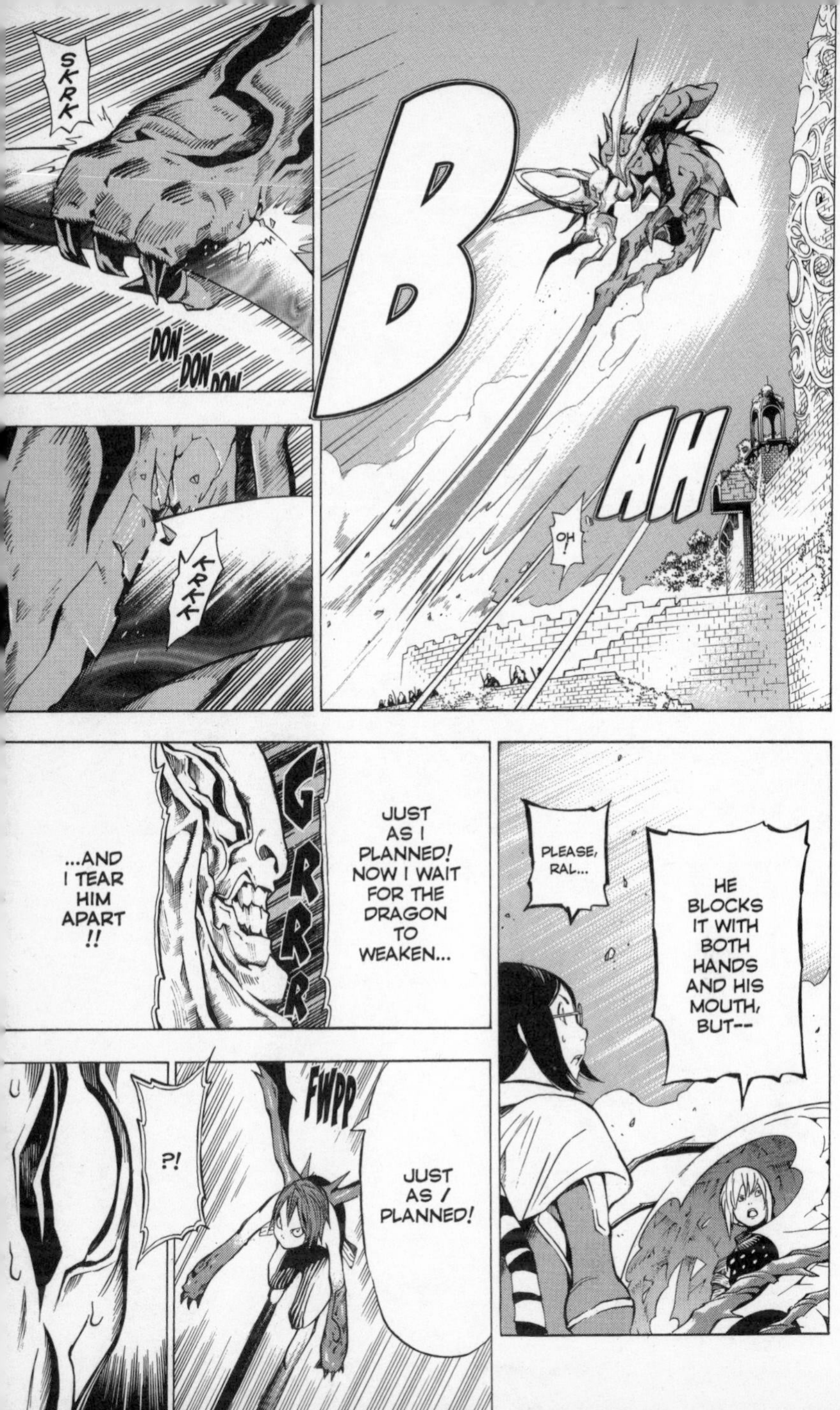
B
AH
OH!
SKRK
DON DON DON
KRKK
HE BLOCKS IT WITH BOTH HANDS AND HIS MOUTH, BUT--
PLEASE, RAL...
GRRR
JUST AS I PLANNED! NOW I WAIT FOR THE DRAGON TO WEAKEN...
...AND I TEAR HIM APART!!
FWPP
JUST AS I PLANNED!
?!

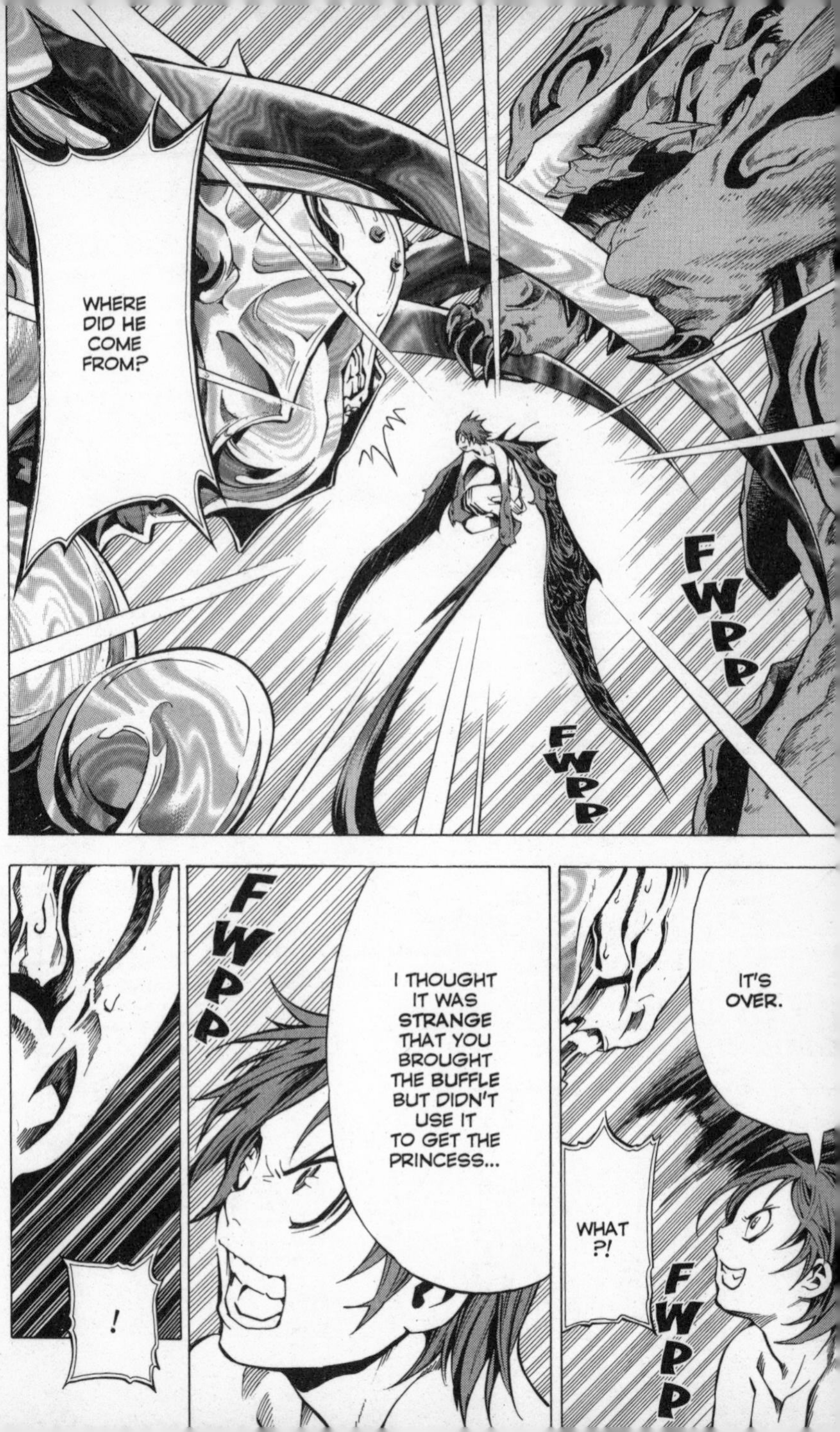
WHERE DID HE COME FROM?
FWPP
FWPP
IT'S OVER.
WHAT?!
FWPP
FWPP
I THOUGHT IT WAS STRANGE THAT YOU BROUGHT THE BUFFLE BUT DIDN'T USE IT TO GET THE PRINCESS...
!

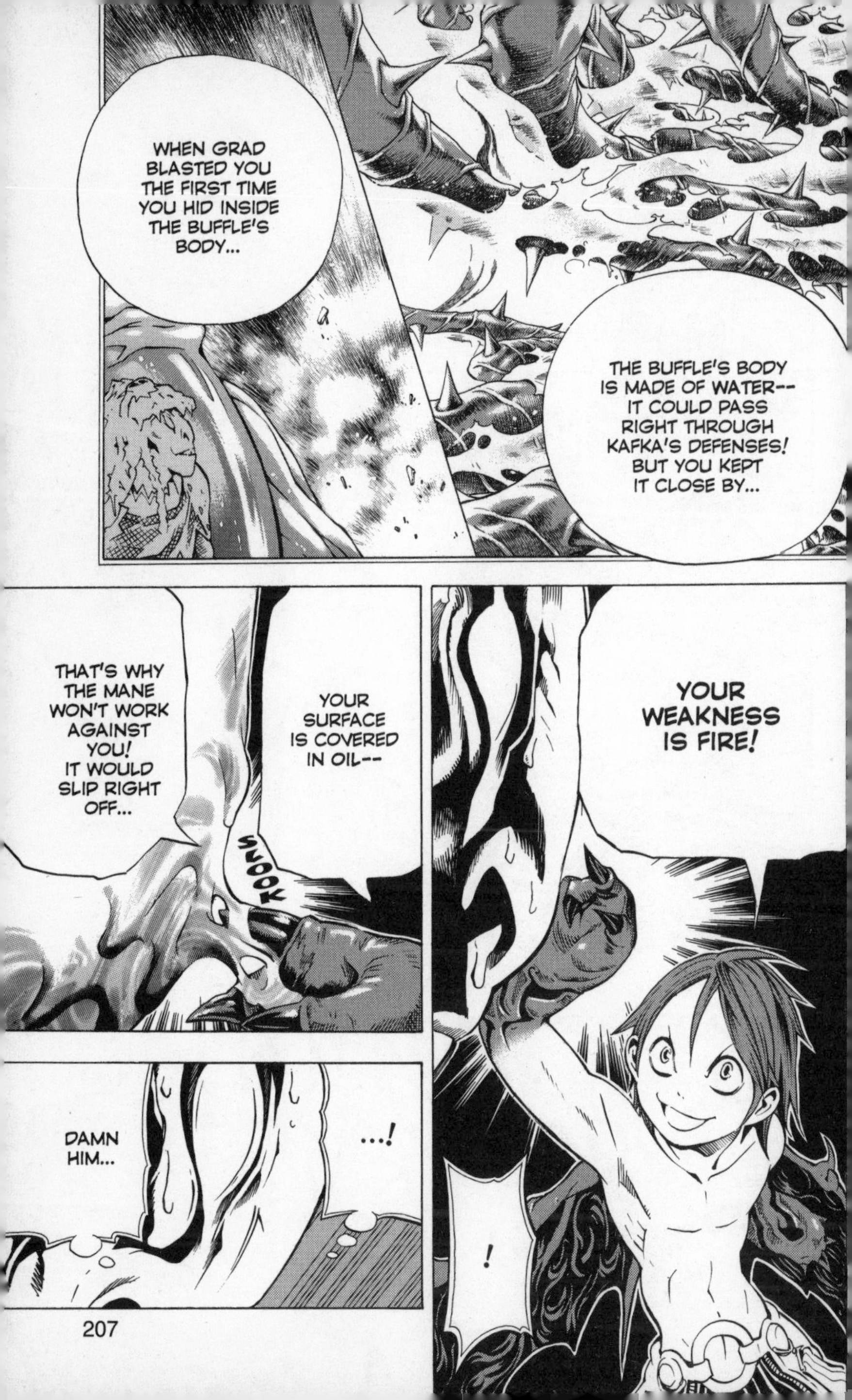
WHEN GRAD BLASTED YOU THE FIRST TIME YOU HID INSIDE THE BUFFLE'S BODY...
THE BUFFLE'S BODY IS MADE OF WATER-- IT COULD PASS RIGHT THROUGH KAFKA'S DEFENSES! BUT YOU KEPT IT CLOSE BY...
YOUR SURFACE IS COVERED IN OIL--
THAT'S WHY THE MANE WON'T WORK AGAINST YOU! IT WOULD SLIP RIGHT OFF...
SNOOK
YOUR WEAKNESS IS FIRE!
!
...!
DAMN HIM...

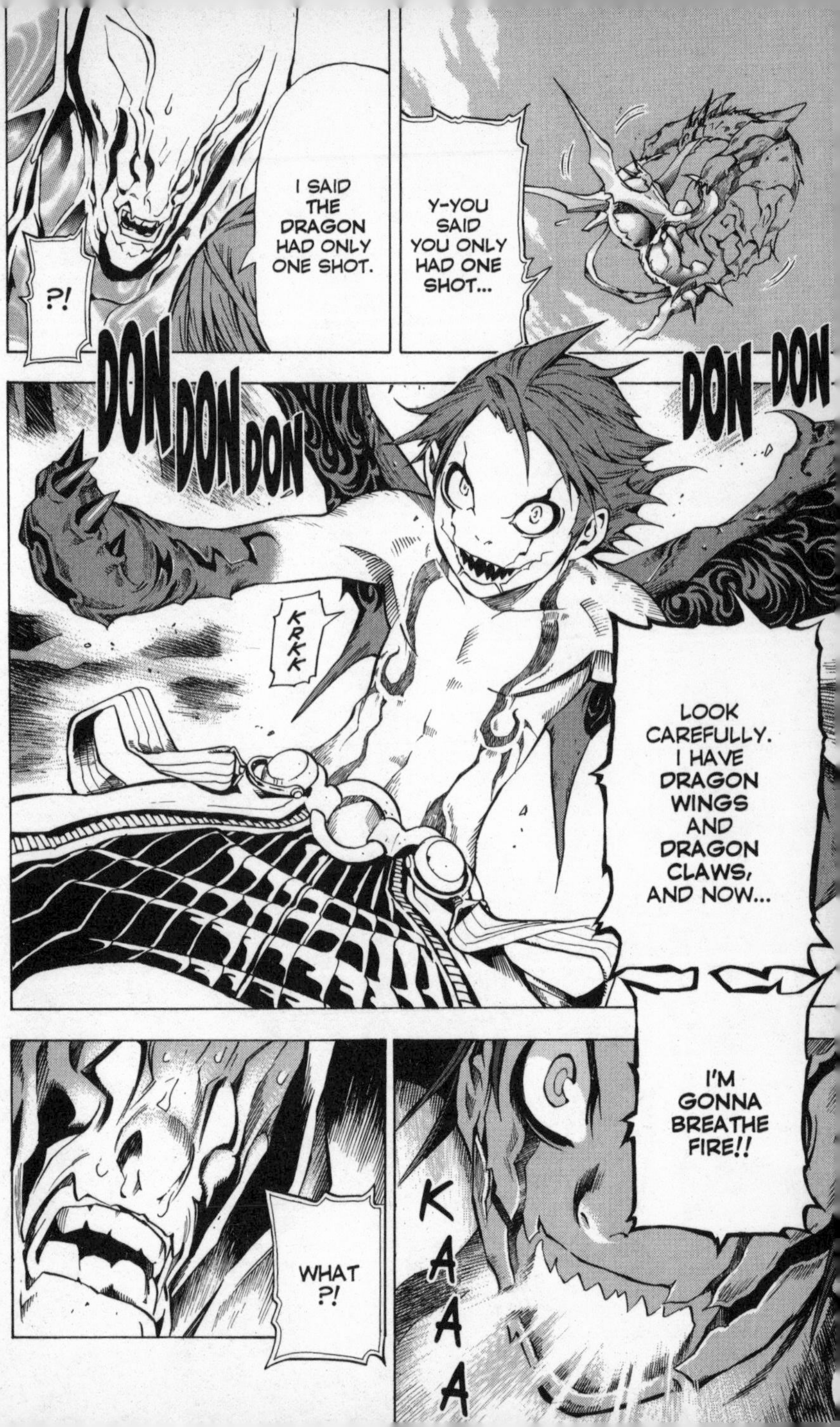
Y-YOU SAID YOU ONLY HAD ONE SHOT...
I SAID THE DRAGON HAD ONLY ONE SHOT.
?!
DON DON
DON DON DON
LOOK CAREFULLY. I HAVE DRAGON WINGS AND DRAGON CLAWS, AND NOW...
KRKK
I'M GONNA BREATHE FIRE!!
KAAAA
WHAT?!

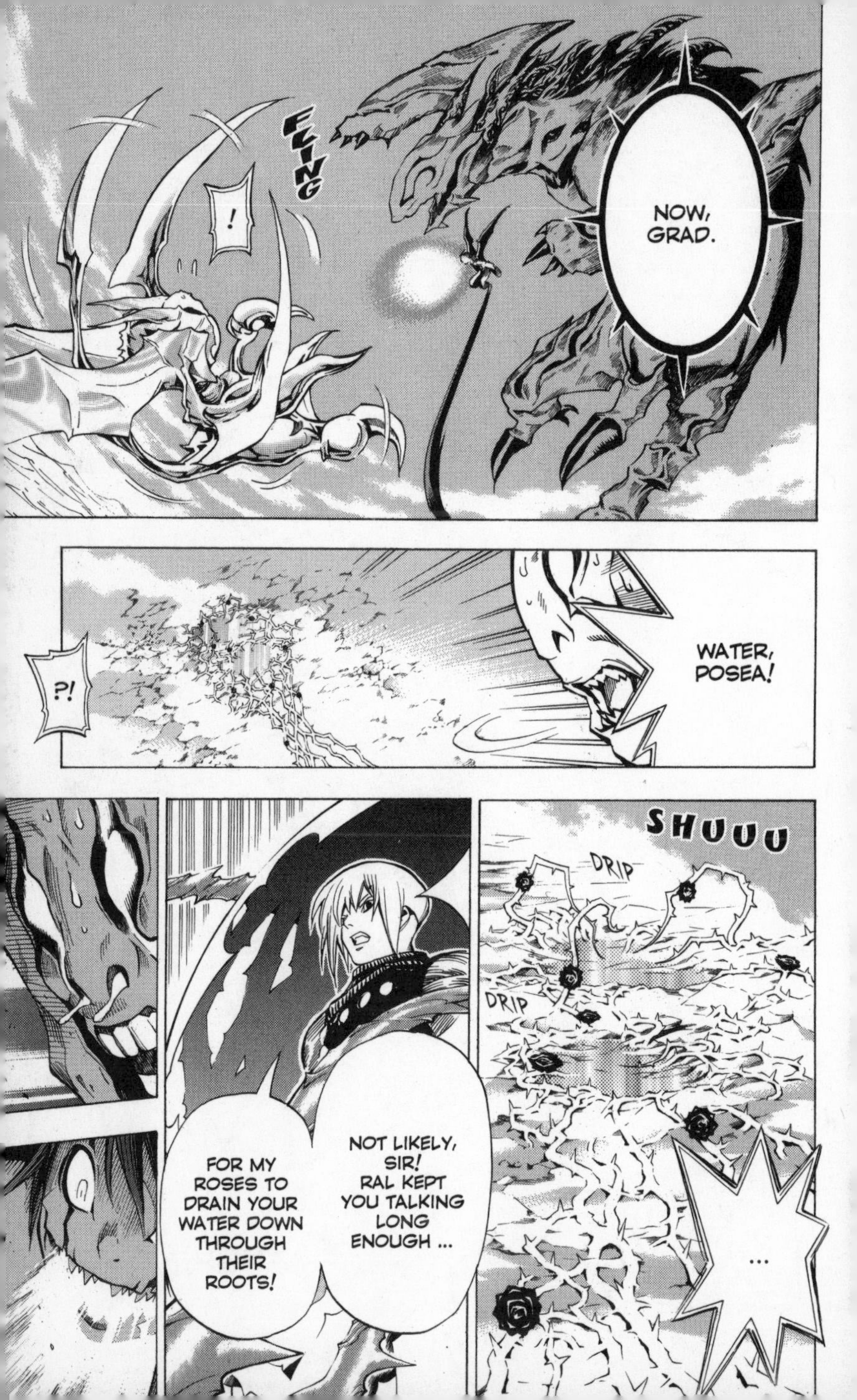
NOW, GRAD.
FLING
!
WATER, POSEA!
?!
SHUUU
DRIP
DRIP
...
NOT LIKELY, SIR! RAL KEPT YOU TALKING LONG ENOUGH ...
FOR MY ROSES TO DRAIN YOUR WATER DOWN THROUGH THEIR ROOTS!

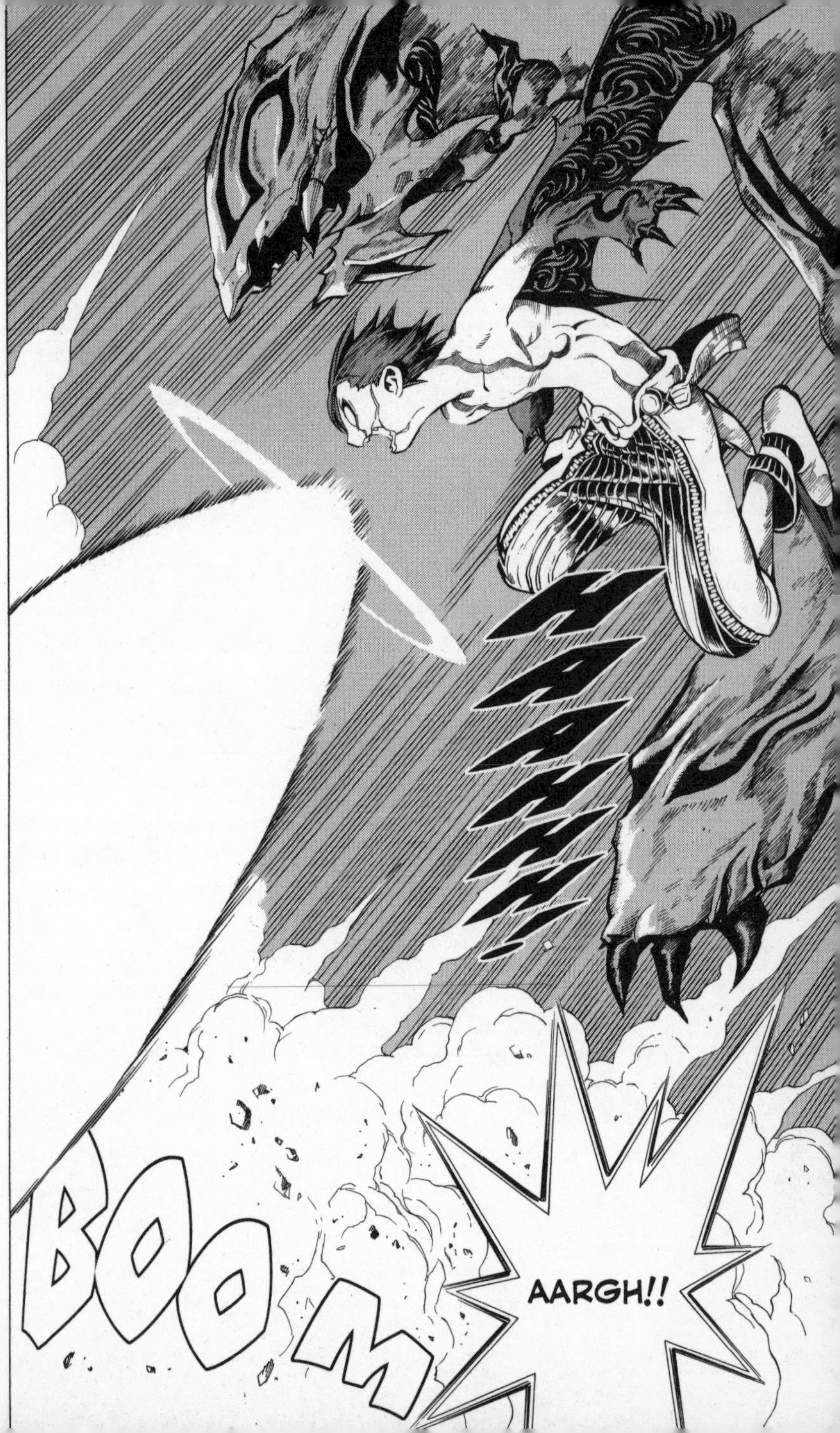
HAAAHH!
BOOM
AARGH!!

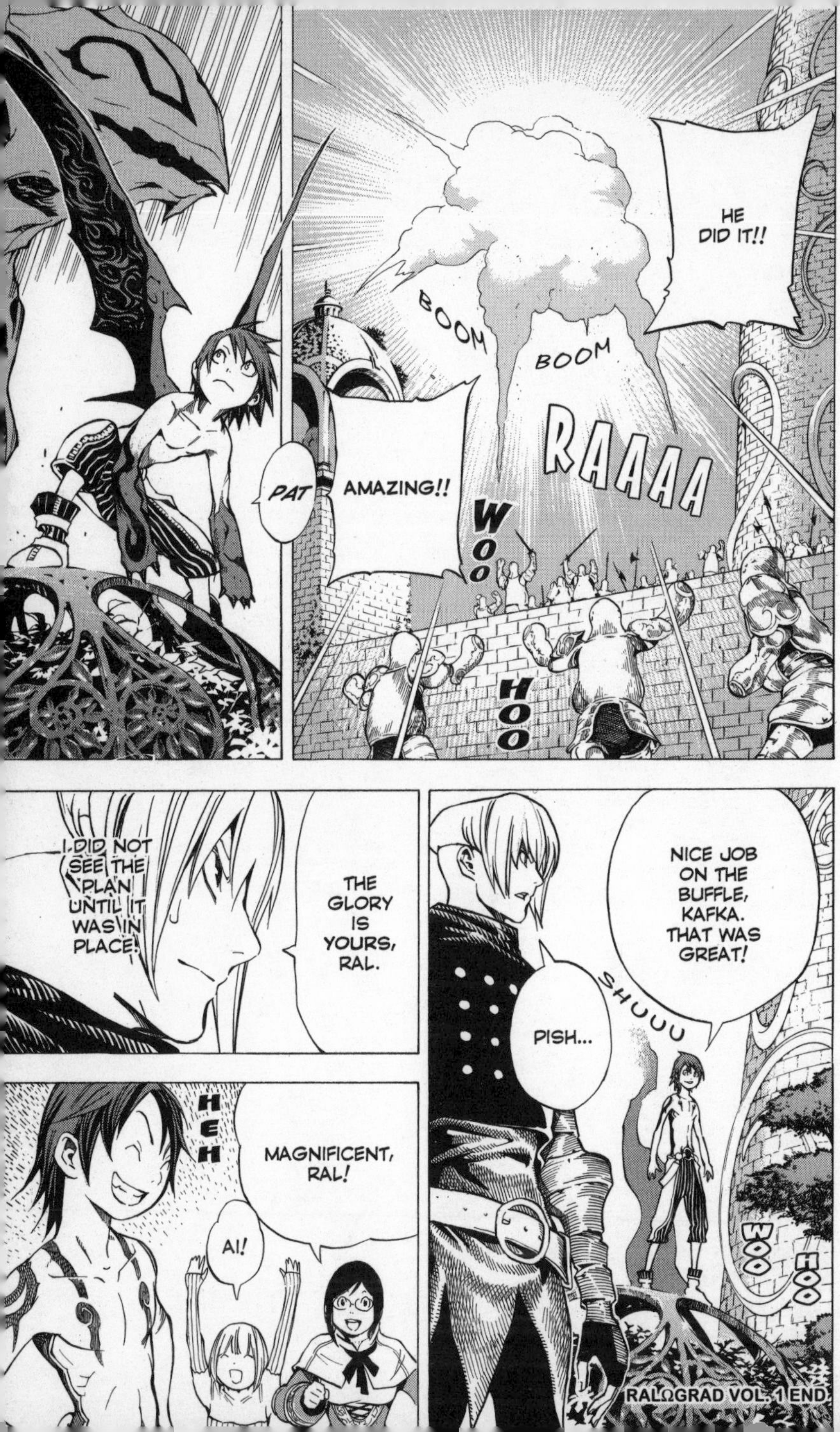
HE DID IT!!
BOOM
BOOM
RAAAAA
AMAZING!!
PAT
WOO
HOO
NICE JOB ON THE BUFFLE, KAFKA. THAT WAS GREAT!
SHUUU
PISH...
WOO
HOO
THE GLORY IS YOURS, RAL.
I DID NOT SEE THE PLAN UNTIL IT WAS IN PLACE!
HEH
MAGNIFICENT, RAL!
AI!
RALΩGRAD VOL. 1 END

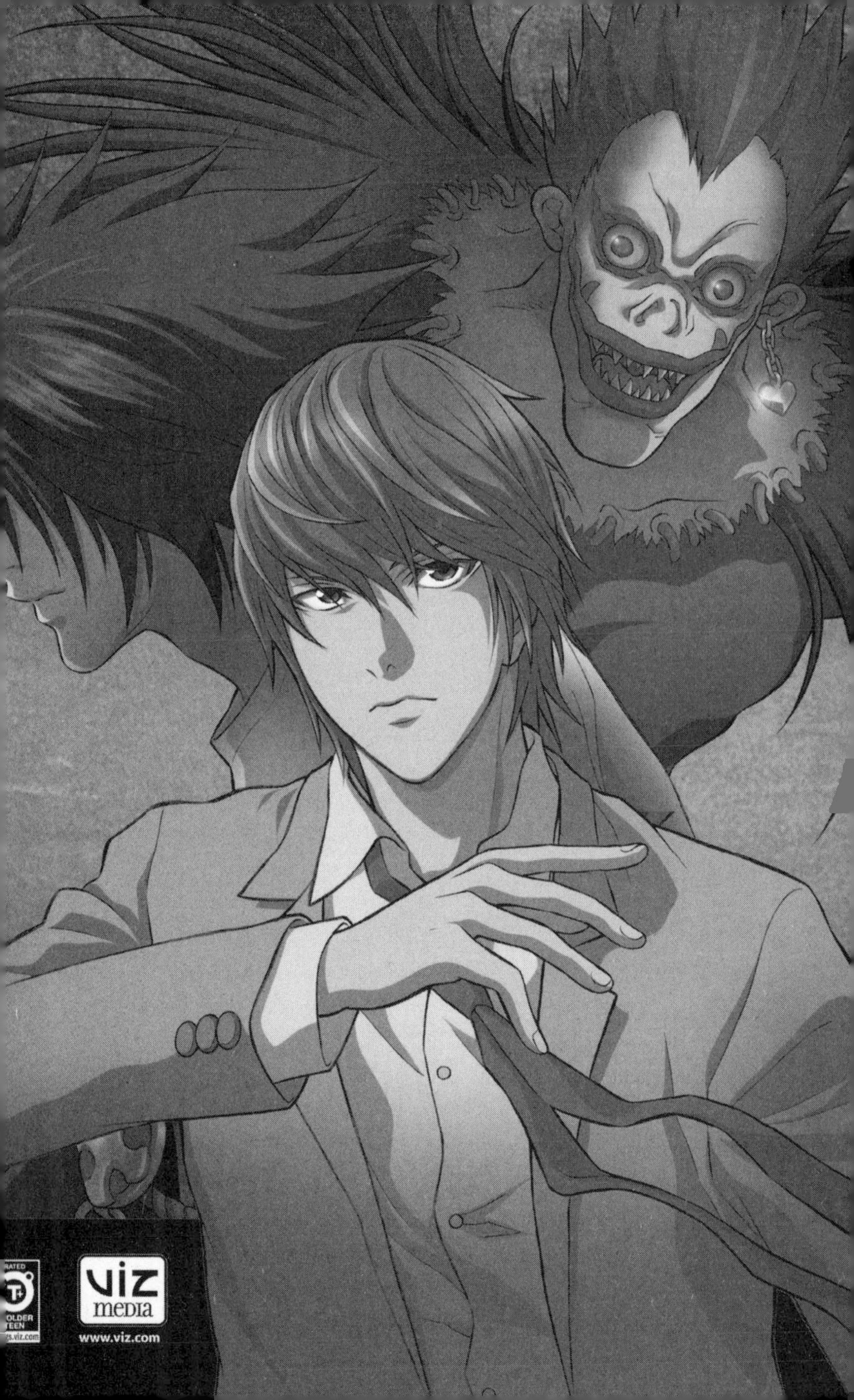

RATED
T+
OLDER
TEEN
viz media
www.viz.com

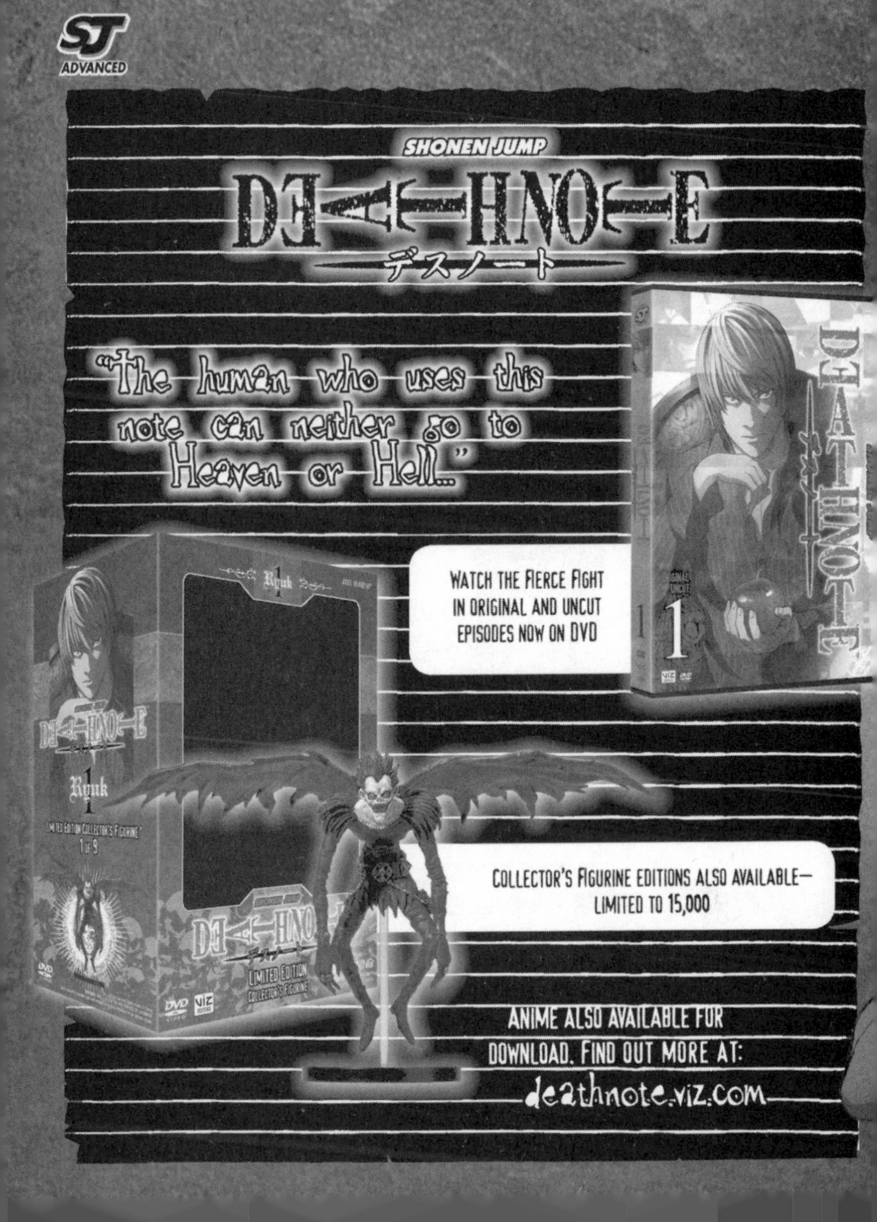

SJ ADVANCED
SHONEN JUMP
DEATH NOTE
デスノート
"The human who uses this note can neither go to Heaven or Hell..."
WATCH THE FIERCE FIGHT IN ORIGINAL AND UNCUT EPISODES NOW ON DVD
COLLECTOR'S FIGURINE EDITIONS ALSO AVAILABLE—LIMITED TO 15,000
ANIME ALSO AVAILABLE FOR DOWNLOAD. FIND OUT MORE AT:
deathnote.viz.com

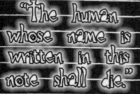

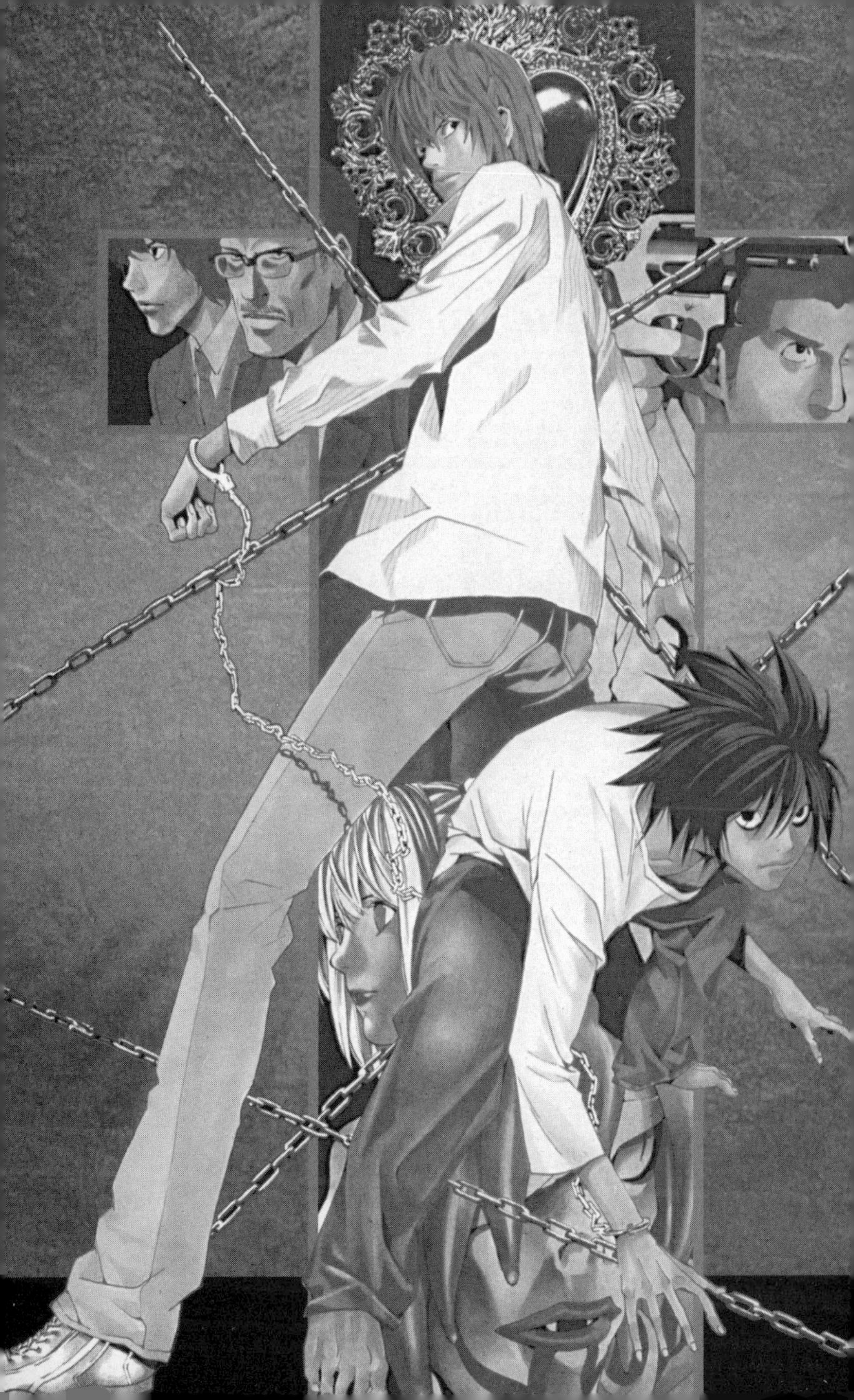

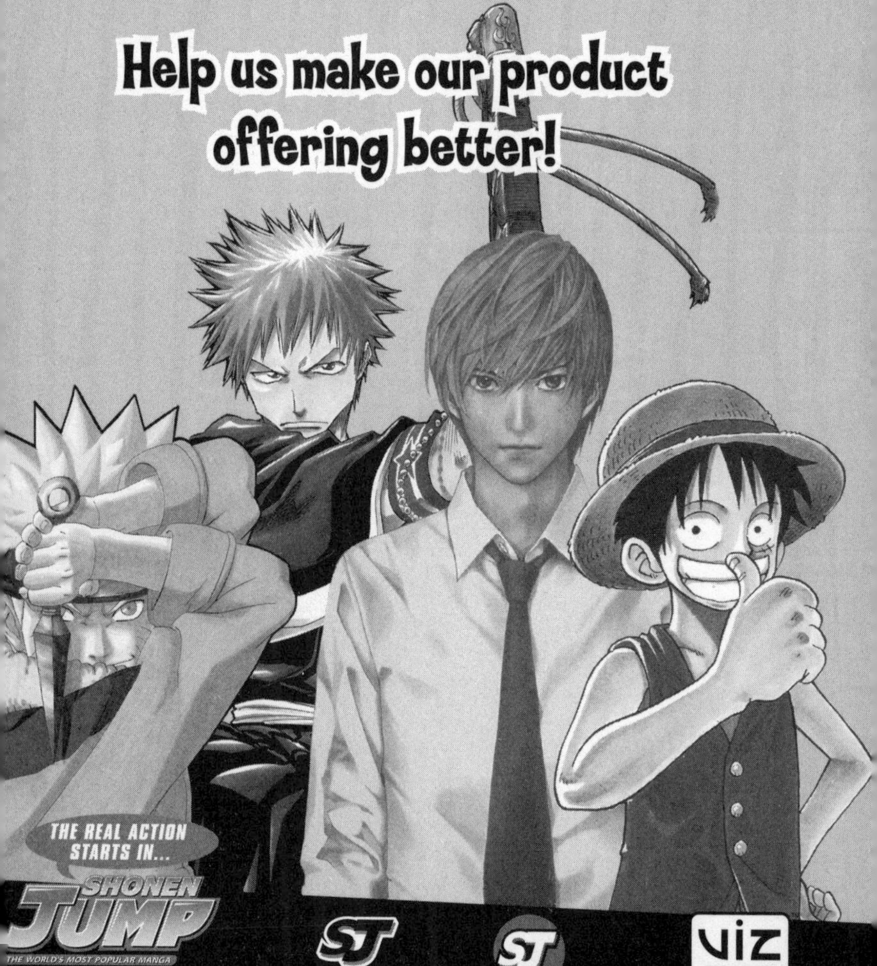

THE REAL ACTION STARTS IN...